HOP UP

The First 12 Issues

**BY HOP UP PRODUCTS
AND MARK MORTON**

MBI Publishing
Company

First published in 2002 by MBI Publishing Company, Galtier Plaza, Suite 200, 380 Jackson Street, St. Paul, MN 55101-3885 USA

The information in this book is true and complete to the best of our knowledge. All recommendations are made without any guarantee on the part of the author or Publisher, who also disclaim any liability incurred in connection with the use of this data or specific details.

We recognize that some words, model names and designations, for example, mentioned herein are the property of the trademark holder. We use them for identification purposes only. This is not an official publication.

MBI Publishing Company books are also available at discounts in bulk quantity for industrial or sales-promotional use. For details write to Special Sales Manager at Motorbooks International Wholesalers & Distributors, Galtier Plaza, Suite 200, 380 Jackson Street, St. Paul, MN 55101-3885 USA.

Library of Congress Cataloging-in-Publication Data Available
ISBN 0-7603-1073-4

Back cover photo from the Pat Ganahl collection.

Printed in the United States of America

CONTENTS

PREFACE

By Mark Morton

Hop Up. It's a verb, a noun, an adjective—and an icon.

For those unable to pay the steep price demanded for that elusive copy of an original *Hop Up*, or are unwilling to grovel at swap meets and estate sales, the following pages make available the historic first 12 issues of the magazine that broke ground and first presented rods and customs together. It is timeless, the definitive tome of the traditional rod and custom movement.

Hop Up was not around long enough to resort to the shotgun theory of increasing readership by including a little bit of everything, be it go-karts, vans with graphics, or Corvettes with flared wheel wells. It has remained unevolved all these years, not unlike James Dean, with its youthful artistic efforts defining what was cool and real, unsullied by changing trends and the increasing commercialism of the hobby and the publishing world. Somewhat fittingly, it died a premature death and is today preserved in our minds and memories as something pure and true.

Today's *Hop Up* attempts to dignify the era of the original magazine, recognized as the most golden of the traditional years, without modifying or evolving it drastically with the new efforts of today. Some new techno innovations are accepted, but the style—Hop Up Style—fits within certain narrow parameters not unlike those precepts in classic cars, classic music, literature, and other examples of timelessness. When it's good, it lasts through the ages. We got that here, Boys. It is truth in motorsport. Not ALL the truth, but it is the truth in rods and customs. Thus our creed: **en hopup veritas**.

You will appreciate the letter from Hop Up Guy Tony Miller who, at 12 years of age in 1952, wrote to the editors about his new L.A. club. He lived vicariously through the pages of the magazine in the early 1950s, and like many of his peers, he remains a Hop Up Guy today. He's still onboard with hot rods and customs, enmeshed in a lifelong pursuit that began with the pages reproduced here.

Nouveau-rodders may find this collection to be a touchstone. If a youngster wants to be informed but has too little time in grade, if he needs some rod and custom intellect to go with his cuffs and ink... then he should soak in the images and text that follow, and it will add 20 or more years to his hot-rod psyche, without the wrinkles.

Hop Up Honor. Stay Honor.

HOP UP

- HOT RODS
- CUSTOMS
- MOTORCYCLES
- RACING
- BOATS

AUG 1951

15¢

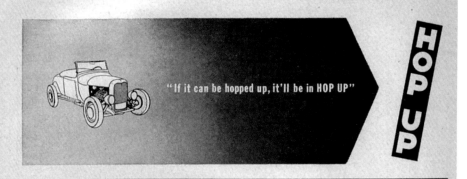

"If it can be hopped up, it'll be in HOP UP"

OUR POLICY

As publishers of ROAD and TRACK Magazine, which is editorially directed toward sports car activities and road racing, we have had many requests to include material on other activities such as hot rods, custom cars (American), motorcycles, speed boats, and various forms of American speedway racing.

Now, with HOP UP, we can cover all of these deserving subjects, without varying the policy of ROAD and TRACK. Also, realizing that many of HOP UP's potential readers may be of a young age group, we have decided on a smaller page size and a fifteen-cent price. Subscriptions will be only $1.50 for 12 issues.

We urgently request our readers to write us—tell us the type of articles you like and what you don't like. Don't pull any punches . . . because we want to make HOP UP into exactly the kind of magazine YOU want it to be. Basically, we intend to cover any engine-driven vehicle that can be "hopped-up," but the amount of coverage given to any one type will be governed by your letters.

EDITORIAL STAFF

Editor.................................Oliver Billingsley
Technical Editor..........................John R. Bond
Historical Editor...................W. Everett Miller
Associate Editor.....................Robert Dearborn
Staff Photographer.................Jerry Chesebrough
Photographers............Jack Campbell, Bob Canaan
Joe Al Denker, Gene Trindl

PRODUCTION STAFF

Managing Editor....................W. H. Brehaut, Jr.
Art Director.............................Louis Kimzey
Art...Jack Caldwell

ADVERTISING

Advertising Manager..................William Quinn
East Coast Representatives......Peabody & Ortgies
276 West 43rd Street
New York 18, N.Y.
United Kingdom.................Kenneth Kirkman
2 Longcroft Avenue
Banstead, Surrey, England

CORRESPONDENTS

Italy.................................Corrado Millanta
England.................Geoff Healey, Spike Rhiando

Contributions—not responsible for the return of unsolicited manuscripts, photographs, and/or drawings unless accompanied by self-addressed stamped envelope.
Mailing address—Box 110, Glendale, California.

Vol. 1, No. 1   **August, 1951**

CONTENTS

HOP UP is published monthly by Enthusiasts' Publications, Inc., 540 W. Colorado Blvd., Glendale, California. Phone CHapman 5-2297. Application for entry as second-class matter is pending. Copyright 1951 by Enthusiasts' Publications, Inc. Reprinting in whole or in part forbidden except by permission of the publishers.
Subscription price $1.50 per year thruout the world. Single copy 15c.
Change of address—must show both old and new addresses.

H
O
P

U
P

2

CORRESPONDENCE

CUSTOMIZED OLDS 88

I am enclosing a couple of snaps of a 1950 Olds 88 which, when completed, looked very nice. We installed an electric lift in the trunk lid, Cad tail lights and a "continental spare." It is nosed over and painted a metallic blue.

Caldwell, Idaho   D. J. Wilkins

WANTS ATLANTA SPEEDWAY PHOTOS

I would like to obtain some photographs of races at the Atlanta Georgia speedway for the events held in 1909 and 1910?

My father was one of the men who built this two-mile replica of Indianapolis. At one time I had many photos of these events . . . I've only one left now.

Clearwater, Florida   Ross Durant Sr.

CUSTOMIZED STUDEBAKER

Here are a few notes and photos for Studebaker fans. The hood has been leaded and the rear trunk has lost the oversized handle. It now works from a hood latch located in the rear arm rest. Twin exhaust stacks come thru the lower part of the bumperettes. This was done by changing the right to the left and then turning upside down and drilling holes thru large end and welding the tubes in place. The body is finished in '50 Studebaker Aqua Green; wheels are Tulip Cream. The only changes in the engine are .020 oversize bore and the head is milled .040. All bearings were replaced and Grant Piston Rinngs were used.

The interior will be redone in yellow quilted plastic trim and aqua-green plaid base of woven plastic. All this at a very low cost if you have access to the proper tools and can do most of the work yourself, as I was able to do.

Miami, Florida   Harold C. Van Ostrand

CUSTOM FORD CONVERTIBLE

All my life I have had a yearning for a sports type open car. One so different I wouldn't meet my waterloo every mile on American Highways. I wanted one in the light car class economical and easily serviced and with power to spare.

So here's the answer: We took a 1949 Ford Convertible, sawed it in two all the way around through doors, front fenders, rear quarters, etc. We lifted upper half off, made another round with the saw taking a strip out 4¼ inches side, put the two halves together and you have a car again. Sounds easy, but Oh! My Aching Back. We pulled instrument panel, built mounds to carry tachometer and several other instruments. Now we wanted some feminine

touch, so we put this on where it should be out in front. We used a special brassiere type front bumper for protection.

Of course seats had to be chopped along with all upholstery to correspond with the now slenderized body. Car stands 38 inches high at cowl, Power top works and everything fits perfectly as a new convertible. Now for that power, we installed a set of overhead valves, a special cam and double exhausts, double ignition and an overdrive. To step on the gas is like pulling the trigger on a machine gun, yet she's quiet as a mouse, corners exceptionally good and is good to look at.

Power is approximately 182 hp. at 4800 rpm. If you think this is easy, try it. Work was started December 11, 1950 and with two of our best body men completed January 12, 1951. All custom work was done by Covington Motor Co., Covington, Virginia   J. A. Wright

CURED HENRY J

My Henry J would rear and buck like a rocking horse until I installed '49 Ford shock absorbers. It now takes dips, corners and rough road with very little lurch or roll.

My parents would rather drive my Henry J on long or short trips than their '50 Ford.

Camp Chaffee, Ark.   Michael Keen

Many thanks for your tip on improving the Henry J. A good many cars could be improved by better shocks. Just a suggestion, next time try the new Chrysler "oriflow" shocks—I have a hunch they are even better. —Ed.

H O P U P 4

JOIN NOW!

WHAT? The AMERICAN HOT ROD CONFERENCE, INC., is a non-profit organization with all timing associations in California as members. Officially recognized by the California Highway Patrol.

WHY? Reasons? There are MANY. (1) to UNIFY all existing activities (rules, events, efforts, publicity); (2) to promote SAFETY; (3) to provide FACILITIES (paved timing strips); (4) RECOGNITION of records.

WHO? You! The AMERICAN HOT ROD CONFERENCE is open to all motor enthusiasts, regardless of type of equipment or affiliation. Memberships are available to both associations and individuals.

WHEN? NOW! Join today. And for further information, see the article on page 6 of this issue.

APPLICATION FOR MEMBERSHIP

AMERICAN HOT ROD CONFERENCE
c/o Harold Osborn, Treasurer
339 N. Barbara Ave.
Azusa, California

Membership fee
$2.00 per year

Name..

Street..

City...State............................

Club or Association, if any...

Type of Automotive Interest..

Membership card and sterling silver pin will be sent upon receipt of application blank and fee.

WANTED...

One Paved Timing Strip!

No amount of words can describe conditions at a lakes meet—you have to be there to understand why the almost desperate need for a paved timing strip. While speed-minded California youths have been using these dried-out lake beds since 1933, the lack of rain in recent years has progressively ruined the once-hard surface. This year it has been necessary to move the course several times during the running of one day's events. The dirt and dust are terrible. Some people may have the idea that these lakes are salt, like Bonneville, but unfortunately, they are not. The dirt surface is still relatively hard but it is easily torn up by repeated use.

For the past several years there has been a growing movement directed toward obtaining a paved timing strip in the Southern California area. Sites proposed are mostly in desert areas, where the crowds and noise will bother no one. The greatest benefit a strip would bring is safety. There have been accidents at these dry lakes meets, but almost all can be blamed on the rough surface throwing a car out of control. A smooth paved surface would eliminate this problem, and would also mean faster speeds! The slippage on the rough dirt holds down speed to a considerable extent.

The cleanliness of a new strip would certainly be appreciated by everyone who has gone thru the grime and grit of a day at the lakes.

The movement to obtain a timing strip is being forwarded in three ways at the present time, and to use the words of one enthusiast, "I don't care who builds the strip, just so I can use it." Motorama, one of the numerous "hot rod" shows, has already made a start towards a strip. The two newly formed national organizations, the American Hot Rod Conference and National Hot Rod Association, also have this as one of their objectives.

The AHRC, which was organized to unify all existing hot rod timing activities, was formed by a combination of the leading California associations, including S.C.T.A. and Russetta Timing Association. However, memberships are open to anyone regardless of location, and type of car he owns.

The NHRA, which has basically similar objectives, is also open to speed enthusiasts thruout the U.S.

HOP UP hopes that thru these efforts it will be possible for everyone with a desire to test the speed of his vehicle to do so. Hot rods, motorcycles, foreign cars, American stock cars . . . events at the timing strip should be held for all types.

HOP UP 6

The "LADY BUG"

This well built streamliner clocked 144.00 mph at the May 6th S.C.T.A. El Mirage meet. Engine is 4-port Riley. Builders are Lobello, Benson, Vesco, and Dinkians of the San Diego Roadster Club.

PHOTO BY TRINDL

El Mirage Story

by Louis Kimzey

Few people realize the time and effort that goes into the colorful activity of a timing meet. Enthusiastic hot-rodders come hundreds of miles from all over Southern California to El Mirage Dry Lakes, located on the desert approximately 100 miles northeast of Los Angeles. The "lake", dry for the past 15,000 years, is 5 miles long and ¾ mile wide. It is ideal for high-speed runs because of its length and the amazingly flat, smooth surface.

During our weekend visit, the Russetta Timing Association was conducting a meet. This organization has thirty-one member clubs scattered from San Diego to Bakersfield. A club must comply with strict requirements before joining the association and even after the club is accepted, there are additional individual safety requirements which must be met before a car is allowed to run at a meet. This policy results in an almost complete absence of accidents during the season.

The 4-mile long course is made up of an approach of 1.2 miles, a stretch of 528

Above, entrance to the "traps". Car breaks beam of light, which activates the timer.

At left, the finish—528 feet from the start. Extremely accurate electronic clock timer.

8

14

feet (1/10 mile) between the timing lights, and a shut-down distance of 2 to 3 miles.

Never have I seen such effort put into an undertaking. These fellows and their friends work on their cars under the very worst of conditions . . . numbing cold at night and almost blistering heat during the day.

One of the amazing things I've seen up at the lakes is the *industry*. All the men are working all the time! They're dead serious about it and I guess a lot of employers would like to see them work as hard at their regular jobs. Imagine! Change plugs by moonlight . . . new rear-end by spot-light . . . look for tools by flash-light . . . One of the true life savers is the lunch wagon, which sells hot coffee, cold drinks and food. If it wasn't for that boiling java about 5:30 in the morning, I think it would be unbearable. There is a very busy atmosphere about the whole deal up there, but I noticed something

Above, Russetta's official timer checks his equipment. Note cracks in the lake surface.

At right, a member of the Technical Committee checks a car for safety before it can be allowed to enter the high-speed course.

else . . . everybody was so friendly. They borrowed from each other and went out of their way to help each other. It was very easy for a total stranger like myself to join any group and wind up friends within a matter of minutes, *providing* you spoke their language . . . and that's cars!

After things were in shape for the next morning's run, many took off for town. There are two towns: Palmdale, 35 miles away and Victorville, 25 miles away. And a dirty, bumpy road between you and both. In town, some concentrate on getting a room for the night, some go to a show, and some just get together and raise hell.

But there are quite a few who don't go to town. When they finish their work, they crawl into a sleeping bag, with as many things as possible on top to keep warm, and they are set for the night. Others sleep in cars, using marker cones as a pillow. Then there are those who get into a trunk and huddle together for warmth (see photo). This is really true love for the sport, and it's fellows like these who have made Southern California the custom and speed center.

In the morning, about four o'clock, they all start heading back with their hopes and dreams of breaking a record. It seems with all their dreams and hopes they are too busy to mind the cold-windy mornings—but brother, *I* sure did.

16

Right, these cars are not built for beauty!

Below, the final achievement of many hours of preparation . . . a fast run!

17

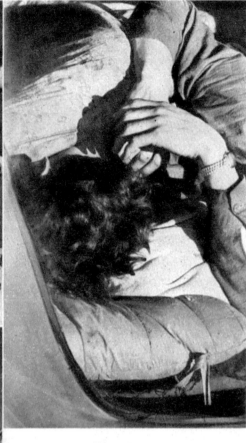

NEW RECORDS

Class	Name	Club	Engine	Speed
A Coupes	Mickey Thompson	Roadents	Merc	129.96
B Coupes	Bob Trout	Coupes	"	123.71
C Coupes	James D. Evans	Rod Riders	"	131.89
D Coupes	Dick Pierson	Coupes	"	141.73
A Roadsters	Johnson Bros.	Screwdrivers	"	127.65
B Roadsters	Bob Thomas	Screwdrivers	"	133.33
C Roadsters	Stecker-Cobb	Rod Riders	"	153.19
A Sedans	Sharon Baker	Coupes	"	122.03
B Sedans	Howard Johansen	A.R.C.	GMC	135.33
B Str'mlnrs	Earl Evans	Hutters	Merc	165.13

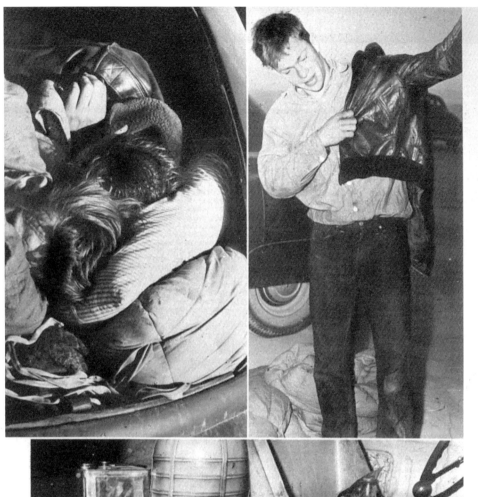

TECHNICAL TIPS

COLUMBIA AXLE, McCULLOCH BLOWER

. . . as yet have found no articles on Columbia rear ends. Very popular in the 1936 to '40 era, I believe it was renamed Skyline Drive and fitted on 1946 Fords. Also McCulloch superchargers, all I know about them is there were several different models made, one that bolted on the stock Ford manifold and another model that the manifold was an integral part of the blower. A very nice article could be written on these subjects and, some technical information could be used.

I plan to use both the blower and the Columbia on a car now under construction.

Sand Springs, Oklahoma   Randall Wells

The Columbia 2-speed axle was built by the Eaton Axle Company, but was discontinued due to the design change in Ford axles and because of Ford's adoption of the more logical Warner Gear overdrive. Also discontinued was the McCulloch supercharger, so we feel that articles on these two items, however interesting and worthy, are not advisable.

Both had a number of serious technical drawbacks. The 2-speed axle was much heavier, and the stock Ford rear end was already extremely heavy, so that the unsprung weight suffered. The gear ratio change from 1 to 1 to about .72 to 1 was much too drastic, and since the planetary gear train was bolted to the differential carrier, it had to be heavy enough to transmit the full engine torque, times the low speed ratio, times the axle ratio. In other words, about 4 times the torque loading of an overdrive unit located behind the transmission.

The supercharger was reasonably successful, tho beneficial only at higher speeds (as is the way with centrifugal types) and the amount of horsepower which was required to be transmitted by only 2 V-belts was, at the higher speeds, rather hard on belt life, a situation not helped by the belt idler supplied to eliminate slippage.

I have a very good friend in Milwaukee who built up a fast road car using the 2-speed axle and the supercharger. The combination of the two is very good as the disadvantages tend to cancel. However, he has not driven the car very much, because of other reasons. No parts or service information is available from McCulloch (he tried) and he had quite a time re-building the thing. By reversing the worn bronze gear and machining new thrust washers, it runs good, but the boost pressure is not up to the 6 psi supposed to be possible.

After much calculating, and some trial, he finally settled on a 4.44 ratio axle for this car—a 1934 Ford convertible coupe. The engine, incidentally, was bored to 3⅜ inches, had a semi-race cam, and 7.5 to 1 aluminum heads. —Tech. Ed.

OVERDRIVE FOR '37 BUICK 40

Would you please tell me if there is any way to install some type of overdrive in a 1937 Buick, series 40. It has the stock 4.44 rear end which is fine for acceleration but much too high for speed. The engine has been worked over to give 125 bhp at 3800 rpm.

Berkeley, Calif.   Bruce A. Moritz

You are absolutely "sunk" insofar as overdrive is concerned. Nothing is impossible but the cost would be terrific. My only suggestion is to compromise on a 3.9 axle ratio.—Tech. Ed.

'50 CHRYSLER ENGINE IN '41 DE SOTO

Have just purchased a new 1950 Chrysler engine to be used in a 1941 DeLuxe De Soto Sedan, six cylinder . . .

Have wanted to convert to Propane. What is your opinion on Propane?

I attended the last Hot Rod show in L.A. and noticed one roadster having a pipe or bar on the front end of frame. A bracket was welded to the bar and the front spring was bolted to the bracket. The spring was transverse using an axle. This appeared to be a good way of lowering the chassis. Is it a safe practice?

Wilmar, Calif.   Harry J. Cox

With thoro safety precautions, the use of Propane is very worth while—in fact, it has a great many advantages. The L-head engine does not permit full utilization of Propane because considerations of volumetric efficiency (good breathing) limit the maximum compression ration to about 8 to 1, whereas the fuel would permit 9 or 10 to 1 without detonation. I know of two stock L-head engines which show a drop in peak bhp when the compression ratio is increased to anything over 7 to 1.

The type front end you describe is commonly called a "suicide front end," but don't let that scare you—properly made for strength, it's perfectly feasible.—Tech. Ed.

CADILLAC IN CHEVY?

I have a 1950 Powerglide Chevrolet four-door sedan. Is it very hard to have a Cadillac engine installed in the Chevrolet? Could it be installed with the Hydramatic transmission? If so do you know of anyone that does this work or makes adapter kits for this conversion?

Warner Robins, Georgia   Ronald Hardman

I hear that OHV Cadillac engines have been installed in late Chevrolets, but have never actually seen one.

The installation is somewhat difficult because the diagonal cowl braces must be cut away, and you have to convert the rear end to an open drive shaft, with Hotchkiss drive.

My only suggestion is that you write Frank Burrell, 17607 Ferguson Avenue, Detroit 35, Michigan, as he might be interested in making your conversion.—Tech. Ed.

1950 FORD IS DEAD

I have a 1950 Ford convertible and I think it is fairly dead. I have dual exhaust but nothing else. How much should be removed from cylinder head to give 8 to 1 ratio. Also have overdrive but which gear ratio would you recommend to give top speed and pickup. Do you think a hot coil and ignition system would help?

Wilton Jct., Iowa   Wm. Tumey

You can mill the heads about .070 to get 8 to 1 compression ratio, but this amount also requires redoming which is probably impossible in your area. If you can afford their cost, I would suggest a pair of aluminum heads.

You are stuck on gear ratio, because 4.55 to 1 or even more would be very desirable, but 4.10 is the highest numerical ratio available.

Better ignition often shows up to advantage when "winding tight" and dual points do seem to give top performance for a longer mileage. —Tech. Ed.

TECHNICAL TIPS

OVERDRIVE FOR '49 PLYMOUTH

What is the approximate time and expense involved in the installment of a Borg-Warner overdrive in my 1949 Plymouth?

I read once of using a syncromesh transmission turned end-for-end with the low and reverse removed.

Either way it sounds like there would be some trouble with the emergency brake.

Marcus, Iowa — Wilmer Hohbach

A 1940 Chrysler overdrive unit will bolt onto a Plymouth transmission housing of the same year. Later Plymouth housing will also work by remachining the rear face to 1940 style. You can also use the complete 1940 Chrysler transmission and overdrive, or install Plymouth gears in the Chrysler case. The Chrysler gears give a 1.55 second speed ratio, while the '41 and later Plymouth gears are 1.83 second for easier starting in this speed (but less top speed). A special hand brake anchor bracket is available, but is not difficult to make one. A special cast iron clutch underpan, replacing the Plymouth sheet metal pan, is necessary to give adequate support to weight added and is available on special order. The propeller shaft does not require changes. A new transmission main shaft (output shaft) is required if you use Plymouth gears and Chrysler overdrive. This is a 1940 Chrysler part.

A good Chrysler parts man, one who knows his parts book, can give you all the part numbers required. Incidentally, you should use at least the 4.10 axle ratio and preferably 4.30 if you can get it. A 3.9 axle with overdrive will not pull the slightest grade or headwind when cruising, since the effective ratio drops to 2.81.—Tech. Ed.

WANTS NON-CONTEMPORARY OLDS 98

I am the owner of a 1951 Oldsmobile, series 98, deluxe Holiday Coupe equipped with Hydramatic drive. My driving is evenly divided between city streets and country highways. I am not dissatisfied with the performance built into my car by its maker, but I feel that I would like something extra to set my car apart from its contemporaries. While desiring better performance, I do not wish to sacrifice any of the car's dependability, economy, or all around usefulness.

What are your suggestions?

West Lafayette, Indiana — Wayne D. Surface

My first inclination is to suggest you leave the car "as is"—you can't really improve performance without sacrificing somewhere.

I would, however, install a dual exhaust system. You can also increase the compression ratio by milling the heads and retain "octane requirement" by using a Thompson or Octa-Gane water-alcohol injector.—Tech. Ed.

BUTANE BURNING NASH STATESMAN

My brother and I have equipped our '50-'51 Nash Statesman with a Butane carburetor. How much can be milled off of the heads to increase the compression ratio to help mileage performance while using Butane and Propane?

Kismet, Kansas — George E. Daley

With butane fuel you can go as high as 9 or 10 to 1 compression ratio. However, the L-head engine of your Nash Statesman can't only be "milled" to the point where the valves (when open) will just clear the roof of the combustion chamber. You can take measurements when you remove the head. In any case, you cannot mill enough off the head of this engine to take full advantage of butane fuel.—Tech. Ed.

CADILLAC ENGINE IN PONTIAC

You mentioned that a Cadillac engine could be transplanted in the Pontiac. Can you tell me just what would have to be done in order to make this a desirable change, such as the cost, changes that would have to be made in the Hydra-matic, and performance. Have heard that the Cadillac is an economical engine (mpg), what effect would putting it in a Pontiac make on that?

Great Falls, Montana — Dwight M. Berner

I haven't seen a Cadillac installation in a Pontiac, but it should be especially easy with the Hydramatic—no changes required there, except for throttle linkage. New front engine mounts are no problem, and exhaust and cooling piping not difficult.

1951 Cadillac engines are not available, but cost was around $680.

You could stand an axle ratio "faster" than the 3.31 of the Cadillac, but this is not available. Thus, the lower weight Pontiallac will probably use about as much gas as before, and possibly even use a little more—a small price for the terrific performance available.—Tech Ed.

WIRE WHEELS FOR LINCOLN CONT.

Can you tell me where I could obtain wire wheels (if possible) for a '48 Lincoln Continental, similar to "Rochester" car.

Lebanon, Indiana — Robert F. Hutchinson

Locating a set of 52 mm hubs for wire wheels is plenty tough. You might try Floyd Dreyer in Indianapolis for a secondhand-set. Then, after you have the hubs comes the problem of having rims made and re-spoked to the correct offset for your particular car. Then you still have to have hub adapters made. There is no one source for all of this work.

I also suggest you write A. E. Ulmann & Associates, 3042 Madison Avenue, New York 17, New York, who have a kit for Ford conversion which should also work on the Lincoln.—Tech. Ed.

BLOWER ON 1941 BUICK

I have a 1941 Buick with a 1950 Buick Special engine in it and would like to get some dope on hopping it up a little.

How would a blower work on this? or is there one made that would fit it?

Monitor, Washington — Keith Cannon

There are no blowers available for Buick engines, and to make up a special installation is very costly.

I know of several Buicks modified with considerable success. One precaution, however—don't mill the heads much, if any. Certainly not over 8 to 1 is absolute maximum with premium fuel. The intake valves from the big engine can be reworked to fit the small engine, and most of the cars I've used the 41 "compound" manifolds, with two carburetors working all the time. Dual exhausts are also easy to incorporate and well worth while.

If you want to go "all out" then a semi or ¾ race cam is the final suggestion, and there's not much more you can do.—Tech Ed.

(Continued on page 38)

H O P U P

15

21

$4000 *roadster goes* 131 *mph!*

This unusual roadster built by Long Beach City College student Les Callahan, Jr., is the culmination of 3 years' work.

Based on a 1932 Ford chassis, transverse springs are retained at both front and rear. A 3-inch dropped Dago front axle is positioned with radius rods. An interesting feature of this car is the pivoting of both front and rear radius rods in line with the universal joint. Steering mechanism and front end running gear are 1947 Mercury. A Pat Warren quick-change rear end provides optional ratios for various types of competition activity.

Les' engine has a 59-A block (Merc), stroked ⅜", 3 5/16" bore, ported and relieved, 30° seats on valves, guides cut, Weiand heads, Smith & Jones 3-carburetor manifold, Scintilla magneto and Zephyr transmission with column shift. The body is from a 1922 Dodge, lowered with channeled flooring. There is a partial belly pan to aid streamlining.

Gaylord and California Auto Top provided the grained yellow DuPont Fabrilite upholstery. Body work and painting was done by Barris. Altho this car was clocked at the dry lakes at 131 mph, Les expects to go even faster this season. During the past year, this car has been first place winner in many auto style shows.

—GEORGE BARRIS

PHOTOS BY MARCIA CAMPBELL

16   **COVER ROADSTER**

22

Trophy Winner

The dream car appearing on the cover this month was constructed over a period of nine months, sandwiched in between transportation runs to classes at U.C.L.A. and work. The owner, Sigma Nu fraternity member Bill Taylor, has been a customized car enthusiast for many years.

Taylor's customized Chevrolet, designed and built by the Barris Kustom Shop, has many interesting features. The grille, made of seamless tubing, is mounted on springs and rubber to provide full floating. Hood and fenders are faired into the new grille contour. Headlights are mounted in a rimless flush opening, adjusting and removal of the lamp unit being performed from inside the fender. Excess chrome trim is removed from hood, trunk and body sides. Taillights from a 1950 Olds were blended into reshaped rear fenders. Rear-bumper is also from a '50 Olds, cut and fitted to the Chevrolet body. Latches for doors and trunk are electrically operated by a dash push-button and by concealed strips under the doors.

Front springs were cut, heated and reshaped to lower the front. At the rear, the body was channeled and the sub-frame sectioned to receive the channeled flooring. Lowering of the chassis at the rear was accomplished by using lowering blocks and

Above, the interior of Taylor's car features white and purple leather, with gray carpets.

PHOTOS BY MARCIA CAMPBELL

re-arching the spring leaves. Windshield was chopped 4 inches, and Gaylord padded top installed. This top features a 3-piece removable full-vision window in the rear. Upholstery, in bone white and gray-purple antique leather, contrasts nicely with gray carpeting. The dash in a two-tone purple and lavender metallic lacquer, with chrome trim, completes the interior theme. Exterior finish is purple lacquer . . . 25 coats! At many West Coast shows, this car has been a trophy winner.

—GEORGE BARRIS

COVER CUSTOM
17

KURTIS-KRAFT
3000 SERIES
INDIANAPOLIS
RACE CAR

18

One of the top American race car constructors, Frank Kurtis has built many Indianapolis winners. The 3000 series is Frank's latest and best design, with independent front suspension and low streamlined body. These construction photographs show the excellent workmanship that goes into the Kurtis-Kraft race cars.

PHOTOS BY CANAAN

19

RECORD BREAKING LAMBRETTA SCOOTERS

Above, the latest record breaker, which made a one-way run of 121.578 mph and a two-way average of 118.363 mph for the flying kilometer. Truly an amazing performance.

Below, interesting details of the Lambretta 125 cc engine, transmission and drive shaft.

Scooter activity in Italy is really something which has to be seen to be believed. Imagine the situation here in America if everyone who owned a car, instead owned a scooter, and scooter-owners owned cars. That is approximately the proportion that scooters represent in Italy, as initial and upkeep costs for a car are prohibitive for the average Italian workers.

Innocenti, who build the Lambretta, are the largest manufacturer of scooters, and their 125 cc model is a real engineering achievement. In various streamlined versions they hold many of the class 4 and 5 world's records over distances ranging from one kilometer to 3,000 miles.

As just an example, riders Brunori, Masetti, Masserini and Rizzi covered 3,000 miles on the 125 cc Lambretta scooter at an average speed (including all stops) of 97.759 kmh. (60.74 mph). This amazing record was established at the Montlhery Autodrome in France.

On the 14th of April 1951, an even more amazing record was set. Romolo Ferri, on or more correctly, *in* a streamlined Lambretta, achieved average speeds of over 120 mph. This time the course was the new Appian Way, near Rome.

SPECIFICATIONS OF STANDARD PRODUCTION LAMBRETTA SCOOTER

No. cyl.	1
Type	2 cycle
Displacement	125 cc
Bore	52 mm
Stroke	58 mm
Horsepower	4.3
Fuel mixture	5% oil
Transmission	3 speed
Wheelbase	48.8 inches
Tires	4x8
Weight	132 pounds
Speed	43.4 mph
Fuel economy	Approx 120 mpg

H
O
P
U
P

20

Tremendous interest in scooters is demonstrated by size of crowd lining course of rally.

In Italy, they even have wedding processions on scooters! Note flowers on groom's sidecar.

21

PHOTOS BY TRINDL

To the Lakes with Barney . . .

by Louis Kimzey

"Barney" Navarro of Navarro Speed Equipment is a soft spoken, easy going fellow who has but one big love . . . and that's building record breaking engines. He tackles a job with such vigor and finishes it with such finesse that one can't help but marvel . . . and maybe even feel a *slight* tinge of jealousy!

Here's what I mean. It all started approximately 39 working hours before the day of S.C.T.A.'s May 6th meet. Barney bought a new block and from here on we'll "keep time" on him.

The first day he ported and relieved. Then he installed a 180° crankshaft; next, a special Winfield cam and Navarro heads.

The following day was spent assembling the various parts, and that evening the engine was ready to "drop in" . . . Whew!

22

Photographer Gene Trindl and I arrived on the scene to record the all night struggle. Frankly, we never thought Barney would get the roadster running by morning. 9:30 p.m. 'till 5:30 a.m., Navarro worked on the engine, wiring, fuel lines, roll bar, (a requirement), and just making sure everything was in its correct place. In the middle of the job, the fuel lines and the water hose fittings turned up missing and nobody was able to find them. None were available at that time of night, so he improvised . . . He scrounged around and borrowed fuel lines. Then he found an elbow joint similar to the one which bolts to the cylinder head. This was welded to a pipe, so he had to cut it off. Then he ground it down and threaded it, all of which took considerable time. If you'll look at the photograph of the engine, you'll see the elbow I'm speaking about. A *small* hose instead of the normal size is used . . . Barney believes that Fords heat-up because the water circulates too fast . . . interesting theory!

About the engine: It has Navarro heads and Navarro manifold (of course!); 182 cu. in.; 3-1/16 bore; 3-1/16 stroke. The body? Perfect '27 T roadster with a cast grille; in short, just the *opposite* of Beatty's roadster. (Page 30). There is no transmission . . . just a "dog clutch" and a quick-change rear end. The bubble on the hood accomodates "Barney's Blower" if, and when he uses it.

At 6:00 Sunday morning, believe it or not, the job was finished, but it was so late, Navarro decided to go directly to the lakes before finding out if the car would run! O.K., we're off to the Lakes!

On the way, while we made a breakfast stop, the roadster was lubricated. At 8:30 a.m., off again . . . next stop, *El Mirage!*

A couple of hours later we arrived at the lakes, after jarring all our teeth loose on the @!!#@!*$? dirty, dusty, bumpy read (and that's putting it mildly) which leads into the lake bed.

The weather was terrible. A cold wind was blowing. The sun was out but you could hardly tell it for the dust. Right here is a good place to put in a plug for the American Hot Rod Conference. After one day at El Mirage, I feel there's something wrong if all the fellows who have been to the lakes and Bonneville don't get together and back this movement. I say, *join today! Let's get a paved strip!*

The first thing you do when you arrive, is get your car checked for safety. If there is something wrong with the car, the Safety Committe gives you tools and makes you repair or replace the faulty parts right on the spot! And you've got to compliment the Safety Committee (of the S.C.T.A.) for it's thoroness of inspection.

24

Finally, the inspector hands you your certificate which shows the car is safe to run. Here's the moment I've been waiting for! Will it run? Will it break a record . . . or just break? All this was running thru my mind as the picture (left center) was taken. It shows me pushing Barney.

As you see (bottom) it ran, and after a little carburetor work he made his first run . . . 101 . . . not good enough . . . but then the engine had only been running a few minutes. After checking carburetion again, (it was running too lean) Barney made another run . . . and this time . . . 109. Still running too lean. He adjusted the pots again and got back in line to await his turn.

(Photo above shows line-up. Barney in front row, with push car directly behind.)

The procedure is this: Get in line when you think your car is in condition to run. Keep moving up till you are in the front row. The starter asks if you are ready. When you are, he gives the signal to take off. A girl above on a platform phones to the other end, to let them know you are coming and gives them your number.

(Photo, right, shows me pouring "alky" into tank prior to the last run.)

25

(Photo above was taken from push car just as the roadster broke away on its 119 mph run. We were going about 65 mph with Gene, the photographer, hanging out the window! You can see the markers and the straight course in front of Barney.)

With the mixture *still* too lean, Barney adjusted the carburetors *again* and got in line for the fourth time.

Photo, above center, shows Barney on last run. He said the tach showed he was doing 135 mph before the fuel back-fired thru the carburetors and caught fire. Part of the standard safety equipment is a fire extinguisher. So Barney had the flame out in no time, and there was little damage. Just after photo at right as taken, I asked him how he felt about the whole thing and he replied, "I know what's the matter . . . the *next* time, I'm installing a bigger fuel line. And then . . . *the record!*"

H
O
P

U
P

26

Trammel's "BATHTUB"

A home town beauty is seldom appreciated until she appears elsewhere. Such was Bob Trammel's experience with his customized car.

During the early stages of construction, it was but a '41 Ford club coupe with the top cut off at the waistline . . . and was soon nicknamed "The Bathtub." 'Twas well named, too, for I actually took a bath when Trammel charged thru a water puddle while the floor was absent.

Over a period of 2 years, Trammel, young race car mechanic, spent all of his spare time shaping the Bathtub into a Beauty. When the removable padded top is in place, Trammel's car stands only 48" high overall. Altho the bottom of the frame rails are only 1" lower than stock, the body was greatly lowered by radical 10" floor channelling — seats dropped into deep wells on either sides of the driveshaft tunnel. This was made possible by reducing the X-member to a very stiff, yet thin strut. Six inches were trimmed off the bottom of the body— four inches from the top. Special windshield frame castings, by DuVall, give a rakish effect.

A Dago dropped axle and rerolled spring eyes brought the chassis down to a Dachshund level. To provide a low hood line, a special radiator was relocated in front of the frame cross-member. One of the most difficult operations was the relocation of controls to conform with the new low seating position.

The engine, a Navarro-built 1941 Mercury, was bored 7/16" and stroked 1/8", ported and relieved, equipped with 8¾" to 1 Navarro heads, a Navarro dual manifold, and a Winfield super 1-R cam.

Brown and tan is the theme of interior appointments, with all upholstery in pleated DuPont Fibrilite by Floyd Tipton. The back of the front seats fold to form a bed . . . for sportsmen. A full-padded dash is a safety feature.

Trammel's Bathtub attracted great throngs of admirers during a trip to Helena, Montana, where the car now awaits a buyer . . . like all customized car builders, Trammel had new ideas before the present project was completed, so is anxious to sell.

MEET THE ADVERTISERS

HOP UP wishes to take you for a visit with the firm of Auto Accessories, presided over by Milton Stanton and George Friedland The firm has long been one of the top accessory stores on the West Coast. With a growing list of 25,000 customers, the popularity of Auto Accessories Company can now be considered world wide.

In addition to their successful career, Milt and George (as they prefer being called) are avid racing enthusiasts and have sponsored a very successful jalopy during the past season. In the recent Palm Springs road race, Milt drove a Singer roadster and was doing quite well until forced out with faded brakes. Milt comes by his racing naturally, having grown up with and gone to school with a chap you may have heard of . . . Johnnie Parsons.

This year Milt and George are sponsoring a race car at Indianapolis. Known as the Auto Accessories Special, it is the ex-Maurie Rose Maserati, powered by a super-charged 3-litre, 8-cylinder engine and piloted by the capable Bud Sennett, who is chief mechanic and installation expert at Auto Accessories. This car should provide some stiff competition for the Meyer-Drake-Offenhauser powered cars.

Auto Accessories' showrooms are located in the center of metropolitan Los Angeles, which has long been considered the home of custom and speed equipment. A 6400 sq. ft. building on Washington Blvd. provides a large showroom and ample parts warehouse. Most recent addition to their line of custom equipment is their foreign car accessories for Hillman Minx. These will soon be augmented by accessories for Jaguar and Austin.

You name any item of speed and custom equipment, and if these boys don't have it in their stock room, they'll probably start building it. That's their way of doing business—please the customers!

PHOTOS BY CHESEBROUGH

H
O
P

U
P

28

Bud Sennett and Milt Stanton install heads on a Ford.

Below, the counters at Auto Accessories are jammed with parts.

BEATTY'S "RUST BUCKET"

by Louis Kimzey

Give me your opinion. Look at the photos . . . the one above shows an upside-down Model A front suspension and a rusted hood. The rear end of the body was welded on a few short hours before it arrived at the lake. And the interior! The steering wheel is stripped to the wire core with friction tape for a grip, and the gauges are taped or wired into place. The engine (photo above, right) has a '41 block with Navarro heads and manifold. The worked-over supercharger is from a G.M.C. two-cycle Diesel. Note oil on top of blower and the complete lack of paint anywhere. Upon seeing the car for the first time, one lady visitor to the lakes remarked, "Oh, look, that poor fellow's car has been all gutted by a fire!"

Well, what *is* your opinion? What do you think she'll do? Here's a typical comment as Tom Beatty pulled up in front of the inspection tent: "How fast will that rust bucket go?" When the inspector looked under the body, he suddenly started banging the frame with a wrench. He had *actually* found a nest of spiders! The few who know owner Tom, guaranteed his car would "go like a tall dog . . . if it holds together."

Frankly, I thought he was taking his life in his hands, driving that "beast" thru the course. But to make a long story short, he passed the safety inspection, which was really a surprise to everyone (but Tom). I moseyed over to the inspector. "What do you think of her?" "That roadster may not be beautiful, but it's one of the *safest* cars here. It has the weight distributed so that it handles like a dream at high speeds and would be a hard one to turn over.

However, on his first run, he clocked 141.96 mph. The record is 143! As I ran over to congratulate him, he was tinkering with the "pots." "Nice going," I beamed. He looked up, sad faced. "My mixture was a little rich . . . I'll do better the next run." I thought, well . . .

He ran thru again. This time he did something that made me feel a little cheap . . . cheap because I had "judged a book by its cover." Still I was so happy for *him*, I forgot my chagrin and ran over to tell him the good news. "Guess what you did, Tom!" "Oh . . . I figure it was about 150 according to the 'tach'." When I told him his speed was 154.63 mph, he said, "Oh, I think she'll do better the next time!"

PHOTOS BY TRINDL

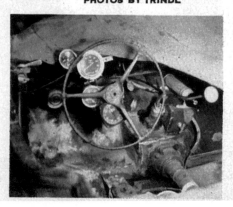

CATALINA GRAND NATIONAL

Steve Ward (Harley 125) flies thru the air.

32

Favored by brilliant smog-free weather, the 1st Annual Catalina Grand National motorcycle race was an outstanding success. Early arrivals were on hand Friday morning. By Saturday, accommodations were at a premium. Late comers, nothing daunted, spent the night in sleeping bags on the golf course.

Genial Frank Cooper (who seemed to be everyplace at once) and the rest of the AMA staff, handled the entire two-day racing program beautifully.

Saturday, the preliminary race for cycles of 125 to 250 cc displacement was run on the 5-mile course, which was 4 rough miles of narrow, mountain trails, balanced by 1 mile of excellent, paved highway. The cycles were started in two groups . . . the larger (250 cc) being the first to start. Unlike the Sunday "go", this was a massed start and the sight of 40 mad machines accelerating on the dirt section will surely gain a mob of new cycle fans. First man around at the end of lap one was Walt

Above, the start of the 250 cc race on Saturday.

Below, Johnny Quick of Compton, Calif., is airborne along narrow path.

PHOTOS BY CHESEBROUGH

39

Fulton on the new experimental overhead valve Mustang . . . which is the *first machine of its type ever run!* What it actually amounts to is a Triumph twin, cut in half.

Walking around the course during the race was an education in itself. One saw many examples of good and bad riding. Outstanding were Walt Fulton on #17 Mustang; Portland, Oregon's, H. C. Simon, on his O. K. Supreme, ohc, which again is the only one on the coast. (Some of the boys better get busy!) Carrying on a grand tradition in beautiful style was Cordy Piper, who is the nephew of Jack and Cordy Milne (you remember both these as world champions).

On lap 8, Fulton and his Mustang retired. This let H. C. Simon into the lead. He gave way to Nick Nicholson (13 laps) who finished the 50-mile race in excellent time. Surprising were the few retirements. The course was not easy, as you can judge by the winner's speed.

Many of the riders were exhausted and those planning on riding in the 100-mile

Above, the youngest rider, Bob Onstine did a wonderful job on a Mustang 222 cc.

Below, Jack Baldwin (BSA) leads #137 down the mountain. Surprisingly few dropped out.

The eventual winner Walt Fulton (Triumph) did a masterful job of riding, passing over 50 other machines on one lap.

Spills such as these were quite common on the rough up-and-down mountain trails. Low speeds reduced danger on steep hillsides.

35

PHOTOS BY CANAAN

#45—Pete Sanatra (Ariel), #81—Dave Hunter (Triumph), and #84—Jack Baldwin (BSA), cornering in town.

PHOTOS BY JACK CAMPBELL

Grand National race retired early as the 50 mile race was only a sample of the 100-mile course laid out for Sunday.

The 150 spotless machines lined up in Sunday's brilliant sunshine with the blue harbor as a backdrop provided a beautiful sight for the huge throng of spectators. Promptly at 2:00 p.m., the signal to start engines was given. All 150 roared to life almost as one. Then, with an ear-shattering roar, the first 5 machines revved up. With precise regularity, the cycles started at 30 second intervals. Streaking into the lead at the start was #6 Nick Nicholson (BSA). In the 21st group was Walt Fulton, now on a Triumph, destined to win the first Grand National, and even at the start, it was obvious to many that here was a brilliant rider on a superbly prepared mount. During the entire race, his average varied only a few seconds per lap. This standard of riding was even better than Saturday's and spills were surprisingly few considering the terrain. During the closing stages of the race, the winner was still an uncertainty due to elapsed time intervals at the start. Preliminary announcements at the finish had Chuck Minert on a B.S.A. as winner. A review showed that Walt Fulton had the lowest actual riding time. An examination of the winning Triumph showed

Eddie Hildebrand (Indian) bounces high on the rough section of the course.

Dick Hutchins (Harley 125) never left his mount and kept right on going after this nasty spill. No injuries were reported during two days of rough and tumble racing.

it to be in excellent condition . . . with *very little tire wear.* Meticulous attention to detail had paid off. Actual preparation of the Triumph had begun weeks before, all nuts were safety wired and tune was probably as good as any factory job.

Notes and Comments:

The islanders as a whole were very happy with the race and with the conduct of riders and spectators. Wm. Wrigley, owner of the island, was an enthusiastic spectator in the sidecar of one of his two Indian fours. He was driven to various vantage points during the race and shot several hundred feet of motion picture film.

A check with the police department revealed no arrests. They said that this was one of the best behaved organizations to ever visit the island. Catalina looks forward to a bigger and better Grand National in 1952.

RESULTS

1st	—	103	Walt Fulton	Triumph
2nd	—	73	Chuck Minert	BSA
3rd	—	78	Del Kuhn	AJS
4th	—	6	Nick Nicholson	BSA
5th	—	16	Wally Albright	AJS
6th	—	68	Ray Tanner	Harley

37

43

(Continued from page 15)

BLOWER SIZE FOR '50 FORD

I own a 1950 Ford convertible, without over-drive, and equipped with 8-1 Edelbrock heads...

What will a supercharger do to the gas economy? How much so? Will the addition of a supercharger mean taking off the heads and replacing them with the original stock heads? How large a roots blower would be necessary for the Ford? When I say large, I mean cubic feet per minute or pounds per square inch delivery pressure. This would be a rating at some specified rpm.

As the rear end is very light the gas tank is kept full for the additional weight but more is desired. Will lowering blocks help or would weights be better?

Alexandria, Virginia   H. C. Weart

A supercharger definitely means returning to stock compression ratio, and since more horse-power is available, it will take more fuel if the added power is used. How much more fuel depends on how you drive it. The old super-charged Graham used to give slightly better economy than the un-supercharged model under steady driving conditions, due to a better mixture, distributed more uniformly. A positive displacement blower should have an output of roughly 30 to 40% more than the engine requirement. In your case, this is ½ the piston displacement (for a 4-cycle engine) or 120 cu. in. per revolution plus the 30 to 40%, or about 162 cu. in. You must also know the volumetric efficiency of the blower, which in the case of a roots type, decreases with increasing speed to values of less than 60%.

It is usually an error to add weight to the rear end of a car, but in such an extreme case as a late Ford, I would suggest you clock acceleration with and without the weights in order to prove what is best. I do suggest you try a set of lowering blocks before adding weight as they help somewhat.—Tech. Ed.

MODEL A FORD JETS & LOWERING

My Model "A" engine has the usual modifications for road use but I don't know what size jets to use for my two Stromberg 97's. What would be the best for economy? Also what can I do to the rear suspension to lower it somewhat, without makeshift changes, using the stock rear axle? Are there any possibilities of using a different spring altogether, or coil springs, or raising the rear cross member higher?

San Francisco, Calif.   Wilbur E. Bullis

Too many things have to be considered to say definitely what jet size to use. I can merely say, start with the stock V-8 jets and experiment up or down as general running indicates. Don't run too lean as exhaust valves will be burned.

Some hot rods use the model T type rear cross-member and spring to lower the rear end. Another method is to "Z" the frame. This involves cutting the frame just forward of the rear axle and lowering the rails about 4 to 6 inches. This is a lot of work and re-splicing of the resultant mismatched frame requires ingenuity to retain strength. The body under-pan of the rear deck section must also be re-worked. Reversing spring eyes gives a modest drop at minimum cost.—Tech. Ed.

DRY SUMP FORD V-8

Do you consider it feasible to convert a Ford engine to dry sump in order to get the hood line down?

Olympia, Washington   John H. Kirkwood, Jr.

The flywheel is the lowest point, especially if the engine sits at 3 to 5 degrees slope as required for a straight drive line. Actually, I do not feel that dry sump lubrication is at all necessary or even desirable for any American engine for any use short of, say, running at Indianapolis, because oil temperatures in our engines are reasonable and well controlled. I am using a pair of Zenith side draft carburetors to get the hood line down but haven't yet made the necessary adapter.—Tech. Ed.

POWER BOAT RACING

Almost all competitive power boat activities are under the control of the American Power Boat Association. To understand the antics of the water-going speed lovers, a brief listing of the most popular classes is helpful.

OUTBOARDS

Owners of "inboards" laughingly call the outboards "shingles with egg beaters hung on the rear." With a hopped-up two-cycle engine clamped to the transom, these highly specialized craft go bouncing about a "watery road course" to the accompaniment of a deceptively loud exhaust bellow.

Each class is designated by engine displacement and minimum weight limits.

Class	Disp.	Hull Wt Empty	Wt/Driver & Engine
M	to 7½ cu in	75 lbs	200 lbs
A	7½ to 14	100 lbs	250 lbs
B	14 to 20	100 lbs	265 lbs
C	20 to 30	150 lbs	315 lbs
D	30 to 40	150 lbs	315 lbs
E	40 to 50	160 lbs	335 lbs
F	50 to 60	160 lbs	335 lbs
X	unlimited	unlimited	

The average speed during races ranges from about 35 mph for class M to 60 mph for class F. The mile record is for outboards.

INBOARDS

The outboard owners jokingly refer to inboard boats as "cabin cruisers." Using hopped up automotive or aircraft engines, these slick, and sometimes very expensive, beauties are divided into nine popular classes (there are many others).

"PODH" — Pacific one design hydroplane — the "poor man's boat." Stock Ford V-8 "60" engines, gasoline only, rigid standardizing specifications. Jokingly called a "rowboat with sponsons," the PODH's carry two (driver and balancing mechanic) aft of the engine and do about 55 mph in races.

Class B Runabout—135 cu in. engine (usually a "60") in a V-bottom sponsonless hull; does about 55 mph in race. Driver only. Engine aft of driver.

135 Hydroplane—135 cu in. engine hopped to the limit in an all-out 3-point hull. About 90 mph in race. Driver only.

"Crackerbox" Runabout—another "poor man's boat" with a 267 cu in. limit on engine (usually Ford V-8) and an almost-flat-bottom hull. Limited to 1 carb venturi for each 2 cyl. Driver and mechanic. Does a wild 65 mph in race. Must be porpoising (jumping) to really go.

Class E Runabout—similar to B Runabout. 245 cu in. engine limit. 65 mph in race.

48 cu in. Hydroplane—usually Crosley powered. So small that one man can easily carry the hull, yet they do 85 mph tops!

Division I, 225—really a misnomer, for 267 cu in. is the limit. All-out hulls and anything goes in fuels. Can use 3-carb manifolds. Do 90-95 in race. Record is 115.045 mph.

Division II, 225—actually limited to 225 cu in. Gasoline only and carburetor limit.

Gold Cup Class—Unlimited, anything goes. The "Millionaire's Class." Allison, Rolls-Royce, and Packard aircraft engines push super-hulls in 85-90 mph races. Record is 160.323 mph.

The most exciting classes are: Division I 225's, because they have plenty of steam and "cross-up" corners like a dirt track race car, and the wild but fast Crackerboxes.

H
O
P

U
P

40

SUBSCRIBE TO HOP UP TODAY!
Use Subscription Blank on Page 3

H
O
P

U
P

41

MORE POWER TO YOU
WITH A *Belond* EQUA-FLOW Exhaust System

ELIMINATE BACK PRESSURE and INCREASE HORSEPOWER!

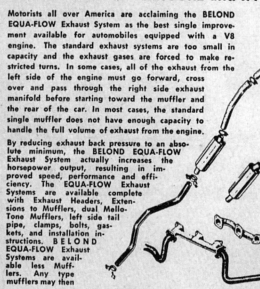

Motorists all over America are acclaiming the BELOND EQUA-FLOW Exhaust System as the best single improvement available for automobiles equipped with a V8 engine. The standard exhaust systems are too small in capacity and the exhaust gases are forced to make restricted turns. In some cases, all of the exhaust from the left side of the engine must go forward, cross over and pass through the right side exhaust manifold before starting toward the muffler and the rear of the car. In most cases, the standard single muffler does not have enough capacity to handle the full volume of exhaust from the engine.

By reducing exhaust back pressure to an absolute minimum, the BELOND EQUA-FLOW Exhaust System actually increases the horsepower output, resulting in improved speed, performance and efficiency. The EQUA-FLOW Exhaust Systems are available complete with Exhaust Headers, Extensions to Mufflers, dual Mello-Tone Mufflers, left side tail pipe, clamps, bolts, gaskets, and installation instructions. BELOND EQUA-FLOW Exhaust Systems are available less Mufflers. Any type mufflers may then

be used, or one stock muffler may be installed to be used in conjunction with the present right side muffler. This combination is quiet as well as efficient. This set also contains all of the necessary parts for installation except mufflers.

The BELOND EQUA-FLOW Exhaust System with stock mufflers is recommended for Oldsmobiles. However, on Fords, Mercurys, and Lincolns, the type of mufflers to be used are a matter of individual choice.

TYPICAL STANDARD FORD & MERCURY EXHAUST SYSTEM

FORD V8 ● MERCURY ● OLDSMOBILE ● LINCOLN V8
For prices and models, see coupon below

CLYMER BOOKS OF NOSTALGIA

Entirely New!

American Horse-Drawn Vehicles

200 ILLUSTRATIONS . . . 106 LARGE PAGES

Contains largest and most complete assortment ever published of carriages . . . wagons . . . buggies . . . phaetons . . . track sulkies . . . skeleton wagons . . . top buggies . . . jump seats and surries . . . two-wheelers . . . hearses . . . fire wagons. All styles and sizes clearly shown. A pictorial album compiled in typical style of the days when many different HORSE-DRAWN VEHICLES were common . . . colorful vehicles of every description.

ORDER NOW! **Postpaid $2.00** ☐

De Luxe Edition with Fabrikoid binding
and gold leaf lettering **Postpaid $3.50** ☐

MOTOR SCRAPBOOK SERIES

Motor Scrapbook No. 6. Latest and best. Profusely illustrated Auto Scrapbook. 224 pages. Ads, photos, details of 250 early cars. $2.00. Deluxe Edition $3.00.
Scrapbook 5 $2.00, Del. $3
Scrapbook 4 $1.50, Del. $2
Scrapbook 3 $1.50, Del. $2
Scrapbook 2 $1.50, Del. $2
Scrapbook 1 $1.50, Del. $2

MOTOR HISTORY OF AMERICA

Complete growth of the automobile industry from its beginning. Stories and anecdotes of the men whose names made auto history: Ford, Buick, Chrysler, Willys, Kettering, Haynes, Winton, etc., $3.00.

Treasury of Early American Autos.

Just out. Clymer's new McGraw-Hill book of historical cars, songs, cartoons, data Vanderbilt Cup, Indianapolis, N. Y.-Paris Races. 22,000 words text, 500 illustrations. Beautiful large gift album. 224 large pages. **$5.00** ☐

HENRY FORD by William Simonds
Authentic story of America's Foremost Automotive Giant. Illustrated $3.00 Deluxe............................$4.00 ☐

HISTORY OF MOTORIZED VEHICLES
Mechanical Traction and Travel—1769 to 1946. 368 carts, photos, drawings of historical vehicles, including steam, gas, electric, Diesel and tractors, with a short history. $2.00 Deluxe............................ $3.00 ☐

THE MODERN STEAM CAR AND ITS BACKGROUND
120 illustrations and a mine of information with specifications and descriptions of ancent and modern steam cars ....$2.00 ☐

SAGA OF THE ROARING ROAD
The story of early auto racing in America with 40 exciting photos from eye witness accounts of De Palma, Rickenbacker, Milton, Chevrolet and others..........$2.00 ☐

STEAM CAR SCRAPBOOK
Lists and describes over 125 makes of Steam Cars. A complete history of steam cars—past and present. Profusely illustrated with early ads and photos $2.00. ☐
Deluxe ....$3.00 ☐

ALBUM OF STEAM TRACTION ENGINES
U. S. and Foreign makes from 1855 to 1929 are shown with 470 photos including 105 makes. Nostalgic pictures and ads of old time farm equipment. Memories of the early agricultural days on the farm...$2.50 ☐
Deluxe ....$3.50 ☐

FASTEST ON EARTH
By Capt. G. T. Eyston, world-famous record holder. 175 pages, 75 photos, charts, drawings. Complete history and speed record 1898 to date. Postpaid $2.00 ☐

"THE SALT OF THE EARTH"
The personal story of Ab Jenkins, former Mayor of Salt Lake City, greatest long distance driver the world has ever known—no other person has ever traveled so far, so fast on land. The history of the Bonneville Salt Flats. Jenkins' record runs described in detail. The MORMON METEOR, Ab's streamlined racing monster, and other racing machines illustrated and described. The record runs of Campbell, Eyston and Cobb. $1.50 De Luxe ☐ Edition $2.50 ☐

FLOYD CLYMER MOTORBOOKS
1268 S. Alvarado, L. A. 6, Calif.

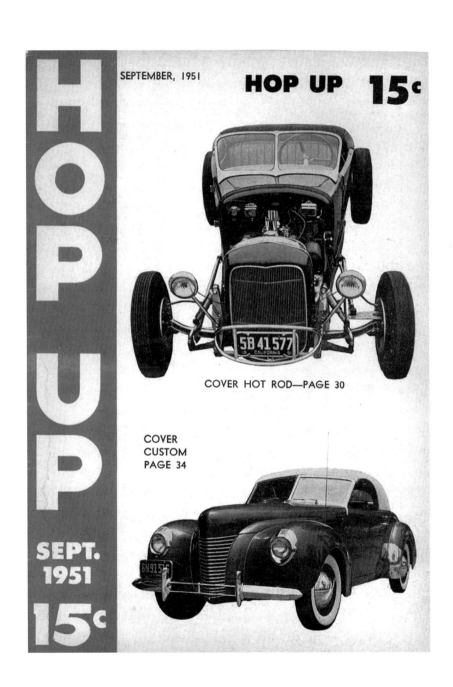

SEPTEMBER, 1951

HOP UP 15c

COVER HOT ROD—PAGE 30

COVER
CUSTOM
PAGE 34

SEPT.
1951

15c

CORRESPONDENCE

CONTINENTALIZED PONTIAC

This is my 1950 Pontiac Super DeLuxe Catalina with rear tire mount which was handmade

except for tire cover. Entire cost was about $50.
Vancouver, Washington   Harold L. Mason

OLD LEAPING LENA LEAPS

Recently made a few modifications on Old Leaping Lena, my 1950 Ford V-8 Custom Deluxe . . . Dual Mellotone Exhaust System, dual point Roemer Distributor conversion plate. 8.5:1 finned aluminum heads, dual intake manifold, with dual Ford type 8BA pots. Now Old Lena looks just as innocent as any other '50 Ford, but actually, she is a Bearcat.

My chief gripe at Ford at present is that confounded single point ignition system that they are using and I wouldn't give 3 cents in Chinese money for a whole load of 'em. Why doesn't Dearborn wise up a bit?
Rapid City, So. Dakota   Thomas L. Squyres

Ford and Mercury (949-51) are greatly improved by installation of dual-point ignition. —Ed.

HIGH COMPRESSION FOR OLDS

Enclosed a few pictures of my very beautiful Olds 98 Holiday which recently won a trophy at the Tracy Drag Races as the best performing and appearing stock. The car is equipped with Belond Equa-Flow system, special racing plugs, and '51 heads with '50 gasket giving it a compression ratio of approx. 8 to 1. This is a good trick, using '51 heads with the comparatively thin '50 gasket since the '51 gasket is

made much thicker but the heads are of a higher ratio.

The car is finished in beautiful aqua-blue green with black rose top and wheels. The fender skirts are special made filling them out to the bottom of the body line. The Olds script and ornaments have been replaced by the very distinguished '50 Caddie V's front and back.
Lodi, Calif.   Bob Bowen

CUSTOMIZED LINCOLN CONTINENTAL

Enclosed please find photo of my '48 Lincoln Continental . . . All body work by "Doray of Miami", designed by yours truly, while engine modifications consist of: a ¾ cam, dual stacks and carbs, milled heads, platinum points,

and lowered rear end . . . installed by Miami Allied Automotive Specialists.

For a heavy car, performance is splendid and cornering is surpassed by none.
Miami Beach, Florida   Benjamin E. Wendkos

SPEED SHIFT BEATS OLDS 88

It seems to me every 88 owner thinks he has a foreign sports car. I have a little ole '37 Ford —not hopped except for 100 hp engine—have taken numerous Olds—both in top speed and pickup. I believe it is just a matter of speed shifting thru the gears.
Clinton, Iowa   Mel Willgrubs

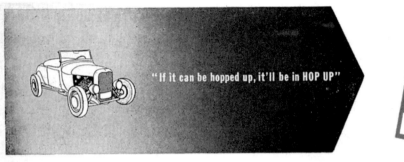

"If it can be hopped up, it'll be in HOP UP"

BONNEVILLE NEXT

During the last week of August, the eyes of the HOP UP world will be focused on Bonneville Salt Flats, Utah.

The third annual speed trials will be held from August 27 to September 2 and will probably be the fastest yet. During the first two meets, timed speeds rose from the 190 mph range to over 200 mph in the streamliner classes. Several new cars are expected to beat the 200 mph mark this year.

Considerable good will and favorable publicity can be the result of this well-organized, orderly program of events.

ACCELERATION TRIALS

Organized acceleration trials, more often referred to as "drags," are becoming increasingly popular. The most accurate test for acceleration is the elapsed time for a standing start quarter-mile run. A rolling start is neither accurate nor comparable with standard tests. Using the "last tenth average" method, the highest mph clocking does not necessarily indicate the lowest time for ¼ mile.

For the sake of recognition and accuracy, it is hoped that the regular elapsed time standing quarter-mile will be adopted by *all* acceleration trials.

EDITORIAL STAFF

Editor....................................Oliver Billingsley
Technical Editor...............................John R. Bond
Associate Editor..........................Robert Dearborn
Staff Photographer.................Jerry Chesebrough
Photographers...........Jack Campbell, Bob Canaan
Joe Al Denker, Gene Trindl

PRODUCTION STAFF

Managing Editor...................W. H. Brehaut, Jr.
Art Director ....Louis Kimzey
Art..Jack Caldwell

ADVERTISING

Advertising Manager.....................William Quinn
East Coast Representatives......Peabody & Ortgies
276 West 43rd Street
New York 18, N.Y.
United Kingdom.....................Kenneth Kirkman
2 Longcroft Avenue
Banstead, Surrey, England

CORRESPONDENTS

Italy ....Corrado Millanta

Contributions—not responsible for the return of unsolicited manuscripts, photographs, and/or drawings unless accompanied by self-addressed stamped envelope.

Mailing address—Box 110, Glendale, California.

Vol. 1, No. 2   **September, 1951**

CONTENTS

HOP UP is published monthly by Enthusiasts' Publications, Inc., 540 W. Colorado Blvd., Glendale, California. Phone CHapman 5-2297. Application for entry as second-class matter is pending. Copyright 1951 by Enthusiasts' Publications, Inc. Reprinting in whole or in part forbidden except by permission of the publishers.

Subscription price $1.50 per year throuout the world. Single copy 15c.

Change of address—must show both old and new addresses.

Darlington "250" Won by Faulkner

Above, Walt Faulkner (#2), Cecil Green (#4), Gordon Reid (#71). Below, Neal Carter (#53), Rex Easton (#39) and Johnny McDowell (#79). Note smooth, wide, asphalt track.

Dynamic little Walt Faulkner (5'5", 128 lb.) walked away with the 250-mile AAA championship race at the new Darlington, S. C., International Raceway on the 4th of July. Setting a new record for the race at 104.239 mph for the 250 miles, Walt drove a sensational race on the Grant Piston Ring Special owned by J. C. Agajanian.

Billy Vukovich, well-known California midget chauffeur, led the race for 26 laps but threw a rod and was forced out of the race. Later he took over the wheel for Walt Brown and finished in 10th spot.

That amazing car, the Belanger Special, driven by Tony Bettenhausen due to the injuries to Lee Wallard, gave us further proof that lower piston speeds are more important than cubic inches. It added a 2nd in this race to its victories at Indianapolis, Milwaukee, and Langhorne.

Left, Walt Brown (#44) and Paul Russo (#7). Right, Henry Banks (#1) finished 7th.

Fin. Pos.	Car No:	Driver:	Car:	Qual. Speed
1	2	Walt Faulkner	Grant Ring Sp.	111.111
2	99	T. Bettenhausen	Belanger Spec	110.837
3	4	Cecil Green	John Zink Sp.	111.940
4	33	Mill Mackey	Iddings Spec.	110.024
5	9	Jack McGrath	Hinkle Spec.	110.294
6	31	Manuel Ayulo	Coast Gr. Spc.	110.837
7	1	Henry Banks	Blue Crown Sp.	110.565
8	83	Mike Nazaruk	Jim Robbins Sp.	110.025
9	8	Chuck Stevenson	Bardahl Spec.	111.111
10	44	Walt Brown (*)	Fed. Eng. Sp.	111.900
11	23	Clif Griffith (**)	Morris Spec.	111.111
12	57	A. Linden(***)	Leitenberger Sp	109.489
13	7	P. Russo(****)	Russo-Nichels Sp	111.662
14	19	Kenny Eaton	Hinkle Spec.	111.111

(*) Brown relieved by Vukovich.
(**) Griffith relieved by Ridger Ward on 153rd lap.
(***) Linden relieved by Roy Sherman.
(****) Russo relieved by Tolan on 146th lap.

Winner Walt Faulkner receives congratulations.

57

MORE POWER TO YOU

WITH A *Belond* EQUA-FLOW Exhaust System

ELIMINATE BACK PRESSURE and INCREASE HORSEPOWER!

Motorists all over America are acclaiming the BELOND EQUA-FLOW Exhaust System as the best single improvement available for automobiles equipped with a V8 engine. The standard exhaust systems are too small in capacity and the exhaust gases are forced to make restricted turns. In some cases, all of the exhaust from the left side of the engine must go forward, cross over and pass through the right side exhaust manifold before starting toward the muffler and the rear of the car. In most cases, the standard single muffler does not have enough capacity to handle the full volume of exhaust from the engine.

By reducing exhaust back pressure to an absolute minimum, the BELOND EQUA-FLOW Exhaust System actually increases the horsepower output, resulting in improved speed, performance and efficiency. The EQUA-FLOW Exhaust Systems are available complete with Exhaust Headers, Extensions to Mufflers, dual Mello-Tone Mufflers, left side tail pipe, clamps, bolts, gaskets, and installation instructions. BELOND EQUA-FLOW Exhaust Systems are available less Mufflers. Any type mufflers may then

be used, or one stock muffler may be installed to be used in conjunction with the present right side muffler. This combination is quiet as well as efficient. This set also contains all of the necessary parts for installation except mufflers.

The BELOND EQUA-FLOW Exhaust System with stock mufflers is recommended for Oldsmobiles. However, on Fords, Mercurys, and Lincolns, the type of mufflers to be used are a matter of individual choice.

TYPICAL
STANDARD FORD &
MERCURY
EXHAUST SYSTEM

FORD V8 ● MERCURY ● OLDSMOBILE ● LINCOLN V8

For prices and models, see coupon below

6

Bill Chambers' '49 Ford

RUSSETTA MEET

Above, Boren & Keldrank's sedan turned 128.11. Below, Howard Johansen of A.R.C., taking top honors with a 141.17.

Below Chet Herbert who makes the famous "roller cams" supervises work on his G.M.C. in a '36 Ford.

Perfect weather for this month's Russetta Timing Meet. Fast times were turned in in all classes, with Earl Evans of the Hutters Club taking fastest time of the day with 165.89. The club standings at this time are: 1st place, the "Coupes" with 226 points; 2nd, the "Hutters" with 222 points; and 3rd, the "Rod Riders" with 217.

The meet had a big turn out as only a Russetta meet can have . . . with every club represented.

The lake was in poor condition and it is certainly not getting better with the constant use, but with the following results it looks like it didn't slow these fellows much. Next month we are going to define the different classes so that you can fully realize what a "C" Class roadster is and the difference between an "A" Class coupe and a "B" or "C" Class coupe. Then there will be a better understanding of the terms used in these "lakes reports."

Car #	Entrant	Club	MPH
	"A" Coupes		
14	Mickey Thompson	Roadents	130.90
131	Fox & Freudiger	Auto Union	118.81
170	Albert Fache	Arabs	118.81
20	Gorton Bros.	Hutters	117.26
	"B" Coupes		
355	Ed Pink	A.R.C.	133.82
225	Mailliard & Cagle	Dusters	122.44
151	Williams & Christensen	Rod Riders	121.62
	"C" Coupes		
38	Cantley & Sylva	Coupes	141.73
45	James Evans	Rod Riders	140.66
30	Jim McGonigal	Arabs	128.57
	"D" Coupes		
69	Bob Rounthwaite	G.C.R.C.	145.74
11	Thomas Cobbs	Auto Union	143.42
308	Bob Comstock	Hutters	132.84
	"A" Roadsters		
83	Bob Wilcox	Hutters	136.88
29	Bill Likes	Couptes	134.32
361	Don Heywood	Arabs	130.43

	"B" Roadsters				B Coupes		
456	Bruce Robinson	G.C.R.C.	144.00		Ed Pink	A.R.C.	137.93
156	George Bentley	Rod Riders	138.99		C Coupes		
15	John Agajanian	Rod Riders	137.40		James D. Evans	Rod Riders	145.74
	"C" Roadsters				D Coupes		
91	Stecker-Fugatt	Stingers	156.52		Dick Pierson	Coupes	150.00
154	Johnson & Wheeler	Rod Riders	144.00		A Roadsters		
339	Irving Brendel	Auto Union	120.00		Bill Likes	Coupes	140.07
	"A" Sedans				B Roadsters		
6	Sharon Baker	Coupes	125.43		{Bill Davis—May	G.C.R.C. }	144.00
312	Bill Bowering	Hutters	124.56		{Bruce Robinson—June	G.C.R.C.** }	
18	Tom McLaughlin	G.C.R.C.	124.13		C Roadsters		
	"B" Sedans				Stecker-Cobb	Rod Riders	163.63
10	Howard Johansen	A.R.C.	141.17		A Sedans		
9	Christensen & Williams	Rod Riders	132.84		Sharon Baker	Coupes	129.03
8	Moon Bros.	Hutters	129.96				
	"B" Streamliners						
41	Earl Evans	Hutters	165.89				
163	Bob McClure	G.C.R.C.	154.50				
287	Carl Lindberg	Hutters	153.19				

EXISTING RECORDS

Names	Club	MPH
A Coupes		
Mickey Thompson	Roadents	133.33

Above, Christensen & Williams' entry for the "Rod Riders" which turned 132.84. Below, Cantley & Sylva's coupe which took first place in the "C" coupe class.

Above, a rhubarb! This "protest" took about a half an hour to settle and maybe I shouldn't say "settle," because it still isn't. The car in question has a belly pan which some believe extends past the body, which is against the rules for its class. They don't agree. The board passed it this one time.

At left, Mickey Thompson's Class C coupe turned fastest time in his class, 130.90 mph.

Below, Bob Wilcox of the "Hutters" turned 136.88 in his class "A" Roadster and won the "Hop Up" trophy for the current month.

10

B Sedans		
Howard Johansen	A.R.C.	141.17*
A Streamliners		
B Streamliners		
Earl Evans	Hutters	165.98*

* New record June meet
** Tied record June meet

George Bentley pictured above came in second to Bruce Robinson in Class B roadsters. George belongs to the Rod Riders Club.

At right, one part "Castro," two parts "metha," six parts "alki." This isn't the mixture this fellow is making, as he has the "mixture" and no one is to know what it is.

Below, Ed Pink with Chet Herberts' G.M.C. engine in his Ford ran 133.82 to win class.

25 Hour JALOPATHON

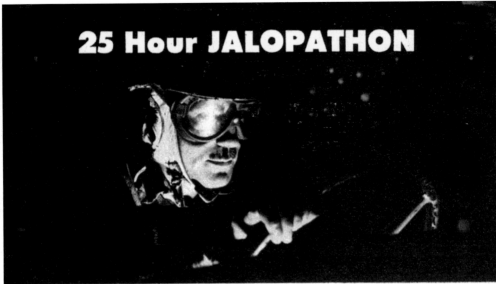

by Louis Kimzey

Jalopathons are not new to the nation, having been run before this in the East. However, Steve Gardner's twenty-five hour endurance race for jalopies at Culver City Speedway (with sprint races every hour to enliven the proceedings) is Los Angeles' first taste of the crash-bang-till-you-drop-from-exhaustion races.

The waitress who "drew the Joe" at the refreshment stand told me that she had ."been watching those darned things go 'round and 'round till I'm dizzy." This comment came during the half way point in the 24-hour run, and I could see what she meant. After two or three hours of watching the pre-1937 cars skid around the oval, one's head *does* get in a whirl.

Procedure with most spectators is to drop in for an hour or two after work, or in the afternoon, and then let it go at that. While there are quite a few hardy souls who seem to get mesmerized and stay on and on, the limit for most seems to be about the time it takes to take in a movie.

Naturally, the crowds must be kept out of the working areas, or pits, but believe me, that is where the real thrills lie. So let me take you "behind the scenes" to the boys who keep the old cars going hour after hour.

An endurance race is just an endurance race until you realize that most of these cars are over fifteen years old and none of them were built later than '37.

12

HOP UP, September, 1951

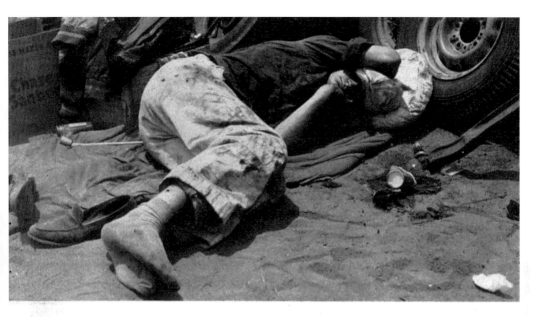

You've no idea of the amount of thought and preparation that goes into this event. One crew seemed really determined to finish. In their pit I counted these extras: eighteen tires and tubes, two axles, two distributors, two fuel pumps *and* a tow truck! With 3000 laps to go, these boys were set for any eventuality.

Anything can go wrong with an old car in a long run, but one fellow I talked to seemed to be blessed with phenomenal luck. Jack Tate (#23), who drove the entire race with no relief (!) went eight hours before he made his first pit stop and then only stopped three times more during the rest of the race. For food, all he had was graham crackers, apples, one lemon and he drank water from a hot water bottle which was hanging overhead with a hose attached. Jack's total time-out for the twenty-four hours was only twenty minutes. His '34

Ford used only one quart of oil and fifty-five gallons of gas. (Tate's fuel, along with that of all the other cars, was donated by Urich's Serve-Yourself Stations, 2500 gallons in all, and the oil and other lubricants by Sta-lube, Inc.)

While Jack Tate's car (and now that I think of it, it couldn't have been luck) had no mechanical failures at all, other drivers were led to fantastic extremes in order to finish. Out of all the tools he brought along, Jack only used his lug wrench, pliers, and a crescent, but I saw one car with its wishbone *chained* in place and another which was running with a broken right rear axle!

Pit crews in some cases worked at lightning speeds. I watched one gang install a rear end in five minutes and another group replaced a broken axle in twenty!

At 13 hours, car #5 ('36 Hudson, driven

Above shows well padded interior of a jalopy. Below is Jack Tate coming into pits after driving 24½ hours of constant racing, with only 4 pit stops for a total of 20 mins.

14

by Joe Heard) threw two rods and was out of the pits in one hour flat! And how was this done? Simple, my dear Watson. Along with the two bad rods, the crew removed two good ones, leaving 1-2-7-8 in operation. Thus, #5 started the race as an eight and finished as a well-balanced four.

Of course blow-outs were the big problem. All thru the day and on into the night, one could hear BANG! BLUMP-BLUMP, Blump-blump, as tires gave way under the tremendous beating. One car used forty-eight changes of rubber during the run!

There were a total of thirty-eight cars at the start. Twenty-eight finished. One car, driven by the Anderson brothers, finished on their sole remaining tire . . . the cord had been showing for over an hour and only blew out as the checkered flag came down! Can you imagine the pit crew sweating that out?

The main excitement for spectators was the series of sprints which occurred every hour. At a given signal, everyone took off like crazy for a chance at extra prize money. All drivers had an equal chance, as the overall position in the race was disregarded during the brief runs.

HOP UP, September, 1951

Thinking back over the event, I find that the thing which lingers strongest in my mind is the fact that the 1st six places at the end of twenty-four hours, were held by '34 Fords! Why won't my old clunker run like that?

Above, with hundreds of tires blowing out under the strain, one of the busiest places in the infield-located pits was the air hose.

Right, the only way to get across track and into the pits was to run in front and in between cars. Kept us on our toes, I'd say!

Below, the "V gap Special" car #7 was a constant winner in all the "jams." It ran the race with no mechanical failures. Amazing!

S.C.T.A.
EL Mirage Meet

Photo above left shows the old yellow water tank, which is the only direction sign showing where El Mirage Lake is.

by Louis Kimzey

Photo above shows Jim Dahm of the Pacers Club being shoved off for his 141.287 run which was fastest time of the day in his class. Below is Clyde Sturdy of the Sidewinders in his Class B Modified Roadster.

S.C.T.A.'s slogan is "Sponsors of the World's Safest Automotive Speed Trials." After watching their technical committee inspect the cars, and observing the proficient manner in which the meets are run, one can readily see why such a slogan. Their meets are some of the best organized timing events I have ever attended.

Let's take their recent meet at El Mirage Dry Lake. The weather was perfect. No wind and so . . . no dust. It was so calm that one fellow remarked, "Honest timing today . . . no wind!"

The top three best times of the meet for each class were:

16

ENTRANT	CLUB	MPH
Class A Modified Roadster:		
Ray Brown	Sidewinders	124.309
Baldwin & Barker	Sidewinders	120.643
Barney Navarro	Stokers	113.636
Class A Lakester:		
Xydias & DeLangton	Sidewinders	131.386
C. W. Scott	Hornets	125.348
Al Schirmiester	Sidewinders	125.173
Class B Roadster:		
Bill Likes	Sidewinders	137.404
Bob Joehnok	Whistlers	132.939
J. Lehman & Schwartzrock	Albata	127.298
Class B Modified Roadster:		
Jim Dahm	Pacers	141.287
Riese & Kaylor	Gear Grinders	136.986
Winston Ranger	Stokers	126.363
Class B Coupes		
Lindsley & LeSage	Gear Grinders	118.890*
Barton & Frostrom	Pacers	111.386
Class B Modified Coupe:		
Dick Pierson	Road Runners	139.103*
Doug Hartelt	Lancers	134.932
Jim Woods	Road Runners	125.523
Class B Lakester:		
Lotze & Patterson	Hornets	142.857
Stanford Bros & Phy	Road Runners	139.534
Lebello-Bensen	San Diego R.C.	137.195

	CLUB	MPH
Class C Roadster:		
Al Barnes	Albata	141.287
Bruce Robinson	Trompers	140.625
Harold Nicholsen	Trompers	138.674
Class C Modified Roadster:		
Akton Miller	Road Runners	155.979
Waite & Bradshawe	Sidewinders	151.006
Del Porto & Errecalle	Sidewinders	137.825
Class C Coupe:		
Harold Miller	Road Runners	123.966
Gray & Erickson	Whistlers	123.796
Class C. Modified Coupe:		
Chas. Abbott	Sidewinders	144.694
Thomas Cobbs	Road Runners	143.769
Flint & Brown	Sidewinders	130.246
Class C Lakester:		
Earl Evans	Road Runners	165.441
Breene & Haller	Road Runners	156.250
Bob McClure	Road Runners	153.846
Class D Modified Roadster:		
Tom Beatty	Stokers	138.461

*Indicates new class records.

Baldwin and Barker's Class A Mod. Roadster, above, clocked 120 mph. Below, Ron Williams flashes thru the traps in his B Roadster.

Unusual roadster above belongs to Max Couch of the Santa Paula Roadsters. It has a '37 Ford front end '27 T body. Below, shows early line up at inspection.

Above is Class "C" Lakester belonging to Hedrich, Perry, Davis of the Stokers.

This roadster has a '23 Dodge body and a Chevy frame. The lowest point is 2½". Has dago front end and dual radiators. The engine is '46 Merc. Belongs to Steve Stephens of the "Hornets." Below, altho this class has a lot of competition with Earl Evans turning speeds like 165 mph, Bob McClure keeps trying as do other enthusiasts in this class.

Above is "Creampuff Too" driven by an out-and-out "lead foot," husky Ed Olsen.

Below, in his "Avenger III" 135 cu in. hydro is Bud Meyer, son of famous Eddie Meyer.

Below, Lorin Pennington in "Copperhead III," and Ernie Bender piloting "Thunderbolt."

Art Maynard winning race in "Restless III."

POWER BOATS

by Louis Kimzey

The word *hydroplane*, according to Funk & Wagnalls, is a noun and means "*a motorboat of extremely light construction driven by submerged screws and moving on water at a speed sufficient to give support thru hydrodynamic and aerodynamic forces alone.*" Mere words or even pictures cannot quite explain the thrill one gets from just watching these boats skim along the water at speeds up to 100 miles an hour in the straights and hitting the turns with such force and determination that awed spectators stand with open mouths, wondering "how do they do it?"

Ever been to a boxing match and during a fast bout found yourself throwing lefts and rights along with the boxer? Well, this race was the same. Standing at the water's edge when the boats streak by, you watch as they go into the turn; two boats side by side, neither one giving or taking an inch, hitting the turn with water flying.

Above, Eddie Meyer of race car fame, piloting "Avenger II," a 135 cubic inch hydro.

Then out of the spray they come down the back straight . . . you're in that boat, *you're* the one who is winning this race! After it's over, you lie down in the sand . . . relax . . . and dream . . . but what's this! another race! 225 cubic inch Hydros! There are the big boys! and you're off . . .

The average person may not realize that these boats are powered by the same engines that are used in the hot rods and family cars. Heads, manifolds, cam, all add up to a "full house." The degree of "hopping up" is decided by what class they are in* To clarify matters, we plan to run an article on a different class each month.

Let me, green with envy, introduce Art Maynard, who, building and racing boats since 1945, now has a 225 cubic inch hydro, division II, called "Restless III." Art threw a rod at a meet prior to this one, so when I arrived at his home, I found him just completing the engine and ready to "drop it in." There are quite a few interesting features about this powerplant. For instance, it has to sit low in the boat, which necessitates a shallow crankcase. To provide for proper lubrication, Art cut the pan at an angle so that the oil, as it returns, will drain to one corner, and then be pumped back thru the engine. There is no room for a radiator, so water is picked up by a metal tube extending from the hull, forced into the water jackets, around the oil cooler and out the other side. The engine is a 225 cubic inch Ford six, with Knudson heads and manifold teamed with a Harman & Collins ignition and cam. Maynard runs 91 octane aviation gas, and the engine can be installed or removed in fifteen minutes! The instrument panel holds fuel pressure, oil and water temperature gauges. The hull weighs 300 pounds and is 16 ft. 8 in. long with a ¼" birch plywood bottom. After Art installed his engine, Gene Trindl shot

Below, Clyde Randall in his "Crackerbox."

Below, Dr. L. J. Novotny, a consistent winner in his speedy "Cherub II" P.O.D.H.

Below, "Lead foot Olsen," piloting an "E" class boat to victory at the Long Beach race.

Below, Burney Edwards in "Mighty Chevron,"

Above is interior of Maynard's boat showing dual pumps and small gas tank. Below, shows steering, dash. Note the clean construction.

a few pictures and then we called it a day and told Art we'd meet him at the Long Beach Marine Stadium the day of the race.

The time trials were underway when we arrived, and Art was just pulling his boat out of the water after making the fastest time in his class. He thought he would do better in the race . . . he was trying out a big prop and would have a smaller one in the race. I didn't quite understand what he meant, but I let it pass with a "swell" and decided to walk around to see the various activities in the pits. The whole meet had a "Coney Island" atmosphere about it. Girls in bathing suits (woof!), men in shorts. People lying in the sand, watching the races while being cooked brown under the bright summer sun.

The Long Beach Marine Stadium is the most spectacular facility of its kind in the United States. Mr. Gus Fan certainly gets a break here. People can line up anywhere about the bank of the "stadium" and still have "50-yard line seats." With the P.A. system announcing the drivers and interesting sidelights, it really provides a wonderful day for one little "buck." Races get underway right on time and when one race is completed, another begins.

The Southern California Speedboat Club is well organized, thanks to its officers: Commodore Bill Collins, Vice Commodore Art Maynard and Rear Commodore Clyde Randel. Their motto is "The Club of Champions," which is no idle boast.

The July 4th Sweepstakes Regatta was sponsored by the West Long Beach Lions Club with all proceeds going toward West Long Beach Lions Club Boys Club.

* See Power Boat Racing column in August issue of HOP UP for review of classes.

Boats are taken out of water immediately after every race. They glide or paddle onto trailer and then are pulled out of water. Below is view of dash and steering wheel.

Art's engine is Ford six, with Knudsen setup.

RESULTS

Pos.	Driver	Boat Name	Engine
48 cu in. Hydroplane			
1.	Victor Klette	Peggy	Crosley
2.	Gillette Smith	Snuffy	Crosley
3.	Louis Meyer, Jr.	Lou - Kay	Crosley
4.	Alex Cockburn	Sol	Crosley
P.O.D.H.			
1.	Elmer Cravener	Pudgy	Ford 60
2.	Dr. Novotny	Cherub II	Ford 60
3.	Marion Beaver	Parker, Ariz.	Ford 60
4.	Dick Blindbury	Destiny	Ford 60
135 cu in. Hydroplane			
1.	Roy Skaggs	Skalawaggs	Ford 60
2.	Eddie Meyer	Avenger II	Ford 60
3.	Bud Meyer	Avenger III	Ford 60
4.	Howard Newton	Maybe	Ford 60
225 cu in. Hydroplane Div. II			
1.	Art Maynard	Restless III	Ford V-8
2.	Dean McGinnis	Quiz Kid	Ford 6
3.	Bill Davis	Sunkist Kid	Ford V-8
4.	James Beyers, Jr.	R U Kiddin	Ford V-8
Crackerbox Runabout			
1.	Ed Olsen	Cream Puff Too	Merc.
2.	Bob Patterson	Hot Cinders	Merc.
3.	Danford Campbell	Miss Fire	Merc.
4.	Rudolf Roskop	Hut Sut	Merc.
225 cu in. Hydroplane Div. I			
1.	Roy Skaggs	Mighty Chevron	Merc.
2.	Bob Sykes	The Dutchess	Merc.
3.	Ernie Bender	Thunderbolt	Merc.
4.	Bill Ward	Balloon Foot	Merc.
E Racing Runabout			
1.	Ed Olsen	Honey Bee Too	Merc.
2.	Bill Douglas	Half Fast	Merc.
3.	Keith Black	Mary E.	Merc.

HOP UP, September, 1951

23

CYCLE MEET

Not to El Mirage this time, but to Rosamond Dry Lake. It's a smaller and slightly rougher lake than El Mirage, but it serves its purpose. An interesting difference at this meet is the use of two courses at once, one for slow cycles and novice drivers and one for fast cycles, with the center of the two lanes used as a return route. The rider of Schaller's #1, which turned the best time of the day (Irwin Lee), got into the return lane thru error and didn't know it till he was almost to the lights, then crossed over to the traps to clock 138.99 mph. Whew!

Photo top of page shows "Schaller Cams" camp. This spot is some distance away from

the course to discourage visitors. Schaller, as a rule, is the speed leader. He had two motorcycles with him this week . . . one with a "blower" and the other with a special fuel injection system. Photo at left shows Walt Fulton on his 19.4 cu in. Mustang with which he set a new record for flat heads in the 21 cu in. class (90.00 mph). In the photo below, left, owner Schaller and rider Lee appear with the record-breaking cycle. Photo below, inside: Schaller's #2 with blower. Didn't do too well because of mechanical failures, but did turn 131.38 mph. In photo above, right, Carey Loftan, movie stunt man, compares times with Delores Stebbles who ran thru the course at 100.27 mph. At left, group of motorcyclists await their turn at the starting line (the girls are holding up their boy friends' "bikes"). Photo at right shows Joe H. Simpson on his HRD which turned 134.33 mph. Below, Jack Dale rides his H-D in the "prone position," to win the class. The reason? As little wind resistance as possible.

MEET THE ADVERTISERS

Our roving camera man selected for this month's issue the main shops of the world's largest firm dealing in racing equipment and special accessories to increase mileage of passenger type cars. Newhouse Automotive Industries, located just east of metropolitan Los Angeles shows one of the most lavish displays of "hop-up" items it has ever been our privilege to witness. Virtually every make and brand of heads, manifolds, ignitions and other equipment is cleanly and neatly exhibited, both on open counters and in mirrored glass cases. Here is a speed shop that answers the hop-up fan's dream.

Newhouse does a tremendous business in dual manifolds, hi-compression heads and all the other power increasing and mileage increasing euipment. A staff of seven girls processes the mail and prepares the invoices and special mailings. Hundreds of letters and orders are received daily to be turned over to the shipping men and the mailing department for reply, packaging, and shipping. It surprised us to learn that in addition to the larger items almost 4,000 of the little carburetor Air-Flow Needles alone are shipped out every month. They are all sold on the "trust" sales plan, payment being made after a trial period in the customer's own car.

An unusual and outstanding feature of Newhouse Automotive Industries is the total absence of "employees." The workers are all known and referred to as *associates*. The term "associates" is very real, as a number of them participate in profits each month by a percentage of the gross business done in their departments. An outside sales force is also maintained . . . dealer orders are written in the field and sent to the firm for filling. The firm itself, with several other California associate firms, exclusively control the national distribution of a number of well-known products and high-performance equipment items.

Newhouse spends over $3,000 monthly on advertising alone. Just to give an idea as to the vast customer interest, three months ago a 100,000 print order of the small booklet, "How to Obtain 150 Miles per Gallon" was distributed at the rate of 32,000 per month. A 300,000 reprint is now being mailed. Their latest heavy promotion is the Gane Economy Club, which offers purchasing advantages to members. The total membership now numbers over 150,000. Newhouse is now testing radio and TV advertising in the New York area, and if it proves successful, the program will be expanded coast to coast.

BUMPER GUARD TAIL LIGHTS

First, obtain the type of bumper guard you prefer; those from almost any model of car can be used. Examples above are 1949 Mercury.

1st step. Outline desired tail light opening pattern with masking tape. Be sure to make opening large enough to conform with legal requirements.

2nd step. Grip guard in vise, taking care not to scar or scratch chrome surface. Cut section out with hack saw, then grind and file to smooth and regular outline. Some guards will require re-chroming, but delay this operation until trial assembly of entire unit has been made.

3rd step. Obtain transparent red plastic (¼" to ⅜" thick Plexiglas or similar) for lens. Mark with scribe or pencil to fit design of opening in the guard. Lens pattern should be ⅛" larger all around than opening. Cut with hack saw.

4th step. Grind and file plastic lens to fit into opening design of guard by cutting ⅛ inch flange around edge. Lens should fit snugly and flush when set in cut-out section of guard.

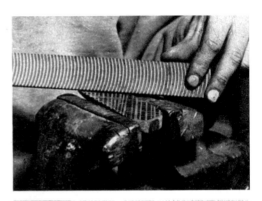

5th step. Grip lens in vise, again taking precautions not to scar, scratch, or crack plastic. Then file diamond pattern ribbing (to reflect light) in back of lens, spacing cuts about ⅛ inch apart.

6th step. Sand lens, with 120-grit wet sandpaper, to a smooth surface. Then repeat with 280-grit wet, follow that with 320-grit wet, and finish with 400-grit wet. Polish lens on a light buffer, using rubbing compound and plastic polish. Make sure you polish both sides of lens.

7th step. Use your original tail light socket by removing lamp assembly from old unit, then weld or bolt base plate to guard or bumper. Position assembly so wires point downward, where it can be led out bottom of guard.

8th step. Install lens in guard by gluing around flange and holding in place until dry. Spring steel clips may also be used to hold lens in place.

9th step. Install guard-light assembly on bumper, hook up tail-light and stop-light wires, and you will be ready to present a distinctive glow to cars you pass.

—GEORGE BARRIS

81

COVER ROADSTER

The "street" roadster, long a common sight on the highways of California, is a very practical and surprisingly economical car for everyday use.

The September cover hot rod is a dark green beauty owned by William D. Piercy of San Francisco, California. Since it is not intended as an "all-out" lakes roadster, the owner kept reliability in mind when building up the engine, which is a 1940 Mercury block, bored ⅛ inch, stroked ¼ inch, and is ported and relieved. Offenhauser 10:1 compression ratio aluminum heads are fitted, as is an Offenhauser intake manifold. A Winfield "R 1" cam replaces the stock grind, and standard Ford-Merc ignition is used. The chassis is '32 Ford, to which is added a '27 "T" body. The rims of the rear wheels are reversed to increase the tread for body clearance. The light weight of the roadster body, plus the increase in size and power of the engine give a weight/power ratio far superior to the average car and correspondingly neck-snapping acceleration.

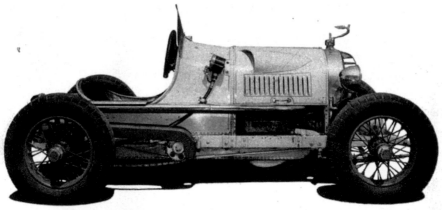

1918
HENDERSON

Above, a view of the "Hendy" showing the speedometer on the side. Below, the compact interior.

The "Hendy" was built in 1918 by Gus Henderson. It is now owned by Louis Ergman, who still drives it around. It has a hard wood frame and a Henderson four-cycle engine. You can't appreciate it until you stop to think that this car has only a 61½" wheelbase, a 38" tread and stands only 37" high! The engine is air cooled, has a Boch "mag" and Winfield SR downdraft carburetor. With three speeds forward, speeds up to 65 mph can be attained. It also has a reverse.

32

Above, note Winfield carburetor and steering rod which runs thru center of fan to chain.

When sitting in it, one's legs straddle the engine with the clutch on one side and the brake and accelerator on the other. The speedometer is on the right, outside of the car, and the starter is on the left side. It is dual chain driven and has chain steering. This car is so unusual that Louis rents the car out for different publicity purposes.

COVER CUSTOM

The cover custom this month is exactly that . . . a true custom car. Designed and built by Coachcraft, Limited, of Los Angeles, in 1940, it was intended to have long-lasting beauty. Now, more than ten years later, it is still an "eye-catcher" and looks as good or better than any of the Detroit production-line "hardtops."

The original Ford chassis was left untouched. Long shackles were not even used. Instead, a complete new body was built around the chassis, and overall height was actually lowered by 10 inches, yet retaining a very comfortable seating position.

Front fenders are now 14 inches longer than stock, and the cowl is also lengthened to match. All of the rest of the body is custom steel panels over ash frames, except for the rear fenders, which are stock.

The steel top is covered with fabric, and unlike the current hardtop convertibles, it is easily and quickly removed.

Now on its 3rd engine, this car has far over 100,000 miles on it, yet, it still is very solid and free from the looseness and rattles associated with the stock Ford convertibles of similar age and mileage.

Here's the World's Record Motorcycle—*180 mph!*

In April of this year, a 39 year old German motorcyclist, Wilhelm Herz, covered a flying kilometer at an average speed of 180.72 mph. His mount was an NSU supercharged 500 cc machine, with fully enclosed aerodynamic body.

The engine of the record smashing NSU has 2 cylinders with two overhead camshafts driven by vertical shafts and bevel gears. The supercharger is located between the engine and gearbox. It is driven by duplex chain.

The record attempts were made on the Munich-Ingolstadt autobahn. The former record holder in this class was Ernst Henne, who covered the measured kilometer approximately 100 mph back in 1937. Henne's machine, a special BMW, also sported a similar streamlined body.

The following international records were also set during the day with this and another NSU machine: Flying Mile—179.17 mph, 350 cc solo flying kilometer—172.3 mph, 350 cc solo flying mile—172 mph. Several sidecar records were also set.

Above, Herz is push started by a mechanic at the start of his record run. Below, Wilhelm Herz, center, talks over matters with the former record-holder (on a BMW) Ernst Henne.

DAGO DRAGS...

Above, finish line and last set of lights. They rent S.C.T.A.'s equipment which includes Crocker's famous precision timing instrument.

Below, one of the really outstanding entries in all their meets is the Miller Crankshaft Special. It has turned (and is improving with every meet) 117 mph for the quarter mile.

by Robert Devereux

The San Diego Timing Association is the only organization of its kind to conduct quarter-mile sprint races with the internationally recognized standing start.* Also, the Association's Paradise Valley Sprint Strip, a 0.6 mile, asphalt-surfaced, ex-AAF fighter strip is the only place in the U. S. where *monthly* road races are held.

The Strip is located southeast of San Diego, three miles out National City's Eighth Avenue. Over its bench-smooth surface, some quick speeds have been attained at the end of a standing quarter. Top record stands at 117.34 mph, established by Art Chrisman, in a Class "A" hot rod. Sports cars, 88.49 mph, R. Collins in XK-120; motorcycles, M. E. Johnson on Vincent; stock car, 78.80 mph, Gib Lilly in Olds Rocket.

The San Diego Timing Association began when a mass meeting of this area's "drag" enthusiasts was called because the Paradise Valley Airstrip, long the scene of chaotic, illegal sprint bashes, had been closed by the authorities. The problem of re-opening the Strip for safety-supervised meets crystalized the group.

At noon the sprint course is transformed into a short (0.7 mile) road circuit by a hundred or so rubber marking cones. In the inaugural road race, Vern Hill, BSA rider, won the motorcycle event (and *Hop Up* magazine trophy). In the first sports car road race, a 15-lap go, Bill Cramer's V8-60 powered MG overcame a long handicap (0.3 mile) by sheer horsepower, leading 1250 cc winner Peter Wold to the checkered flag by many seconds.

*See editorial entitled "Drag Meets" on page 3.

HOP UP, September, 1951   39

V-GAP SPARK PLUG

The V-Gap spark plugs features dual firing, that is to say,
the "V" shaped ground electrode has two surfaces that
receive the spark from the
center electrode. The spark
never divides itself; therefore,
it fires on one side and then
the other. This establishes
positive or surer firing as a
single lane firing spark plug
has but one surface to fire on
and when this surface is
blacked out by oil or additives
from the gasoline, then power from that
particular cylinder is lost due to non-firing.
The manufacturer makes the following claims:

Shop block tests, road and race track tests
have shown the V-gap spark plug to produce
the following benefits: quicker starting,
smoother idle speed, snappier acceleration,
reaching high speed with less throttle and at
a shorter distance, high speed, more power,
less fouling and a longer life to the plug.
These are not all produced in any one engine
but a majority will exist in every engine.

PHOTO CREDITS

Cover photos: Lower, Bob Cannan: Upper,
          Jerry Chesebrough
Pages 4 & 5: Jack Cansler
Page 7: Jerry Chesebrough
Pages 8 thru 25: Gene Trindl
Pages 26 & 27: Jerry Chesebrough
Pages 28 & 29: Marcia Campbell
Pages 30 & 31: Jerry Chesebrough
Pages 32 & 33: Louis Ergman
Pages 34 & 35: Bob Canaan
Pages 36 & 37: Erich Bauer
Page 38: Gene Trindl

40   HOP UP, September, 1951

93

TECHNICAL TIPS

NEWER BUICK ENGINE IN BUICK SPL.

I have a 1938 Buick Special I am very fond of and want to rework the engine for better performance without sacrificing too much low speed or "lugging" performance.

Do you feel a ¾ grind on my cam would be too severe for the twenty-five to forty mile an hour speed range? There is also a "semi" grind for Buicks.

The 1951 Buick Super engine seems to be the same size (externally) as my 1938 engine. Do you know if any 1951 engines will more or less "drop" into place in a '38? If any model Roadmaster engine can be adapted to my car, I think it would be the berries.

Oakland, California   John McNab

I have often said that the 1938 Buick was the best one ever built. Trying to use the Roadmaster engine is "out"—there isn't room without drastic reworking. The series 60 "Century" model was merely the series 40 car with 4" more wheelbase to take the larger engine. The new 263 cu. in. Buick engine will "drop right into" your 1938 chassis, and it is very desirable unless your 248 cu. in. engine is in exceptionally good condition. The ¾ grind cam and the 263 would satisfy your needs best, while a semi-cam would appear better for the old engine. I say this because the larger displacement would more than offset the slight torque loss of a ¾ cam against a semi-grind. Noise is not increased in the more conservative grinds.—Tech. Ed.

RACE ENGINE BEARINGS

I would like to have some information concerning main and connecting rod bearings for racing engines.

Minneapolis, Minnesota   Guenter H. Schmidt

The so-called silver-grid bearing as developed by Allison is probably the best bearing to date. However, nearly all race engines now use steel backed copper-lead alloys. Pressures go up to around 6000 psi, but PV factor or unit pressure times rubbing speed is of more importance. A PV factor of 30,000 is usually good practice and 55,000 is considered an extreme condition.

Surface finishes on both bearings and journals run between 10 and 20 RMS micro-inches (a lapped surface) and journals must be at least 280 Brinell hardness for use with copper-lead bearings. Standard clearances are .0015 per inch of diameter for these bearings and oil temperatures as high as 275° F are considered safe but not encouraged if avoidable.—Tech. Ed.

'46 HUDSON ALMOST HOPELESS

I would like to know if there is any way of improving performance of a 1946 Hudson Commodore six. Our company mechanic says that he does not believe much can be done.

Winter Haven, Florida   Harry S. McDowell

The 1946 Hudson 6 Commodore had a bore and stroke of 3 x 5 = 212 cu. in. and was advertised at 102 bhp at 4000 rpm. On the dynamometer it will not show over 95 actual bhp, even with the optional 7.1 to 1 head, all accessories removed, and no muffler.

There are only three gravity fed main bearings and the extremely short 8-3/16) connecting rods are offset with poured babbit bearings of 1-15/16 diameter. The cylinders are siamesed in groups of three, and the valve seats are not completely surrounded by water jackets.

While nothing is impossible, I am very much inclined to agree with your mechanic when he says not much can be done. Just as a suggestion, why not install the Hudson 8 engine? I think the Commodore model had room under the hood for either powerplant.—Tech. Ed.

DUALS FOR OLDS 88

I am considering installation of a Southern California Belond-type dual exhaust system on my 1949 Olds Rocket 88. I thought that I would use stock mufflers since this car is used for general passenger use. My question is, with this system would I experience valve trouble?

Manhattan, Kansas   Lot F. Taylor

I definitely believe that dual stock mufflers are well worth while on any V-8 engine since both performance and economy are improved. There is absolutely no danger of valve trouble; in fact, theoretically the reduction in back pressure on the system should reduce valve temperature and increase valve life.—Tech. Ed.

MORE "GO" FOR '42 PONTIAC

I own a 1942 Pontiac "8." How much should be milled off the head to reach 8.00 to 1 compression? Also would the 1941-42 Buick dual manifold be suitable on a 1942 "8" Pontiac?

Wenatchee, Wash.   D. C. Spayd

In the case of a 1942 Pontiac 8, there is very little or no gain in peak bhp by going over 7.5 to 1 compression ratio. This ratio is available as optional equipment on the later models, and you can get the combustion chamber depths by comparing the two heads at your local Pontiac parts counter. As a rough guess, mill about .050 to .060 off the 1942 heads.

I've never heard of anyone installing Buick manifolds on a Pontiac, and I doubt very much that they would fit. Even if they would fit, you would have an impossible situation in the sloping feature of the R. H. Buick manifold when transferred to the Pontiac L. H. side, since the ports of these two engines are on opposite sides.—Tech. Ed.

OVERHEAD VALVE vs. FLAT HEAD

I think the public is being sold a bill of goods on these so-called new ohv passenger car engines. I'd like to stir up a hassle on L head vs. push rod ohv for passenger car and semi-sports cars. Meaning pump gas and therefore compression ratios under 8 to one.

The Mobilgas runs, Nascar Daytona race, Bonneville, Jalopy racing—where are the ohv cars and why? Exactly what can the costly ohv engines do that Ford-Merc-Lincoln-Hudson-Plymouth-Pontiac can't do as well? Never mind advertised hp and gas mileage. Review Nascar and Mobilgas results over the last two years.

I'm the first to admit the ohv engines are the thing above 10/1, and 6000 rpm, with methanol, but dollar-for-dollar, why Chev over Ford? Why Olds over Hudson?

Arcadia, California   J. N. A. Hawkins

Yes, in many ways I'll have to agree with you that the importance, need, and advantages of the ohv engine are being exaggerated. Still, I'm very much in favor of the ohv engine, and the arguments you give as to results can be readily explained.

To take just one example, economy, there is surely no question that given two identical cars, one with an L-head, the other with ohv, which one is the most economical. To be more specific, if you were to install a 216 cu. in. Chevrolet engine into a 1951 Ford chassis, I'll bet the Chevrolet would be more economical than the stock Ford 6. Heat loss to the cooling water alone will prove this: an ohv engine has 25% lower heat rejection rate than an L-head; therefore, less fuel is being wasted.

Nevertheless, I will admit that the talk of 10 and 12 to 1 compression ratios is absurd in the light of fuel possibilities in the foreseeable future.—Tech. Ed.

115 MPH LINCOLN V-12

Have just purchased a '41 Lincoln Cabriolet . . . how much planing on stock heads to reach 8.2? Would also like to use O. 88 intake valves. Could the planed heads be made to accommodate them?

As to speed vs. pickup, I lean strongly to more pickup rather than higher speeds. A top of 110 or 115 is plenty. With this in mind would you recommend the original cam, ¾ grind, or something in between? While on cams, what would you suggest for tappets? Will it pay to cut down the flywheel weight, and if so, how much?

Grand Island, Nebraska   L. W. Scheel

I suggest you mill and redome the heads from .060 to .070 which will give just under 8.0 to 1.

I haven't looked into a Lincoln V-12 for a long time, but I am fairly sure Olds valves will not work. Thirty degree seats on the intakes are good enough if you want mostly acceleration. I would suggest a ¾ cam and adjustable tappets (hydraulics are not adjustable and "float" at high rpm). Reduce the flywheel weight to about 20 pounds for better acceleration, but it must be re-balanced.

It will take about 200 honest brake horsepower to go 115 mph in a Lincoln, and you have about as much chance of getting this performance as flying without wings. The best clocked time on an LZ I ever saw was 90 mph, and a lot of them wouldn't go over 83—actual mph, not speedometer readings. I would say that if you get 150 bhp and 100 honest mph out of your car, you will be doing very well.—Tech. Ed.

BURNED PISTONS IN CROSLEY

I recently put an I.T. blower on my Crosley Hot-Shot. In less than 100 miles have blown one piston and seriously damaged two others, necessitating major repairs: As counter-measures, have installed Lodge platinum plugs and a straight-thru exhaust. Would cast-iron pistons help? Or lower-compression?

Ridgeway, Pa.   J. R. Curry

The piston failures are due to too high a temperature. This, in turn, due to one or both of two things. (1) too lean a mixture (2) detonation. The cure for the 1st is obvious. The cure for the 2nd is either lower compression ratio or higher octane fuel.

Cast iron pistons will not help, in fact they may hurt because of their lower rate of heat transfer. Lower compression ratio appears to be advisable, tho you do not state what ratio you are using and I can only suggest, therefore, that you consider the alternatives of water-alcohol injection or experimenting with fuel additives such as benzol or alcohol, before getting special pistons.—Tech. Ed.

CHRYSLER 6 HOP UP

I have a 1940 Chrysler 6 block—bore .060 over (3⅝ STD) Twin pots, ¾ or semi cam. Split exhaust manifold, Mallory ignition, milled stock head. I want to put it in a '40 Chrysler coupe and enter in it the Modified Stocks here in the east. What else can you suggest?

New York, N. Y.   Skeety Wyman

I have very little to add to your proposed modifications. One trick is to mill the DeSoto read rather than one from a Chrysler because the DeSoto head has a slightly smaller initial combustion chamber volume than the Chrysler.

I think you will find that your combination will be plenty hot but wil not take the turns very well. Out here, the softly sprung, heavy front end cars are very much improved by installing the caster adjusting screws backwards so that the wheels do not cant at the wrong angle in turns. I also notice oversize tires on the right front only and chains at the left and right rear corners to reduce roll.—Tech. Ed.

SUPERCHARGER FOR '41 CADILLAC 62

Can you help me locate a supercharger for a 1941 62 Cadillac?

Fellows, Calif.   John W. McGinn

Sorry to discourage you, but there is no supercharger available for the L-head Cadillac engine. The only possibility would be to re-work the McAfee supercharger (made only for the ohv Cadillac). The ohv kit costs $882, plus the cost of converting to your engine.—Tech Ed.

HOPPING UP HENRY J FOUR

Being an ardent "Big Car" and "Midget" racing fan, I have recently begun to indicate an interest in "hopping-up" my Henry J (4), but at a minimum of cost.

New Cumberland, Pa.   L. H. Payne

Aside from axle ratio changes, you can contact a Willys dealer for an engine exchange. Get the F-head with optional 7.8 to 1 ratio. This is the easiest and best way to more power from the 4. Two carburetor manifolds will most likely be available soon. You can have the camshaft reground if you don't mind a slightly rougher idle. These changes should give 85 to 90 bhp and your modified 4 would then easily out-perform the stock 6. Incidentally, Willys is supposed to be tooling for an F-head for the 6. With all the above changes on the 4, incorporated on the 6, you would have a miniature hot rod for sure.—Tech. Ed.

WHAT RATIO FOR '50 FORD

I own a '50 Ford with overdrive and the standard rear axle ratio of 4.11. Which axle ratio should I use to get the biggest top speed and the best high speed performance, 3.73 in "regular" or 4.55 using overdrive?

The engine produces 135 bhp. Top speed in second year (4.11) is 77—how many rpm?

Hudson, So. Dak.   D. R. Buckwalter

A 3.73 rear axle in conventional drive will give you the best combination for maximum top speed. You understand, of course, that with an engine "hopped up", you will notice a drop in low speed performance in this gear as compared to the regular 4.10 ratio.

Wheel revolutions per mile for a 6.70-15 tire is given as 740. 740 x 4.10 x 1.602 (2nd gear) x .70 (OD) = 3400 engine rpm at 60 mph or 4360 rpm at 77 mph in 2nd gear—Tech. Ed.

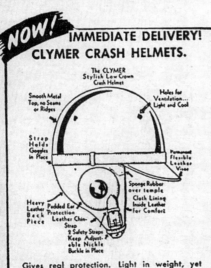

HOP UP   15¢

HOP UP

COVER
CUSTOM
PAGE 7

LET'S RIDE IN A
"CRACKERBOX"
PAGE 18

COVER
HOP UP
PAGE 16

OCT
1951

15¢

CORRESPONDENCE

6.70 x 15 TIRES ON '41 CHEV

What would be the effect on riding ease and gas mileage of replacing the 16" wheels on a 1941 Chevrolet with 15" wheels and 6.70 x 15 tires?

Los Angeles, Calif.   Donald B. Peters

Switching to 6.70 x 15 tires will make your car ride softer, handle mushy, and squeal like a pig on the turns.—Tech. Ed.

125 MPH HUDSON HORNET

I have a new Hudson "Hornet" coupe with standard transmission and overdrive. Is there a supercharger made that can be adapted? How many rpm could I obtain before running into trouble with piston speed?

What is highest ratio for maximum top speed? My car has a 4.10 rear end; with overdrive should be around 2.8. Should I exchange it for a 4.55 rear end, then it would be 3.10 with overdrive?

I would like to make my Hornet hit 125 miles an hour.

Los Fresnos, Texas   Dennis Schmitt

The Hudson Hornet is unquestionably one of the highest performing automobiles ever built in this country. There is no supercharger kit available for this engine. Cost of adapting a 4 cylinder GMC Diesel roots type blower would be almost prohibitive . . . suggest you forget the supercharger.

Because the engine is quite new, I have no definite information on souping it up. You can follow the more or less standard practices: i.e., milled heads, ¾ cam, etc. The 4½ in. stroke gives an engine speed of 3335 rpm at 2500 fpm piston speed for cruising and 3500 fpm corresponds to 4660 rpm, an absolute maximum for occasional use only. Do not exceed about 8 to 1 compression ratio. It would be advisable to relieve the block to avoid breathing restrictions thru the combustion chambers. (Some of the early 264 cu in. blocks were relieved by the factory.)

To do 125 mph in this car would take at least 200 bhp and I doubt very much if such an output is possible from modifications outlined above. The Hudson axle is a little on the delicate side for the 308 cu in. engine, especially with a standard transmission. When you change the ratio from 4.10 to 4.55, the axle shafts are stressed higher in the same proportion, which might prove to be the "last straw", but on the other hand, the 3.18 ratio obtainable in overdrive is much more suitable for developing the ultimate maximum speed than any other available combinaton.

From the foregoing remarks, you can understand why I am not making any definite recommendations.—Tech. Ed.

MORE ACCELERATION FOR '39 BUICK SPL.

I have a 1939 Buick Special Coupe . . . I'm really not interested in increasing the top speed of the car, but I am interested in the acceleration . . . I would like to keep the fair gas mileage that I have been getting.

I would like to have your opinion on the use of a blower without modifying the engine.

Bronx, New York   Vincent A. Forte

Yes, I agree with you, that adding a blower to your '39 Buick would be very nice. The trouble is that no conversion kits are available and it would cost close to $1000 to make a special kit using some stock supercharger of correct size.

I have driven a '41 Buick Special running 8 to 1 compression ratio, big Roadmaster valves, two Ford carburetors and water injection. It ran smoothly and quietly, and accelerated slightly better than a late Ford V8. The addition of a cam and possibly a lighter flywheel will affect the idle somewhat but should give quite a bit more acceleration. You will then have an engine with a bhp output very close to the Roadmaster with one of the lightest Buick models ever built. One project possible on the '39 Spl. is the installation of a 1937 or 1938 Buick Century (Model 60) transmission. Of the four bolts which attach the transmission to the bellhousing, two line up perfectly and the other two require new tapped holes. This installation would also require a 3/16" spacer between the bellhousing and transmission case, plus some juxtaposition of the peculiar arrangement of parts used in the 1939 Series 40 and 60 cars to join the rear end of the transmission to the ball joint of the torque tube. This would be quite a project but would have considerable advantage in providing a more rugged, quiet, and closer ratio transmission.—Tech. Ed.

INTAKE PORT MATCHING

I own a 1941 Pontiac 6 . . . can you describe to me the process of matching intake ports when installing a manifold? Do the intake ports need enlarging or are they large enough for 265 cu ins?

Omaha, Nebraska   John Kuhns

Matching ports can be done in several ways, tho I think the best way is to use a sheet of 32nd aluminum, cut and filed to match the ports in the block and then transferred to the intake manifold, using stud holes as locating dowels. The inlet ports on this engine are definitely restricted, particularly at the point immediately below the valve seat.—Tech. Ed.

BETTER RODS IN '28 MODEL A FORD

Where can I get a high compression head for my 1928 Model "A" Ford? Also rod bearings that would stand a higher compression ratio. Are there hydraulic brake units available for a Model "A"? Would a new type Marvel-Shebler carburetor fit on it and would it give better gas mileage?

St. Paul, Minnesota   Elvin Gilyard

I think most of the answers to your questions are in the Bell Auto Parts Catalog. Ansen Automotive Engineering Co., 6317 So. Normandie, Los Angeles 44, California, makes the most reasonably priced hydraulic brake kit available. To get rod bearings that will really stand up, will require the heavier Model B or C crankshaft which will not fit the Model A block. Both Bell and Ansen rework Pontiac connecting rods to fit this heavier crankshaft. They also supply special heads and special intake manifolds which use the Ford V-8 carburetor.

There is no basic reason why one carburetor can give any better gas mileage than another since the design of the engine determines the leanest mixture which it will burn without overheating. Any carburetor of the correct throat size can be "re-jetted" to give this best economy mixture.—Tech. Ed.

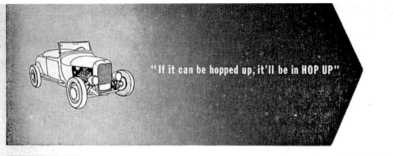

"If it can be hopped up, it'll be in HOP UP"

Crosley, The Poor Man's Merc

We've been wondering why someone hasn't gone after some of the international and American speed records with a streamlined Crosley. Here is a rugged short-stroke overhead cam engine, with all the ingredients to be a real winner. It surprises us that some of our Timing Associations' members haven't turned out some International Class H streamliners. "Goldie" Gardner's 159 mph record isn't too far out of reach, and the 24- and 48-hour records are 76.30 and 64.10, respectively. The 5-mile record is only 128.08 mph. Crosley parts are very reasonable, blowers are available, and the know how is here in the U.S. Let's show that we can do it too! Bonneville is right in our own backyard.

Fenders On Hop Ups?

There's been a lot of talk lately about enforcing various state laws requiring fenders on cars. Putting the stock fenders back on would ruin the looks of many a beautiful car. On the other hand, fenders would certainly be worthwhile in rainy weather. "Cycle" type fenders don't hurt appearance, don't add very much weight, and can be easily removed. Except for the expense of converting, it shouldn't cause too many headaches.

EDITORIAL STAFF

Editor..Oliver Billingsley
Technical Editor................................John R. Bond
Associate Editors.............................Louis Kimzey
Robert Dearborn
Staff Photographer..................Jerry Chesebrough
Photographers............Jack Campbell, Bob Canaan
Joe Al Denker, Gene Trindl

PRODUCTION STAFF

Managing Editor.....................W. H. Brehaut, Jr.
Art Director...Louis Kimzey
Art...Jack Caldwell

ADVERTISING

Advertising Manager.....................William Quinn
East Coast Representatives......Peabody & Ortgies
276 West 43rd Street
New York 18, N.Y.
United Kingdom ....Kenneth Kirkman
2 Longcroft Avenue
Banstead, Surrey, England
Italy...Michele Vernola
C.P. 500
Milano, Italy

CORRESPONDENTS

Italy ....Corrado Millanta

Contributions—not responsible for the return of unsolicited manuscripts, photographs, and/or drawings unless accompanied by self-addressed stamped envelope.
Mailing address—Box 110, Glendale, California.

Vol. 1, No. 3   **October, 1951**

CONTENTS

HOP UP is published monthly by Enthusiasts' Publications, Inc., 540 W. Colorado Blvd., Glendale, California. Phone CHapman 5-3397. Application for entry as second-class matter is pending. Copyright 1951 by Enthusiasts' Publications, Inc. Reprinting in whole or in part forbidden except by permission of the publishers.

Subscription price $1.50 per year thruout the world. Single copy 15c.

Change of address—must show both old and new addresses.

3

BONNEVILLE PREVIEWS

Every speed shop thruout the nation has the *Bonneville* fever! With applications from forty-four states, this meet promises to be the largest national speed trials that Southern California Timing Association has ever sponsored. Speed enthusiasts, whether they have the conveniences of a speed shop or do their building in their own garages, all have one ambition . . . the fastest time of the day! With everyone building and testing, the August Russetta meet was ideal. Being exactly one week prior to Bonneville, it looked like *everyone* had turned out for this event. There was a serious, sober atmosphere about this meet. Everyone was busy, for they had to "get it runnin'" *now* . . . Bonneville was only a week away!

One group of fellows came all the way from Berkeley, California,—a distance of over 500 miles—just to test their rear-engine coupe. This is just a small example what these guys will go thru just to make absolutely sure their engines are at the peak of condition. You can expect to see a lot of "creations" at this meet . . . rear engines, dual engines, low bodies, streamlined bodies. The emphasis is on speed and each individual has his own idea how to get it.

Pictured above are Frank Parker, Bill Cullen, and Ed Swan who came over 500 miles just to test their car at El Mirage. They belong to the Cal-Neva Timing Asociation.

Below is Howard Johansen, manufacturer of the famous Howard Cams with his newly built Crosley bodied sedan. The first time it ran it did 141 mph and the second time he broke the class record with 148 mph!

4

HOP UP, October, 1951

Above are Bob Cantley and Paul Sylva with their class "C" coupe. It just turned 148.14!

Below are Bill Davis and Jack Reilly with their "Ansen Special." It has turned 133 mph, hopes to turn 150 mph at Bonneville. The salt flats are considerably faster than El Mirage.

MORE POWER TO YOU

WITH A *Belond* EQUA-FLOW Exhaust System

ELIMINATE BACK PRESSURE and INCREASE HORSEPOWER!

Motorists all over America are acclaiming the BELOND EQUA-FLOW Exhaust System as the best single improvement available for automobiles equipped with a V8 engine. The standard exhaust systems are too small in capacity and the exhaust gases are forced to make restricted turns. In some cases, all of the exhaust from the left side of the engine must go forward, cross over and pass through the right side exhaust manifold before starting toward the muffler and the rear of the car. In most cases, the standard single muffler does not have enough capacity to handle the full volume of exhaust from the engine.

By reducing exhaust back pressure to an absolute minimum, the BELOND EQUA-FLOW Exhaust System actually increases the horsepower output, resulting in improved speed, performance and efficiency. The EQUA-FLOW Exhaust Systems are available complete with Exhaust Headers, Extensions to Mufflers, dual Mello-Tone Mufflers, left side tail pipe, clamps, bolts, gaskets, and installation instructions. BELOND EQUA-FLOW Exhaust Systems are available less Mufflers. Any type mufflers may then be used, or one stock muffler may be installed to be used in conjunction with the present right side muffler. This combination is quiet as well as efficient. This set also contains all of the necessary parts for installation except mufflers.

Steel packed mufflers are quite loud on the Belond Equa-Flow System for the Oldsmobile. Therefore, the use of stock mufflers is recommended for this car. The type of muffler used on Fords, Mercurys, and Lincolns is a matter of choice.

TYPICAL STANDARD FORD & MERCURY EXHAUST SYSTEM

FORD V8 ● MERCURY ● OLDSMOBILE ● LINCOLN V8

For prices and models, see coupon below

de Ville Mercury

Because he works in a General Motors body shop and sees Oldsmobile Holidays, Chevrolet Bel Airs and Cadillac de Villes day in and day out, Glad Ellis just didn't feel right about his stock Mercury convertible. He wanted to be up to date and the envy of other Merc convertible owners, so he started building a removable hard-top convertible, one which would be both pleasing to the eye and practical. He ordered Cad de Ville parts direct from the factory, as he wanted the finished top to look as smooth and professional as a production line hard-top.

When the parts arrived, he found that a section had to be added to the rear deck. At this point, Valley Custom Shop (Burbank) took over. The section turned out to be 14 inches from the top of the trunk lid to where the new top joined the body. The front of the new top was attached to the original convertible front bow so that removal would be easier. The rear window was quite a problem . . . only recently, in fact, solved. The one used in the Cad-

illac de Ville top is made of Herculite, which cannot be cut or worked in a hardened form. This made it necessary to use a workable-type plastic. Lucite was selected because it can be cut readily and is easy to shape. Using patterns, the Lucite was cut and shaped to the proper dimensions, then fitted to the already completed top.

As the days passed with the car being left in the sun, it was found that the Lucite started to crack from internal stresses. When this was noticed, plans were made to make new windows, this time thoroly heating the Lucite, as in an annealing process.

With the top satisfactorily in place, work began on the rest of the car. The rear deck was cleaned off and leaded, and the gas filler pipe was concealed under the hydraulically operated trunk lid. "Shaving" the nose and use of a solid grille bar completed the front end. The result is a really "different" car, which is the envy of all who have seen it.

DE VILLE MERC

FORREST CYCLE

Howard Forrest, who heads the experimental department of Mustang Motorcycles, has completed a project that really commands attention . . . a home-designed and built motorcycle. The neat frame is of his own design and construction, altho it bears some resemblance to the Mustang. The powerplant for this bright yellow and chrome beauty is a 1931 Ariel "square four" of 500 cc displacement. A regular foot shift—hand clutch, 4-speed Burman gearbox is used along with a foot starter. High efficiency steel brake drums, hubs and the 12" wire wheels were made up specially, then chromed to please the eye. Kelsey-Hayes rims were drilled, dimpled, and then

HOP UP, October, 1951

mounted with 4.00 x 12 tires. The front brake is operated by the right hand while the rear one is actuated by the left foot. Many of the parts for the Forrest, such as the drive chain cover and instrument panel, were special castings.

A tachometer, which is driven from the right side of the engine, and an oil pressure gauge, make up the simple but effective instrument panel. Gasoline and oil tanks hold 2 gallons and 2 quarts, respectively. This cycle is sprung much the same as the Mustang with approximately the same caster angle to produce the remarkable handling characteristics for which the Mustang is well known. A hand-tooled seat is the crowning glory of a motorcycle that anyone would be proud to ride.

Above, Arlen Kurtis in the Kurtis sports car. He turned in 71.57 mph. At side, Pat Reese in his hot roadster. Below, Bob Rounthwaite just shifting into second. Equipped with a Weiand 4 carb. manifold and heads, Howard cam, and a Scintilla mag, this was one of the most powerful cars at the meet. It seems that the "hottest" cars are running now at Saugus.

SAUGUS

by Louis Kimzey

A few miles north of Los Angeles is a new "drag strip," set in a small valley between beautiful rolling hills. A slight breeze, not enough to slow cars, but just right to keep everything cool . . . big trees to sit under . . . cokes, ice cream and hot dogs. Here is the setting for a perfect Sunday afternoon. Hot rods, customs, cycles, and scooters . . . you'll see them all blazing down the ¼ mile strip, racing against time.

12

DRAGS

Above, the big tree where Rich Doherty has a refreshment stand . . . nice cool atmosphere and stuff. Below, airplanes attend the meets.

Bottom, Kenneth Shearer in Ford takes on Olds for match race. The starter stands between cars. Some entrants are from Bakersfield, a distance of 77 miles from Saugus.

Some are so powerful that they burn rubber the full length of the course. Then there are match races . . . cars against cycles . . . '36 Ford and a '50 Buick . . . your car against your buddy's, to forever stop his cracks about his roadster beating your iron . . .

When I went to high school (gad! what a memory) we would meet behind the school and "drag it out." No time clocks or anything. I would look over at him and yell . . . "ready?" He would nod and we'd be off! Down the block we'd go, never thinking what if a kid ran out in front of us? What if a tire blew? Na! all we thought about was that Joe Leadfoot called my roadster an "iron," I'd show him!

Even tho I went thru a stop light, spun around, landed in a gas station, hmm! I showed him and I've got the traffic ticket to prove it!

But now there is no need for such *illegal* drags. If your car meets the safety requirements, you can prove its merits by going to *legal, supervised* drags. Lou Baney, President of Russetta Timing Association, is in charge of this wonderful new strip. The timing is by E. C. Huseman, the same fellow who clocks all of the Russetta meets.

Ernest Hashin's neat roadster really spins a lot of heads when it goes by. It has a '27 "T" body on a model "A" frame. Everything is chromed . . . wheels, axles, radius rods, etc. The engine has a Weiand 3 carb. manifold, Evans heads, Iskenderian cam. Over $2100 has been invested in this roadster. Top speed is 102 mph. He uses it as a street roadster.

At side, seats are removed from the neat interior in preparation for a really fast drag!

Below, the immaculately clean engine is a feature of this beautiful and very fast roadster.

14

Just when you think you've seen everything in the way of automobiles . . . Boom! Here comes a completely different roadster or a custom. Good looking or ugly, these cars interpret the feelings of the owner on how to get the best time of the day (btd). Lou Baney and Lou Senter, of Ansen Automotive, present a $25 savings bond for the best time of the day, along with nine trophies for the various classes and two trophies for cycles.

Yes, sir! regardless of whether you are running a car or are just a spectator, you can have *fun* at a drag race!

COVER 'HOP UP'

16

by Louis Kimzey

While at the San Diego drags, there was a mob of people crowding around a car . . . I'm as curious as the next guy, so I went over to have a "look see."

It was a 1927 Ford touring, all primed with gray paint and sporting huge chrome headers on each side of the engine. The body, frame rails, windshield and much other equipment are original "T". A white tonneau cover over the back seat and white canvas windwings topped off with a little horn. With a '40 Ford column shift, this "bathtub" was a sight to behold. I could see why such a crowd gathered.

The very proud owner is Bob Williams of Burbank, California, who now is with Uncle Sam in the United States Army. Altho this car has the original radiator shell, Bob had a special oversize radiator made to cool the big V-8 which is equipped with a Navarro manifold, Engle super cam and chopped flywheel. It has also been ported, relieved and bored.

In order to get these pictures, we had to tell the crowd to stand back. This done, the photographer got one picture before the crowd closed in . . . so we had to make a date to shoot the car later. I asked him how he liked all the attention. "Oh, I like it, but

my girl is a little bashful," he replied. I could see why . . . with all these people staring, it's enough to give a person a complex!

Photo at top of page sixteen shows beautiful Clark header, canvas windwings, high windshield, and monster bulb horn (?) on top.

Photo at bottom of page sixteen. Note radiator cap and shell. Also the clean engine.

Above, owner Bob Williams and Mary Carlice.

Below, compare height of windshield to body.

CRACKERBOX

by Louis Kimzey

"Wanna go for a spin?" Clyde Randall's voice intruded on my thoughts like a dash of cold water. "Sure," I grinned toothily, wondering what I had gotten myself into *this* time. "I'll see if I can find a helmet to fit ya." "Better make it about a 7½," I gurgled, my heart tangling up with my tonsils. As Clyde hurried away, I was already mentally circling the course in the slight Cracker-Box—and *not* enjoying it. What if we should flip? These little boats *do* jump around a bit. What if I bounced out . . . and got caught in the prop? It turns up well over 5000 rpm, you know. What if . . . ?

"Here's your 'crunch-bonnet'. I got it from Olsen." I wondered what Olsen had against

me, but I reluctantly accepted the protective head-shell and started squeezing it down on top of noggin. It looked like a soup bowl perched on a watermelon.

I resigned myself with a sigh and climbed aboard as the little craft slid into the water. It's only fair to tell you I am a landlubber from way back . . . tho I *have* made a few voyages on the Staten Island Ferry. So there I was, sitting in that eggshell, struggling into a life (?) jacket and worrying. I wanted this ride with Randall, and then again I didn't . . . know what I mean?

Now . . . time stops dead still as the boat floats slowly backward. Clyde settles himself and thumbs the starter button. A hollow grinding, and then silence . . . I

18

clear my throat to ease the tension as the starter rasps the second time. The V-8 roars into life and with a surge we move ahead, the bow rising at a 45° angle. We get underway with a series of kidney-cracking bumps. This little canoe isn't missing a wave!

"She'll smooth out when we get movin!" Randall's yell was snatched away in the general racket and turmoil. When we get moving? *Oh great!* But sure enough, as we skipped and roared toward the end of the stadium, the bumps *were* smoothing out! When the boat gets up speed it only hits about every third or fourth white-cap . . .

But my problems had only just begun. As I saw the turning buoy rush up to meet us I wondered whether I had made out my will. Jumping and bucking we began our wide bank around the marker. Clyde yelled again. I'm not sure what it was, but I think he said we would get moving as soon as the engine warmed up. *Oh brother!*

The farther we went, the *faster* we went, until we got in the back stretch, with the boat leaping into the air, landing . . . leaping . . . landing . . .

Realizing that we *might* not flip after all, I began to enjoy myself . . . for about ten seconds, that is. My fun was short-lived, for I looked ahead and saw that we were going into a turn, faster than ever. Man, are you *mad?* We can't turn at this speed! I grabbed the gun'l (or whatever the side rail is called) and around we went . . . headed *straight* for the marker . . . we're going to hit! But no . . . bam . . . bam . . . with a series of crashing bounces

Above, Ed Brown and L. Gordon in Ed's "Bouncy Barby." Has Wayne Chevie engine.

Below, Louis Meyer, Jr, winning another race in speedy record holding "Lou-Kay."

Below, Bob Patterson in "Hot Cinders", another "goin" Cracker Box during the race.

Below, Marion Beaver of Parker, Arizona, in his "Littl' Beaver" P.O.D.H. class at speed.

Above is Chuck Powell in "Keeno" who, after the throttle broke, drove complete race with one hand on wheel and one on the throttle.

we were around the turn and down into the front straight. After two runs around the course, I thought, *Well!* This wasn't so bad after all. I even sat up straight and began looking around at the people! No sir! Not bad at all. I think I like this! We screamed passed something in the water and Clyde waved at the blur. Must have been another boat, and then . . .

Aw, phooey! We're going in. As Clyde turned the engine off, we glided over to the trailer which had been run down into the water in order to beach the boat.

Clyde's wife was standing at the water's edge. "Well, how'd you like it?" (I wondered if she knew how scared I had really been) "Swell! Better than a rolly-coaster." As Clyde leaned over and kissed the Mrs. he said, "I thought he looked sorta worried a couple of times." (If he only knew!) I told him it was a little like trying to sit down while riding a pogo-stick, and that

l was ready to go again any time. (Yeah, who?)

Incidentally, Randall's about the most modest guy you'd want to meet. When I told him about the proposed HOP UP article, he said, "Aw, you don't wanna write about me. Besides, the boat isn't running right. And awayway, we just race for the fun of it." This, from the guy who built one of the first "Cracker Boxes" and has held *all* of the records in this class at one time or another.

Chuck Shields has ridden with him for four years and Mrs. Randall rode with him before that*. (You can imagine how silly I felt when he told me *that*) Clyde's first boat was the "Alley Cat," followed by his "Ski-Bee," and now it's the "Hot Box" which claims his attention.

Hot Box is pushed along by a full house 267 cu in. Ford V-8. The record speed for this class is 68.562 mph to date. And on water, that's moving!

Scared or not, if Clyde ever needs a rider, I'm his man. I asked him how he accounted for the steady gain in Cracker Box popularity.

"All we have to do is get somebody who is mildly interested in boats, and take him out for a ride. After we whing-ding a couple of corners at full-throttle, he can't wait to get home and start building a Cracker Box of his own."

Anybody got some ¼ inch plywood they don't want?

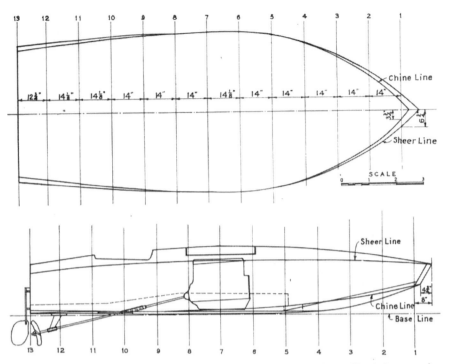

CRACKER BOX CLASS

The Cracker Box is a special class. Unless otherwise stated, **General Racing Rules for Inboards** and **General Rules for Inboard Runabout Racing** will be applied, in addition to rules below.

1. Boats must be in accord with these rules and official drawings.
2. Match consists of two or more heats of 5, 6, or 10 miles in length. For international races, heats may be 9 or 15 miles in length, upon approval of Racing Commission.
3. The total max. displ. of engines used shall not exceed 267 cu. in. No tolerance above.
4. Single engine, 4-cycle, 2 valves per cylinder and 1 carburetor venturi to each 2 cylinders. Electric starter required. Battery or magneto ignition. Total engine cost not to exceed $750. OHV allowed only if standard equipment. Changes in power plant only if parts can be purchased by other owners at same price. Price of such parts to keep total cost of engine within limit specified.
5. Vee drives or gear boxes not permitted.
6. Not more than 15' 6" long or less than 13' 6", (bow to transom). Deviations not to exceed 1" at frame from No. 4 to No.

13. Forward of frame No. 4, bow may be altered. Cockpit must be between stations 9 to 12 with engine mounted forward of cockpit. No longitudinal or transversal steps, including relieved chine or concavity, on bottom hull to be of wood frames covered with plywood not less than ¼ inch thick.
7. Boat raced with two persons on board except at option of drivers.
8. Spring-loaded throttle release. Rudder assembly, shaft size and angle optional.
9. Cracker Box boats carry number with suffix "P" painted on bows.

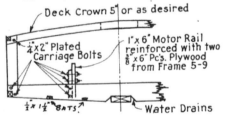

TABLE OF OFFSETS													
INCHES & EIGHTHS OF INCHES TO OUTSIDE OF PLANKING													
		1	2	3	4	5	6	7	8	9	10	11	12	13
HALF	CHINE	3-6	15-0	22-7	29-0	32-6	34-0	34-0	33-6	33-5	32-2	31-1	29-7	28-6
BREADTHS	SHEER	6-6	16-4	23-6	29-3	33-0	34-0	34-0	33-6	32-6	31-3	29-7	28-1	26-1
HEIGHTS	KEEL	11-4	6-6	3-0	1-0	0-2	0-0	0-1	0-2	0-3	0-3	0-5	0-6	0-7
FROM	CHINE	11-7	9-2	6-7	5-0	3-4	2-4	1-7	1-5	1-3	1-3	1-7	2-0	2-1
BASE	SHEER	21-1	22-1	22-5	22-7	22-7	22-6	22-5	22-4	22-0	21-3	20-3	19-0	17-5

21

Jim Skonzakes of Dayton, Ohio, has taken a '41 Buick, added Cad fenders and bumpers, a removable hard top and cocktail bar.

1st place winner of 1951 Indianapolis show. B. F. Harris of Champaign, Illinois, owner. Car is entirely hand-built, exhibits the utmost in perfection inside and out. Engine was built of two Austin engines.

HEY! How about you fellows in the East sending more pictures of your custom cars?

This beautiful '32 channeled roadster belongs to Lynn Wineland who lives in Dayton, Ohio. It has a "full-house," boat windshield and all-leather upholstery.

This very beautiful 1939 Merc longs to Ray Zuend of Dixon, nois. Grille made of ⅜" stai steel. Owner claims 120 mph sp

22

INDIANAPOLIS CUSTOM SHOW

This car, believe it or not, is a '49 Ford! It has been channeled and with the addition of a different grille Continental kit, and bumpers, has the appearance of a high priced car. Belongs to J. A. Wright, Covington, Va.

Bill and Don Cunningham of Indianapolis are the proud owners of this 1939 Merc, with a removable top and unusual swivel front seat.

bert Hamke won the Detroit, Chicago, uth Bend, and the 1951 Indianapolis shows th this 1927 T pick up. It has a full race Merc engine. Two-speed rear end, entire gine, front & rear axles are chrome plated.

BELL
TIMING MEET

Above, Jay Lightfoot's modified roadster superimposed on a photo of the lake bed. Note the cracked, baked mud on which these fellows run. Below, Leland Klob, a member of the "Dra-gons Club. He turned 110.94 mph.

Below, Dana Boller runs his father's Cad thru at 90 mph. Dana had bet it would do 100.

by Louis Kimzey

The weather was perfect for this month's Bell Timing Meet . . . that is, up until 11:00 a.m. when all "h" broke loose. A wind (I use the term loosely) came up and it blew so hard that it cut the speeds down to low "nothings." One fellow got *so* mad because he couldn't do a fast time that he dropped his car in *low* gear and ran the *full* length of the course in that cog, turning a timed 74.24 mph. The car looked and sounded like it was going to blow up!

Because of the wind, the meet was called off at noon, which was a big disappointment to the fellows who didn't get a chance to run their cars. Everything went like clockwork, as all of Bell's meets do. Cars representing all the affiliated clubs were in attendance.

Bell Timing was founded in 1948. Altho many of their members have joined the armed forces, the group is still very active. This association has no restrictions as to what type of car runs at their meets, provided it meets their safety requirements. So you fellows who have a car that you think is faster than your buddy's, well, come on out to their September 12th meet and find out. The association is also interested in the enrollment of more clubs, so if you're interested, write: Ed Thurman, 4940 58th Place, Maywood, California, and he'll give you all particulars. The Bell Timing Association is a charter member of, and is solidly behind the *American Hot Rod Conference!* Their President, Ralph "Rip" Car-

24

Under hood is Dick Peterson, at front is Lynn Peterson, and at side is Nate Jones. They are removing stock heads and manifold and will install speed equipment borrowed from the Billy Morgan's '39 sedan in background.

Center, this 1939 Ford turned 86.85 mph while bucking strong headwinds. Owner and driver is Billy Morgan of the "Centenarions."

Bottom, '41 Merc, the driver of which became disgusted with high winds, dropped it in first to turn the amazing speed of 74.24 in low!

ter is the representative to this fast-growing federation and is also Vice-President of the "Dra-gons," one of the many clubs in B.T.A. The friendly atmosphere prevailed here as at the other meets. Fellows borrowed from each other and even pitched in to help put a competitor's car together. The crew of a convertible coupe was borrowing a dual manifold and hi-comp. cylinder heads from a "full house" two-door sedan. This was quite a sight to see these guys take the stock equipment off, install the other fellow's speed parts, run the course a couple of times, then repeat the process all over again. (Whew!) With that I think I'll leave . . . I'm tired, I just changed a tire . . .

Doug Hartelt is proud owner of this fast '34 coupe. In preparation for Bonneville, Doug entered his coupe in this meet to iron out bugs before the big national meet August 27 to September 3. This car has a Weiand four-carb. set-up, Evans heads, Potvin ignition and cam on a 248 cu in. Ford engine. Doug belongs to the "Lancers" of Orange, California. Above, Doug on his way to a 133.31 mph run. Side, Doug installing new set of spark plugs. Bottom, immaculate interior of this extra clean car. Extra heavy "roll bars" (behind seat) protect driver in case of accident. Plexiglas windows, safety belt, and quick fuel cut-off are other visible safety features. All-important "tach" is mounted prominently on steering column. Fuel pressure pump and "nitro-alky" tank are located at the driver's right.

26

Ralph "Rip" Carter (above, left) is the President of Bell Timing Association. He is also V-Pres. of the Dra-gons and representative to the American Hot Rod Conference. Just a word for the American Hot Rod Conference . . . There is a representative from each of the *active* timing associations in California to the AHRC (Valley Timing Assn, Oakland Schools Auto Assn, Cal-Neva Timing Assn, Fresno Rod Benders, So. Calif. Timing Assn, and Russetta Timing Assn). The officers are Dean Batchelor (SCTA), president; Felix Dal Porto (VTA), V.P. for N. Calif; Lou Baney (RTA), V.P. for S. Calif; Dean Bradley (FRB), secty: and Harold Osborne (TRA), treas. How about joining today!

Above right, if a fellow is having trouble, you can bet your bottom dollar he'll have help in a very short time. Such is the case of Jim Chapkis, when David Foster came over to help.

Below left, Billy Morgan gives technical advice (?) to Gerald Roberts. Both of these fellows belong to the "Centenarions," a new club which recently joined the Bell Timing Association. The club is at present seeking some new members in the Los Angeles area.

Below right, Nate Jones, President of the Centenarions, working on engine. Nate, who has been active in speed events for years, is founder of club. He operates a muffler shop.

EASTERN AUTO

Eastern Auto can truthfully claim to be the oldest accessory and custom firm in the business, having been started in 1919, by Joseph Kraus, to feature speed and custom accessories for the model "T" Ford.

Alex, his son, grew up with the business, working there after school and on Sundays,

Since graduating from UCLA in 1939, Alex has devoted full time to the store. Eastern Auto pioneered many items now taken for granted in the custom accessories line, such as "bull noses" for Fords, Plymouths, etc. (the first being the 1936 Ford) While long shackles and lowering kits had been used for some time on California cars, Eastern Auto was the first to apply mass production tech-

MEET THE ADVERTISER

nique to these items and make their popularity nation-wide, as well as lowering the cost. Also among Eastern Auto's firsts are solid hood sides and grille panels, which, in the middle and late '30s accounted for a good volume of their business.

Thru the years, this firm has established an enviable reputation for fast service, excellent workmanship and fair dealing. Their guarantee of satisfaction is no idle claim. In addition to their retail store, Eastern maintains a large manufacturing division. There, a research department constantly adds to their ever expanding line of custom accesories. Included are such items as chrome air cleaners, chrome wire looms, and chrome dash-boards. In fact, Eastern Auto claims to have one of the most complete lines in the business. While government restrictions may temporarily curtail introduction of some new items, Alex assures us that with the lifting of restrictions, they will offer more, better, and newer "automotive goodies" than ever before.

AIROADSTER

Will it "go" or "blow"? Jot Horn and Norm Taylor intend to find out and we should know the results by next month's issue of HOP-UP. The boys, who both work at Bell Auto Parts, are spending all their spare time on the project. Toying with the idea of putting an airplane engine in the chassis of Norm's '32 Ford roadster, they were lucky to find an engine (complete with plane attached) for 100 bucks. From the P.T. 19 Trainer, they salvaged what they could, including a "bucket seat," and discarded the rest.

The engine is a six cylinder Ranger, 185 hp. The single overhead cam acts on roller rocker arms, with inclined valves. Rods are steel "I" beam. Twin mags take care of the electrical system. The dry sump oil system has a 17 qt. cap. and is cooled by an oil radiator. Mounted upside down and backwards, a crank connector was made for the prop shaft and fitted to a Ford flywheel. The engine plate was made to fit a '49-'50

30   **HOP UP, October, 1951**

Ford bell housing and a '39 Ford transmission was adapted to that. The rear end is a '32 Ford with shortened drive shaft and radius rods, and Halibrand quick-change center sectiton. The rear wheels have special 18″ disks and will mount 7.50 x 18 Indianapolis tires. The stock 1940 Ford front end will have Firestone ribbed racing tires.

A 27-T roadster body will make up the "coachwork."

Norm and Jot don't anticipate any trouble unless it's from overheating the air cooled engine. For this problem, they're working on a system of baffles to direct the flow of air across each cylinder and the head. For the time being, the engine will be left stock except for the installation of four Ford carburetors and a homemade intake manifold.

Here's wishing them luck and we'll be looking forward to the results from this low fly'n monster.

BLOWN SAMPSON SPRINT CAR

Something new has been added to an already successful Sampson-engined sprint car combination. The little-heard-of Sampson engine, originally built for Alden Sampson, is a 16-valve, double overhead cam, four-cylinder, with a displacement of 100 cu in. A Borg-Warner, roots type supercharger installation was conceived and carried out by Mel Hansen with the help of Marvin Faw and Dan Quella. The blower

is driven by chain from the rear of the
crankshaft between the engine block and
the "in and out" gear box. To eliminate
the carburetor, a Hilborn fuel injection
system was adapted from parts that were at
one time used on a Maserati. Air is supplied to the blower thru a giant air cleaner
located under the cowl between the dash
and firewall. This installation required the
frame, hood, and front radius rods to be
lengthened.

STUDIE CUSTOM

George Jules of Huntington Park, California, is the proud owner of the Studebaker shown here. The custom work was done by George Arny, who did an exceptionally fine job of fitting a Cad grille and smoothing off the body. The top (not shown) and upholstery are by Gaylord. The engine is stock L-head Studebaker, but George plans to install a new V-8 Studie soon.

The improvement in appearance over the standard Studebaker by removing excess chrome and fitting a small conservative grille is remarkable.

34

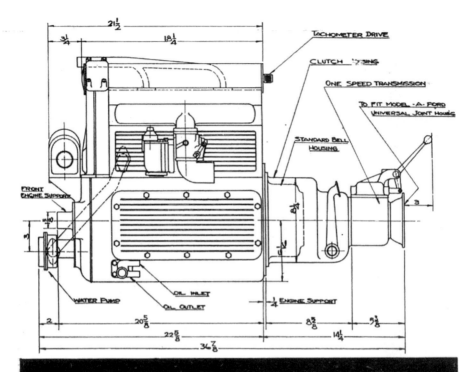

OFFY MIDGET ENGINE

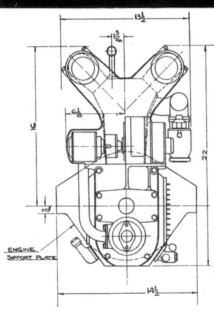

The Offenhauser "Midget" engine is world-renowned as the foremost midget race car power plant. The drawings show an early version of the "Offy." At that time, the 97 cu in. unblown engine was credited with a mere 90 hp at 6500 rpm. Today, with 105 cu in, and fuel injection, developed horsepowers of over 140 have been reported, using alcohol based fuels. The photograph shows a later Meyer-Drake built version. Note the compact construction.

CUSTOM MERC

134

Johnny Hagen, who owns and operates a custom shop in Glendale, Calif., took simplicity as the theme when he customized his 1950 Mercury convertible. The low, long look of the Hagen Merc has been accomplished by removing 2½ inches from the windshield, wind-wings, rear, and side windows. To carry the simplicity motif further, frenched headlights have been worked into the front fenders, and '50 Merc skirts were installed. When the Carson top is removed, a beautiful full tonneau cover, made by American Top Shop in Lynwood, Calif., covers the seats to protect them from the sun. In the future, Johnny hopes to have the tail lights set into the rear bumper, then the whole rear of the car will be smooth. The engine is completely stock except for a Kong ignition, but there is talk of a "full-house" treatment later on.

REJUVENATED INDIAN

This 1928 101 Indian Scout has been in the process of being rebuilt and modified since early in 1948. After almost four years and approximately $1000 dollars expenditure, little remains of the original bike.

The engine still retains the 1928 crankcase but has been converted to a dry sump oil system by using a 1933 oil pump. Fly-wheels from a 1912 "Altoona' Chief are used with 'Bonneville' Scout rods and crank pin. A complete Bonneville valve set up replaces the original assembles and are actuated by stock Bonneville cams and lifters. A Chief transmission has been installed. The gentleman who performed this exacting work is owner-builder Everett Duncan of Glendale, Calif.

38

137

THEY'RE HERE AT LAST! New Simplified plans for Building the Fastest Boats in the World. We now have a complete line of 18 sleek racing boats from 6 foot outboards to 20 foot inboards. Why not send for your new illustrated catalogue today. Just send 25c to CHAMPION BOATS, Box 9038 Dept. 46-J, Long Beach, Calif.

PHOTO CREDITS

"The Cam of Records and Successes"

Bigelow Gimmy produces 248 H.P. equipped with the $40 Iskenderian rocker cams. A special brochure detailing the conversion of the GMC for racing or fast road car use is available FREE. Ask for it when sending for our catalogue.

For the most complete and informative booklet ever published on Racing Cams send only 25c. Profusely illustrated. We also include without charge a pocket-size calculator and "The Secret of Cooling the Ford V8."

ED ISKENDERIAN   5000 W. Jefferson Los Angeles 16
REpublic 3-7587

WEAR THE MASCOT OF THE
SPEEDWAY DRIVERS!

"LADY LUCK" in Four Colors
10" Felt Jacket Emblems....$1.00
7" Felt Jacket Emblems..........50c
Decals—15c — Stickers—15c
"T" Shirts with Design.........$1.50
(no COD's)

Complete Catalog of Popular Emblems, including Club items, Racing Novelties, Garments, Decals, Special Emblems: 25c.

STYLIZED EMBLEM COMPANY
1356-U N. Western Ave.
Los Angeles 27 Calif.

40

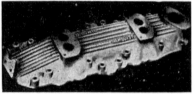

TECHNICAL TIPS

FORD 6 ECONOMY COMPLAINT

I have a 1950 Ford "6" Fordor . . . Bought it for advertised "Economy" features—However, every V-8 I've owned has given me better economy. Everything has been checked . . . can't get over 17½ miles per gal. at 60.

Imagine the gas consumption . . . I make as many as 3 starts and stops in one city block! Is there anything I can do to increase my mileage? With all the progress made in every phase of engineering in the last 10 years, it seems strange they haven't improved such an important "sales feature" in the American auto.

San Antonio, Texas   J. R. Jacobson

In answer to your complaint on the gas mileage of your Ford 6, I think 17½ mpg at 60 mph is darn good, and the car must be in excellent condition. Did you ever stop to think how much improvement in gasoline consumption has been made in the last 20 years? In 1930, 20 mpg was a fair average for owners of the big three cars. They developed 40 to 50 bhp and weighed roughly around 2400 lbs. These same cars today have nearly 100 bhp, weigh over 3100 lbs., are cruised at much higher speeds, and still give about the same gasoline mileage.

Door to door driving is something else again, and no car, even a small one will give better than, say, ⅔ the mpg that it gets at 60 mph steady speed.

An outline for better economy is about as follows:

1. Higher compression cylinder head, an automatic booster of mpg only if fuel octane requirement is met.
2. Leaner jets and/or smaller carburetor reduces performance and tends towards high internal temperatures.
3. Sodium cooled valves and/or stellite seats on the exhaust valves to alleviate item 2.
4. More heat—200° F water thermostat . . . . more heat on intake manifold reduces performance.
5. Reduced exhaust back pressure. On a six, the most efficient method is to completely separate the front 3 from the rear 3 cylinders. Nothing is available to do this and still meeting item 4.
6. Higher gear ratio. A 3.31 axle would help mpg and seriously affect performance.
7. Miscellaneous items such as using 1 oil ring per piston instead of 2, lighter lubricants, higher tire pressures, etc., all of which have objections.

This outline is not complete, and of course does not mention driving habits or technique, also if you try any or all these combinations you will drive it one day and go back to the stock set-up. Newhouse Automotive Industries has a good book that covers this subject much better than I can in a letter. The title is "How to Get 150 Miles Per Gallon."

Finally, don't try to improve mpg by working on the carburetor. Thousands of poor dumb inventors have tried—overlooking completely the simple fact that this much maligned unit already supplies the leanest mixture possible which will burn in the particular engine—assuming of course that the carburetor is in proper working order.

Sorry I got a little wound-up on this subject—actually, I'd buy a 4-cylinder Henry J for your job.—Tech. Ed.

HIGHER COMPRESSION FOR CHEVY

I have a 1951 Chevrolet in which I have installed a 3.727 ratio rear axle (4.111 standard) I would like to install a higher compression head than the standard 6.6 . . . am wondering what ratio I should use for **general highway** and **driving use** without overloading crankshaft and main bearings. What effect would Hi-Lift rocker arms have on performance?

Belding, Michigan   William B. Davis

You can safely mill .090 from the cylinder head of your Chevrolet, which will then give 7.0 to 1 compression ratio. But, there's more to it than that! Intake valves must be seated deeper into the head to prevent their hitting the piston. Also you must place .045 shims under each rocker arm shaft support bracket. This is to restore the geometry to normal.

Re the hi-lift rockers, I had hoped by this time to have some actual performance data on the improvement, but the car on which they are installed still hasn't been road tested. Unquestionably they will help performance.—Tech. Ed.

HOW TO BUILD A STEERING WHEEL

On my A-V8 roadster I was using a '30 Chevrolet steering box with the original, wood rim steering wheel and sheet metal spokes. I removed the spokes and found a cast iron "spider" that formed the center and which contained the hole for the steering column. I bought four pieces of annealed spring steel about eight inches long, 1½ inches wide, and 1/16 inch thick. I tapered and bolted the four spokes onto the "spider" with three small set screws. I then drilled a small hole in the outer end of each spoke, cut four slots in the wood rim and inserted the spokes, holding them in place with a pin passing thru rim and spoke. The wheel was then dismantled and, while the spokes were being tempered, I wrapped the wood rim with venetian blind cloth and lacquered it several times. Next I cut slits in the wrapping so the pin could pass thru rim and spoke. I stretched ⅝ inch surgical rubber tubing about an inch long next to the rim over each spoke, which protected the hands from damage by the thin steel spokes and hid the slits in the wrapping. The pin holes were hidden by short lacquered pieces of cloth. Finally, aluminum was lathe turned to a pleasing shape to cover the center.

The wheel cost me $2.00 which is a considerable saving over a new one, and the appearance is very workmanlike indeed.

John J. Hunholz

MORE "GO" FOR '36 CORD

I have been informed that if I shaved .05 (which seems quite a lot) from the heads of my 1936 Cord engine #FB 256 and had ¾ grind cam the horsepower would increase 25%.

If this were true (just considering the heads) what would the compression ratio be? Wouldn't the engine run real hot?

Is the Cord preselector primarily the same as the Wilson preselector?

Is there any reason why there are not more Cords and Auburns used in stock car races?

Memphis, Tennessee   E. A. Draisey

If I had a Cord in good shape, I'd go easy on engine modifications. Of course, .050 isn't much to remove from the head of an average '36 car because fuels have improved since then.

TECHNICAL TIPS

Grinding the cam is tricky because of those funny little rockers which upset all normal calculations as to how to regrind. Further, I doubt very much if you'd gain anything like 25% in power. Driven exactly the same, a higher compression ratio gives better economy and cooler running—provided it is not detonating.

The Cord pre-selector is somewhat similar (for the driver) to the Wilson, but the comparison ends there. The Wilson box uses epicyclic gears operated by bands, while the Cord has constant mesh helical gears engaged by syncronized dog clutches. I highly recommend conversion to a manual shift on this car to save the transmission as much as possible . . . available from R. G. Sceli, 317 Asylum Street, Hartford 3, Connecticut.

I think there are two good reasons you don't see Cords and Auburns in stock car races; one, they aren't eligible according to the rules as to year built, and two, no owner feels like beating up a good car that can't be replaced.—Tech. Ed.

ECONOMY HOP UP '41 BUICK

I own a 1941 Buick Special sedanet with a stock dual carburetor system. Would like to get better mileage and more power from my car; should a high-compression head be first or perhaps a dual exhaust system. Can you advise me what should be the first and most important equipment to put on my car and what should follow when I have the dough.

Berkeley, Calif.   Fred Mok

I would say that the order of procedure on your 1941 Buick might be about as follows:
1. Dual mufflers—stock mufflers are straight thru and are okay.
2. Mill the head. Special heads are not available. You can't mill very much if you use the 1941 .015 "thin" gasket. It's already 7.0:1 and very prone to knock, as you surely know.
3. Consider a semi-reground cam, or maybe Barker hi-lift rockers will be available for your car by the time you are ready for this.
4. Try a pair of Ford V-8 carburetors without the Buick "cut-in" feature. This isn't quite as good as "compound" carburetion, but it will stay in tune much better.
5. Roadmaster intake valves can be re-machined to fit the Special. Ports and seats must also be re-machined.
6. Throw the engine away and put in the larger F-263 engine and start all over again with item 1.
                                  —Tech. Ed.

MODEL A HOP UP

I have a Ford A and I would like to hop it up. Will a supercharger be better than twin carburetor?

Morris, N. Y.   Lester Thompson

There is no supercharger available, and the engine would not stay together very well if it were supercharged. In fact, for a really hot engine, it is strongly recommended that you start with the B block, rather than the A, and use the C crankshaft. This gives much larger bearing surfaces to stand up better under the higher power and rpm you contemplate.—Tech. Ed.

'50 FORD WITH A ROAR

My '50 4-door with overdrive has a disagreeable roar or rumble at 48 miles per hour. At 55 to 65 this car is very quiet; at 66 to 69 this roar comes back and gets louder as my speed increases. I bought the car new . . . have 15,000 miles on it and have had it 6 months.

The roar is very noticeable when the engine is under load. It is quiet when going down hill or when the engine is not pulling. It rumbles in and out of overdrive and at the same speeds. Sometimes it is more noticeable than others. It is very annoying—nearly drowns out the radio.

Middletown, Ohio   George Breitenbecker

I am almost positive that the vibration in your 1950 Ford is caused by the front universal joint of the driveshaft. One of the changes incorporated in the 1951 Fords is the raising of the rear motor mounts by 1½ inches. This was stated in Ford publicity releases to have been done to reduce propeller shaft vibration. Front floor pan clearance has to be increased accordingly to make this change on a '50 Ford and I also suspect that the angle of the rear springs seat pads have been changed.

I believe that all Ford service managers have received official service bulletins on this problem and what corrective measures to take.—Tech. Ed.

HOPPING A '51 STUDEBAKER V-8

I own a '51 Studebaker Commander V-8 and am interested in raising the compression inasmuch as I understand that this is the easiest way to increase gas mileage and performance.

What compression ratio would you recommend? I do not want to sacrifice durability nor dependability. According to my calculations, a ratio of 8:1 would require planing off .058"—correct? Will the intake manifold still fit on the heads after lowering them this much?

Approximately, what horsepower and gas mileage increase could I expect?

Does anyone make a dual exhaust system for this car?

Will increasing the compression ratio decrease ring life?

Eugene, Oregon   Malcolm E. Manley

I feel you would be wise to stick to 8.0 to 1, and this will definitely give better mileage and performance. You will also have to use premium fuel to retain close to stock ignition timing.

The intake manifold will not fit after milling the heads until it is also milled an amount determined by measuring the angle of the mating surfaces and solving by trigonometry.

A good guess on power increase would be 10 bhp, and certainly more if you add dual exhaust (write Southern California Muffler Company, 11039-49 Washington Blvd., Culver City 6, California for this). You can reasonably expect 1 to 2 more miles per gallon, provided that you drive it exactly as before. With an engine so well designed as the Studebaker, you have no fears as to ring life. Incidentally, the stock engine develops 105 bhp "as installed" with all accessories, muffler, etc.—Tech. Ed.

CLASSIFIED

AUTOMOBILE SUPPLIES

"WATER INJECTION" Also "Economy and Power" Methods. Send for your Free Life Membership Card. "Water Burners" of America, La Verne 5, Calif.

TUCKER CARS, parts, frames, body front & rear hoods, engines. Build yourself a sport car or race car. High frequency coils for over 5000 rpm. New Cadillac Engine and Heavy Hydramatic Transmission $350. Hillman Demonstrator cars. Schlipf Auto Sales, Metamora, Illinois.

AIR HORNS. Beautiful. Powerful. Blast like Dynamite! Send postcard for free new catalog: Tom MacCanna, 148-B East 40 Street, New York 16.

TOOLS AT WHOLESALE direct from factory. Full line of top quality, fully guaranteed, chrome, factory-new, mechanics hand tools. You save half regular price for tools of this quality. Our Permanent Price Protection Plan guarantees you wholesale prices. Write today for free catalog. Mechanics Co-op, Dept K, Oakland 8, Calif.

CARS FOR SALE

5 AAA MIDGETS, 4 cyl. ready to run, no junk. From $125.00. Will buy used Jaguar, Aston-Martin, Jupiter, Allard. Ramsay Enterprises, 1210 E. 55th, Chicago.

1941 GRAHAM HOLLYWOOD Sedan, Super-charger, good running condition, solid body. Write 143 Glendale Ave., Glendale, Calif.

1912 OVERLAND TOURING, New Tires & Tubes. In running condition. R. V. Goodman, 2907 48th St., Des Moines, Iowa.

1930 CHRYSLER CUSTOM IMPERIAL. Engine recently overhauled. Two side mounts only one spare. One new tire. Recently made a 1,200 mile trip with no trouble at speeds in excess of 50 mph. Address correspondence to Donald A. Dunn, 136 High St., State College, Penna. All offers considered.

1937 SUPERCHARGED CORD Convertible, factory re-built perfect, radio, heater. Cost $3700, take $2500 or swap for Rolls or Lagonda. J. B. Petty, Box 1010, Gastonia, N.C.

SPEED EQUIPMENT

SPLIT MANIFOLD PARTS. Special cast iron welding fitting permits installation of dual exhausts on Chevrolets, Plymouths, and most other in-lines. $3.75 each postpaid. Gotha Automotive Specialists, Box 141-T, Harvey, Illinois.

McBAR ADAPTORS-HOUSINGS permit installation of 49-51 Lincoln V-8, 49-51 Cadillac, 49-51 Oldsmobile, 51 Chrysler V-8 Firepower, engines in Ford, Mercury, Zephyr, Lincoln & Lincoln Continental, Allard. List $65.00 Inquiry invited. Custom installation if desired. McBar Machine Shop, 65 North Miami St., Peru, Ind. Phone 6200.

MERCURY CARBURETORS and other big 4-bolt flange carburetors adapted to Ford V-8s and others. Custom adaptor $4.00 postpaid, Gotha Automotive Specialists, Box 141-T, Harvey, Ill.

MISC. FOR SALE

"T" SHIRTS IMPRINTED with your club name & design in any 1 color. $9.50 doz. Free Sportswear Catalog #D-2. Agents wanted. R. Smith, 217 BB Centre St., New York.

PHOTO ALBUMS Duesenberg Model A. 12 5x7 photos showing standard & custom bodies, engine and chassis. Order from PRINTS, Room 102, 1951 University Ave., St. Paul 4, Minn.

DUESENBERG BOOK, just published! Details of chassis, custom bodies, everything about this mightiest American car. Models A, J, SJ. 225 photos, plus 50 drawings, cutaways. 8½x11", 165 pages, $5 postpaid. Motor Classic Bookhouse, Arcadia, California.

44

HOP UP 15c

COVER HOP UP
PAGE 26

BONNEVILLE
NATIONALS

17-PAGE
BONNEVILLE
STORY
STARTS
ON PAGE 7

230 mph KENZ

HOP UP

NOV.
1951

15c

145

CORRESPONDENCE

OHC FOR AMERICAN CARS?

When are we going to get overhead camshafts on U.S. cars?

Great Neck, L.I., N.Y.   Ted Powell

I seriously doubt if we will ever see ohc engines in production American cars . . . and for two very good reasons: One is that it obviously costs a great deal more money, and don't ever forget that the manufacturer really squeezes the pennies! As one wit said, "every so-called mechanical improvement is actually the sales department's excuse for some cost-saving idea devised by engineering." Secondly, American car engine speeds are gradually going down, not up. By this, I mean revolutions per mile and not peaking speeds. The point here is that rocker arms are OK in an average size engine, so long as speeds do not exceed 4500 rpm.—Tech. Ed.

HUDSON-ESSEX DATA

You refer to the 1931 Hudson and Essex Speedsters that were factory produced at that time . . . also to the exhaust system used on the 1932 Hudson race cars that ran at Indianapolis. I would like more data on these subjects.

Philadelphia, Pa.   Chas. L. Betts, Jr.

Apparently, the Essex speedster was not built in 1928. In 1929 it re-appeared with a single seat rumble. In 1930 none were built, but in 1931, both the Hudson 8 and the Essex (which by then had interchangeable bodies) were offered in a new speedster body having more "flair" to the boat tail section. To my knowledge, only the 1931 was "cataloged."

I've heard that the engine in the '32 Hudson "Indy" cars had a specially cast block with the exhausts running straight out of the block (horizontally) and the intake ports having an extra 90° turn to facilitate multiple downdraft carburetion. This would be exactly the reverse of the ports as used today on the 8.—Tech. Ed.

V-8 IN '41 PACKARD 120

Would it be possible to install the new Chrysler V-8, the Cadillac, or the Lincoln V-8 engine, complete with its own respective standard clutch and transmission, in a 1941 Packard coupe? I'd like to retain the Packard overdrive.

Travis Air Force Base, Calif.   Paul E. Maddox

I've never seen a V-8 installed in a Packard, but I see no good reason why it can't be done. There is plenty of length available, but watch for steering column interference with the left-hand cylinder bank and exhaust pipes. To check this, measure from the centerline of your Packard cylinder bores to the steering column. This dimension must be 13" to clear the Cadillac engine, or 14½" to install the Chrysler.

Neither of these two engines can be used with overdrive, without solving the problem of attaching your excellent Packard transmission. No kits are available to do this, so you are on your own . . . it might involve a special casting.

While I much prefer the other two engines, the Lincoln would be the easiest to install if you require an overdrive. My principal objections to the Lincoln are: weight (862# less trans.), and cooling requirements.—Tech. Ed.

If it's hopped up, it'll be in HOP UP

BONNEVILLE

The Southern California Timing Association deserves great praise for the success of the 1951 Bonneville National Speed Trials. Long-range planning and careful construction produced a group of outstanding cars whose sizzling speeds established a new set of class records. The Kenz Twin-Ford one-way time of 230.8 mph rocked critics of the "hop-up artists."

Of even greater significance are the over 180 mph averages attained by Tom Beatty's Auto Accessories-Hop Up Magazine Special and the Evans Speed Eqpt. Special . . . both approached within reasonable striking speed of the International class C record now held by the late Bernd Rosemeyer in the 500 hp Auto Union at 219.5 mph for the flying mile.

It is certainly reasonable to assume that either of these cars, provided with a streamlined all-enclosed body, would closely approach the record and . . . equipped with a properly engineered supercharger installation, could easily break the record.

And, speaking of records, special praise should go to Otto Crocker, whose timing equipment performed faultlessly for 1000 runs. During the previous week, failure of the famous AAA timing wrecked the record-breaking attempts of Lt. Col. Goldie Gardner who had brought his MG and crew to the perfect surface of the Bonneville Salt Flats.

Perhaps the professionals might well take a lesson from the amateur?

EDITORIAL STAFF

Editor..Oliver Billingsley
Technical Editor...............................John R. Bond
Historical Editor..........................W. Everett Miller
Associate Editor............................Robert Dearborn
Staff Photographer...............................Gene Trindl
Photographers..........Jack Campbell, Bob Canaan
                                                   Joe Al Denker

PRODUCTION STAFF

Managing Editor.......................W. H. Brehaut, Jr.
Art Director..Louis Kimzey
Art...Jack Caldwell

ADVERTISING

Advertising Manager.......................William Quinr
Motorcycles...Bill Bagnall
East Coast Representatives....Peabody & Ortgies
                                                   276 West 43rd Street
                                                   New York 18, N.Y.
United Kingdom.............................Kenneth Kirkman
                                                   2 Longcroft Avenue
                                                   Banstead, Surrey, England
Italy...Michele Vernola
                                                   C.P. 500
                                                   Milano, Italy

CORRESPONDENTS

Italy...Corrado Millanta
England...............Geoff Healey, Spike Rhiando

Vol. 1, No. 4   November, 1951

CONTENTS

Contributions—not responsible for the return of unsolicited manuscripts, photographs, and/or drawings unless accompanied by self-addressed stamped envelope.

Mailing address—Box 110, Glendale, California.

HOP UP is published monthly by Enthusiasts' Publications, Inc., 540 W. Colorado Blvd., Glendale, California. Phone CHapman 5-2297. Application for entry as second-class matter is pending. Copyright 1951 by Enthusiasts' Publications, Inc. Reprinting in whole or in part forbidden except by permission of the publishers.

Subscription price $1.50 per year thruout the world. Single copy 15c.

Change of address—must show both old and new addresses.

TECHNICAL TIPS

LINCOLN CONTINENTAL

About to purchase 1940 Continental convertible. Compare 1940 model with later model Continentals. Compare 1940 Continental with present automobiles.

Waco, Texas   John D. Burnett

The pre-war Lincoln Continental is already a prized collector's item, and unquestionably will continue as such, with very little or no depreciation. You can't compare it with present cars because its handling and roadability are much better than anything we have today, and its styling will never be dated to the extent that today's car will be.

Many people (including me) think the 1940 and 1941 models are vastly preferable because of the simpler, less ornate treatment as compared to the 1942 and later models, an incidental, but important point is the fact that for some unknown reason each years model got 100 lbs heavier.

The Continental is a car well worth maintaining and the rather sad powerplant can be replaced by any of several others.—Tech. Ed.

MORE MILEAGE AND FILLING HOLES

I have a 1947 Chevrolet sedan on which I would like to make some minor mechanical and body changes.

I would be very grateful if you could supply me with information on how to increase miles per gallon.

In reference to the body, I would appreciate information about removing chrome and leading in the holes underneath.

Irvington, N.J.   Frank J. Cangialosi

There isn't a lot you can do to get more miles per dollar out of your Chevrolet. I say miles per dollar advisedly, because a milled head gives more miles/gal., but not miles/dollar. A 3.73 axle is available and will help economy with some loss in low speed performance.

There are several ways to fill holes. If they aren't too big, use a large drill to countersink the hole. Then apply a spot of brass with the aid of a torch and brass rod. This takes a definite technique . . . most welders can learn by practicing on an old sheet. You can check the job by making sure there is a good fill or slight bulge of brass on the back side. Finish by facing off with a disk sander. Larger holes require a piece of sheet steel cut to fit and welded in place. This is very difficult to do unless you have a really good body man. Finishing requires both hammer work and filing.—Tech. Ed.

WANTS '32 FORD ROADSTER

I want to buy a '32 Ford V-8 roadster. Could use a 4 cylinder but prefer a V-8. Send photo and describe condition.

1835 Cherokee   Mack Weston
Baxter Springs, Kansas

NAVY CUSTOMIZER

Before coming into the Navy, I owned a '40 Buick club coupe which I was undertaking to customize and rebuild . . . Would like to correspond with anyone interested in customized automobiles and would like help with mechanical or body work of project in this area.

VUY Box 15 NAF   R. J. Amelong, HA, USN
Chincoteague Island, Va.

HENRY J SIX VS. FOUR

After driving several new cars and considering performance and price, I have decided to get the new Henry J. I would appreciate it if you could answer a few questions for me.

As the cars stand now, the J-6 will far outperform the J-4. What I want to know is if, considering costs, the 4 cylinder couldn't be hopped up to perform about as well as a hopped up 6. Do you have any information as to what hp the 4 would put out with say ¾ cam, 8.5:1 heads, dual or oversize carbs, and a better exhaust system? Also included on the treatment on the new engine will be a reboring job and if available, stroked crank with rods and pistons.

Washington, Indiana   Glen Inman

I have some definite opinions on your Henry J questions—but remember they are only "one man's opinion."

For the extra cost, the six is a much better car than the four, because you can easily spend the difference between them on making the 4 go as well as the 6—so what have you gained except experience? You might even get, say 80 bhp (or even more) out of the 4, but look at those long rods (8.75″) and the 4¾ stroke, and compare with the 6. You can use the F head Willys 4 to get big intake valves and mechanical octanes. You can even use the 1930, 4.75″ stroke crankshaft (no counterweights) and the corresponding shorter rods for more displacement, but it always costs more than you estimate; and frankly, hopped-up engines are always a little less reliable and a little more troublesome than the stockers.

Still, if you want four barrels, go to it—it should be a very interesting project.—Tech. Ed.

DE SAXE PRINCIPLE

(1) What is "quench area"? What factors does it affect?

(2) Are any engines presently being built on the De Saxe, or "offset con-rod," principle? Do you believe this type has any merit?

Detroit, Michigan   Donald Scott

To answer your two questions—first, quench area is the low clearance area (about .060″ deep) used to "quench" the last 15 to 40% of the charge in the burning process. The percentage is figured on linear flame travel from the spark plug, not volume, and the effect is to suppress detonation thru the cooling effect of a high surface to volume ratio. Quench area is absolutely essential with today's fuels and compression ratios.

Generally speaking, the De Saxe principle is passé today. Ford still uses a 3/16 inch offset, but the very small theoretical advantages are of doubtful value. I expect the new ohv Ford engines to have the crankshaft in line with the cylinder bore. On the other hand, Cadillac showed (in the SAE Transactions for July 1949) that a wristpin located off-center in the piston had certain advantages in reduced piston slap and in giving equal piston side thrusts. Olds has done this for many years. Ford adopted this for 1950 (along with the DeSaxe crank). There may be other De-Saxe engines in production today, but the 1932 thru '51 Ford-Mercury V-8 is the only one of which I am positive.—Tech. Ed.

TECHNICAL TIPS

REWORKING '36 FORD ROADSTER

Am installing '51 Ford V-8 engine in my '36 Ford Roadster and I also wish to install a Zephyr transmission. I wish to move the engine aft 12 to 18 inches which necessitates moving of the cowl—this to more equally distribute the weight. How may such be done? My problem seems to be (1) shortening of the driveshaft which I fear will not produce too good results or installing a shorter driveshaft of what kind I know not; and (2) how, oh how will I provide for the steering shaft with the cowl being moved so far aft, the present one being too short?

I understand that the Zephyr transmission alone requires the moving of the engine forward so if this be true the problem becomes even greater.

Louisville, Ky.   Ralph W. Sullivan

The problems you mention are easy . . . what I am wondering is whether you realize that the whole X-member has to be reworked to get the engine back, as well as the pedals, etc. It's a lot of work, but it can be done.

Your present drive shaft and torque tube have to be shortened by a good machine shop, who will retain alignment and concentricity of the parts involved. Use the solid drive shaft for its desirable torsional flexibility, in preference to the earlier tube, even tho the tubular shaft is easier to shorten.

The steering column can be cut off about 6 or 8 inches above the gear and a 1936-37 Cadillac wheel and column substituted. This has a pair of universal joints and a connecting shaft (which can be made any length required). Another way is to cut the thing in the middle and weld in sections—just the opposite of your drive shaft and torque tube problem. I have seen this done, but it takes good welding on a part which must not fail. Better yet, a machine shop could make up an entirely new steering column of required length.

The Zephyr transmission case is exactly the same length as the Ford and you can put Zephyr gears into the Ford case.—Tech. Ed.

MORE LINCOLN CONTINENTAL

I have a 1948 hard top Lincoln Continental . . . thinking of installing a different engine . . . either the new Chrysler 180 hp, the Cadillac 150 hp, or the new Lincoln V-8.

Aspen, Colorado   Leonard Woods

I suggest you use the ohv Cadillac 160 bhp engine. The new Lincoln and old Cadillac are too heavy (roughly 850# against the new Cadillac at 700#) while the Chrysler weighs around 750# complete with an adapted flywheel and clutch. Actually the Chrysler would be first choice if it were available, and if it were not so difficult to add a conventional flywheel and clutch. Also, no McBar adapters have been announced for this engine, so there are serious "marriage" problems. I have never been able to get an accurate weight on the V-12, but it certainly weighs at least 700# and probably more. The Cadillac will not change handling qualities in any way except for the better.—Tech. Ed.

SURPLUS BLOWER

I have a chance to purchase a Borg-Warner, roots-type blower (war surplus). If adapted to a late Ford manifold, would boost be satisfactory?

Watertown, Mass.   Joseph Linehan

With regard to the surplus roots blower, we have had several inquiries re this little gem. I have never looked at one but understand the rotors are not straddle mounted.

Just to fill the cylinders of a Ford V-8 requires 208 C.F.M. at 3000, and it takes at least 25% over capacity from the blower discharge to insure a boost. Roughly you would need eight (yes, 8) of these units to get a 4" pressure head. If the "inches" are in mercury, that is a boost of only 2 psi. This assumes running them at crankshaft speed, of course, but I wouldn't advise running them any faster. Sorry!—Tech. Ed.

MORE GO & MPG FOR '46 FORD

. . . give me a little advise on how to get a little bit more power and mileage from my '46 Ford V-8 with the minimum of cost.

What I had in mind was to mill the heads down, use water injection, an electric fuel pump and duals with stock mufflers. Just how much should I mill the heads down?

U.S.S. Shannon   Gerry Watts

Your ideas on the '46 are OK, tho I'd better point out that water injection works best when mixed 50-50 with alcohol. Also there's no real reason for using electric fuel pumps that I can see, except as stand-by units.

You can safely mill about .040 off the heads. More than that requires a form tool for "redoming," so that the pistons will not hit the head. By re-doming, you can mill up to .070 off the heads.

A good "wrinkle" on the '46 V-8 is to replace the stock (for that year only) 3.54 axle gears with 3.78 ratio. This gives a lot more performance.—Tech. Ed.

FIRE-PROOF CLOTHING

A recent AAA bulletin contained the following useful information:

"All drivers are urgently requested to treat their uniforms and other clothing in fire preventative solution before every race. The solution is very easily concocted and has been certified by physicians to be harmless in every way. It consists of eight ounces of boric acid and four ounces of Borax, dissolved in two quarts of hot water. All the clothing should be prepared at home before the race. After cleaning, clothing must be redipped."

All competition drivers would be wise to follow this advice.—Ed.

5

1951 BONNEVILLE NATIONALS

Record "A" Lakester, Xydias and De
Langton of Burbank, 147.0106 mph.

The Bonneville Salt Flats were first tested as a high-speed race course in 1912. Since then, the flats have been used for breaking most of the outstanding world's speed records. In 1912, the world land speed record was 141.732. On September 16, 1947, John Cobb literally *flew* over the course at the phenomenal speed of 394.2 mph!

The flats are a salt deposit left by the receding of ancient Lake Bonneville. The deposit covers 159 sq. miles. The salt is white, crystalline aggregate, porous and so hard and rigid that it can support tremendous weights.

The first Bonneville Nationals were held in 1949. At the 1950 Nationals when the Xydias and Batchelor "C" streamliner turned 208.9271, people shook their heads and wondered, "Where in the heck's it goin' to end?" "How they going to improve *that* speed?" "Yep, I think they've hit their limit!" But, as the 1951 Nationals rolled around, it was quite evident that no record from last year would be left standing. True to the prognostications, *all* but one of the 1950 records fell and fell *hard!* To start

the ball rolling, the Kenz streamliner turned an astounding 221 average the very first day. Later on in the week, with Willie Young driving, the Kenz turned 227.848 mph!

Tom Beatty in his Auto Accessories' Special turned 185.8097, a new record for the Class "D" Lakester and the fastest time ever turned in a lakester. Tom did 188 mph the first time he ran. He set the new record the second time down the course. It's interesting to note that while waiting for his return run, instead of putting water in the tank, he used ice cubes! Earl Evans was next in line with his Class "C" Lakester and, with Bob Ward driving, turned 180 mph average to beat the old record of 175 mph. These are but a few who did outstandingly well. There were also C. T. Automotive, Carillo E. Hartelt, Hernandez & Likes, McClure and Ray Brown, to name a few. There were hundreds more who either set a record or beat their own top speed.

There were over 197 entries from all over the United States . . . they made 1,689 runs thru the traps!

Bill Kenz's beautiful, low, baby blue, aerodynamically perfect streamliner was the outstanding entry in this year's meet. This twin engined Floyd Clymer Special turned a speed of 227 mph with, it seemed, the greatest of ease. Using one engine, it turned 173.076 and set a new record of 221.4795 with both.

Photo top of page . . . Willie Young getting underway on his record run. Right, a member of the Kenz crew checking plugs on rear engine. Note other engine in front of driver's seat. Below, Tom Wingo, Frank Liston, Ed Leeman, all members of the Kenz crew, check engine preparatory to the next run. Willie Young (lifting goggles) drives.

These fellows deserve a lot of credit. They first started using Ardun heads in '49, took much kidding from friends, but with a lot of determination and effort, they went on to prove their engine by establishing a new Class "C" roadster record. Running in the most contested class at Bonneville (thirty-three competitors) this year, they really had the guys talkin'. Don Clark, Harrison Haggard and Clem Tebow pictured above are the proud owners of this roadster. They belong to the Roadmasters Club and are running a Chet Herbert roller cam, Silvo-Lite pistons and a Halibrand rear end. The powerplant is a 1945 Ford V-8 with fuel injection.

Altho plagued by all kinds of trouble early in week, Mailliard and Cagle (Clark Header Special) stuck it out and came thru with new record for "C" coupes. 133.6680.

10

Cantley and Sylva's "B" Modified Coupe, altho qualifying for a record, blew a head gasket on return run and lost chance for for record. They took first place in their class with 146.1869 mph.

Lanthorne Bros. & Gray's GMC powered "C" Modified Coupe turned in 153.061 mph.

Bell Auto Parts Special owned by Bill Burke & Dahm Bros. has a '39 Bantam body, tubular frame. Engine has Evans heads, manifold, ignition and Weber cam. It took second place in its class with 141.509.

Bill Boren, "Gerald" Keldrank & "Muskrat" working on their "C" sedan. Took 2nd in class.

Mal Hooper in his Ray Brown Special. This is just one of the 33 entries in this class.

Popular Ak Miller in his aerodynamic roadster. Engine was built by Nelson Taylor and Johnny Ryan. He turned 161.870 mph to take his class.

After 1689 runs thru his precision timing instrument, J. Otto Crocker, instead of seeing stars, sees cars! It must be very gratifying for the fellows running their car thru the traps to know that Crocker with his faultless timing device is up in the stand, recording their time down to a thousandth of a second.

Above is Osborn & Garrett's "Anteater" which turned 146.8189 in the "D" Modified Roadster class. Left, is same roadster with hinged body up. Above, Paul Schiefer with his "C" modified roadster. With 274 cu in. '51 Merc. engine it did 150.753.

Above, Bob Meeks watches as Fran Hernandez makes final adjustments on his engine. This roadster turned 160.142 to take second. Below, Because of the corroding action of the salt, all cars had to be washed every day.

Above. Side view of Doug Hartelt's "C" Modified Coupe. It took second with 158.450.

Top, right, Johnson & Wheeler's class "C" Modified Roadster. It turned 156.521 mph.

Below. Because Clyde Sturdy's roadster was too heavy to buck others in his class, he took engine out and put it in Brown and Hooper's tank, which set a new record of 163.7736.

by Dean Batchelor

The third annual Bonneville Speed Trials were run off with great success. Speeds over the salt flats were truly phenomenal . . . 16 of last year's records splattered all over the landscape! One of the two stock-bodied "C" roadsters which topped 160 mph was clocked thru at 162.4595 average and a modified "C" coupe clicked off 164 mph.

The beautiful Kenz twin-Ford-engined streamliner qualified with 230 mph, and 221 mph was its average on a two-way record run over the measured mile.

For the first time in history, A.M.A.* and S.C.T.A. have run together at the same meet . . . ten motorcycles being invited to participate. And this is one of the best moves made by either organization in a long time! The bikes under official A.M.A. sanction broke 8 records, some of which have stood for as long as fourteen years! The cycle boys, good sports all, made a good impression and I for one hope to see them at the 1952 Bonneville Trials.

The motto of the S.C.T.A., "Conductors of the World's Safest Speed Trials," was upheld 100%. Tho several of the cars caught fire, none of the drivers were hurt . . . damage being confined to wiring and paint.

It is gratifying to see the interest in amateur racing catching hold thruout the U.S. Sixteen states were represented this year; some came from as far away as Maryland!

Those who worked hard to make the meet a success deserve a lot of credit, especially Bozzy Willis, Jim and Phyl Lindsley, J. Otto Crocker and Multy Aldrich. This gang normally does the work of ten at the lakes meets—at this one they did the work of 20.

Inclement weather didn't help matters. The lake bed was completely under water the week before the event, which meant that the course had to be set up in a different location from that planned. Some of the record runs were made during a light sprinkle, which caused Crocker to take protective measures for his timing equipment and this delayed running a while.

I'm sure that valuable lessons were learned this year and that next year, even with an increase in participation, the meet will go off as smoothly as the first two Bonneville Trials.

*American Motorcycle Association

Harrison & Lean entry turned 152.801 mph. Has a 296 cubic inch 1939 Mercury engine.

This "B" Lakester, owned by Stanford brothers & B. Phy, took second at 160.427 mph.

Bill Waddill, owner and driver of this clean "C" Modified Roadster, turned 130.813 mph. Waddill, Don Onyon, Bruce Westfall and Harold Smith are all from Flint, Michigan.

Above, Ray Brown having mechanical troubles. Below, Lee Chapell's crew are making minor adjustments before the next day's run. His Class "C" streamliner turned 174.418.

Below, Brown, Hooper & Sturdy's "B" lakester on its way to 163.7736 mph run.

1951 BONNEVILLE RECORDS

"O" Streamliner		80.9823
Robert Alberts	San Jose	
"A" Lakester		147.0106
Zydias & DeLangton	Burbank	
"B" Roadster		144.24195
Bill Likes	Los Angeles	
"B" Mod. Roadster		158.2775
Miller & Taylor	Whittier	
"B" Lakester		163.7736
Sturdy, Brown, Hooper	Hollywood	
"B" Mod. Sedan		109.9545
Selway & Baker	Los Angeles	
"C" Roadster		162.4595
Clark & Tebow	Hollywood	
"C" Mod. Roadster		172.0437
Miller & Taylor	Whittier	
"C" Lakester		180.6848
Earl Evans	Los Angeles	
"C" Coupe		133.6680
Mailliard & Cagle	Norwalk	
"C" Mod. Coupe		160.1324
Dawson Hadley	Pomona	
"C" Mod. Sedan		149.2623
DuBont & Herbert	Los Angeles	
"D" Mod. Roadster		143.1151
Buzz Wagner	Huntington Pk.	
"D" Lakester		185.8097
Tom Beatty	Glendale	
"D" Mod. Coupe		155.3202
Thomas Cobbs	Santa Monica	
"D" Streamliner		221.4795
Bill Kenz	Denver	

RESULTS

"A" Modified Roadster

Name	City	MPH
Barney Navarro	Glendale	126.050
Multy Aldrich	Mentone	79.787

Class "O"

Robert Alberts	San Jose	98.792
Vanderlip Conway	Annapolis Md.	68.754

"A" Lakester

Xydias & De Langton	Burbank	145.395
Purdy & Scott	San Bernardino	141.065
Stewart & Howe	San Diego	136.363

"B" Roadster

Bill Likes	Los Angeles	153.583
Al Barnes	Los Angeles	143.0842
Bob Joehnck	Santa Barbara	138.461

"B" Modified Roadster

Miller & Taylor	Whittier	161.870
Winston Ranger	Altadena	155.440
Carrillo & Hartelt	Orange	154.109

"B" Coupe

Bud Fox	Van Nuys	126.582
Gorton Bros.	Norwalk	123.966
Simpson & Conyers	Cypress	122.282

"B" Modified Coupe

Cantley & Sylva	Inglewood	146.1869
Burke & Dahm Bros.	San Gabriel	141.509
Doug Hartelt	Orange	138.888

"B" Lakester

Sturdy, Brown, Hooper	Hollywood	161.290
Stanford Bros., Phy	Alhambra	160.427
Edward Miller	Culver City	146.341

"B" Modified Sedan

Howard Cams Spec.	Los Angeles	131.964
Selway & Baker	Los Angeles	114.795
Albert Maple	Los Angeles	87.976

"C" Roadster

C. T. Automotive	Hollywood	162.162
Hernandez & Likes	Los Angeles	160.142
Robinson & Zabel	Los Angeles	154.373

"C" Modified Roadster

Miller & Taylor	Whittier	172.744
Carrillo & Betz	Monrovia	172.413
Blair Auto Parts	Pasadena	161.579

"C" Coupe

Mickey Thompson	San Gabriel	141.065
Mailliard & Cagle	Norwalk	137.614
John Quinton	Santa Barbara	137.404

"C" Modified Coupe

Dawson Hadley	Pomona	164.233
Hartelt & Leon	Orange	158.450
Bob Rounthwaite	Glendale	154.905

"C" Lakester

Earl Evans	Los Angeles	183.299
Xydias & DeLangton	Burbank	178.217
Bob McClure	Los Angeles	170.132

"C" Streamliner

Lee Chapel	Oakland	174.418
Bill Kenz	Denver	173.076

"C" Modified Sedan

Du Bont & Herbert	Los Angeles	154.373
Boren & Keldrank	Venice	145.161
Alan Crain	Santa Ana	130.246

"D" Modified Roadster

Buzz Wagner	Huntington Pk.	149.253
Garrett & Osborn	Azusa	146.818
George Du Nah	Pasadena	133.729

"D" Coupe

Bill Edwards	South Gate	115.532

"D" Modified Coupe

Thomas Cobbs	Santa Monica	154.639
McClure & Rounthwaite	Los Angeles	146.341

"D" Lakester

Tom Beatty	Glendale	188.284
Harold Nicholson	Pasadena	179.282
Bob McClure	Los Angeles	179.282

"D" Streamliner

Bill Kenz	Denver	227.848

"D" Modified Sedan

Howard Cams	Los Angeles	156.521

Above is Mickey Thompson who, tho having more than his share of trouble, came thru with the fastest time in his class. He turned 141.065 and won the HOP UP Trophy for "The Most Determined Effort." Below are five roadsters from Cheyenne, Wyoming. All are members of the Cheyenne Roadster Club.

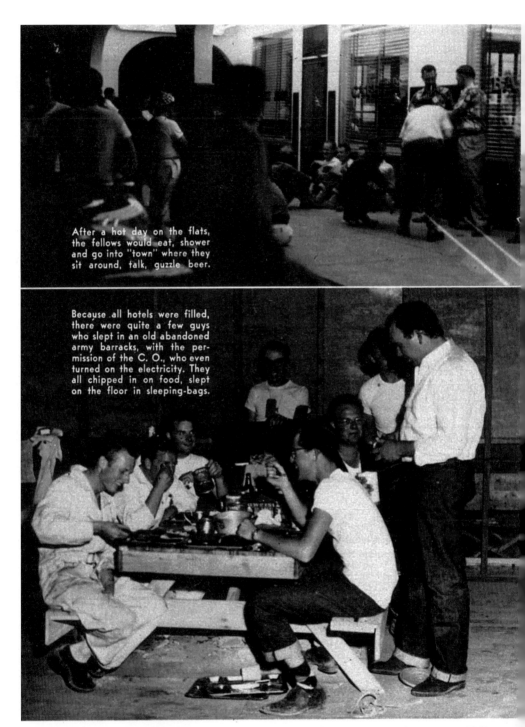

After a hot day on the flats, the fellows would eat, shower and go into "town" where they sit around, talk, guzzle beer.

Because all hotels were filled, there were quite a few guys who slept in an old abandoned army barracks, with the permission of the C. O., who even turned on the electricity. They all chipped in on food, slept on the floor in sleeping-bags.

Don & Bob Alberts and Bill Riesenbeck slept under a tent right in their pit and cooked their food on a butane stove.

While a lot of fellows went into town to relax, there were quite a few working on their engines 'way into the night.

163

Above is Bill Burke of the Road Runners making last minute adjustments. Photo above right shows clutch housing on Bob Alberts' Class "O" Crosley-powered streamliner after hitting 10500 rpm in second gear . . . the clutch actually exploded. Bob turned 98 mph and hit 9000 rpm in second gear with ease!

Below. Milt Stanton, sponsor of Tom Beatty's "D" Lakester, is putting ice cubes in tank prior to return run in which Tom set a new record of 185.8097. Tom and his wife watch Milt.

20

Howard Johannsen helping Harold Nicholson get ready for his 179.282 mph run. Harold took second place in the big "D" lakester class.

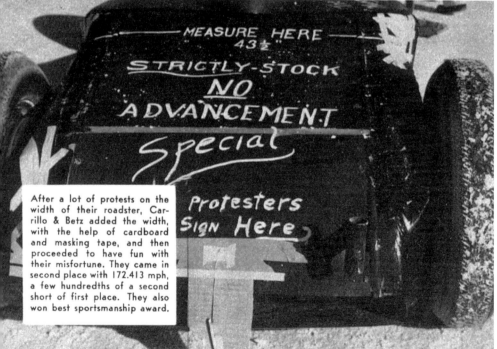

MEASURE HERE
43½"
STRICTLY-STOCK
NO
ADVANCEMENT
Special
Protesters
Sign Here

After a lot of protests on the width of their roadster, Carrillo & Betz added the width, with the help of cardboard and masking tape, and then proceeded to have fun with their misfortune. They came in second place with 172.413 mph, a few hundredths of a second short of first place. They also won best sportsmanship award.

Right, DuBont & Herbert's record breaking "C" Modified Sedan. It turned 149.2623.

Below, Dawson Hadley's "C" Modified Coupe which set a new record of 160.1324 mph.

Below, one of the best looking lakesters at the meet belonged to Edward Miller. He came in third with 146.341.

Bob Alberts' record holding Class "O" Crosley-powered streamliner. He set a new record of 80.9823 mph.

Hap Alzina's BSA, with Gene Thiesen riding, broke the class "C" 30.50 record with 123.694; class "C" 40 cu in., with 128.9445; and the class "A" 40 cu in. record at a speed of 143.5477. He also has a claim in for the 10-mile standing start, 10-mile, 20-mile, 30-mile, 40-mile and 50-mile flying start records—all of which has to be confirmed by the A.M.A.

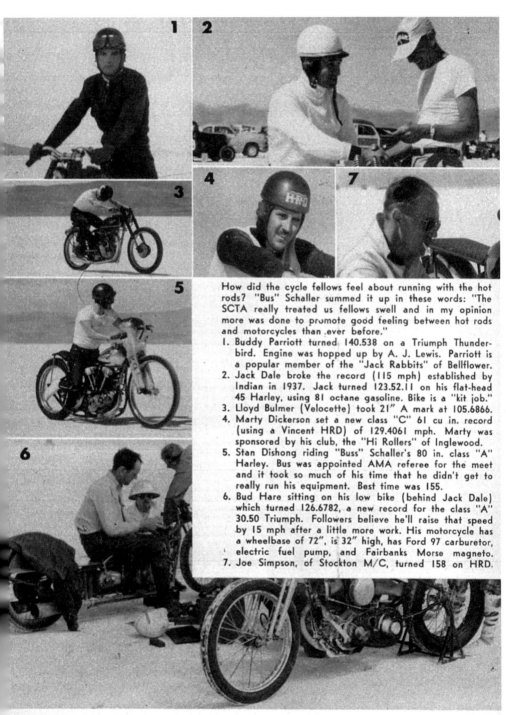

How did the cycle fellows feel about running with the hot rods? "Bus" Schaller summed it up in these words: "The SCTA really treated us fellows swell and in my opinion more was done to promote good feeling between hot rods and motorcycles than ever before."

1. Buddy Parriott turned 140.538 on a Triumph Thunderbird. Engine was hopped up by A. J. Lewis. Parriott is a popular member of the "Jack Rabbits" of Bellflower.
2. Jack Dale broke the record (115 mph) established by Indian in 1937. Jack turned 123.52.11 on his flat-head 45 Harley, using 81 octane gasoline. Bike is a "kit job."
3. Lloyd Bulmer (Velocette) took 21" A mark at 105.6866.
4. Marty Dickerson set a new class "C" 61 cu in. record (using a Vincent HRD) of 129.4061 mph. Marty was sponsored by his club, the "Hi Rollers" of Inglewood.
5. Stan Dishong riding "Buss" Schaller's 80 in. class "A" Harley. Bus was appointed AMA referee for the meet and it took so much of his time that he didn't get to really run his equipment. Best time was 155.
6. Bud Hare sitting on his low bike (behind Jack Dale) which turned 126.6782, a new record for the class "A" 30.50 Triumph. Followers believe he'll raise that speed by 15 mph after a little more work. His motorcycle has a wheelbase of 72", is 32" high, has Ford 97 carburetor, electric fuel pump, and Fairbanks Morse magneto.
7. Joe Simpson, of Stockton M/C, turned 158 on HRD.

Complete Equa-Flow Exhaust Systems are shipped all over the world from the packing and shipping department shown here.

Various assemblies are made up in the storage room. Large stock assures fast delivery.

Fourth stop in HOP UP's tour of advertisers is the well-known Southern California Muffler Company in Culver City, California. Sandy Belond, the quiet, reserved owner, did most of the manufacturing and assembly of the Belond Exhaust Systems in the early days when the shop was a mere shack. Even today he may be occasionally found under a hoist, working on a particularly difficult development job. The well-known Equa-Flow Exhaust Systems now account for a considerable portion of So. Cal's business. Proof of the increased performance can be gained by quizzing most any speed mechanic or by writing for literature . . . usually Belond Exhaust Headers are one of the first items used in setting

Special hoists at the large, modern Southern California Muffler Company shops allow adequate working space under customers' cars.

MEET THE ADVERTISERS

up a competition engine. This year, Sandy expects to install the Equa-Flow Exhaust System on a good portion of the cars entering the Mexican Road Race. Under this year's regulations, modifications to engines and chassis are allowed. However, due to the nature of this race (which permits flat-out speed for long stretches), most mechanics hesitate to increase performance at the expense of reliability. A glance at Floyd Clymer's Mexican Road Race book of last year shows the alarming percentage of blown up engines. The Belond Equa-Flow Exhaust System is one of the few positive methods of increasing performance and horsepower without sacrificing reliability. In fact, the installation of a Belond Equa-Flow Exhaust System will usually show a gain in engine longevity.

Equa-Flow Exhaust Systems are available for Ford V8, Mercury, Lincoln V8, Oldsmobile and Cadillac. Chassis Dynamometer tests consistently show an average gain of 10% in road horsepower.

Before any Belond products are placed on the market, a thoro and searching road test is undertaken and if the system does not meet minimum gain requirements, the project is either abandoned or further modifications are made.

In addition to the manufacture and installation of Exhaust Systems, Sandy devotes considerable time and effort to sponsoring competition cars. Included are lake jobs, roadsters and a dark horse entry in the AAA Pacific Coast Championship Races. Rumor has it that next year an Indianapolis entry may fly the Belond colors.

COVER HOP UP

This month's Cover Hop Up belongs to Dick Flint of Glendale, California. Dick's roadster has a Model A chassis and body and a 1940 Merc engine with 3-5/16 bore and 4-1/8 stroke. The engine has an Edelbrock 3-carburetor manifold, 9:1 heads and Fleischmann ignition. A 3:27 rear axle ratio, and 7:00 x 16 rear tires are used, with 5:00 x 16 tires on the front wheels. Zephyr gears are installed in the Merc transmission.

Dick did most of the mechanical work himself, the Valley Custom Shop doing the body work. Upholstery is by Tipton of Burbank. One of the nicest features of this car is the full belly pan, which contributed to the high speed (143.54 mph) reached at El Mirage. The weight, ready for action at the lakes, is 1900 lbs.

26

HOP UP, November, 1951

Considerable time during the 4 years of construction went into this neat interior. Below, the neat tubular bumper was designed and built by proud owner Dick Flint.

171

KURTIS 4000

The new series 4000 boasts many new features not found on previous Kurtis models, most important and radical being the frame. This consists of two oval section tubes fabricated from flat chrome-moly sheet and welded. Large diameter holes are stamped in these members for lightness. Torsion bars, located inside the aft end of each tube, provide the rear springing. Two piston type and two vane type shock absorbers are used at the rear while two piston type only are used at the front. A transverse leaf spring is used at the front.

The fuel tank is fabricated from metal sheet and is formed to fit into the tail section. Customers are given a choice of

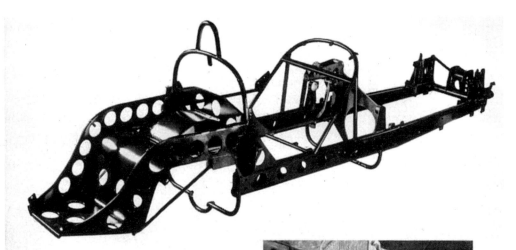

brake systems, several have requested the Goodyear disc type. Wheelbase is 96 inches and weight of the completed car, approximately 1500 pounds.

Many of these cars have been purchased, among them one to Jack Hinkle of Wichita, Kansas (which Jack McGrath is driving), one to Ed Walsh of St. Louis (which Johnny Parsons is driving), and one to Hart Fullerton of Santa Monica (Johnny McDowell driving). All of these well-known drivers are very enthusiastic about the new cars and have been doing exceptionally well in them.

—R. E. Canaan

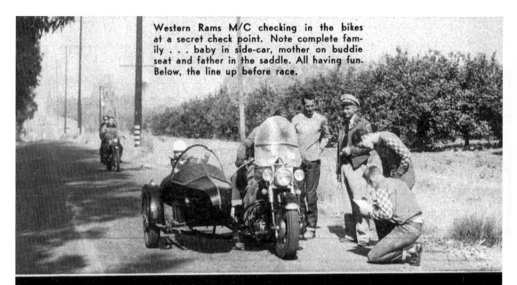

Western Rams M/C checking in the bikes at a secret check point. Note complete family . . . baby in side-car, mother on buddie seat and father in the saddle. All having fun. Below, the line up before race.

RAMS TOUR

"Oh, hell! Maybe *you* can start it." He jumped on and pumped a couple of times. "Gimme a push!" and he climbed aboard, "maybe that'll do it." So there we were . . . trudging down the street . : . pushing him on this @c!!?$#% contraption.

A window banged open . . . came a voice . . . a *woman's* voice. . .

"Git da hell away from my house, ya jerks! I wanna sleep!"

We started pushing faster . . . the "Harley" sputtering and coughing—this cycle (for it *was* a cycle that was giving us the

early morning blues) was hopped-up, which made it a little beyond this writer's mechanical abilities. "You push *me* awhile, I'm pooped!" After a mild argument about which gear was best to start off in, we changed places. A block later we *both* decided we'd better take the car . . . even if it was an MG.

But wait a minute! What will the fellows say when they see the MG? I wonder . . .

"Why'd you have to take a cycle in the first place?" My sleepy-eyed friend was disgusted. I looked at him sheepishly.

"Well, the basic idea was that riding along with the crowd on a motorcycle would

give me a better perspective on this event. You know, ride with the gang, do the same as they do—just get in and get to know everyone. Bill said . . . "Better ask Frank Cooper*, maybe he'll let us go along with the cycles in the British puddle-jumper." By hook or crook, we finally got to the Los Angeles Coliseum on time and got Frank's okay. He grinned at the MG, but said we could bring 'er along.

All the contestants were in line, paying their fees. We lined up with them and got our instructions . . . just as if we had a bike. This done, we put the MG top down (*and they're just as windy as a motorcycle, brother!*) and with a half hour to kill before starting time, we grabbed a bite.

I guess you're wondering what this is all about. Well, you're now at the north side of the Los Angeles Coliseum on Exposition Blvd., waiting for eight o'clock to roll around so you can get started on a 150-mile Gypsy and Endurance run. This particular event is sponsored by the Western Ram Motorcycle Club and is primarily designed for the average motorcyclist who, under the rules, can vie for trophies on equal terms with professional riders. It is AMA sanctioned and is the first of a series of interesting, supervised events to help build motorcycling as a sport. You have your direction cards with the low average speeds on them and it's almost eight, so let's turn gypsy and go on the Ram's tour.

We leave at one minute intervals in parties of four as Bill Francis, our navigator (and partner-in-crime from the start) told us where the first turn off was. You have to watch average speeds and look for land marks . . .a lot of fun!

Above, last check point before a nice cool swim at the beach near San Juan Capistrano.

Below, Frank Cooper, who directed the race with help of Vern Hancock of the Rams M/C.

A pair of dubious characters in the MG.

Above, Dick Fox of the San Gabriel Valley M/C having a little mechanical (?) trouble.

Below, left, is another check point. Note participation of husband and wife teams.

Below, right, shows type of roads in tour. The course by-passed towns, reducing stops.

32

Look here! A motor and side-car with the rider's wife navigating! And there's a couple of single riders with the instruction cards taped to their gas tanks . . . so they can read them easily.

The most difficult task of a tour is to maintain the low speeds in spite of miles of open, straight hi-way in front of you. It's an awful temptation to crank 'er full on! Frank Cooper, Vern Hancock, Sereno Silva and Noel Deveraux who laid out this tour, really did an outstanding job. It includes every type of scenery from mountains . . . to desert . . . to ocean. With the weather perfect, and everyone so friendly, we are all having one swell time!

The run came to a climax at the Salt Creek Beach (about 5 miles from San Juan Capistrano, Calif.) where everyone sprawled on the sand, leering at petite Lois Johnson (who proceeded to walk away with the "Miss Southern California Motorcyclist" title for 1951). The winner of the sweepstakes was Victor Sirna. The top three solo drivers were: Floyd Burke, first; George Clark, second; and F. Heacox, third. Winning girl riders were: Alice Wombsley; Dottie Ellison, and Lucille Meeker, tied for second; Etta Onan was third. In the doubles teams, the Messrs. & Mmes. Dick Murry, Gary Sherman and George Widder, also in that order.
*In charge of meet with Vern Hancock.

Above (inset) is pretty Lois Johnson, "Miss Southern California Motorcyclist of 1951."

Above, the beach where the run ended.

Below, THIS is a MOTORCYCLE. Art Weyandt of Cleveland, Ohio, is owner and rode.

Above, shows Boren and Keldrank's "B" sedan with Bob Kuydendall's "C" roadster sitting in the pre-dawn stillness on the lake.

Below, Mary Morgan helping with the Harris and Lindberg entry. She lives in Victorville, if anyone else wants a tire changed!

RUSSETTA

If you drive on to the lake bed and see the hundreds of cars attending, you can be darned sure that it is a Russetta Timing Meet. Why? Because: 1. Russetta has the largest membership of any timing association on the West Coast. 2. All of the individual clubs which make up the association are in a hotly contested battle for first place. Because of this, every club is on hand at every meet, working hard to earn as many points as possible.

This particular meet happened to fall one week before the big Bonneville National Meet. So . . . everyone was working feverishly, getting the cars in the peak running condition before the trip to Utah.

As you see below, very fast times were turned in by all entrants. w.o.t.h.o.w.*
* without the help of wind

RESULTS

Entrant	Club	Time
"A" COUPES		
Albert Fache	Arabs	123.28
Garrett-Henry	Prowlers	114.64
Bentley-Wheeler	Rod Riders	113.75
"B" COUPES		
Mailliard-Cagle	Dusters	132.35
John Wolf	G.C.R.C.	130.43
Harris-Lindberg	Hutters	128.11
"C" COUPES		
Cantley-Sylva	Coupes	148.14
W. G. Brown	G.C.R.C.	140.07
Willingham-Franzman	Coupes	139.53

34

"D" COUPES

Bob Rounthwaite	G.C.R.C.	137.40
Don Fergeson	Rod Riders	133.33
Thomas Cobbs	G.C.R.C.	126.76

"A" ROADSTERS

Paul Andrews	Roadents	137.40
Johnson Bros.	Screwdrivers	134.83
George Cromer	Hutters	127.65

"B" ROADSTERS

J. Agajanian	Rod Riders	146.93
(George Bentley	Rod Riders	145.74
(Bruce Robinson	G.C.R.C.	145.74
Ray Beck	Coupes	141.17

"C" ROADSTERS

Stecker-Cobb	Stingers	162.89
Al Lyons	Rod Riders	150.62
Johnson-Wheeler	Rod Riders	148.76

"A" SEDANS

Tom McLaughlin	G. C. R. C.	133.33
Donald Green	Hutters	125.43
Alan Crain	Dusters	124.13

"B" SEDANS

Howard Johanssen	G.C.R.C.	148.76
Boren-Keldrank	Screwdrivers	141.17
Christensen-Williams	Rod Riders	137.40

"A" STREAMLINERS

Arlen Kurtis	King Pins	104.65

"B" STREAMLINERS

Bob McClure	G.C.R.C.	157.89
John Stauffacher	Pace Setters	111.45
Tom Sellberg	Aristocrats	109.09

CLUB STANDINGS & POINTS

Place	Club	Previous	August	Total
1	Rod Riders	306	91	397
2	G.C.R.C.	296	96	392
3	Hutters	306	62	368
4	Coupes	272	45	317
5	Screwdrivers	238	69	307
6	Arabs	170	17	187
7	A.R.C.	112	12	124
8	Roadents	104	17	121
9	Dusters	79	22	101
10	Auto Union	80	--	80

Above, altho the majority stayed in motels, there were quite a few who slept right on the lake bed. Such is the case of Johnny Harris, Carl Lindberg and their crew. They're playing cards by moon and fire light.

Below, C. D. Hunter on his 118.03 run.

Below, Stecker-Cobb entry on a 162.8 mph run. He is a member of the Stingers.

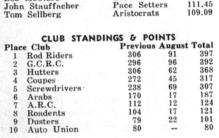

One of the many outstanding Class "D" coupes in Russetta belongs to Bob Rounthwaite of the G.C.R.C. Bob has turned 146.84 mph in his beautiful coupe. He's running Weiand heads, Weiand four carb. manifold, Howard cam, Scintilla mag. An unusual feature of Bob's coupe is that the body comes off (note below) with a minimum amount of effort, which facilitates easy access to the engine.

Bob put in a new engine prior to this meet and was checking it out before Bonneville. Not the least bit satisfied with the times he was turning, he went home in disgust, tore town the engine to find out the cause for such *low* speeds. He turned 137.40, but to a fellow who's constantly turning speeds up in the one-forties, this is a low figure. Don't you wish your coupe would do 137.40 mph!

36

Bruce Robinson, who also is a member of the G.C.R.C., is employed by Phil Weiand, famous manufacturer of Weiand equipment.

Bruce's "A" roadster has Weiand heads and a Weiand four carburetor manifold (of course!), Howard cam and a Scintilla mag. It has turned 152.54 mph. Photo above, owner Phil Weiand with Bruce Robinson in the front entrance of Phil's modern shop. Above side, a quick tire change. Below, Bruce, just like so many of the other fellows, does his personal engine building after work.

1942 BUICK

Chuck Porter has over $7000 in this month's custom. It is, or maybe it *was*, a 1942 Buick Roadmaster. Chuck has added a '47 Cad hood, a Carson padded top, hydraulic lifts on hood, 1948 ¾ race Buick engine, '41 Cad bumpers in front, '49 rear and '48 Cad tail lights. The top has been chopped 2½". With electric doors, black leather upholstery, and the deck filled, this is really *the* car!

PHOTO CREDITS

Cover Photos:
    Upper: Jerry **Chesebrough**
    Lower: Kenz & **Leslie**, Cloyd Teter
Pages 7 thru 23: **Duane Alan**, Ted Buford, Joe Moore, **Dean Batchelor**, California Bill
Pages 24 & 25: **Ralph Poole**
Pages 26 & 27: **Jerry Chesebrough**
Pages 28 & 29: **Bob Canaan**
Pages 30 thru 33: **Gene Trindl**
Pages 34 thru 37: **Gene Trindl**
Page 38: Gene Trindl

FLASH!

"Blackie" Bullock on a Triumph Thunderbird set a new 40 cu in. class "C" mile record with an average speed of 132.1607 mph. This is the fastest speed ever turned by any class "C" displacement motorcycle in the United States. It was prepared and tuned by Johnson Motors Inc., Pasadena, Calif. Blackie also set a standing 20, 30, 40 and 50 mile record. These speeds broke the records set a week before by Gene Theisen at the Bonneville Nationals.

Sam Parriott on an Ariel Square 4 set a new class "C" (61 cu in.) mile record with an average speed of 131.9539. The bike was prepared and tuned by A. J. Lewis of the Long Beach Motorcycle Speed Center. This breaks the record that Marty Dickerson had set at the Bonneville Nationals. All of the above records were set at Bonneville with AMA sanction a week after the National Hot Rod Meet.

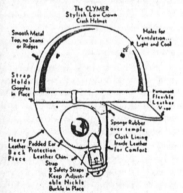
187

Floyd Clymer's POPULAR Motor Books

New Catalog Reprints!

DUESENBERG INSTRUCTION BOOK

We offer this excellent 64-page reprint for owners and collectors. 25 photos of cars . . . charts drawings, cutaway views of engine, oiling system, camshaft and valves, instrument panel, chassis transmission differential, wheels, brakes, complete wiring diagram. Interesting and authentic data on care and operation of the world-famous Model J "Duesie," with parts numbers and description . . . Order Reprint No. 4JDR . . . Postpaid ....$1.50 ☐

CORD OWNER'S MANUAL

This 36-page book gives all driving instructions and necessary servicing information for Cord V-8 cars. Complete specifications. 20 photos, charts, drawings. All about care of engine, trans., front drive, clutch electrical equipment, timing, cooling system, fuel system, lubrication, front steering data, universals, alignment, hydraulic brakes, shocks and tires. A "must" for every Cord owner or enthusiast interested in design of this unique front-wheel-driven car. Order reprint No. 2-C0810. Postpaid...................................$1.00 ☐

MERCER CATALOG REPRINTS

Complete data on this World-famous car of early days. Photos and specifications of all models and body styles, including the outstanding RACEABOUTS. Series "5" 4 cylinder models. Order Reprint No. 5-Mer.
Postpaid ....$1.00 ☐
Series "6" 6-cylinder O.H.V. models Order Reprint No. 6-Mer. Postpaid......................................$1.00 ☐

STUTZ CATALOG REPRINT

25 photos, specifications all famous 4-cylinder Stutz series "E" cars including the fabulous "Bearcat," Roadster and Touring models, in both 4 and 6-cylinder-powered cars. Order No. E-STU. Postpaid $1.00 ☐

MARMON MODEL 34 CATALOG REPRINT

Probably the finest and most informative catalog of early day cars. 46 large pages, complete and beautiful photos, unique body styles, engine, chassis every feature minutely described and illustrated, cutaway views of engine and other units. A collectors item without comparison. Order Reprint No. 34-Mar. Postpaid...............$1.00 ☐

MILLER RACING CARS AND ENGINES

Here is a brand new reprint of the original 1927 booklet of information on the famous Miller racing engines and cars. Gives complete specifications, service data, types and styles built. Also notes all records, on land and sea, achieved by Miller units up until that date. 36 pages, 25 illustrations. Order Reprint No. 27-MIL.
Postpaid ....$1.00 ☐

NEW YORK TO PARIS RACE, 1908

76 Pages . . . 109 photos. This book tells of World's Longest Race, won by a Thomas-Flyer. Photos of cars in all countries. Start at Times Bldg., N.Y.C., snows in Mid-West, sagebrush and sand in Wyoming, Alaska, Japan, Russian soldiers, Trans-Siberian Railways, Mongolian giants, the return to Times Square. A colorful story about an unbelievable around-the-world race in 1908. The Thomas-Flyer was then acclaimed the "World's Champion Endurance Car." A real book of Americana . . . Postpaid.............................$1.00 ☐

New Motorcycle Books!

CATALOG OF 1951 BRITISH MOTORCYCLES

A brand new book of reference, for the enthusiast, owner, all persons interested in motorcycles. Covers every make and model machine now made in England, names and addresses of manufacturers. 160 pages, 83 sharp illustrations..Postpaid $2.00 ☐

THE MOTORCYCLIST'S WORKSHOP

Contain valuable advice on the care and maintenance of your own shop, proper care of tools, handy hints on bench work, and a special chapter on speed tuning your machine. 152 pages, 95 informative charts and drawings.
Postpaid ....$1.50 ☐

SPEED—HOW TO OBTAIN IT

160 pages, 142 pictures and drawings. Deals fully with theory and practice of engine tuning. Includes articles on design, essentials of speed, materials, fuels, supercharging, oil and lubricating system etc. Discusses in detail the factors that influence high performance.
Postpaid ....$1.50 ☐

QUESTIONS AND ANSWERS

1951 Revised Edition of the popular motorcycle book by "Uncle Frank", noted authority. Now contains new, comprehensive data on motorcycle repair and maintenance, including information on the new Mustang, Powell, Indian, and Harley-Davidson. Most complete on the market.
Postpaid ....$2.00 ☐

**MODERN MOTORCYCLE MECHANICS
AND SPEED TUNING**

Probably the most thorough treatment of the subject ever published. Covers design, construction, operation and care of any and all American and British machines, including War models, special motorcycle units. Complete informtion given on engine work, such as balancing, piston pin and ring fitting, lower-end work, etc. Emphasizes speed tuning for racing and hill-climbing. Truly a necessity for the motorcycle man. Postpaid........$4.00 ☐

ENGLISH MOTORCYCLE SERVICE MANUAL

72 pages, 140 illustrations. Gives complete, authentic factory information on all well-known English makes and models. Interesting and educational. Postpaid $1.50 ☐

BRITISH CAR OWNER'S HANDBOOK

This Autocar Handbook, compiled by the staff of "Autocar," is a fine service manual for the owners of new British cars. Contains data on engine repair, lubrication, carburetion, electrical, etc. 252 pages, 240 illustrations. Revised up-to-date information.............Postpaid $2.00 ☐

1951 GRAND CANYON ECONOMY RUN

32 American stock cars competed from Los Angeles over mountains and desert to Boulder Dam and Death Valley, ending at Grand Canyon. A.A.A. Sanction. 64 pages . . . 150 photos, charts and drawings. Articles by automotive authorities . . . Technical engineering details . . . . . . Rules . . . data each car . . . See how your favorite car performed! . . . Auto Editor's stories . . . famous personalities . . . Travelogue by Clymer . . . photos and data on interesting Boulder Dam and Grand Canyon . . . An impartial, colorful report on world's greatest Economy Test. Postpaid.............................$1.50 ☐

Floyd Clymer, Dept. 11-UP

*World's Largest Publisher of Books
Relating to Automobiles, Motorcycles,
Motor-Racing, and Americana*

1268 So. Alvarado St., L. A. 6, Calif.

Read Floyd Clymer's Test Reports on new cars monthly in Popular Mechanics Magazine

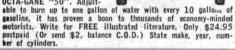

HOP UP 15¢

COVER HOP UP—SEE PAGE 36

Moon Bros. **141** mph Sedan

see page 8

DEC. 1951

15¢

If it's hopped up, it'll be in HOP UP

HOP UP

DECHROMING

The annual "face-lifting" of American cars quite often produces, in the opinion of many, unhappy results. The same basic body panels are usually retained for several years (for example: 1942, '46, '47 and '48 Ford) and the yearly face-lift consists largely of additional chrome trim. This "trimming the Christmas Tree" routine can, and sometimes does, completely change the stylist's original conception.

To me, the clean lines of the 1949 Ford have been spoiled by the "bathroom molding" trim which encircles the '51 model. The "California custom advocates" are following a much more aesthetical motif . . . removal of chrome to produce larger expanses of pleasing curves. It is hoped that Detroit will eventually do likewise.

ROADSTER HILL CLIMBS

Something has to be done for roadster activities. So many organizations use El Mirage Dry Lake (the only suitable place to run at the present), that the surface is made rougher by the week. It is becoming almost impossible to operate safely there at speeds the majority of cars now attain. It would seem that the next logical step should be reliability runs, hill climbs, maneuverability trials (gymkhanas), and possibly road racing. First, they must improve the handling and braking of their cars—two qualities they sadly lack. To start the ball rolling, the American Hod Rod Conference is organizing America's first Roadster Hill Climb. Run on private property, the winding ½ mile, asphalt course may prove to be the first of a whole new group of badly needed activities.

EDITORIAL STAFF

Editor..Oliver Billingsley
Technical Editor..........................John R. Bond
Associate Editors...........................Louis Kimzey
Robert Dearborn
Staff Photographer.........................Gene Trindl
Photographers..........Jack Campbell, Bob Canaan
Joe Al Denker

PRODUCTION STAFF

Managing Editor....................W. H. Brehaut, Jr.
Art Director.....................................Louis Kimzey
Art..Jack Caldwell

ADVERTISING

Advertising Manager............................Bill Quinn
Southern California......................Dean Batchelor
Motorcycles..Bill Bagnall
East Coast Representatives....Peabody & Ortgies
276 West 43rd Street
New York 18, N.Y.
United Kingdom........................Kenneth Kirkman
2 Longcroft Avenue
Banstead, Surrey, England
Italy...Michele Vernola
C.P. 500
Milano, Italy

CORRESPONDENTS

Italy..Corrado Millanta

Vol. 1, No. 5   December, 1951

CONTENTS

HOP UP is published monthly by Enthusiasts' Publications, Inc., 540 W. Colorado Blvd., Glendale, California. Phone CHapman 5-2297. Application for entry as second-class matter is pending. Copyright 1951 by Enthusiasts' Publications, Inc. Reprinting in whole or in part forbidden except by permission of the publishers.

Subscription price $1.50 per year thruout the world. Single copy 15c.

Change of address—must show both old and new addresses.

Cover Photos: Chesebrough & Trindl
Trindl: 7 thru 12, 18 thru 21, 30 thru 35
Kent Hitchcock: 13 thru 17
Chesebrough: 24-25-26-36-37-38
Canaan: 27   Marcia Campbell: 35

TECHNICAL TIPS

CHEVROLET PERFORMANCE

I own a sweet little '50 Chevy convertible. With a higher speed rear-end I figure that I can have a pretty fair top speed and still get good acceleration because of Powerglide. Am I right?

I have never clocked my car at top speed, but I know that when my speedometer says 80, it means just that, because I drove an 80-mile stretch between two towns in one hour flat and I never lifted it over 80. By the speedometer, top speed is 92 . . . I'm not saying that I can beat an 88 or a Cad on pick-up, but I have beat Ford 6s and most other cars . . . I have made several guys with '49 and '50 Mercurys eat my dust on pick-up. I beat a couple of Mercs in a top speed run, too, but I don't think those were in top operating condition.

Montgomery, Alabama   Eugene W. Rothlanf

You already have the highest ratio axle made for the Chevrolet, 3.55—that's all there is, but it's a very good ratio and a stock Powerglide Chevrolet with this gear will clock around 85 honest mph. Chevrolet speedometers are among the very few at this time that are reasonably accurate.

The following performance table will interest you—taken from road tests of unquestioned accuracy. The Powerglide figures used lo range to best advantage and neither the Ford 6 nor Mercury had overdrive. Best timed speed on the Powerglide Chevrolet was 89.1 (one way); average of 4 runs gave the 85.1 figure. —Tech. Ed.

	0-60	0-70	Clocked	Speedom.
Chev. Standard	20.7	30.7	83.0	85
Chev. Powerglide	22.0	30.7	85.1	90
Ford 6 Standard	16.0	23.7	90	100
Merc. Standard	19.2	27.8	86.5	93

MERC-FORD HOP UP

I am building a hop up and need advice. Will use a '46 or '47 Mercury engine and build from there on . . . have either a '37 Lincoln Zephyr or '38 Lincoln transmission lined up and would like to know which of these would be best. What kind of axle should I use in the rear? Would like to cruise at 60 to 75 mph. Hope to use either a '32, '33 or '34 coupe body and chassis. How about milling the heads? Am thinking of dual carburetion but am told that this

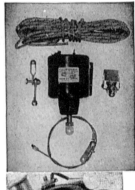

TECHNICAL TIPS

wouldn't work without my cam being ground.
Kenosha, Wisconsin   Blake Smith

For your rear axle, use the one that comes with the chassis you buy. A ratio of 3.78 is probably the best all-around compromise. Neither a '37 or '38 Zephyr is anything special—same gears as Ford. The real "premium" gears are Zephyr 1942 to '48. Second choice is Zephyr '40 or '41. You can't mill Ford heads very much without also "re-doming." Don't let anyone tell you you can't use two carburetors without a reground cam. On the other hand, a reground cam does permit you to use a higher compression ratio than does a stock cam. It's all a matter of compression pressure—135 psi is about the limit for Fords with cast iron heads and premium gasoline. —Tech. Ed.

NEW DEAL FOR CHEVY

In the near future I plan to buy a Chevy . . . could I possibly put in a Buick Fireball engine?
Fort Stockton, Texas   William Van Landingham

I would say it's impractical, if not impossible. There is a "new deal" for Chevrolets now. It consists of using the 270 cu in. GMC engine, modified for still more power. You will find complete information on this in California Bill's Chevrolet Speed Manual. —Tech. Ed.

WANTS CROSLEY TO BEAT CADS

In my '47 Crosley I want to give the Cadillacs and Oldsmobiles a run for their money at the stop-lights and be able to zip around the slow-pokes on the open road. In other words, accent on acceleration rather than top speeds.

Can the little Crosley do it and still retain the ability to run at low speeds for long periods of time? What would be the most economical way of getting this performance?
Ennis, Texas   Walter Jones, II

A Crosley coupe weighs about 1200 pounds so to even equal our "hottest" stock cars having 26-28 lbs/hp would take 46 bhp from the Crosley. To get over one horsepower per cu in. is not impossible, but it's "stretching things" plenty in the Crosley. The hopped-up Crosleys I've ridden in were flat at low speeds and very good from 50 to 75 mph. I've never driven a supercharged Crosley, but I seriously doubt whether it could stay with the Olds or Cadillac at a stop-light, primarily because of the poor 3-speed transmission. —Tech. Ed.

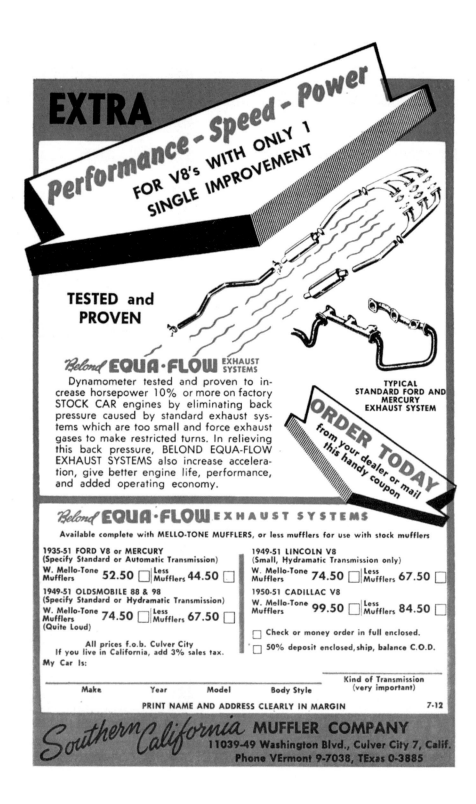

Bob Muccilli's Hudson

Bob Kuykendall being pushed to starting line. Bob turned 140.07 in his "C" class roadster.

Tony Capana, who has been active at Lakes meets for years, now sells hot fuel "mixtures."

To the Lakes with the "Screwdrivers"

Each of the twenty-three clubs in the Russetta Timing Association has a specific duty to perform at each lake meet. For example: The "Pile Drivers" set up the pit area, the "Hutters" handle the P.A. system and the "Pace Setters" clean up the lake bed after each meet.

Of all the assignments allotted the clubs, the one that takes the most thought and planning is setting up the course. Those responsible for choosing the location have to find one that is not only fast, but also *safe!* With the lake bed getting so rough, it is no longer possible to find a stretch that is ideal Rough spots are a constant worry. As you know, the boys who lay out the strip also drive on the course . . . so, they're doubly careful!

The "Screwdrivers," who are handling this chore currently, are located in West Los Angeles (Culver City). With twenty-nine active members, they have participated in

8

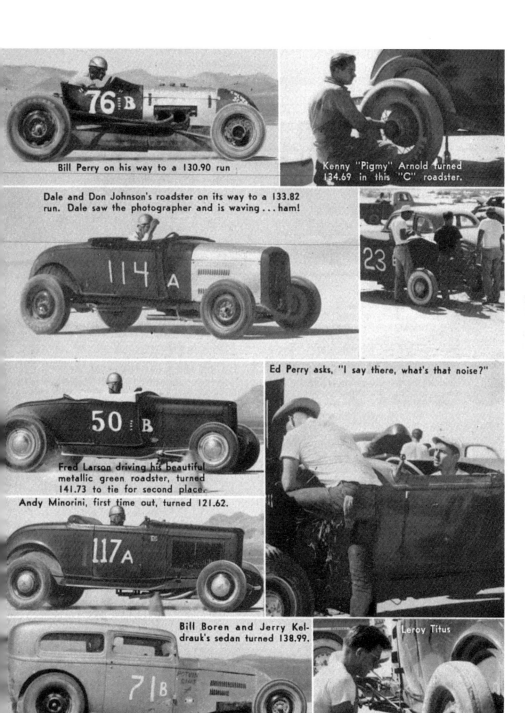

Bill Perry on his way to a 130.90 run

Kenny "Pigmy" Arnold turned 134.69 in this "C" roadster.

Dale and Don Johnson's roadster on its way to a 133.82 run. Dale saw the photographer and is waving...ham!

Ed Perry asks, "I say there, what's that noise?"

Fred Larson driving his beautiful metallic green roadster, turned 141.73 to tie for second place.

Andy Minorini, first time out, turned 121.62.

Bill Boren and Jerry Keldrauk's sedan turned 138.99.

Leroy Titus

lake meets since 1948.

Meeting every Monday night (with over 90% attendance), Screwdrivers are a very agreeable group, so why don't we go to the lakes where we can watch them at a typical Russetta Timing Meet?

A few of the gang leave Friday night before the meet, but the majority leave around 4:30 Saturday morning. The first stop is a little cafe on the way, where everyone eats breakfast, discusses the troubles they had getting their engines together . . . what they hope to do at the meet . . . and so on. Next stop, El Mirage.

Three hours after leaving home and after a wild ride on the "washboard,"* the lake hove in view . . . fifteen cars already there. After borrowing a truck from the "Rancho El Mirage"** and loading equipment, the first job was to locate a suitable course.

It took forty-five minutes of careful scrutiny to find a stretch that was safe. Even *it* had a rough spot, but the Screwdrivers moved the course forward so the cars would be going slow when they hit it. The course laid, E. C. Huseman, the official timer, arranged his equipment. The "King Pins"

erected the portable official's stands and the "Pile Drivers" set up the pit area. At last, the boys could focus their attention on their respective cars.

After inspection, a series of runs, tests and adjustments until noon, then they shut down for lunch. Quite a few work on their cars right thru the lunch hour, munching on hot dogs and gulping cokes from the nearby lunch wagon, but the majority go to the Ranch House, at the end of the lake bed.

The afternoons are the same, with everyone working hard to get his car running right, before the meet shuts down. At five o'clock they head for Victorville, some twenty miles from the lake. The Screwdrivers have chosen the Green Spot Motel to stay in because of its adjoining rooms. The Green Spot is a veritable madhouse. You can imagine the scene, with everyone exhilerated by the day's events . . . exchanging various bits of information . . . comparing times with one another . . . shouting predictions on the next day's trials. And all this amidst the finest atmosphere of friendship you ever saw.

Ed "Axle" Stewart on his way to a new "A" streamliner record.

Howard Johansen turned 148.29.

George Bentley tied for second place with a speed of 141.17

A consistent winner, Tom McLaughlin turned 129.49 to take first place in "A" sedan class.

Bill Likes turned 141.73 to set a new class record.

Leadfoot "Crash" Baney, driving Jack Midgett's '49 blown Cad, turned 108.64 mph with a converted G.M.C. blower

The Screwdrivers are typical of all the other clubs, whether they be "Rod Riders," "G.C.R.C." or "Coupes" . . . they're all good sports and work hard to earn as many points as possible for their individual club.

---

* That **freeway** leading from the main hi-way to the lake.
** The closest cafe within twenty miles . . . !

RESULTS

"A" COUPES

Name	Club	Time
Albert Fache	Arabs	123.28
Gorton Bros.	Hutters	111.80
Bentley-Wheeler	Rod Riders	110.76

"B" COUPES"

Fox-Freudiger	G.C.R.C.	136.88
A. Wheeler	Rod Riders	129.96
Mailliard-Cagle	Dusters	126.76

"C" COUPES

Cantley-Sylva	Coupes	144.00
W. G. Brown	G.C.R.C.	137.93
Jim McGonigal	Arabs	136.36

"D" COUPES

Thomas Cobbs	G.C.R.C.	149.37
Gordon Clayton	Hutters	128.11
Eugene Husting	Aristocrats	125.00

"A" ROADSTERS

Bill Likes	Coupes	141.73*
Paul Andrews	Roadents	136.88
Ray Beck	Coupes	135.33

"B" ROADSTERS

Allan Thomas	Screwdrivers	141.73
Fred Larsen	Screwdrivers	141.73
Robt. Weeks	Rod Riders	141.17
George Bently	Rod Riders	141.17
Smith-Brice	Stingers	140.07

"C" ROADSTERS

Stecker-Cobb	Stingers	150.00
Bob Kuykendall	Screwdrivers	140.07
Donald Montgomery	G.C.R.C.	135.33

"A" SEDANS

Tom McLaughlin	G.C.R.C.	129.49
Don Green		124.56
Sam Comstock	Roadents	123.71

"B" SEDANS

Howard Johansen	G.C.R.C.	148.29
Christensen-Williams	Rod Riders	142.29
Moon Bros.	Hutters	141.17

"A" STREAMLINERS

Ed "Axle" Stewart	Prowlers	119.20*
Arlen Kurtis	King Pins	113.92

"B" STREAMLINERS

Earl Evans	Hutters	155.81
Bill Wacker		150.00
Lloyd Finch		145.16

---

* New record

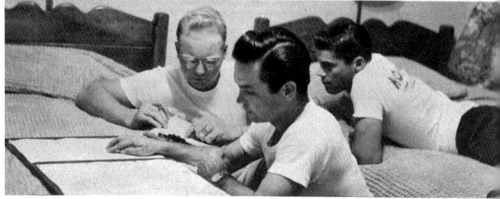

12

The winner! Lou Fageol in the cockpit of Slo-Mo-Shun V.

1951 Gold Cup Race

by Kent Hitchcock

The Gold Cuppers and the big Unlimited Hydroplanes are about thru for the season . . . comes time now to review some of the major events and actually put a value on outstanding performances. Lou Fageol, driving Stan Sayres' new **Slo Mo Shun V,** was the winner of the 44th Annual race for the American Power Boat Association's historic Gold Cup. The accident of the **Quicksilver** forced cancellation of the third heat with Fageol far out in the lead at the time, but **Slo Mo V's** victory was a clean-cut, first place in both the first and second heats and new records for a single lap and a thirty mile heat. The Gold Cup looks just like any

other hydroplane race and the casual follower of the sport assumes that each driver is out to get the lead and keep it. Actually this is seldom the case. The contest for the coveted cup is governed by rules that put a premium on ruggedness and dependability as well as on speed. To understand any account of the Gold Cup Race, it is necessary to understand the point system. As in any other A.P.B.A. race, each boat receives points for the position in which it finishes each heat. The points for the first five places are: 400, 300, 225, 169, and 127. In addition, the boat finishing in the least elapsed time is given a bonus of 400 points and the boat turning the fastest thirty mile heat is given a bonus of 400 points providing it finishes.

Remember that the race for the cup consists of three grueling thirty mile heats and the present crop of cuppers are capable (in top form) of turning a lap at 100 mph which means a probable 140 mph on the stretches. The boat itself is a pretty small package wrapped around a powerplant delivering from 1450 to 3000 hp. Rarely can one of these temperamental parcels win all three heats with the pressure from competition. Mechanical failure is common and so this event is far from the usual wire-to-wire wide-open scramble.

The problem is to complete the 90 miles and at the same time gather enough points to top the rest of the field. Team racing puts the finishing touches to the complicated situation. Several owners will improve their chances by entering two or more boats. If these dual entries hold together the race becomes a duel of speed rating and good strategy can win the event. An owner may instruct one of his drivers to get the lead at any cost (forcing some of the opposition to break up under the killing pace), while his other entries maintain a pace calculated to last the entire race up near the front and to gather enough points to win if the leaders break up under pressure. Examine just one of the score of combinations

(under the bonus system) and you will readily see where rating and strategy play a big part in the Gold Cup Race. In this particular instance, we will have four boats, all very fast and evenly matched. Boats No's 1 and 2 (from different teams) immediately get into a wide open battle for the lead, each one, of course, hoping to hold together but primarily trying to force the other into a breakdown. No. 1 runs the fastest heat of the contest, wins the second but breaks down in the third . . . As he has not finished the contest, he is not eligible to receive bonus points for the fastest heat. Boats No's 3 and 4 have been riding the consistency groove for two heats waiting for the leaders to break up. As No. 1 breaks down in the third heat, No. 4 turns loose all the stuff he has and sneaks by No. 3, catches No. 2 and takes the lead with No. 3 in hot pursuit. No. 2 holds on for two laps, trying to keep the pace with the new leader but develops a miss and wisely takes off the pressure in an attempt to finish. It's No. 4's move now and he pours on the coal with No. 3 sticking a hundred feet behind, but making no move to pass. Into the final lap they go! They're together coming out of the first turn, neck and neck thru the back stretch. No. 4 holds the lead to beat 3 out by less than a boat length at the line!

Here's the way the heat points came out: No. 1, 800 points (two firsts); No. 2, 727 points (two thirds and a poor fifth a lap behind the field); No. 3, 750 points (two thirds and a second); and No. 4, 738 points (two fourths and a first). There will be no bonus points for the fastest heat. No. 1 set that mark but failed to finish. No. 2 lost his chance for the fastest 90 miles with his poor fifth in the third heat. No. 3 beat out No. 4 by a hundred feet in the first two heats, thus building up a slight time margin. In the final heat, he (3) drove to finish within a boat length of No. 3, protecting his fractional second time margin. This gave No. 3 the shortest elapsed time for the 90 miles and the 400 bonus points. So we have

14

204

Such Crust

the winner. He won with two thirds and one second. The combinations are infinite. In 1949 at Detroit, Robert Stanley Dollar of San Francisco drove his **Skip-A-Long** to the fastest ninety miles of the race but still lost the trophy to Horace Dodge's **My Sweetie** which garnered the 400 bonus points for the fastest heat and just enough placing points to beat out the California boat.

Now, with the strategy and scoring system in mind, have a look at this year's race (Lake Washington, Seattle). For twenty years Western sportsmen have been trying to bring the race to the West Coast. Detroit has held a strangle hold on the Cup, and a jinx has followed each attempt to win it away from the Motor City. In 1950 Stan Sayres caught the Detroit clan asleep and won the cup with three straight heat wins. The Mid-Westerners were determined to take the cup back this year, and several months before the race the challenger's strategy was clear. Included in the six boats that would represent Detroit Yacht Club would be the Dossin Brothers' **Miss Pepsi**. A capable competition boat not to be discounted in any race, **Pepsi** wound up the 1950 season with practically a clean sweep of the competition records including a 2½ mile lap mark of 95 mph and a ten mile heat record of 107 mph over a 5 mile course. Lightning fast on the turns, **Pepsi's** straightaway top speed was an unknown factor. Sayres (Slo-Mo IV) saw the scribbling on the stucco. Just how good some of the other DYC boats might be was unknown but it was a cinch that the **Pepsi** was going to run the course in the high 90's. She had never run anything longer than a 45 miler before and just how she would hang together at full bore was another unknown to Sayres . . . and he couldn't afford to gamble. Slo-Mo-IV would have her work cut out for her with the ever present chance that she might come unstuck. Even if **Pepsi** should unravel, the Seattle boat would still have to deal with the team tactics of the DYC jobs, anyone of which might be a world beater!

Sayres went into action two short months before the race. Ted Jones whipped out a design for **Slo-Mo-Shun V** and Anchor Jensen built it . . . in record time. This new addition

to the family differed little from her sister ship. Length, powerplant, gearbox, and general design were identical to **IV**. The big difference was an addition of 8 inches of beam which went into broader non-trips* for faster and safer turning. If **IV** had changes in her planing surfaces, they were not apparent in her appearance or performance. Externally, the boats look alike tho **V** was a single seater. She was built quietly and probably came as a surprise to the challengers.

It usually takes a full season to work the bugs out, and some times an outfit won't reach peak performance until the end of the second year. With minimum changes, Sayres wasn't faced with bugs. Nevertheless "ole lady luck" sure came along for the ride, and **V** was ready for the show on time. With two boats Sayres was in a position to combat the strategy of the challengers.

The Gold Cup contestants must turn three laps of the 3-mile course at 65 mph average, and Horace Dodge's venerable **My Sweetie** held the qualifying record (92.402 mph). Here's a run down on 1951 qualifying trials, and final results.

---

* "Trip-chines" generally extend outward 45° from rear corners of hull, act as stabilizers.
   —Ed.

Specifications:
Both of the **Slo Mo's** are four pointers (a three pointer with a bow plane), powered by single Allisons (registered at 1750 hp but probably hopped up far beyond that), installed with hub end sternwards; Western Gearbox (1 to 3 step up) studded to engine in place of hub housing (no intermediate shaft); H.I. Johnson club type racing prop 14x25.

Hurricane IV is a three pointer with propulsion equipment identical to the **Slo Mo's** with stock Allison. This job, changed over from Vee drive rig only two weeks before the race (no time for trim testing) was obviously out of balance, tail heavy. Went like a bomb when pressed but driver made no effort to stay with pack as she handled badly. Plagued with loss of oil pressure in gear box.

Hornet, brand new three pointer, plagued

End of first lap of the first heat. Such Crust, Slo Mo IV, and the Hurricane battling it out for fourth place. Hurricane came thru between boats to take the spot.

Miss Pepsi blistering along in second spot.

with minor bugs . . . fast and pretty wild. Single Allison with separate Arena Gearbox.

Dee Jay V (three pointer with same propulsion set up as Hornet). Had nothing but trouble, first in carburetion and finally blew gearbox, failing to qualify.

Gale II, another brand new boat. With Arena at the wheel, ran into trouble during qualifying, split steering bearing bracket . . . broached off and ripped out transom. Prompt action by rescue boat caught her as she sank. Hurriedly patched up she was ready for race and showed surprisingly good speed and handling. Refused to start for second heat. Arena climbed on with the driver . . . started engine and dove overboard.

Such Crust and **Gold'n Crust** (twin three pointers powered by 2000 hp Rolls Royce with separate step-up gearboxes) was tough luck team of race. Proved boats with plenty of speed. **Such Crust** after constant mechanical trouble turned in blistering qualifying lap of 97.035 mph but refused to wind up at all in race . . . quit cold in the fifth lap, first heat. **Gold'n Crust** had blower trouble, then blew an engine, finally qualified. Broke up her steering on test run, didn't start the race.

Miss Pepsi (big multiple step hydroplane powered by two Allisons in-line coupled to single gearbox, prop shaft passing under rear engine. The prop nearly amidship). Turned fastest qualifying lap ever (104.247 mph). Twisted off crankshaft in one engine on fifth lap of first heat.

My Sweetie (multiple step hydro, single Allison, Vee drive, prop just about amidship). Turns fast but limited straightaway speed. Has won the Gold Cup and her share of big races . . . simply outmoded now. Leaked like a sieve, trouble with carburetion during qualifying. Was in race as a safety boat for the **Hornet**. Was driven far from full bore at all times.

Quicksilver (step boat packing hopped up Rolls Royce, separate Vee drive gearbox, prop back near the transom). Handled poorly on turns, porpoised, plunged on straightaways.

This comprised the eligible field. The weather was ideal. Practically no wind, and smooth water. A tremendous crowd of spectator boats were assembled long before race time (estimated 250,000 persons lined the Lake Washington shore line). The nine starters appeared on the course and just as the clock started, the two **Slo Mo's** left the rest of the field and disappeared thru the approach span of the Lake Washington Bridge. As the field started to straighten out for the line, the two Seattle boats came blasting back under the bridge at full bore to catch the rest of the pack just before they reached the starting line. Lou Fageol in the **V** had timed his long run back thru the bridge perfectly and led them over the line just one second after the gun signalled that the race was on. Close behind the leader were **Hornet**, **Pepsi** and **Gale** with the rest of the boats scant seconds behind. Fageol set a terrific pace and Chuck Thompson **(Pepsi)** moved into second place, coming out of the first turn and immediately set out to catch the leader. Ted Jones **(Slo-Mo IV)** was in fifth place at the end of the first lap with **Hurricane IV** closing rapidly and **Such Crust** just a boat length behind. At this point, Sayres' strategy was apparent. He couldn't afford to risk **Slo-Mo IV** in a speed duel with the Detroit flyers, so he assigned her to the inglorious position of "safety" boat. With countless hours of racing and testing this boat, Ted Jones could undoubtedly get more out of her on the turns if the new **V** blew up and left him the job of battling the challengers. Fageol, a terrific driver in any boat was assigned the handling of the untried **V** and was apparently instructed to get out ahead of any challenger and stay there until somebody came unstuck. The first four laps were the most thrilling I have ever seen, with **V** and **Pepsi** thundering around the three-mile oval as tho tied together with string . . . first lap, 94.89 mph and the second, 97.89 mph. It would be hard to say whether Fageol or Thompson was setting the pace. **Quicksilver** and **Sweetie** were lapped on the third circuit. **Hurricane**, with plenty of speed handled badly, dropped back. **Hornet** was riding full 20 seconds behind the leaders . . . then came **Gale** and **Slo Mo IV**, the latter running smoothly, ready to go if needed. Four dizzy laps the two leaders reeled off. Then in the back stretch **Pepsi** stopped. Fageol took off the pressure, turned the fifth lap at 91 and the rest at about 89 . . . lapped **Hurricane** . . . **(Such Crust** quit under the pressure). Near the end of the heat, he lapped the field, lapping **Hornet** in the last mile.

Consider strategy. Why didn't Fageol back off for an easy win over the second place boat instead of lapping him? Because **V** was the expendable outfit of the Seattle team. **Pepsi** might return in perfect shape and **V** might lose the next heat. The obvious move was to shoot for

Hornet

HORNET   G-31

16

Slo-Mo-Shun IV

that 400 bonus point (for fastest heat). As it worked out, he got the points at 91.7665 mph, but didn't need it to win. But if **Pepsi** had come back in good shape, Fageol could have backed off in the latter stages and that 400 points could have been the winning margin.

The second heat started with **Pepsi** back on the course, but **Such Crust** was thru and **Quicksilver** was unable to make repairs in time. Dan Foster relieved Bill Cantrell in **Hornet** and Dollar, Jr., replaced Visel in **Hurricane** which was giving the driver a rough ride. The two So Mo's again made a beautiful start, Fageol out in the lead, followed by **IV** and the rest. **Pepsi** lasted less than a lap, was out for good. **Gale** a lap and a half behind the field went well. Foster caught **IV** in the second heat . . . they raced even for a stretch with the **V** well ahead. Jones, playing "safety," moved back to

third. There was little more action as Fageol won at 89.977 mph. The third heat was a beauty. Visel, back in **Hurricane,** adopted Sayres' starting technique and came out with the two defenders at full bore in a terrific race for the line. Foster (**Hornet**) broke up the race by coming in sharp off the upper turn, forcing **Hurricane** to give way. They got away with **Hornet** hot on the heels of **V,** but the Detroit boat didn't last the lap. **Quicksilver** was back in the race, crashed, with 'fatal results.

This was the first fatal accident in the 44-year history of the Gold Cup. The race was finally stopped and the first two heats declared a contest. Next year Lake Washington again will be the scene of the Indianapolis of Motor Boat Racing. Already in Detroit, builders are working on new muitiple engine jobs to attempt to recapture the big cup.

SUMMARY OF 44TH GOLD CUP RACE

Boat Club	Owner Driver	Hull Size	Qualifying Speed	(Heat 1) Speed Position	(Heat 2) Speed Position	Total Point Score
Slo-Mo-Shun V Seattle Y.C.	Stanley S. Sayres Lou Fageol	Jones-Jensen 28' 6"x12'	91.370	91.766 (1st)	89.977 (1st)	1600
Hornet Detroit Y.C.	Horace Dodge Bill Cantrell	Cantrell 30'x12' 4"	82.129	81.558 (2nd)	85.673 (2nd)	600
Slo-Mo-Shun IV Seattle Y.C.	Stanley S. Sayres Ted Jones	Jones-Jensen 28' 6"x11' 4"	90.406	79.946 (3rd)	84.905 (3rd)	450
Hurricane IV Lido Isle Y.C.	Morlan Visel Morlan Visel	Visel-Moore 29'x10' 9"	90.067	71.343 (5th)	81.374 (4th)	296
Gale II Detroit Y.C.	J. A. Schoenith J. L. Schoenith	Arena 30'x11' 9"	84.705	75.901 (4th)	69.390 (6th)	264
My Sweetie Detroit Y.C.	Horace Dodge Dodge-Walter Kade	Hacker 30'x10'	71.967	58.473 (7th)	80.808 (7th)	198
Quicksilver Portland Y.C.	Orth Mathiot Orth Mathiot	Mathiot 31'x7' 6"	68.038	63.829 (6th)	D.N.S. —	95
Miss Pepsi Detroit Y.C.	Walter & Roy Dossin Chuck Thompson	Hacker 36'x9' 3"	100.558	D.N.F. —	D.N.F. —	—
Such Crust Detroit Y.C.	Jack Schafer Dan Foster	Ventnor 30'x12'	93.344	D.N.F. —	D.N.S. —	—
Gold'n Crust Detroit Y.C.	Jack Schafer Roy Duby	Arena 30'x12'	74.654	D.N.S. —	D.N.S. —	—
Dee Jay V Ocean City Y.C.	Dan J. Murphy, Jr. Norman Lauterback	Ventnor 27'x11' 6"	D.N.Q. —	—	—	—

Gale II

Note "Frenched" headlights and beautifully constructed grille.

License plate has been sunk into bumper. At end of license plate is the light. Typically a Barris creation, along with the bumper guard tail light.

18

Bob "Moose" Muccilli is one of those guys who never keeps a car very long. You know the type. Buys a car. Fixes it up. Becomes the envy of the neighborhood. Then he sells it! No particular reason. Just seems to got bored with the whole deal and wants to start all over.

Such is the case with Moose's 1950 Hudson Pacemaker. Not satisfied with its looks, he started modifying . . . at George Barris' Kustom Shop. First, George took off all excess chrome ("garbage," he calls it) and then nosed and decked* the Hudson. This done, he molded the fenders to blend with the body; set the tail lights in the bumper guards**; frenched front headlights*** and installed *two* '49 Cad grilles . . . one on top of the other.

Moose now has a car any guy would give his right eye for. Guess what he wants to do. That's right. Sell it!

* Nose chrome, trunk handle, etc., taken off, body leaded smooth.
** See "Bumper Guard Tail Lights" by George Barris in September Hop Up.
*** See page 34 of this issue.

COVER CUSTOM

The Bell Auto Parts main building.

A section of the machine shop.

Meet the Advertiser

The efficient billing and filing department, where over 30,000 customers' cards are on file.

Mailing department. Merchandise is usually shipped same day order is received.

One of the oldest and largest speed shops in the world . . . that's Bell Auto Parts. The big Bell catalog is almost an encyclopedia of "go-fast" equipment, covering nearly every manufacturer in the business, as well as many highly specialized race car parts made in Bell's own well-equipped machine shops. Orders are regularly received from such places as Africa, South America, Australia, England, etc., making Bell Auto truly an international institution. A recent addition to the ever-expanding Bell organization is the foreign car department which retails MG, Morris, Riley and other fine cars from a modern sales and service center.

Owner Roy Richter has done a bit of driving in the past, including midgets. More recently, he won the Santa Ana Road Race in his Bell Auto Merc-Allard . . . this car also made best time of the day at the 1950 SCCA drag races, while running an experimental vane type supercharger.

Bell Auto, in addition to selling speed equipment, is now actively engaged in defense work, the machine shop turning out essential war materials.

HOP UP, December, 1951

20

The latest addition to Bell Auto Parts is the Foreign Car Sales and Service Division, presided over by Thatcher Darwin, well-known sports car figure.

Interior of speed shop, where everything from a spark plug to a complete competition engine may be purchased over the counter.

Tom Beatty's 188 mph Tank

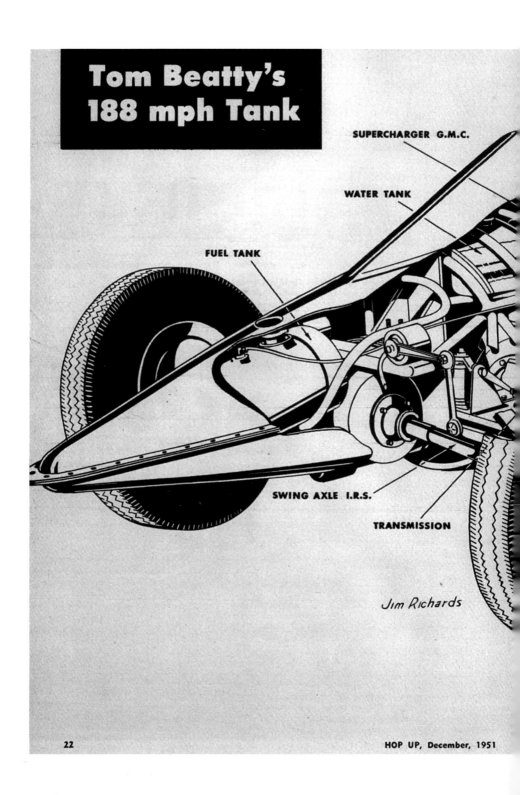

SUPERCHARGER G.M.C.

WATER TANK

FUEL TANK

SWING AXLE I.R.S.

TRANSMISSION

Jim Richards

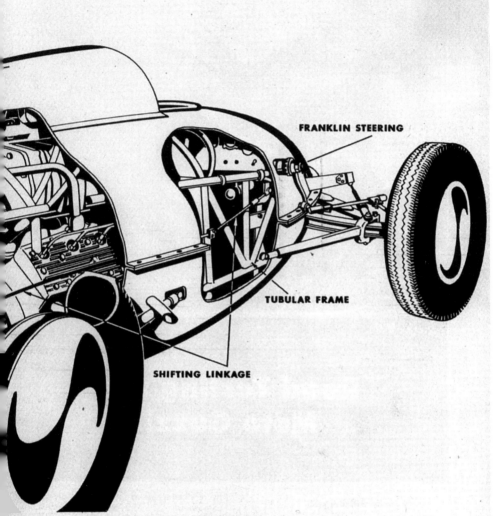

FRANKLIN STEERING

TUBULAR FRAME

SHIFTING LINKAGE

Finally an original "tank" has come along —built by Tom Beatty (August *Hop Up*). Since the day Bill Burke brought the first surplus drop-tank bodied car to the lakes, all other cars of this type have been carbon copies of his first efforts. Burke's car was ahead of everything else at the lakes in those days—but now it is about to be outmoded.

For his new creation, Tom Beatty uses a truss type tubular frame, with the roll bars, engine and seat mounts, etc., built as part of the frame. The transmission (stock Ford)

was selected for use on the short El Mirage courses, where acceleration is needed. This unit would be of little use on a long course such as Bonneville, where direct drives are sufficient and better.

The outstanding feature of Beatty's new tanker is the swing axle independent rear suspension. Since the speed of any car is dependent on how much power can be transmitted to the road thru the wheels, constant contact must be maintained with the ground. Cars with unsprung rear wheels (such as other belly-tankers) will soon be outclassed.

Road Testing the Moto Guzzi

by Bill Bagnall

A newcomer to the American motorcycling scene, and a welcome one, is Italy's fabulous Moto-Guzzi. These machines, recently imported, are the first quantity shipment to arrive on these shores.

The other day Hop Up phoned and asked me to road test the Guzzi. This was quite an honor; first, for having the privilege of riding this beautiful machine for several days and, second, to think that my humble opinions were worthy of setting in type. True, I have ridden almost every make of domestic motorcycle, but to ride a complete-

ly new concept of motorcycle design and engineering . . . this was really something!

That afternoon, I hurried to Branch Motor Sales (U.S. Distributor for Moto-Guzzi) and left there aboard a 500 cc Falcone, one of the six models turned out by the factory in Como, Italy. (Incidentally, all six models are here and available for immediate delivery.) This was not my first ride on the Guzzi, as I had ridden this same machine several weeks before . . . just enough to "whet my appetite."

The ride home (thru downtown Los Angeles' and across streetcar tracks and dips to see how it handled in traffic) was a real pleasure . . . at *any* speed. With its remark-

24

able suspension the bike never "bottomed" once. A most comfortable ride for rider as well as pillion passenger! Even with its comparatively high gearing thruout the four speeds, once underway, the Guzzi really steps out in front. From a standstill start, the clutch has to be slipped for the first few feet. Before we go any further, I would like to establish that the suspension and maneuverability was *unquestionably* the finest I have seen on a bike of this size. Also let it be understood that this cycle is designed as a touring bike and was tested with this in mind. Result? The machine never left the pavement while in my hands.

The following day I tried the Guzzi on some good high speed *winding* roads . . . up, down, around, and double-twist. Without a speedometer it was rather hard to give my accurate speed, but I can honestly state that the wind was rippling the flesh on the cheeks of my face as I approached the curves (from previous experience this happens at about 65 mph). Usually, I backshift into third gear and take such bends under power. Not once did I lose faith in the handling of the Guzzi. I have noted on other sprung-frame machines, that the rear wheel has a tendency to weave outward on fast bends. This was not the case with the Moto-

Guzzi . . . each curve was made with hairline accuracy! This ride completely sold me on the Guzzi's frame design and close ratio gearbox, for in any gear it was possible to backshift without over-revving or stressing the engine.

Next day came some "highway" riding to see if the Guzzi was successfully designed as a high-speed tourer. Practically straight all of the way . . . I covered the distance in rapid time. The rear springing arms are fitted with easily adjustable friction dampers and above 50 or 60, I found it advisable to take up a turn or two on the thumb screws to keep the ride from being "spongy." With its high top gear (3.98 to 1) cruising speeds of 70 and 75 were easily held indefinitely. Even at this speed the engine is ticking 'em off rather lazily.

Observations and Comments:

The large bore and short stroke of this engine, coupled with its slow turnover and high gearing, all add to give an extra margin of life to the cylinder wall as well as the moving parts. The engine revolves backwards (the flywheel rotating in the opposite direction to the front and rear wheels). Two reason I found for this: First, the crankshaft acts like a scoop and throws oil to the top side of the cylinder wall (remember now, the cylinder lies **horizontally**) thus relieving any dry or hot spot that might develop there if the engine rotated in the other direction. Next, with the engine ro-

tating backward, the primary chain is eliminated and a gear on the crankshaft drives directly into the gearbox, reversing the power into the right direction again. The flywheel, mounted on the outside of the crankcase on the left side of the machine, is highly polished so no chance of catching your clothing on it. The flywheel and crankcase are both marked with a timing arrow, eliminating guesswork and saving the owner's time and patience in tuning the engine. Also, with the flywheel "outdoors" the crankshaft cases are smaller, thicker, stronger. Both shafts in the gearbox are ball bearing mounted. Oil from the oil tank lubricates both engine and gearbox. Front and rear fenders are mounted independently of the wheels, lessening the unsprung weight. The gas tank is fitted with a true racing type cap that opens or closes at the flick of the lever. Riding position and handlebar layout were found satisfactory, with the handlegrips being larger than those on most imported bikes . . . after a day's riding no "rider's cramp" in the hands. The kickstarter is located on the left side of the machine and feels quite natural after a few kicks. There are two locking tool boxes, one on each side of the rear fender . . . (Lou Branch failed to give me the key for them, but my ride was trouble-free, so I had no problem there). A switch, located on the headlamp, cuts into the hot wire leading from light to battery, thus when the Guzzi is idle, there is no drain on the battery. Ignition is by magneto . . . lighting equipment and generator looked very satisfactory. Red and chrome finish of the machine was A-1 altho rust was noticed on the spokes. Alloy rims are used front and rear, both wheels fitted with 8-inch brakes that really work! No engine vibration was felt at any speed.

In conclusion, I can honestly say that this was a most enjoyable weekend and the Moto-Guzzi is an ideal machine for the everyday rider as well as the connoisseur.

HOP UP, December, 1951

Power is supplied by a 500 cc BSA single, using the Gold Star piston, rod, and cams; BSA four-speed transmission is also used. Frame is of the "spring frame" type and is fabricated from 1" and 1¼" chrome molybdenum tubing. The wire wheels and hubs are Chuck's handy work also.

GARDNER MOTORCYCLE

This potent little package of dynamite is owned by Chuck Gardner, an employee of the Mustang Motorcycle Corp. of Glendale. Chuck built the bike in his spare time to prove a few ideas of his own. Exclusive of the engine and transmission the whole outfit was made and assembled by Gardner.

Performance-wise it's a real powerhouse. Acceleration is terrific; full throttle in low gear will not only lift the front wheel off the ground but will send the whole motorcycle arcing over your head. A quick run thru the gears requires both hands on the bars and your knees glued to the gas tank.

MORE "HORSES" THRU CHEMISTRY

by Barney Navarro

Chemistry, responsible for much of our progress in this Atomic Age, is sometimes diverted from practical channels. The use of fuel additives at dry lake meets and track races is a prime example of an impractical application of chemistry. Even the annual Indianapolis Race, which is often called a proving ground of the automotive industry, is partially dependent on fuel additives for faster qualifying times. Much of what has been learned thru racing and time trials has been, and will continue to be, applied to the betterment of passenger automobiles. But, the knowledge of fuel additives obtained from these sources will *never* be used to improve the performance of your family car.

Increased production reduces the cost of many commodities but it will never drop the price of nitro-methane, benzoyl-peroxide and hydrogen peroxide to a point where their use could be commonplace, and there are some additives which cost even more than nitro-methane, which retails for $4 per gallon, benzoyl-peroxide, $1.80 per pound and hydrogen peroxide at $4 per gallon. When added to alcohol in amounts ranging from 10 to 40%, it can readily be seen that these "speed cocktails" are quite expensive; when used at the rate of 3 miles per gallon, one

28

can easily see the futility of this path to power.

A large number of the Dry Lake record holders are sponsored by speed equipment manufacturers who bear part of the expense involved. These same record holders also benefit by the manufacturer's research, so they have a two-fold advantage over independent competition. Those who lack the right "connections" thereby lack the speed to compete with the lucky minority. Many entrants are discouraged from competition because of the obvious impossibility of ever attaining the speeds of the "chosen few." (As an example, only three records were established without the aid of fuel additives at the 1951 Bonneville National Speed Trials.)

In the past, the majority of cars competing at the Dry Lakes were street roadsters. This was often used to illustrate the manner which the lake meets eliminated street If the airstrips weren't used for racing, street racing would again become a problem, because the true street roadsters (which burn gasoline) cannot compete with the specialized fuel burners that are never operated on the streets.

Increasing the supply of liquid fuel to an engine is no problem. In fact, it is as simple as pouring a can full down the carburetor. However, such practice is not going to increase horsepower because gasoline (or alcohol) must be burned with proper quantities of oxygen. Increasing the amount of oxygen that an engine breathes is the big problem. Air only contains 21% oxygen, the remaining 79% is made up of nitrogen and other inert gases. A supercharger can double the quantity of oxygen by compressing the air to double atmospheric pressure, but it also doubles the quantity of the inert gases. This doubling process can come close to doubling the horsepower of an engine, but the blower absorbs part of this power for its pumping action. The addition of oxygen bearing compounds to the fuel changes the quantity of oxygen without the power absorption disadvantage of a supercharger. This procedure is much more practical under existing regulations because there is no handicap placed on fuels such as is placed on superchargers. Whenever a supercharger is employed, a displacement handicap is imposed on the engine to offset the advantage . . . "the powers that be" should officially recognize the supercharging effect of fuel additives.

The fuel additives that are being used at the present time are not the best available and the use of better ones can produce horsepower increases best described as phenomenal; the only limitation to horsepower developed being the strength of the engine

parts and a satisfactory cooling system. Present engine failures attributable to fuels are caused by pre-ignition, *not* by the high horsepower developed. With this in mind, it is obvious that higher horsepower can be produced without engine failure. This is particularly true in the displacement classes where engines do not require boring and stroking, as those engines will have higher safety factors.

You may say to yourself that these statements are only theoretical, but *someone* is going to go faster with a stock engine than has the hottest hot rod and prove the soundness of the theory. When this happens, it will be too late to place restrictions on fuel; for a record will be established that will never be broken with straight alcohol or gasoline. This record will always have to be explained and will exist as an oddity. Already the fuel situation has gone too far. And the necessary restrictions will cause many present records to stand for a long time before they are broken without the aid of additives.

If, at the present time, one wants the ultimate in horsepower increases, rocket fuel can be employed. Rockets must carry their own oxygen, which is burned with alcohol, so they use liquid oxygen. Liquids do not require the use of an intake valve so they may be injected directly into the combustion chamber. This eliminates the carburetor, the intake manifold and all breathing problems. This ideal condition does away with the main constituents to the combustion chamber. Your natural reaction will be to assume that such a fuel mixture will behave in the same manner as an acetylene torch inside the engine. This is quite possible if too large a quantity of fuel is used, but there is a very simple method to remedy the situation if large quantities are desired for even more power. Water, the best cooling agent known, mixes readily with alcohol and can be added in sufficient quantity to control the heating problem.

The foregoing will serve to illustrate what can be done if cost is no object and if fuel restrictions are non-existent. If the right brains and money are concentrated on a maximum horsepower project, years of dry lake trial-and-error fuel experimentation can be crowded into a few days in an engine laboratory. The damage already done to the speed sport promises to be much worse if fuel isn't regulated. The changing of rules will naturally meet with objections because it is impossible to alter a situation of this type without stepping on someone's toes. But, unless fuels are regulated, auto racing and speed trials will become such frauds that they will cease to be sports.

Al Brooks, of the Pace Setters, in his "A" modified roadster. The engine is a four-cylinder Willys overhead valve conversion

Valley Timing

The Valley Timing Association was founded in 1949 by Ezra Erhardt. The objective was to promote a competitive spirit between the existing clubs and to bring them into closer contact with each other.

The V.T.A. covers an area of about 150 miles, with clubs in Sacramento, San Joaquin, Stanislaus and Alameda Counties of California. Most of the members travel 400 miles one way just to time their cars at El Mirage. In 1949 there were only three clubs; now, since the founding of the association, there are twelve. The original three were: Mid-Cal Stockers, Stockton Auto Club and the Century Toppers. The present twelve are: Pace Setters—Stockton, Century Toppers—Modesto, Thunderbolts—Sacramento, Torquers—Sacramento, Head Hunters—Hayward, Westside Auto—Newman, Central Valley—Stockton, Franklin Syndicate—Stockton, Foot Hill Flyers—Oakland, Stockton Auto—Stockton and the Throttlers—Modesto.

When one stops to consider the distance these fellows travel just to time their cars . . . "Greater love hath no man . . . !"

Al Dal Porto & Errecalde turned the fastest time of the day with 143.42 mph. They belong to the "Mid-Cal Stockers."

HOP UP, December, 1951

Jack Hofmann, of the Mid-City Stockers, turned 115.38 mph with his 274 cu in. Merc.

Gene Winfield of the "Modesto Century Toppers" in his "B" modified roadster. He's running Evans heads, Navarro 3 carb. manifold.

One good example why we need a timing strip!

Looking down course.

Both of these roadsters were completed a few short hours before the meet. Arriving late, they only made one run.

What a man looks like when he sees his cam fall out on the ground in pieces. Below, President of the V.T.A. putting his mufflers back on, before the long grind home to Stockton.

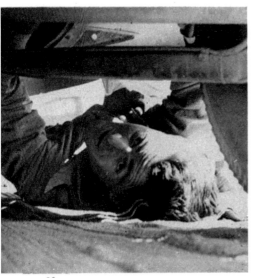

32

Ghan and Schaffers' "B" modified roadster turned 116.51. They are members of the "Pace Setters."

Edwin Horst, of the Mid-Cal Stockers, turned 91.83.

Slayton and Frora's "C" modified roadster, equipped with Ardun heads, turned 127.20.

First run of the day (108.43 mph).

Custom Hints

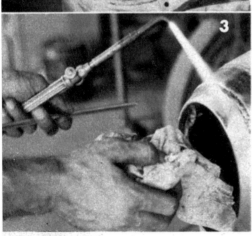

Believing that the readers would like a graphic description of the manner in which headlights are "frenched," Hop Up paid a visit to the Valley Custom Shop in Burbank. Neil Emory and his partner, Clayton Jensen, who are pretty handy with this type of custom work, were in the process of removing 5 inches from the middle of a '50 Ford Club Coupe. At our request, they knocked off long enough to do the headlight work so we could photograph it for you. They claimed they didn't mind the interruption because the headlights had to be done eventually anyway.

You won't run into too much difficulty if you follow directions closely, and if you have done some simple body work before.

First, remove the sealed beam unit and headlight bucket assembly from the fender. With these cleared away, you should next weld or braze some small bolts to the fender, remembering that the bucket must be installed from the inside, which, of course, means that the bolts must face toward the rear and out of sight. You will notice that the bracket has a flange which must be flattened so that this member will slip forward into place.

The rims used on this particular job were taken from a late model General Motors product. Use these for your modification and save yourself a lot of trouble. The rims from the GM cars are brass and can be brazed, whereas the Ford type are stainless steel which cannot be brazed to the fenders.

You may (depending on the make and model rim) have to fit the seal beam unit by cutting the rim . . . and be sure to remove all chrome before you get on with your brazing operation.

And now for the pictures, which will give you the next important steps toward making your car one of the smartest looking in the neighborhood.

1. The surface which is to be leaded is first cleaned with a wire brush. Be sure that you carefully remove all traces of dirt, paint and rust.
2. Now you can see how the area looks after cleaning and before "tinning" is begun.

3. The tinning process, which is one of the *most important* operations, is done so that lead will stick properly. There is no objection to the use of lead in body work as long as it is used sparingly and ap-·plied correctly.
4. A wooden paddle is used to smooth the lead (body solder) as it is applied.
5. Here you see the installation partially leaded with the lead in its rough state, before filing and sanding.
6. Now the job is completed . . . ready to be surfaced and painted.

The complete, customized Ford, by Valley Custom Shop, will be run in an early issue of HOP UP.

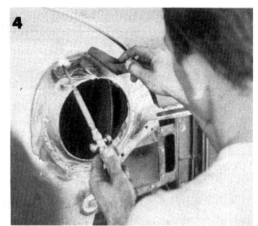

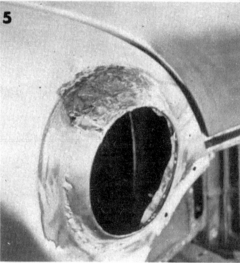

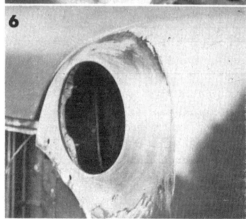

COVER HOP UP

Walt Gussenbauer (active in the hop-up field for over 16 years) wanted his proposed coupe to go fast, *but* he also wanted it beautiful. So, after Slim's Speed Shop in Long Beach had finished building the "square" engine (3⅜" bore *and* stroke, heads and manifold by Evans, Smith and Jones cam, Scintilla mag and specially-built oversize valves), it was dropped into the chassis and sent over to Coast Car Company for radical customizing.

After chopping the top, the right-hand door was leaded-in and a hole was cut in the roof . . . the cut portion being replaced with canvas. Next, the steering gear was moved over to the center, which meant, of course, moving the clutch and brake pedals . . . not too much of a problem until you consider that the '39 Merc engine was mounted in the rear! After some difficulty,

a Rube Goldberg shift was installed to connect remotely with the '37 Zephyr gearbox. The rear engine position resulted in cooling problems . . . there wasn't room for a radiator! Coast Car solved this one by using two G.I. five-gallon cans which (with two water pumps) worked better than the original set-up.

Firewall, paneling and floorboards are aluminum; instrumentation consists of two water temperature gauges, tach, altimeter, oil and fuel pressure gauges.

After spending $3000 and eleven months' time, Walt (who is Bell Timing Association's secretary), finally got his coupe the way *he* wanted it. Painted cream and dark maroon, and weighing 2400 pounds, the finished product is a sight for sore eyes.

36

HOP UP, December, 1951

Above, this '34 coupe is a good example of clean compact design. CO2 nozzle behind G.I. can is aimed at engine to make short work of possible fires. Below, Einstein couldn't have done better on the gear shift.

Side, sturdy roll-bar reinforces aluminum interior while driver sits on pad, holding '41 steering wheel in one hand and gear shift in the other. Aluminum dashboard comes complete with full instrumentation, including two water gauges and an altimeter for high flying. Below, water entering top of G.I. can (which is attached to head) circulates thru engine and is pumped back thru tank.

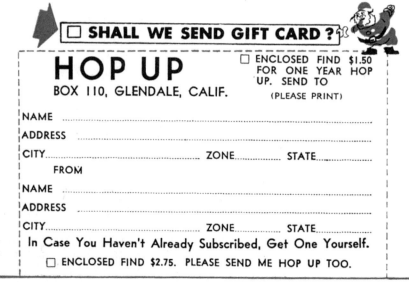

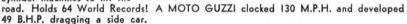
44

STUDEBAKER V8

GAINS
13% to 15% Horsepower

BY REPLACING THE STOCK EXHAUST SYSTEM WITH "PRESSURE-FREE" EXHAUST HEADERS

Fits All Models

Set #1 $59⁵⁰ Includes right and left headers & extensions to mufflers, left tail pipe, 2 steel pack mufflers (1st quality), complete set clamps & brackets.	**Set #2** $49⁷⁵ same as set no. 1 without mufflers. Stock mufflers (or 2 of your choice) may then be used on both sides.

Pr. Headers.................................... $34⁵⁰
                                    $11⁵⁰
Extension to muffler.....................
Anyone can install—only 2 small holes to drill.
No burning or welding—
Installation instructions included in kit.

Send Money Order for full amount or 50% of purchase, balance C.O.D. In Calif. Add 3% Sales Tax
All prices f.o.b. Norwalk

KAYWELD INDUSTRIES, 11144 E. Firestone, Norwalk 12, Calif.
"Experts in Our Line for 8 Years"

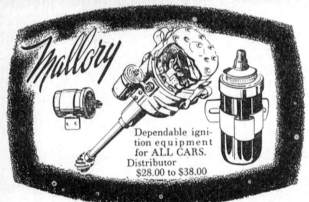

Dependable ignition equipment for ALL CARS.
Distributor
$28.00 to $38.00

The MALLORY DISTRIBUTOR, CONDENSER and "BEST" COIL are a premium piece of merchandise, designed to eliminate all "spark handicap" that would otherwise rob many engines of their maximum horsepower and economy.

Condenser   2.25
"Best" coil   12.75

STEERING ARM

Designed for late Ford cross steering spindles adapted to drag link type side steering. Ball joint can be mounted on top or underneath.

Cadmium plated 6.50
Chrome plated   8.00

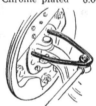

SEND 25¢ FOR EQUIPMENT CATALOG FOR ALL CARS

BELL *Auto parts*

3633 E. GAGE AVENUE, BELL, 8 CALIFORNIA

HOP UP 15¢

JAN.
1952
15¢

Yank Breaks European Speedboat Records...see page 18

NEWS

INBOARD SPEEDBOAT RECORDS FALL

With a total of 14 states and Canada represented, the 1951 Salton Sea Regatta will go down in history as one of the most outstanding meets of all time. A total of 201 boats took part in the 4 day trials . . . . the hottest contest of the year; and, of the twenty-three existing inboard records, twenty-one were smashed. Every class except P.O.D.H. set new records.

Outstanding record breakers were: Paul Sawyer (page 18), who screamed over the course in his "Alter Ego" at 120.085 mph; Ed Brown, who piloted his cracker-box "Bouncy Barby" to a new mark of 72.054 mph; and Pete Pierce, who turned 79.330 mph in his Crosley-powered 48 hydro. Otto Crocker, of course, timed the mile-long course.

February Hop Up will carry the exciting story of this record-smashing meet.

PHOTO CREDITS

Cover photos: Trindl & Alan
Pages 7 thru 17; 24 thru 27; 30 thru 35; 38: Trindl
Page 18 thru 20: Hitchcock
Pages 36 and 37: Batchelor

HOP UP, January, 1952

If it's hopped up, it'll be in HOP UP

HOP UP

HOP UP—SPORT CAR ROAD RACE

By the time this issue reaches you, the American hot rod will have run in its first genuine road race. Three street type roadsters are being invited by the California Sports Car Club to compete in the first annual Apple Valley Road Race (California), December 9th.

This marks the first time that the California brand of hop up has competed with the foreign sports car in a road race. This is a golden opportunity to erase some of the misconceptions and misunderstandings between the roadster enthusiasts and the sports car advocates . . . definitely a step in the right direction.

MOTORCYCLES TOO . . . .

Motorcycles were also invited to participate in the Apple Valley Road Race. We congratulate the CSCC for their splendid cooperation and good fellowship.

OUR POLICY

Hop Up is a magazine with a purpose . . . . a very realistic objective.

By furnishing the enthusiast with news of "faster-and-better-than-normal" automobiles, motorcycles, and boats, we hope to advance the development and growth of this fascinating sport-hobby. It is our desire to give you new ideas, useful data, guidance, and a bond of good fellowship with other hop up enthusiasts.

Because we have a vital interest in the welfare of these activities, we refuse to exploit sensationalism . . . . you will find no crash and smash photos in *Hop Up* . . . . nor will you read lurid tales of "thrills, chills and death." (Only a simple-minded drip would drool over the misfortunes of others.) *Hop Up* is written for the progressive thinker, the clean sportsman, the sincere builder.

EDITORIAL STAFF

Editor ....Oliver Billingsley
Technical Editor..................................John R. Bond
Associate Editors....................................Louis Kimzey
                                  Robert Dearborn
Staff Photographers............................Gene Trindl
                               Jerry Chesebrough
Photographers.......... Jack Campbell, Bob Canaan
                               Joe Al Denker

PRODUCTION STAFF

Managing Editor.....................W. H. Brehaut, Jr.
Art Director....................................Louis Kimzey
Art ....Jack Caldwell

ADVERTISING

Advertising Manager.....................William Quinn
Southern California.......................Dean Batchelor
Motorcycles ....Bill Bagnall
East Coast Representatives......Peabody & Ortgies
                          276 West 43rd Street
                          New York 18, N.Y.
United Kingdom......................Kenneth Kirkman
                          2 Longcroft Avenue
                    Banstead, Surrey, England
Italy ....Michele Vernola
                                   C.P. 500
                                 Milano, Italy

CORRESPONDENTS

Italy ....Corrado Milanta

Vol. 1, No. 6   **January, 1952**

CONTENTS

HOP UP is published monthly by Enthusiasts' Publications, Inc., 540 W. Colorado Blvd., Glendale, California. Phone CHapman 5-2297. Application for entry as second-class matter is pending. Copyright 1951 by Enthusiasts' Publications, Inc. Reprinting in whole or in part forbidden except by permission of the publishers.

Subscription price $1.50 per year thruout the world. Single copy 15c.

Change of address—must show both old and new addresses.

WHAT IS *ONE* HORSEPOWER?

by BARNEY NAVARRO

How much is **one horsepower?** There are more misconceptions regarding this term than any other in automotive usage. Part of the confusion is caused by the fact that horsepower is no longer connected with a horse but is a term of strictly technical nature. Even more confusing is the fact that the "power" half of the word does not mean pulling ability as is popularly believed. Usually, an automobile's ability to climb hills in top gear is attributed exclusively to power, but this is wrong, there are other contributing factors.

Power, to a physicist, means the ability to do a given amount of **work** in a given length of **time.** A simple illustration of this fact can be made by picturing two men, one twice as heavy as the other, climbing a stairway. In equal periods of time, the thin man **runs** up two flights and the fat man **walks** up one flight. The thin man did as much work as the fat man but he had to travel twice as fast to accomplish this feat. Truck engines and race car engines can be compared in the same manner. A pint-sized race car engine produces as much horsepower as a large diesel but it turns three to six times the rpm to produce this power. If the proper gear ratio were applied to the race car engine, it could pull the truck with the same ease as the diesel. Of course, this type of usage would cause the race car engine to wear out much faster than the truck engine, making this type of application impractical—except for comparison.

When most people use the term **power,** they are really talking about **torque.** This term has a high sounding ring to it but it simply means **twisting ability.** A Ford engine is capable of producing 187 pound-feet of torque, but this twisting ability can be duplicated by most men and some women. This statement will cause most people to ask, "How can this be, for a Ford engine is more powerful than a man?" They will be right but the above comparison is not an illustration of power but one of torque. Given a 1 foot long crank a man can apply 187 pounds of twist on the handle, thereby producing 187 pound-feet of torque, but he cannot turn it 1800 revolutions per minute as does the Ford engine. Thus, man and engine both produce the same **torque** but not the same **horsepower.**

The term **horsepower** originated in Southern England many years ago when horses were used to raise mine shaft elevators with the aid of a rope and pulley. It was found that the average horse could raise 550 pounds a distance of 1 foot per second. And the horse could maintain this lifting speed over the full travel of the elevator. This gave rise to the establishment of the standard for 1 horsepower: the ability to do 550 foot pounds of work per second. If you state this as a formula, it becomes: 1 hp = 550 foot pounds per second; or 1 hp = 33,000 ft. lbs. per minute. If we analyze this standard and its derivation, we see that there are three elements, a force (or weight), a distance, and a period of time. But, we must recognize that the distance must be in a straight line.

Now, if we transfer all three elements (force, time, distance) to the circular motion of an engine, we will find a method of measuring and analyzing the horsepower of an engine. These elements may be expressed in standardized terms: torque, rpm, and feet.

Torque (the twisting ability of an engine) uses a 1 foot lever arm acting on a scale as a standard of measurement. If a force of 200 pounds is being exerted at the end of the torque arm, then we have 200 lbs x 1 foot (length of arm) or 200 pound-feet of torque.

Rpm stands for "revolutions per minute" and is a term for expressing speed of rotary motion (just as mph expresses straight-line motion).

Distance, of course, is measured in feet and to find the distance over which force (torque) is being applied, we again consider the 1 foot torque lever arm. When it is rotated, the tip of the arm describes a circle, the arm itself being the radius of this circle. The circumference of the circle, of course, is the distance travelled by the tip of the 1 foot lever arm. To find the circumference, we multiply 2π times the radius (1 foot) which equals 6.2832 feet.

Now if an engine produces 100 pounds of force at the end of the 1 foot lever arm, it has produced 100 pound-feet of torque. If we maintain this 100 pounds of torque at 6000 rpm, we find we have 3,769,920 foot pounds of work per minute. We arrive at this figure by multiplying 6.2832 ft. by 100 lbs, times 6000 rpm.

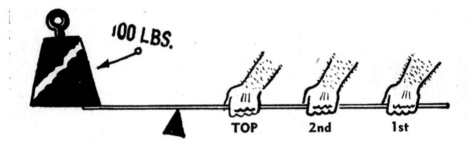

TOP   2nd   1st

We know that 1 hp equals 33,000 ft-lbs of work per minute. But our engine has produced 3,769,920 foot pounds (per minute), which is 114 times more work than 1 hp produces. Therefore, the engine has produced 114 hp.***

A definition has been established illustrating that horsepower is related to time. This will enable us to see what determines the top gear* hill climbing ability of an automobile.

Variations of an automobile's hill climbing ability are brought about by exchanging distance for torque . . . by using various rear axle gear ratios so as to multiply the existing engine torque.

Ratios of at least 3 and 4 to 1 are absolutely necessary if an automobile is to be practical—because automobile engines are incapable of pulling a car without multiplying their feeble torque. For example: an engine producing 100 lb-ft of torque will produce 400 lb-ft at the rear wheels, if you use a 4 to 1 rear axle ratio. And the higher** the rear axle gear ratio, the better the pulling ability. Of course, when you raise the gear ratio, to improve the pulling ability, you are "robbing Peter to pay Paul," i.e., you lose top speed in the inverse proportion. You also get an adverse effect on economy . . . as you will find if you drive in 1st gear continually.

If your car has a 1st gear ratio of 3 to 1, and a rear axle ratio of 4 to 1, the combined ratio would be 3 times 4, or 12 to 1; giving 1200 pound-feet of torque at the rear wheels (disregarding frictional losses).

An automobile may have terrific pulling power in first gear, but everybody knows that it won't go as fast in first as it will in top gear. By the same token, if too low a rear axle ratio is used—say 2 to 1—there won't be enough torque at the rear wheels to overcome wind resistance at high speeds. There are many cars

which experience this difficulty in overdrive . . . having a top speed in overdrive which is actually lower than their direct drive top speed.

Pulling ability at normal speeds is affected by other factors that govern torque, besides gear ratios. Rpm also governs torque. An engine's produced torque varies with its rpm, and is **never** maximum at the same point where it develops maximum horsepower.

As a matter of fact, maximum torque is usually obtained at a point midway between zero and the point at which maximum hp is developed. Some engines produce maximum torque at lower rpm than others, so they will climb hills at lower speeds in top gear . . . they will "lug" down farther. This type of hill climbing is more dependent on engine torque than on horsepower.

A good example can be had by comparing the Chevrolet and the Ford. Using identical gear ratios, the Chevrolet will climb a hill at a slower speed without faltering than the Ford . . . even tho the Ford has a higher horsepower rating. This difference in performance is a result of the fact that a Chevrolet produces maximum torque at 1200 rpm, while the Ford develops its maximum torque at 1800 rpm.

*When referring to a transmission, we use the terms "1st gear," "2nd gear," and "top gear" . . . rather than the more commonly used (and less correct) "low," "2nd," and "high."

**Numerical (4.00 to 1 is numerically a higher ratio than 3.00 to 1, but the 4.00 to 1 is commonly referred to as a "lower" gear because at the same rpm it produces a lower speed. Numerical usage is technically more correct).

***Simplified formula for computing hp.
$$hp = \frac{torque \times rpm}{5250}$$

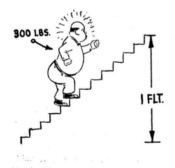

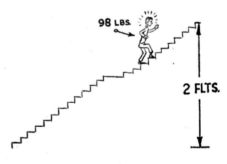

Carl Cerny's 1949 Chevrolet

243

This beautiful 1949 Chevrolet belongs to Carl Cerney who, with his brother George, owns a body shop in Compton, California. Between the two of them, they have taken this "Chevy" notch-back and cut 4 inches out of the top in back and 3 inches in front. Thus, they have a subtle curve which blends into the trunk. This completed, they installed a curved '50 Olds windshield. The side posts have been slanted and the corners of the doors have been rounded. They installed '50 Olds tail lights, '49 Olds rear bumpers. They "nosed" and "decked" it (page 30), and frenched the headlights (December issue of Hop Up). The grille consists of a '50 Olds top bar and a '51 Olds center bar. The upholstery is maroon and white leather and to complete the job they painted the car a beautiful metallic maroon.

8

Custom of the month

245

A small part of the huge crowd that attended.

Russetta

Rusetta Timing Association ended its 1951 season by setting 6 new records at its last meet.

Bill Likes broke his old record for "A" Roadsters (141.73 mph) by over 7 mph. His new mark: 148.76.

Howard Johnson, in his "B" Roadster, moved the record up over 9 mph . . . . went thru at 159.29 mph (old record: 150.62) and this was a '29 A roadster chas-sis with a G.M.C. engine.

Other new record holders: Bob Rounthwaite, "D" coupe, 151.89; Tom Mc Laughlin, "A" sedan, 136.88 (another G.M.C. . . . . in a Cord sedan chassis); Earl Evans, "A" streamliner, 177.33 (fastest run ever made at a Russetta meet).

The turnout of spectators was gratifying . . . . the largest of the season.

Kenny Arnold leaving line on 143.42 mph run.

10

Bill Davis, member of G.C.R.C., did 144 mph.

Clark and Clark B streamliner turned 132.35.

Ed "Axle" Stewart giving pointers to his son.

Arlen Kurtis turned 111.80 mph.

Bob Stanclift leading in first turn.

California
Roadster Association

Hank Henry in Farmer and Boyd's roadster leading Howard Gardner and Bob Stanclift.

Bob Denny in lead with Dick Webb and Bill Norton in hot pursuit. Bob is the top driver in the California Roadster Association this year, and was the Champion driver last year.

Date: Early part of 1946.
Place: A plot of land—Wilson's Ranch.
Event: A race called the "Ash Can Derby" which consisted of a helmet dash, and a couple of heat races, with a 20-lap main event.

So what? Well, simply this: "Wilson's Ranch" wasn't a race track. The "Ash Can Derby" wasn't a legally sanctioned race and the participants weren't nationally known drivers (at that time anyway). To explain: Jim Sheridan, Harry Stockman, Joe and Walt James, Jimmy Davies, Kenny Stansbury, to name a few, used to jump into their cars and go to what was then called Wilson's Ranch in San Bernardino, California. There they removed headlights and all excessive weight and proceeded to have what they called the Ash Can Derby . . .

Preparation for the next race . . .

Walt James trying to pass Colby Scroggins who is driving Allen Heath's regular ride. The large front tire is to make the front end stick on the turns of this hard dirt track.

Walt Jámes, President of the C.R.A.

no safety requirements, no crash walls, just a love of racing.

There was a slight admission charge and after the race the drivers "split the gate" while sitting around in the infield. The spectators sat on top of their cars and watched what they could thru all the dust . . . and at their own risk—the majority being friends of the drivers . . . only a few being curious passersby. Cokes were sold off the end of a pick-up . . . water was in a trough in the infield . . . for radiators and drinking. The only restriction was that no hard tops could run . . . only roadsters and sprint cars.

It was here, at such a weekly race, that a man was seen teaching his son how to drive. It was terrific! First, dad would drive a race. Then he let his son drive the next. At the completion, the son would be told his

Buddy Lee starting his spin, which ended in the infield. Barely missing him is 81 driven by Lou Figaro, N.A.S.C.A.R. contender.

14

Coming around for the start . . .

mistakes. As the years passed, this son went on to national fame. The father's name was "Pop" Ruttman. The son's name was Troy.

This is just one example of the caliber of men that attended these meets. The meets continued until Chuck Leighton, Pop Ruttman, Tom Sloan, Babe Ouse and Johnny Walker decided to unite and draw up the by-laws for a group that is now the California Roadster Association.

The C.R.A. enjoyed a big season in 1947-1948, but the fickle public let them down in 1949 and '50. Now, after a two-year lull, roadster racing is picking up interest again. A lot of credit should go to Walt James, the very capable president of C.R.A., for the increased popularity of roadster racing.

For complete specifications on a track roadster, turn to page 22.

Champion Bob Denny.

Buddy Lee spinning into infield.

Morrison's Roadster

Photography alone cannot express the true beauty of Walker Morrison's 1932 Ford Roadster . . . . which appears to be nothing unusual, but is, in reality, one of the cleanest examples of roadster building in Southern California.

Painted dark maroon with natural leather upholstery, the '32 is set off well by its white top and liberal use of chrome.

Now about this chrome question: the shiny plating can be used in both design and building—*if* it is used correctly. And Moe used chrome as a builder should . . . . on parts which need cleaning most often.

Because the Morrison Roadster was intended for street use, with competition a secondary purpose, appearance was most important. However, he didn't slight the engine compartment too much: Merc, $3\frac{3}{8}''$ bore, 4" stroke; Evans heads; Navarro triplet manifold; Scintilla Vertex magneto; Potvin 38 - 83 cam; the transmission carries 25-tooth Zephyr gears and the rear end ratio is 3.54 to 1.

Moe got Duane Spencer to build the chrome headers and split wishbone . . . . and the car turned 134.50 at a S.C.T.A. Lakes Meet—not exactly crawling in a car built mainly for the streets.

Paul Sawyer

By Kent Hitchcock

You're a pretty hot hydro jockey when you consistently beat the local talent in the dizzy sport of hydroplane racing. If you can knock off both world's records in the hotly contested classes . . . . then beat the best in the country over a full season's racing, you will be in that select list of World Record Holders in addition, to the honor of carrying the coveted U.S. 1 and the U.S. Shield on your outfit. Add a whirlwind invasion of Europe . . . . a clean sweep of the International Championships and you have a thumbnail sketch of Paul Sawyer, owner/driver of the 225 Class Hydro, **Alter Ego.** This transplanted New Yorker (racing headquarters: Long Beach, California) is no flash-in-the-pan—no johnny-come-lately, with a hot rig and a lot of luck. Driving ability is a prerequisite to championship performance and it takes plenty of racing experience to hit the line on the nose, know when to make your move and how to get thru the field when the going is tough. A power plant has to put out peak horsepower in short spurts and still be capable of standing the abuse of a full race . . . . you must be up in front in every race to win a championship. Someone on the boat crew has to build up an engine that won't come unstuck. The championship hull may look just like its sister ship but slight differences in underbody dimensions and angles spell the difference. Some champions have reached the top with driving ability alone, leaving hull design, balancing, testing, and engine development technical experts, but not Paul Sawyer. Rich Hallett builds the hulls, but Paul decides length, width and depth of sponsons, dihedral and angles of attack; design of afterplane and non trips. **Alter Ego** has marked differences from the standard Hallett hull . . . . these too are Paul's own ideas. He built his engines at Buddy Reuter's shop in Texas. The power plant is a 264 cu. in. Ford, Edelbrock heads, three jug manifold carrying Stromberg 97's, Scintilla Vertex Magneto, standard Ford crank, 8BA rods, JE pistons, Madis oil pump, dry sump and Smith & Jones cam. The shaft (1" K Monel) carries a HI J Racing Prop.

With all of the ingredients put together, Paul starts testing to achieve balance, riding trim, handling, and acceleration. Countless hours go into test runs . . . . in and out of the water . . . . change this . . . . change that until finally the right combination is reached. Actually there are several combinations: one for rough water, another for glassy stuff . . . . one for single buoy turns, another for long sweeping curves . . . . one for long courses and another for short ones that are nearly all turns . . . . and finally a combination for the straightaway mile trial. All this takes a lot of experience but a glance at Paul Sawyer's background explains his success.

Paul started racing in 1929, with outboard hydros and very soon was riding with the leaders . . . . racing on an intercollegiate team as well as regular circuits and he wound up many successful seasons with a trip to Paris where he astounded the continentals by whipping their 1000 cc Class X Outboards with a 500 cc job!

Before leaving college he won seven Eastern Divisional Championships . . . . was Intercollegiate Champion and member of the Championship Intercollegiate Team. When the World War II got under way he had passed his bar exam in New York and was still working the bugs out of a Class X Outboard Hydro, looking forward to a shot at Frenchman Jean Dupuy's all time world record of 79.04 mph. Paul had the background and legal training that could have placed him in the services with a commission but he couldn't visualize himself at a desk job. Uncle Sammy couldn't seem to find a place in the picture where boat driver and engine expert Paul Sawyer could put these talents to work so Paul simply closed up his private affairs, put his racing equipment in moth balls at Buddy Reuter's shop in Texas and enlisted in the Navy. At boot camp (San Diego Naval Training Station) he arranged for a mile trial during a weekend leave. Lake Elsinore was selected, survey accomplished, timing installed and the "X" trailered out from Texas. Class X is the unlimited division of the outboards and just about anything goes, including tractor lower units which are barred from use in the regular racing classes. There are no hull or engine limitations except that the power plant must be an outboard type and be hung on the transom.

Sawyer was tangling with a real wildcat in this record try. A few months previous on the channel (Brownsville, Texas) veteran Frank Vincent flipped during a tune up run on Junior Wood's **Satan's Go Cart,** a "not nearly big enough" conventional hydro powered with the terrific six cylinder Italian Sorriano outboard. A pair of fisherman pulled Vincent unconscious from the water, saved him from drowning, but the accident left him with a broken leg and other injuries as the screaming "X" went over backwards at about 90 mph. Paul's "X" was a four cylinder opposed job, much like the Draper's and Eldridge X's engines. The hull was a slightly overgrown conventional F hydro. Three times, on that blistering day on Lake Elsinore, the "gob on leave" tried the mile and each time nearing the 90 mph mark the outfit became airborne and flipped. Most drivers would have given up the attempt after the first spill. It was a major miracle that he emerged from each flip with nothing more serious than bruises. And it was a second miracle that Paul and crew were able to run the "X" again after each dunking. Sunset put an end to the trial and Dupuy's record is still on the books. This was Sawyer's last fling in outboards, but he amassed several hundred trophies and priceless experience that made it possible for him to reach the top in inboard ranks.

Paul's rise in the Navy was a meteoric flight from one specialist's school to another. Uncle Sam needed apt scholars in electronics, so in a very short time Ensign Paul Sawyer went overseas (Pacific Theatre) as an officer in Radar. Home from the conflict and discharged with a Lieutenant's stripes he decided to enter inboard competition.

It was a windy, rough day on the Lido Isle course (Newport Harbor, Calif) when he took

18

"Alter Ego" air borne and on the way to the new one mile record at Salton Sea, California.

his first inboard hydro ride as mechanic, with world record holder and national champion Dr. Louis Novotny in **Cherub II.** You will have to go a long way to find a rougher riding boat in a chop than the Pacific One Designs and the "Good Doctor" never backs off as long as the boat is right side up, so Paul got the ride of his life. Things started to come unstuck as the **Cherub** came over the finish line, so Doc headed for the pits and none too gently put the boat on the beach. Unprepared for the sudden stop Sawyer's chin made contact with the dash and the lights went out.

During the winter of 1947, Paul worked with Willard Campbell of Long Beach on the design and construction of his first 225. This was a Division II job, powered with a Ford 6 and named **Belligero.** The new boat didn't set the world on fire, but Paul arrived at a pretty fair combination by the end of the 1948 season and won the National Championships for his class. During the winter, 1948, Hallett built two new hydros for Sawyer: **Belligero II** and **Alter Ego**—the former (powered with the 264 cu. in. Ford previous described) to race in the 225 Class and the latter (Ford 6) to race in 225 Division II. These two classes, have the same hull restrictions but different engine limitations. The 225 Class may not exceed 266 cu. in. with pretty broad permissions for modification and use of replacement parts. Division II may not exceed 225 cu. in. with **strict limitations** on modifications, replacement parts, fuel and permissible engine cost. Both of the new boats had a whale of a season in 1949. It takes a good man to keep one outfit on top of the heap and a wizard to race **two classes** at each regatta and win in both. By Fall, Paul found the combination for **Belligero II** and in Cincinnati, in September, he set up a

sparkling new 5 mile competition record of 78.192 mph—to erase from the books Joe Taggart's long standing (1941) figure of 73.170 mph. Next the two Sawyer boats won both National Championship events: the one mile record, 225 Class, of 88.786 mph, (set by Dave Forman in 1940) was taking quite a kicking around but Paul put his name on it in no uncertain way at Salton Sea, in October, when he blistered that famous one mile trap for a two way average of 99.820 mph. **Belligero II** amazed the racing clan by doing a one way mile at better than 100 mph, the first boat (other than Gold Cupper or Unlimited) to top the century mark.

1950 was the pay off year and Sawyer's boats cleaned house regularly. Winning both National Championships and gathering enough points to win the National High Point Title for both classes (which entitles him to carry on the hull the Stars and Stripes Shield and the "U.S. 1." Along the way Paul raised the Division II five mile competition record from 73.1 mph to 75.188 mph. Back in California readying for the Annual Salton Sea scramble, Sawyer decided to shoot for the world's first 100 mph limited hydro mark. The Ford 6 was removed from **Alter Ego,** the outfit was re-registered (225 Class) and powered with the spare 264 cu. in. engine. After several weeks of testing, tho both boats were now identical twins, **Alter Ego** appeared to stay on the water a little better at full bore, so Smith & Jones replaced the carburetion with the Hilborn-Travis fuel injection system: The first attempt to use injection on a limited hydroplane, and an idea Paul had been toying with for some time.

Water conditions on the Big Salton (November 17, 1950) were ideal. Without fanfare or testing **Alter Ego** scorched (two ways) thru

Sawyer at Lake Elsinore trying to set a 90 mph Class X Outboard record.

the electrically timed trap at the astounding average of 115.045 mph. Officials and the racing clan stood with butterflies in the solar plexus while the air-borne hydro negotiated the trap without a bobble. Then **Belligero 11** was put thru at an average of better than 104 mph. This was a safety move, for **Alter Ego** (just transferred from Division II) had yet to place in the first three spots in competition before the record would stand. Most of the best boats in the country were in the competition. Paul made no attempt to lead at the start . . . . apparently satisfied to cinch third in this first heat, to qualify his record, but on the second lap he moved easily out ahead of the leader, obviously seeing easier going in untroubled water, away from the close quarters racing. It was an easy win . . . . the record was in the bag.

So far we have neglected to mention that actually it was the Sawyer racing **team** that accounted for these successes. And the "team" is Mr. and Mrs. Paul Sawyer—and Erminie is right there every minute of the time during planning, building, testing and competition. To say the Sawyer's were "done in" after two years of keeping two racing outfits on top of the heap, would be a masterpiece of understatement. They were exhausted.

During the winter came an invitation from Europe to send a U.S. representative to the International Races in Italy and Switzerland. Paul Sawyer was certainly the man qualified to represent the U.S. and the Sawyers decided to make the trip. Preparations for the trip and racing under unfamiliar conditions, so far from a base of supplies, presented many problems. The Italian Motorboat Federation had foreseen the biggest headache, that of transportation of the boat and equipment not only across the Atlantic but also on the Continent, and as a part of the invitation had agreed to take care of all of the details of shipment including the not insignificant item of expenses. It goes without saying that Paul's preparations were thoro and meticulous. The entire outfit, including spare engine, was torn down to the smallest part, re-assembled, tested on the water and then "pickled" for shipment. The four wheel trailer was converted from a two boat to a single boat outfit and balanced to carry the extra engine. A full description and weight of the whole assembly, together with a drawing of the trailer hitch, was sent to Italy. A fifty gallon drum of alcohol was sent on ahead by freighter, as regulations forbad transportation of volatile fuels on passenger liners. The trailer was "deck cargo" on the liner

Sawyer in "Alter Ego" at Salton Sea with a new 115.04 mph one mile record for the 225s.

256

The language problem was a worry, too. It would be one matter to get the wants of an ordinary traveler understood, but obviously quite another to get the complicated jargon of boat racing from one language into another. Paul didn't know it, but this problem had been foreseen and taken care of by Valvoline Oil Co. wh'ch provided a capable interpreter. Dr. Enzo Salera with a command of excellent English had practically a 24 hour job, should have a medal for his interpretations of the discussions on the technical details of hydroplanes, engines and fuels. Imagine, if you can, listening to the speeches at the many banquets thru the softly repeated words of the interpreter and . . . . even tougher . . . . just imagine giving your trophy acceptance speeches thru an interpreter.

As the trailer came off the steamer immediately arose transportation difficulties; that is to Paul . . . . but not to the Italians. Towing hitches on the continent are a "hook and eye" affair . . . . on the towing vehicle . . . . high off the ground. Paul's tow hitch at bumper level was useless but the Italians, undaunted, simply hoisted the whole trailer on a truck. This was the beginning of practically every known method of transporting **Alter Ego,** except by direct towing. It was hauled on railroad cars, on a wagon pulled by a tractor, shoved and pulled by the willing hands of squads of Italian soldiers, and finally craned onto a barge and towed to the side of the ship on which it was to go home. **But not once** did the carefully balanced outfit ride down the highway attached to a car by its own trailer hitch! The Europeans have no trailers for their racing boats. Each boat has a cradle mounted on skids and at each regatta the unit is unloaded, by crane from a truck or from a railroad car and placed in the pit area.

The United States entry, Paul Sawyer's **Alter Ego,** was beautifully finished in the U.S. colors: the hull bright red, trimmed in white and blue and carrying the Stars and Stripes Shield of the National Champion on the deck. In International Racing the Continentals have followed the pattern of auto racing; each boat carries its national colors: U.S., bright red; Italy, dark red; France, light blue; England, green; and Germany, white. After a day of thoro looking-over the U.S. entry was dubbed "the doll house". Paul didn't find out just what brought about this descriptive name, but apparently those who coined it decided that the contraption had a beautiful paint job but was a bit fragile for the rigors of racing.

Milan was site of the first race. There, followers of the sport were disappointed to find the U.S. entry carrying conventional carburetion instead of the injection system (used at Salton Sea). The contestants felt sorry for Paul . . . . they learned he was using straight alcohol and offered to supply him with their mixture (benzol/gasoline). They were positive he would get no place burning alcohol. Consternation also reigned when **Alter Ego** did not appear at the course immediately for test runs, and on succeeding days the Sawyer's were besieged by everyone. Paul's explanation that the boat had been thoroly tested in California and was ready to race was met with polite but incredulous looks. This was indeed an unheard of way to prepare for a race!

Space had been made available to the Sawyers at the civilian airport, a very short distance from the course and here Paul and Erminie spent most of their time right up to the day of the race. This translation from one of the Italian newspapers tells the story: "With a care which many people would find exaggerated, Sawyer inspected thoroly his boat, checking everything, not leaving the boat

for one moment." No one said so out loud, but it was probable that the extremely race minded Europeans were unanimous in their opinion that this American was really crazy to come all those thousands of miles, from California, for a boat race, and then not even test out his boat before the event!

The course at Milan was a body of water known as idroscalo . . . long years ago a sand pit, converted during the days of Mussolini to a seaplane base and later turned into a very beautiful park. A modern covered grandstand seats only part of the tremendous crowds, and below, on the waterfront, is what can best be described as a sidewalk cafe. What a contrast to the American scene where such facilities are unheard of! Inboards, incidentally are known in Italy as "motoscafi" and out-boards, as the "fuoribordo" the two divisions both included at the big regattas. The inboards race on a 2 Kilometer circuit (roughly 1¼ miles) and the outboards on a 1200 Meter Course (roughly ¾ miles). Paul points out that here lies one of the outstanding differences between European and American Racing. American courses are standardized at either one or one and two-thirds miles, for both inboards and outboards with a few 2½ mile circuits for the inboards. The outboards never race over 5 miles per heat and only in the case of a very few special trophy races do the inboards exceed this distance. The Europeans (as Paul explains) like. to see a lot of racing so the inboards run either 10 or 12 laps per heat (12½ or 15 miles). Class A Outboards run 8 laps of the 1200 Meter Course (6 miles), Class C runs 12 laps (9 miles) and Class X runs 15 laps (11¼ miles) Paul says "You can quote me as being heartily in favor of these long races. It makes a much more interesting race for both driver and spectator and it is a real test of equipment." Quoting again from Paul's statement on the vast differences in the general boat racing picture here and abroad: "The Europeans are sport conscious and motor boat racing ranks high in the list of favored events. The European drivers are spectacular and are master showmen. They make every race a thrilling spectacle, an art that the American drivers have never learned, and the spectators are on their feet constantly cheering their favorites." (Note: This is quite a contrast to the reactions of the crowd at the average race in America, where the announcer has to urge the crowd to applaud as the boats return to the pits.) Another sharp difference is the layout of the courses. Whereas nearly all of our courses have either single buoy turns at each end in narrow waterways, or conventional two straightaway courses with semicircular turns at either end, the European courses are of every conceivable shape. Here, we go to great lengths to fit a conventional course into a body of water and if this fitting puts the course out where the spectators can't distinguish between boats without binoculars, it is "just too' bad". We go to any lengths to avoid dog-legs on a straightaway and frown on a course that parallels a sea-wall (where the slop can bounce back to make the going rough).

The Europeans are not bound down by any conventions in this respect. The course is made to fit the body of water. If there is a dog-leg in the shore line, they simply put a dog-leg in the course and this keeps the racing right in the laps of the crowd. If one end of the waterway is very narrow, the course gets a single buoy turn and if the other end is too wide to bring the racing within reasonable distance of the shore line, they pust toss .another straightaway in the turn.

(Continued next month)

Track Roadster

WEIAND 4 CARB MANIFOLD

This car is a typical C.R.A. member roadster. Owners Bruce Robinsen and Ruey Whiting not only race on the track, but also at drag strips and on the dry lakes. Some of the track roadster requirements of the California Roadster Association are:

Block   American production only
max. displ.   300 cu" unblown, 183 blown

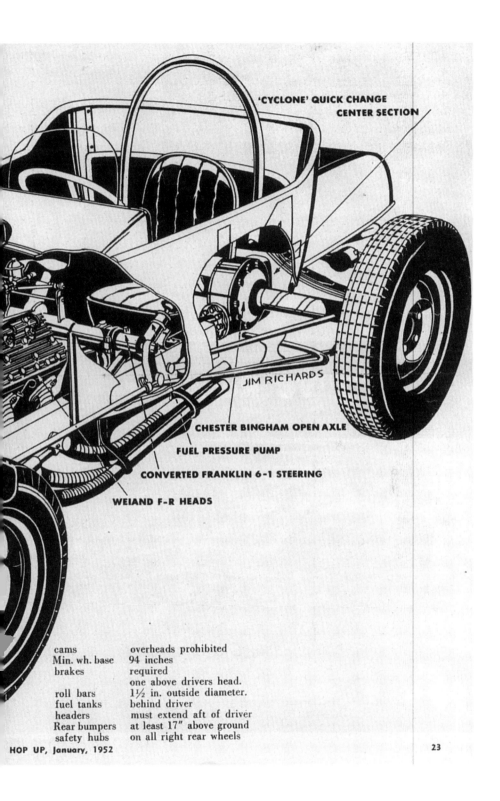

'CYCLONE' QUICK CHANGE
CENTER SECTION

JIM RICHARDS

CHESTER BINGHAM OPEN AXLE

FUEL PRESSURE PUMP

CONVERTED FRANKLIN 6-1 STEERING

WEIAND F-R HEADS

cams	overheads prohibited
Min. wh. base	94 inches
brakes	required
	one above drivers head.
roll bars	1½ in. outside diameter.
fuel tanks	behind driver
headers	must extend aft of driver
Rear bumpers	at least 17" above ground
safety hubs	on all right rear wheels

"T"V8 Roadster

Here's news for those who like to tinker, have some extra time, a little mechanical ingenuity . . . . *and* a fondness for old cars.

Tom Powels took this 1927 T Roadster and restored it to better-than-original condition . . . and you'll find that any ordinary genius can do the same.

After Tom found (and bought) a 1948 Mercury Army Staff sedan, he started tearing it down for the parts. And most of these parts went straight into the T.

It took all of Powels' thought and effort to fit the '48 Merc engine in the stock T body. He found the block had to be lowered into the frame at an angle and then lifted back into position. And he assembled the engine *after* the block had been bolted in place!

Next, Tom used the staff car's axle, column shift, transmission, hydraulic brakes and wishbone. Then he turned his back on the Merc to use a '36 Hudson steering unit; special, thick (four inch) radiator core, Lincoln wheels (rear) and Ford wheels (front); Navarro manifold and milled heads. Also in position Tom has a '40 Ford steering wheel, '34 Dago axle, dual pipes, and is running 6.00 x 16 front tires and 7.00 x 16 rear.

Not satisfied with one example, Tom Powels is hard at work on another '27 T (Merc

engine), a 1913 Ford Touring, and, to prove his love of the old timers, a 1910 "Torpedo" Model T. . .

"T" V8 Coupe

What is it? . . . Watcha got in it? . . . Wanna drag?

These are just a few of the queries that Bob Creech is confronted with every time he takes his '26 T coupe out for a spin. Imagine what *you* would think, if you were riding down the street and *swish* . . . a '26 T passed you as tho you were tied to a tree? You would probably (after the shock wore off) catch up with him and shout the same question. We did.

In answer he would say: "It's a 1926 model T Ford coupe. What have I got in it? Well . . . (deep breath) it has a 1938 Ford V-8 "60" engine, Edelbrock heads, 1940 Ford column shift, 1936 Ford rear end, model A wishbone, 1936 Ford axle, 1926 T springs, Kelsey wheels and drums, 1940 Ford steering wheel, 1936 steering, Hudson radiator core, sealbeam headlights, 1929 Gardner dash, 1936 Graham-Paige gas tank, 1940 Oldsmobile radio, 1941 Studebaker dome lights (that switch on when the door is opened), 1924 Packard door handles, and it's undersealed. I have between 1300 and 1500 dollars invested in it. The crank handle is fake and the top speed is around 85 mph." (Whew!)

One thing Bob forgot: he did all of the work, including the upholstery, and has been working on this jewel since 1949.

26

HOP UP, January, 1952

Readers Customs

My 1936 Ford sports a modified 1951 Merc. engine, Lincoln transmission gears and a 3.78 to 1 rear end.

The body is stock in height, features a metal top, shaved deck, restyled grille, (using ¼" welding rod), and molded fender-running board combination. The tail lights are 1936 Chrysler. Upholstering by J. J. Berfanger of Indianapolis.

Indianapolis, Indiana   Jerry McKenzie

I started with a '39 Ford convertible back and frame, my own ideas and designing, no drawn plans or specifications, a neighbor's garage, what tools I could borrow, and a lot of time and hard work. It took two years, eight months to build at a cost of $3000.00, not including my labor.

My '39 Ford was built with parts from Cadillac, Ford, Packard, Plymouth, Lincoln, Mercury, Willys, Pontiac, Chrysler, Buick, Kaiser, Frazer, Oldsmobile, Nash, Dodge, Chevrolet, Hudson, and De Soto, and also parts from Chevrolet and Ford trucks, including models from 1926 to 1951. There are parts from eight different cars on each door. The latches work by push-button mechanism and the windows by an electric-hydraulic system.

The gas tank flap is controlled by a button on the dash. The dash is a chrome-plated '41 Ford instrument panel.

Glen Allen, Virginia   Clarence L. Patterson

My car is a model T roadster body on a '32 Ford frame, with a '36 Ford engine, a ¾ cam, and heads. The engine and interior are chromed in every possible way . . . is upholstered in bright red leather and finish is metallic bronze. It was clocked at Linden, New Jersey at 117 mph.

Philadelphia 34, Pa.   Mr. William Casentino

28

This 1941 Plymouth has a completely sealed body, fadaway fenders, continentalized rear, with Stude Land Cruiser tail lamps. Grille is completely original, being made of Chevy, Pontiac, K-F and Dodge parts, large spinner is a '34 Dodge headlamp reversed. The dash is inlaid mirror . . . interior of white pleated leather. Has a 1948 Dodge engine with a full house of chrome.

Long Island, N.Y.   Hank Fredericks

My '37 Ford has $875 worth of work in it. Solid hood panels, Plymouth bumpers, whitewalls, Hollywood hubs, dual spotlights, license plate cut in rear, chrome eye-lids on lights, and 21 coats of black lacquer. Engine is a 1948 Merc. with Mallory coil and distributor, dual ignition, Edelbrock heads, Edelbrock camshaft, Lincoln transmission, and hydraulic brakes.

Chester, Pa.   Mr. Edward Buxton

My 1939 Ford Coupe has a '49 Merc grille, '48 Ford front bumpers, '50 Cad. fenders, '49 Cad bumper, '39 Buick spare tire cover, '51 Pontiac fender skirts, '49 Merc. steering wheel, '51 Nash dash panel, pipes with two Smittys.

Cad. fenders were shortened 20". Pontiac fender skirts fit perfectly . . . the bumpers were shortened 6½". Later on I will chop the top and extend front fenders. I paid $130 for the car and the way it stands today it has cost me $700.

Kenosha, Wis.   Domenick Jeardine, Jr.

The car, a 1935 Chrysler C-1 Airflow coupe, with 1948 Cad. fenders and rear bumper, was built up in early 1949 at Riverside, Calif.

The original hood has been filled, dechromed, and the grille has been shortened about 8 inches.

Engine is stock except for a 17" Smitty muffler, which incidentally, turned out to be quieter than the stock job on this car. Running boards were removed, and strips of Plymouth chrome, backed by steel plates, were installed to cover the running board mounts.

S.F., Calif.   Red Blanchard—KCBS-CBS

Custom Hints

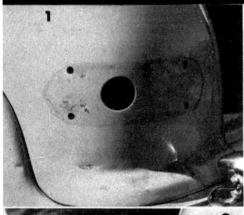

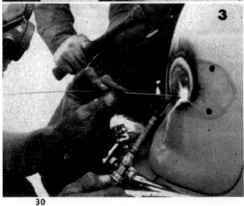

Let's talk about filling holes . . . . and don't make any cracks about using rocks . . . . it's holes in automotive bodies we're referring to. OK, so you don't have any holes in your car *now* . . . . you *will* have when you start to customize. Remove the stock taillights, rip off the chrome strips, take off the deck lid handle, and what's left? Holes . . . . little ones, big ones, and ugly ones. All of them must be filled up before the super paint job is slapped on so let's visit the Valley Custom Shop in Burbank where we can study the actual operations.

The car being worked on is a 1949 Mercury club coupe, but the same would apply to any make or model . . . . in fact, the finished examples are various types.

Filling taillight holes—Remove the taillight assembly and fill in all small holes by welding. Cut and fit a patch to fill the large holes as shown in figure 2, making sure that none of the patch overlaps surface level. After welding in place, beat the weld to a smooth finish by heating (cherry red) a 1″ to 1½″ section at a time and working with hammer and dolly. If carefully done, this process (which should be applied to welds on small holes too) will eliminate traces of the weld on the finished job. Next, file the patched area to smooth finish, picking any low spots with a pick hammer. We are now ready for surfacing and painting.

Filling deck lid holes—Remove deck lid chrome, handle, lock, license plate bracket, nameplate, and any other ornamentation on this be-cluttered panel. Cut away the interior paneling under the holes to be filled, this makes it possible to work from both sides. Remove and discard the brace which is spot-welded to both inside and outside panels of deck in the area of the lock and handle. Weld all small holes closed and fill in large hole with same proceedure as used for filling taillight holes. Now, carefully weld the inner panel in place to give the deck strength. Install the latch and connect a cable to the lock so that it may be operated from front seat. (Note: This

30

installation will be described in an early issue). You are now ready to surface and paint a really elegant deck lid.

1. These are the holes to be filled when the taillight has been removed.
2. A sheet metal patch is cut and fitted into place. Note that patch is fitted to inside of hole and does not lap over edges.
3. Patch is now welded in place.
4. The large hole in this deck has been filled using same procedures as shown in figures 2 and 3. Weld is now being hammered.

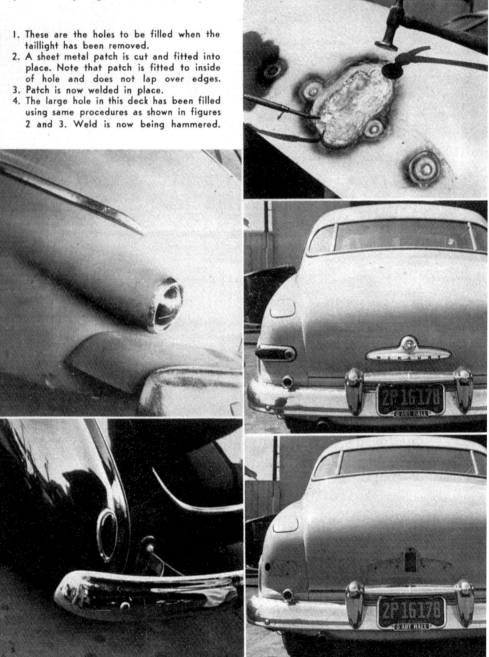

BSA
Road Test

BSA's bid for the lightweight market, the 125 cubic centimeter "Bantam," appeared in this country about a year ago. Its popularity was immediate.

It was my pleasure the other day to have one of these machines at my disposal; to report to you readers my comments and observations on this Bantam from Birmingham (the initials BSA stand for Birmingham Small Arms, world's largest manufacturer of motorcycles).

At Milne Brothers Motorcycle Shop (1951 E. Colorado Blvd., Pasadena), Cordy Milne led me to the rear of the shop where he was fueling up the "Beezay." The first novel feature that struck my eye was the oil measuring spout connected to the under side of

32

the gas cap (as with two-stroke engines, it is necessary to mix a small amount of oil with the gasoline). The engine came to life on my second kick and purred contentedly while warming up. A compression release was found on the handlebars, but was unnecessary 'when starting. Shifting is by foot lever with low gear being at the bottom end of the scale. Second and third cogs are engaged by lifting the shifting lever with one's toe. A gear indicator is visible on the left side of the bike.

Thru city traffic the Bantam's light weight of 160 pounds made maneuvering especially easy. Acceleration was good enough to get the jump on traffic leaving a stop stgnal, and in low gear the bike would creep down to a snail's pace if the situation demanded it. The smoothness of the BSA's engine was impressive and comparable to most vertical twins. Riding position was surprising for a man of my "six feet plus" frame, and there was no feeling of "rider's cramp" so evident on some machines. A detachable bracket under the seat made possible a two inch lower seating position for a shorter rider.

On the open road the Bantam cruised effortlessly at 40 to 45 mph . . . top speed was in the neighborhood of 50. However, on a long grade it was necessary to backshift into second. Front forks were telescopic and a little on the hard side . . . may have been due to newness.

Front and rear brakes were adequate but could be improved for quicker stops. The control cables were exceptionally husky and should last almost the life of the machine. This particular Bantam was fitted with a rigid frame, but I would just as soon pay

the slight additional price for the spring frame model.

Some of the *Hop Up* staff were eager to ride this BSA . . . several of them gave it a whirl around the block. All were impressed by its ease of handling. Only trouble encountered on the day's run was a fouled spark plug.

Summing up: The BSA Bantam was a most enjoyable mount and equally suited for beginning or experienced rider; for utility or pleasure. Yes, sir, this is one Bantam that can roost in my garage any day.

Features I liked:

Quality workmanship.
Clean lines and design.
Integrally housed engine and transmission.
Smoothness of engine.
Maneuverability.
•Riding position and variable adjustment of the saddle.

Features I disliked:

Difficulty of finding neutral.
Wide ratio gears (would like a 4-speed close-ratio transmission, if engineering wouldn't make price prohobitive).
Brakes.

Collins personally supervises...

Meet the Advertiser

Latest equipment is used at Harmon & Collins.

270

Everything in its place.
Cams...cams...and more cams.

Because of the current interest in cams, this month *Hop Up* visits Harman and Collins, one of the foremost cam grinders in the U.S. Harman and Collins have ground cams for everything from motorcycles to Allison aircraft engines (which were used in boat record attempts). While the firm is perhaps best known for their highly successful efforts in the landspeed field, it is also true that among boats their success has been outstanding. Many are the record breakers who have relied on Harman and Collins. And we must not overlook magnetos. Those turned out by this firm are known thruout the world.

Especially in the small displacement class, most power boats rely on Harman and Collins for peak performance. As you can see, from the interior photographs, the machine shops maintain unsurpassed standards for cleanliness and the well known phrase "you can eat off the floor" is literally true . . . . visitors always carry this impression as their most outstanding. However, it can be truthfully said that workmanship standards are just as high, all cams and magnetos being subject to extremely rigorous tests before final O.K. is given.

At the rear of the magneto final assembly department, cams are prepared for mailing.

Eddie Miller's Pontiac 6 engined lakester turned 139.103 first run.

SCTA

In spite of the poor surface condition of El Mirage Dry Lake, the records continue to fall. Tom Beatty, in his supercharged Merc-engined belly tank (*Hop Up*, Dec. '51), broke the all-time, one-way speed record for the California dry lakes, by clocking 181.451 mph.

Tom Cobbs set a new "D" class modified coupe record at 148.210 mph. His car also was powered by a supercharged Mercury.

Until recently the "flat-head" boys had things pretty much their own way in lakes competition; but since Bonneville, the overhead valve engines . . . in the form of Ardun-Ford set-ups and converted GMC light truck engines . . . are giving them fits. With more U. S. manufacturers converting to ohv V-8s, the faster competition cars will probably be switching from L-heads to rocker arms soon.

Bob Reise at the wheel of the Reise and Kaylor "B" modified roadster. Members of the Gear Grinders club, they turned 135.351 mph for second spot. Instead of using a radiator, the water is pumped thru the tubular frame.

36

Tom Cobbs' "D" modified coupe took first place, a record at 148.270 mph. The bubble (?) on the hood covers 4 Strombergs and a "Gimmy" Roots type blower.

Al Schirmeister of the Glendale Sidewinders with his V-8 60 tank.

Holden Bros. "B" class modified roadster. (S. D. Road Ramblers)

Barton & Frostrom "B" coupe received first place winner's trophy.

V-8 60 "A" class lakester entered by C. W. Scott of the "Hornets" club turned 134.128 for second.

What d'you think?

In the December issue of Hop Up Barney Navarro wrote an article against the use of "hot mixtures." How do you feel about that? What do you think about establishing a new class limited to gas?

FRED LARSON
"I think it's a darn good idea. It certainly would be practical for the average guy. I spend around twenty bucks a meet *now*, where if it was gas it would only be a couple of bucks. It's not only the money, but the chance a guy takes in blowing up his engine every time he runs it. There are a lot of guys I know who use their cars just for transportation and I'm quite sure *they* would run if there was such a class. There's no use running *now*, they would be just up against guys who *could* afford fuel and take the risks involved. Of course there are lots of guys who drive to the lakes on gas, and switch to fuel, which takes a lot of time. Wouldn't it be easier to simply come to the lakes and run? Yep . . . I'd sure like to see such a class."

BOB THOMAS . . .
"Yeah! I think it's a swell idea . . . if it were possible. I don't know why it wouldn't be, tho. I've heard that the Santa Barbara "Drags" have two classes; one for gas and one for "mixtures" and they say it's working out good. I think the average income guys will be for it, but there's always a group of "radicals" who are against anything. Then there are those who have the time and the money to tinker with fuels . . . or anything *else* they desire. As for me, I can't . . ."

JACK STECKER . . .
"Well, the way I feel about it is this: If a guy is going to travel this distance to run his car he might as well go all out! I know for myself . . . I want to go fast and if a mixture will make me go fast, then that's for me! If a guy wants to run gas then let him go to a drag race! A guy goes thru a lot of trouble and expense just to see how fast his car will go . . . We don't get money for running up here. All we get is trophies . . . and on MY trophies I want the fastest time my roadster can do. I don't want to have to say ". . . and that was on gas!'"

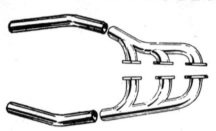
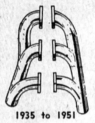

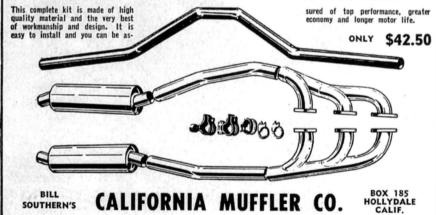

NOTE: The three finished example photos in the article "Custom Hints" on page 35, December Hop Up, were taken by Marcia Campbell, and the body work was by the Barris Kustom Shop, Lynwood, California.

SUBSCRIBE TO HOP UP TODAY!

HURRY! HURRY!
TIME IS RUNNING OUT TO GIVE A
HOP UP
SUBSCRIPTION FOR CHRISTMAS

**HOT RODS   CUSTOMS
MOTORCYCLES   RACING
SPEEDBOATS**

If it can be hopped up, it'll be in HOP UP ....

only $1.50 for next 12 issues

□ **SHALL WE SEND GIFT CARD ?**

HOP UP
BOX 110, GLENDALE, CALIF.

□ ENCLOSED FIND $1.50 FOR ONE YEAR HOP UP. SEND TO
(PLEASE PRINT)

NAME ....

ADDRESS ....

CITY... ZONE............... STATE.....................

FROM

NAME ....

ADDRESS ....

CITY... ZONE............... STATE.....................

In Case You Haven't Already Subscribed, Get One Yourself.

□ ENCLOSED FIND $2.75. PLEASE SEND ME HOP UP TOO.

43

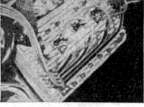
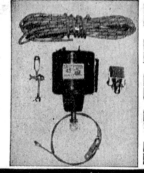

44

280

HOP UP

15¢

Airoadster — See Page 20

Drag Races — Pages 18 and 30

FEB.
1952

15¢

Forrest Water-Cooled Motorcycle...see page 26

TECHNICAL TIPS

TAIL LIGHT '49 STUDE CHAMP

I have a 1949 Stude Champ, 2-door sedan. The car is very light in the rear. What should be done about this? What can be done to substantially increase power and speed? The car has overdrive . . . would that and the standard gear be good enough with increased power you recommend? If I hop up the Champ, will it stand up under general usage?
Richland, Wash.   T. B. Mitchell

You can't do anything about the light rear end. It's your duty to complain to the factory. For more power and speed, there is no better source than Frank Morgan, Marysville, California. Write for his catalog. It is not necessary or advisable to change the 4.55 axle or overdrive unit. The Champion is a rugged little engine, but, of course, notoriously "rough." It will stand hopping up, but it certainly doesn't get any quieter or smoother in the process. Also don't expect any more pulling power on hills—the engine is just too small for a car which in 1939 weighed 2500 lbs. at the curb, and now is almost 500 lbs. heavier.—Tech. Ed.

125 MPH '36 FORD SEDAN

I have a 1936 Ford 4-door sedan that I would like to hop up. Would like it to do a good 125 mph and I'm willing to pay the cost.
Glendale, Calif.   Clifford Noa

To get 125 mph at the lakes from a '36 Ford sedan will require an all-out job on the engine to get 200 plus horsepower.—Tech Ed.

JIMMY AND CHEVY WEDDING

I have a 1940 Chevy special in very good condition with exception of engine. Can I install either a 1948 - '50 Chevy or any GMC above 1940? Have been told Chevy has not adopted inserts in the rods as yet. Is this true? Also want to install another transmission from another year Chevy or GMC to giver a higher top speed but retain Chevy pick-up.
Norfolk, Virginia   R. F. Johnson

If I had a '40 Chevrolet, less engine, I'd install a 270 GMC engine. The Chevrolet transmission will fit and you have to move the radiator core forward about two inches.
Chevrolet still does not use insert rods, and there is no choice on transmission except Chevrolet, since there has been no change in ratios from 1937 to date. You can use a '39 to '48 Ford transmission case, with either Ford or Zephyr gears, by using the McBar adapter. This gets expensive because you also have to adapt the Chevrolet torque tube ball to use Ford parts at the rear of the transmission.
You should have California Bill's Chevrolet Speed Manual. This describes in detail how to install the GMC in a Chevrolet, as well as how to hop-up the GMC, advice on rear ratios, etc. —Tech. Ed.

COMPRESSION RATIO AND MANIFOLD

I plan to build up a Merc engine for '50 Mercury. Have a '48 (59-A) block with a '49 Merc crankshaft and a three-quarter grind cam. The block is bored to 3-5/16 and is ported and relieved. Also plan to buy a 12-lb. flywheel and J.E. full-skirt racing pistons. I would like to know what compression ratio to use and difference between "regular" and "super" type manifolds. Would a "super" help acceleration?
Los Angeles, Calif.   Paul Cote

If you are running this car on the street, I would say that 9 or 9½ to 1 would be about as high as you can go on compression ratio and still have any reliability in conjunction with performance.
Most heads have the compression ratio stamped on them but you must realize that this is figured on a stock block. With your stroke and bore, a 7½ to 1 head would probably come out about 9 - 1 in the final ratio.
The regular type manifold will give much more performance in the lower speed ranges but the super will work better at higher speeds. Also, the regular manifolds with heat risers will be a little smoother around town, will warm up quicker in the morning and will give a little more economy. A super will definitely help acceleration but it is debatable whether it will be better than a regular.—Dean Batchelor

TIRE SIZES

What tire sizes are most commonly used on hot rods for street, dry lake, or track use?
Alburtis, Pennsylvania   E. W. Batterson

The tires most commonly used on the front of roadsters are 5.00 x 16, either Firestone or Ward's Riverside Ribs. The next size in order of preference is 5.50 x 16. Rear tires are generally 7.00 x 16, with some 6.50 x 16. Some of the boys are switching to 15-inch wheels, in which case they use 5.50 x 15 in front and 7.00 x 15 in the rear.—Dean Batchelor

(Continued on page 42)

2

If it's hopped up, it'll be in HOP UP

H O P U P

PROGRESS

In the past few months two important landmarks in the path of American two-wheel and four-wheel sporting competition progress have been passed . . .

(1) The Southern California Timing Association invited motorcycles to run along with cars at the highly successful 1951 Bonneville Lakes Meet; (2) three roadsters were invited by the California Sports Car Club to compete with sports cars at the Del Mar Road Race.

The roadster owners did not run (they felt not enough time was available to prepare their cars for an event totally different from anything in their past experience) . . . they "took a rain check" and expressed a desire to run next time.

And now, the SCTA Rules Committee has proposed to its membership that motorcycles and foreign cars be allowed to join up and run in all 1952 events . . .

Hop Up congratulates the progressive thinkers responsible for these invitations and proposals and offers its full support to all who are working for a closer understanding and friendship between motorcycles and cars . . . and among the various automotive categories.

1952 CATALINA GRAND NATIONAL

Probably the most successful motorcycle event of the year was the road race held (May 1951) on the beautiful Island of Catalina, just 27 miles towards Hawaii from Los Angeles Harbor. Thru the cooperation of enthusiast-sportsman William P. Wrigley, the people of Avalon, and the American Motorcycle Association, the race will be run again this year on May 3rd and 4th. The race course has been reworked to give both spectators and riders a better weekend of watching and riding. If properly developed, the Catalina Grand National will become one of the world's greatest motorcycle events.

EDITORIAL STAFF

Editor ....Oliver Billingsley
Technical Editor...... ....John R. Bond
Associate Editors...............................Louis Kimzey
      Robert Dearborn
Staff Photographers............................Gene Trindl
      Ralph Poole, Jerry Chesebrough
Photographers............Bob Canaan, Joe Al Denker

PRODUCTION STAFF

Managing Editor...................W. H. Brehaut, Jr.
Production Manager..........................Louis Kimzey
Art Director.............................-..............Jack Caldwell

ADVERTISING

Advertising Manager......................William Quinn
Southern California........................Dean Batchelor
Motorcycles....................................Bill Bagnall
United Kingdom.......................Kenneth Kirkman
      2 Longcroft Avenue
      Banstead, Surrey, England
Italy ....Michele Vernola
      C.P. 500
      Milano, Italy

CORRESPONDENTS

Italy ....Corrado Millanta

Vol. 1, No. 7   February, 1952

CONTENTS

HOP UP is published monthly by Enthusiasts' Publications, Inc., 540 W. Colorado Blvd., Glendale, California. Phone CHapman 5-2297. Entered as second class matter at the post office at Glendale, California, under the Act of March 3, 1879. Copyright 1951 by Enthusiasts' Publications, Inc. Reprinting in whole or in part forbidden except by permission of the publishers.

Subscription price $1.50 per year thruout the world. Single copy 15c.

Change of address—must show both old and new addresses.

HOP UP, February, 1952   3

NO MIRACLES!

By Barney Navarro

There is no easy path to high horsepower. No gadget or item of speed equipment will convert your sluggish family bus into a "supersonic rocket". If such things did exist, Detroit would use them and save millions of dollars. The power output of an engine is governed by sound engineering principles dependent on physics and chemistry, not witchcraft.

The hopping up of an engine consists of improving the two basic factors which govern the horsepower rating, namely, torque (twisting ability) and RPM (revolutions per minute, engine speed). Any change that improves one or both of these factors, without sacrificing too much of the other, will raise the horsepower rating of an engine. If torque is doubled and RPM remains constant, horsepower will be doubled. The same holds true for RPM, if it is doubled with the same amount of torque, horsepower is again doubled. Such conditions rarely if ever exist in actual practice but are only used as an illustration. Actually, torque drops off considerably at the point where maximum horsepower is developed but the percentage of drop is less than the percentage of RPM increase.

In the majority of cases, when the hop up treatment is applied to the family bus, torque increases are desired. Such increases aid acceleration and hill climbing ability in top gear. On the other hand, the performance of the family car will meet with great disfavor if the hopping up process leaves it with less hill climbing ability and acceleration in top gear. This condition can be, and is quite often, brought about by making changes that increase RPM but reduce torque. Why, you may ask, do we lay so much stress on torque? Simply this, horsepower is totally dependent on two factors, torque and RPM. The only way that horsepower can be developed thru an RPM increase without a torque increase, is by changing to a lower rear end gear ratio. Of course, the majority of enthusiasts will object to this type of change because they like to limit their alterations to the engine only.

If you wish to add a single item of speed equipment to help you pull a trailer coach, don't choose a race-grind camshaft as that item. This may sound silly but it is being done occasionally. There is no race cam grind on the market that can improve the pulling ability of a stock engine. Some modified cams do less to destroy the original pulling ability . . . . but none of them improve it (stock passenger car camshafts are designed to produce maximum torque without too great a maximum HP sacrifice). Of course, if you wish to change your rear end gear ratio from 4 to 1 to 5 to 1 in order to take advantage of the higher peak RPM, this will help you pull the house trailer, by developing more horsepower at the same road speed.

Race-type cams are equipped with valve timing that enables an engine to get a heavier charge of fuel at high RPM. This is accomplished by holding the valves open longer. The intake stroke of an engine has a duration of 180° when considering the piston travel only, but the intake valves are kept open much longer. There are many reasons for this longer duration, but one of the main ones is due to the fact that the fuel mixture has inertia. In other words, it is difficult to get the flow started into the cylinder as the piston starts down on the induction stroke and, at the other end of the stroke, the fuel has enough momentum at high speed to continue flowing even after the piston starts traveling upwards. This momentum increases with RPM so the intake valve can be left open longer with a high RPM engine. Of course, the long valve duration will cause some of the fuel to be pumped back into the induction system at low engine speed. This will cause the engine to develop less horsepower at low speed with race timing than stock timing. Everyone wants a cam that will produce maximum acceleration and maximum horsepower but you can't "have your cake and eat it too".

The simplest change causing the most effective torque improvement can be attained by installing high compression heads. This makes a very noticeable improvement because pulling ability is increased the most in the driving range between 30 and 50 mph. But again we cannot accomplish miracles by this change alone. Many fantastic claims have been made for compression increases but the small increase in ratio that is possible with a passenger car will rarely, if ever, raise the horsepower more than 10%. The low octane rating of pump gas limits the compression ratio of L-head (side-valve) passenger car engines to 8 or 8½ to 1. These ratios are only made possible by the use of aluminum alloys in the manufacture of high compression heads. Aluminum has a faster rate of heat conductivity, consequently, the surface of the combustion chamber is kept cooler during the early part of the combustion cycle, the period where detonation takes place. By keeping the chamber cooler, the tendency toward detonation and pre-ignition is reduced. Even with the use of aluminum, higher ratios than those outlined above will cause detonation and pre-ignition.

Another item of speed equipment about which many misconceptions center, is the dual intake manifold. The misinformation surrounding this item is almost as bad as the impossible expectations of a cam. "Doesn't a dual manifold use more gas," most people will ask? This question cannot be answered with a simple yes or no but the answer is nevertheless a simple one. An engine requires just so much fuel to deliver a given amount of horsepower, so the addition of another carburetor won't make it consume more unless you place a greater power demand on the engine. Under increased power you will use more fuel because, after all, you are not going to get something for nothing. The basic reasons for installing a dual manifold are to get a more even fuel distribution and to improve the breathing ability of an engine . . . . the latter being the principal reason. Unlike the high compression head, a dual manifold does not improve the torque or horsepower output of the average engine unless it is turning more than 2000 rpm . . . . converted to miles per hour, this would be between 40 and 45 in top gear. The useful speed of the manifold is, of course, much lower in 1st and 2nd gear, which is self evident when accelerating thru the gears. At speeds over 15 mph in first gear the average Ford will have its acceleration improved by a dual manifold. However, maximum advantage is not derived from this unit until the engine is close to the RPM where maximum horsepower is developed. This horsepower increase will range between 7 and 8% with a Ford V-8 engine.

Big men are more powerful than little men, and it is the same with engines. A large engine has a better chance of producing high torque than a small one. Being that torque is still the factor in which we are most interested, increasing the size of an engine is the best way to effect an improvement. There is no single item of speed equipment that will make as much difference in torque as is gained by boring a Ford V-8 to 3⅜" and stroking it ⅜ of an inch. This procedure will add 57 cubic inches to the displacement of the engine and will allow your car to climb hills in high gear that it used to struggle on in second. Now that the ideal has been illustrated, you are probably wondering about the disadvantages. As is always the case when you reach for the best, cost rears its ugly head. Fifty-seven cubic inches will cost you $234.00 for parts and services even if you do all of the work of disassembling and assembling.

Magicians may pull rabbits out of hats, but horses are a much bigger problem.

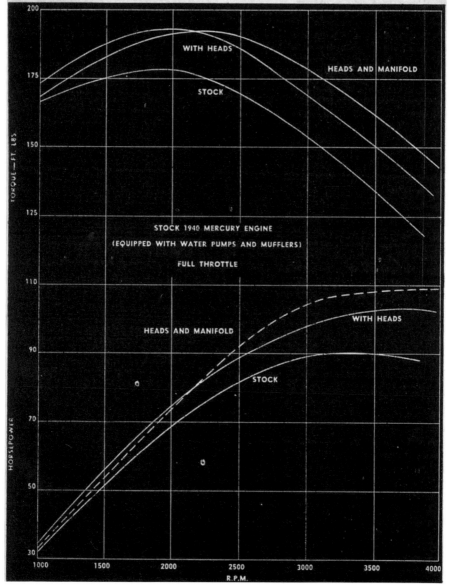

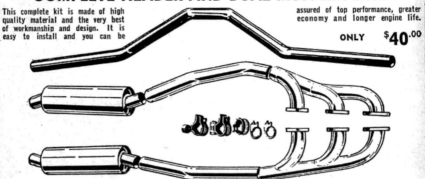

Ralph Jilek's 1940 Ford

This month's custom is the proud possession of Ralph Jilek of North Hollywood, California. The sleek black '40 Ford convertible was built at the Valley Custom Shop in Burbank under Ralph's direction.

To make for lowness and yet more ground clearance than the average custom car, a 4-inch section was taken out of the body above the fender line. This gave the car a slim, lengthened-out look, but it was still not low enough.

The next step was to kick up the frame 5 inches in the rear and install a dropped axle in front. While this work was being done, the springs were sent out to have the eyes reversed, and the front spring was de-arched 1 inch.

At this point, Jilek discovered the front wheels rubbed on the fenders when a turn was made up an incline (such as entering a gas station or driveway). The wheel openings in the front fenders were then raised 2 inches to correct this situation.

To finish the outside of the car, the deck lid was filled and the hood shaved before adding the peak which can be seen in the photograph.

Not being satisfied with the stock '40 instrument panel, Ralph altered it to accommodate six Stewart Warner instruments (tachometer, speedometer, oil pressure, water temperature, fuel gauge, ammeter) and a 1950 Ford radio.

The windshield frames and garnish molds are chrome and an addition below the garnish mold on each side blends into the instrument panel. The blue and white upholstery (leatherette) by Floyd Tipton of Burbank will complete the interior as soon as Tipton has tailored the rug floor mat.

* Bumpers: '46 Chevy; license plate brackets: '49 Chevy; tail lights: '41 Studebaker Champ.

Custom of the Month

291

Chuck Crawford in Chevrolet 4 rear-engined modified roadster.

S.C.T.A.

The Southern California Timing Association brought the 1951 season to a dusty conclusion at Goldstone dry lake, 25 miles north of Barstow, California.

Credit should go to SCTA for a good try, even tho the event was not as successful as was originally hoped. The 20-mile dirt road leading into the lake couldn't have been worse, and the lake itself—even tho it seemed a better place than worn-out El Mirage—turned out to be too soft.

As the cars began to run thru the traps,

they soon chopped the course so badly it became almost unusable.

Speeds were further hindered by a direct, 25 mph headwind.

To change the course around, allowing the cars to run with a tailwind, would have taken too much time, besides making it difficult for the faster cars (belly-tanks, etc.) to get stopped in the available length of the course.

In spite of all the adverse conditions, a rigid inspection by the technical committee

Paul Scheifer getting underway in his red '27 T modified roadster.

Bob McClure in his "D" Class Lakester.

made it a good meet from a safety standpoint.

As the season ended, Jim Lindsley and Burke Le Sage came out on top in point standings, thus earning the right to carry the numeral 1 on their coupe next season. You'll find No. 2 used by Ak Miller, while Earl Evans will be No. 3 and Bill Likes No. 4.

Club standings found the Road Runners with the most points, and the Glendale Sidewinders (last year's champs) 2nd with the Glendale Stokers 3rd.

Whiteman's modified roadster turned 110.867.

Marvin Whiteman's engine—stock except for magneto, manifold, and oxygen injection.

New engine in Mailliard & Cagle's '34 coupe with Ardun overheads and Howard fuel control. Water hoses go to storage tank in rear.

Running as a guest from Bell Timing Association, Walker-Rounds turned 120.805 mph.

Sawyer leading Selva. Races are run under bridges.

The Milano Free-for-All or Grand Prix in which **Alter Ego** was to run was advertised as a 12-lap race (15 miles). The Europeans immediately demonstrated the wonderful sportsmanship that so impressed Paul Sawyer. Knowing that the American boats are built for short races, they questioned that **Alter Ego** could run the distance on a tank of fuel. Paul had installed an 11 gallon tank, the largest he could get into the boat, and he felt if he could run ten miles with a smaller tank he could make 15 miles with the larger tank. His hosts suggested that it would be better to be on the safe side, so they promptly shortened the race to 10 laps (12½ miles). Racing rules too differ considerably from those used in America. Where we use four minute balls, targets, or lights to indicate time before the starting of the clock, the Europeans use five and the fifth one remains in sight while the clock is running. Paul remarked that he liked this system and thought that in many instances it would assist the driver. The green flag (indicating the last lap) is not used in Europe, but after a rules discussion with Sawyer, the green was used at Milan—another instance of Italian cooperation. The starting line disqualification rule is also different. If you jump the gun by four seconds (or less) you may return and restart; or failing to do so, 20 seconds will be added to your total elapsed time for each second you were ahead of the gun. If ahead of the clock by over five seconds, you are disqualified.

At Milan, Paul says the water was fairly smooth except for the lumpy run-back from the seawall. He made a perfect start next to the buoy, took the lead and that was the boat race. Second and third were two Italians, Mario Verga and Ezio Selva, followed by Frenchmen, E. Eminente, Louis Delacour and Maurice Bouchet. Both Verga and Selva drove Abbati hydroplanes manufactured in Como, Italy, powered with the popular B.P.M. racing engine. Piston displacement is 2800 cc with BMW type cam and push rod arrangement, single cam and overhead valves, hemispherical combustion chambers, domed

Paul Sawyer
By Kent Hitchcock

pistons, forged con rods, fully machined counterbalanced crankshaft and magneto ignition. Technically this is a wet sump engine with a very deep pan and a powerful pump, but actually it has dry sump operation with the deep pan replacing any separate oil tank. The engine comes (from the factory) with 2 carburetors and developing about 160 hp. As used by Selva (14 to 1 compression, four carburetors) Sawyer believes the bhp would be in the neighborhood of 190 hp at 6000 rpm. The European boats carry no batteries . . . it takes a pair of great big heavy-duty 12 volters to start the engine. Factory equipment includes built-in thrust bearing, no clutch, 1-to-1 in-and-out gear and water pump (so engine can be run at dock). The batteries are plugged at dock and engine warmed up. When everything is set engine is turned off, water pump disengaged, gear engaged and engine started again. As boat leaves dock, battery lead-plugs pull out and engine is on magneto. Several boats in the 2800 class are using Ferrari V12 which Paul believes will be a very successful racing engine in the near future. The Alfa Romeo supercharged racing engine is not for sale, but it may be available soon.

Followers of American closed course racing would have been stunned at the race staged at Milan by the Marina Militare (Coast Guard). An 8 boat hydro team under a Commander was assigned to put on an exhibition. Extra buoys were placed about, changing the course to resemble a ski slalom run. Soon after the start Paul recalls boats going in and out of the buoys, with wonderful skill but with abandon and disregard for life and limb on which continental drivers flourish.

Sawyer's story of his International Circuit tour follows the deeds of Ezio Selva, whose **Musketeer** we described. Selva is in the silk business, as well as being a machine tool designer and manufacturer. He has his propellers forged from billet steel and has built a machine for grinding and finishing them. The props look pretty much like the American Hi J Racing prop, Sawyer says, except that they are a true screw. Paul's props were examined with interest but he noted a lack of enthusiasm (stemming from European lack of confidence in bronze props). Thinking to make a nice gesture, he posted as a prize a brand new Hi J prop and was a bit surprised to find that the winner thought so little of it that he fastened it to the wall with the rest of his trophies. "We must remember," Paul remarks, "that this is only the second season the Europeans have raced three pointers. Up to the time of Bob Bogie's tour of the continent last year, (225 job **Blitz 111**), most of their jobs were conventional hydros. Given another season, they will race with us on a par with the same type of hull and displacement."

Before the races at Turin, many parties were held. Paul recalls that Selva was always present. Arriving at the Turin pits, he passed Selva's hydro on the skids . . . HOLD ON! Something looked different and he returned for a closer look. Completely rebuilt . . . a beautiful job. The new underbody was practically a counterpart of **Alter Ego**. Sponsons had been shallowed off . . . riding surface narrowed and covered with dural plate, likewise the afterplane. A foot and a half had been cut from the length, a new strut of forged steel installed and a shortened shaft. The tail had been shortened and the whole rig beautifully refinished. After Paul examined the job, Selva shrugged his shoulders, raised his hands and smiled with that Latin gesture that simply means, "Well, there it is." How had he done this thing while attending all the functions? One of his mechanics remarked later that Selva hadn't

Would you like to view a boat race from this beautiful stadium . . . or dine at the sidewalk cafe in front of grandstand?

Win, lose or draw . . . good sports. Selva, after losing race, points out fast first turn made by Sawyer.

Selva out of water . . . like American hydros.

Sawyer running in rain . . . . forgot goggles. He is lapping another boat.

slept for three nights. Paul brought home a little piece of the plywood cut away from **Musketeer** in the modification. It is ¼ inch, 7 ply of birch and mahogany with a bit of a longitudinal hull member glued and copper riveted. Believe me, the glue job is superb. Those men can learn from us in design, but Paul says their construction is superb.

After the Milan Race, Paul says "The honeymoon was over. This fellow Selva was really going. Turin was a two-day meet with an 8 lap heat each day. It was quite rough with bump from a seawall on the mile-long straightaway with a dog leg. We had to pass under a bridge going and coming. I rode in third place for several laps. Selva and Verga both were driving like demons. I finally won both races but I knew I had been in a boat race."

The races at Zurich (Switzerland) wound up of the International Circuit for this year. The course was nearly a constant curve on one side, a half mile straight on the other, and a single-buoy turn on one end . . . ten laps, laid out on one shore of a large lake with choppy water and rollers. There were 8 start-

ers. It is interesting to read a translation (Italian into English) published in "La Gazzetta dello Sport": Headline: MOTOR BOAT RACING . . . SAWYER IN ZURICH ONCE MORE . . . and the subhead: The Italians Were Exceptionally Good.

"ZURICH—8. The second day of the Nautical International Meeting in Zurich ended late in the evening. It so happened that the American Sawyer who took part in the last race of the day, the motorboat race, left like the other competitors a few seconds before the signal was given. This, according to the international rules, implies a fine of 20 seconds per each second acquired at the beginning. Sawyer, aware of this regulation, came back to the starting point after the first turn thus, losing almost 1½ minute. Then he went back into that race where he has shown to be the fastest, reaching the fantastic average of 102.992 KPH striving strenuously in front of the Italian Selva, who with an engine of 2800 cc, averaged 101.910 KPH; the American had also the famous 4½ litre Ford engine. We are sure that a boat powered with a 158 Alfa Romeo engine would have certainly changed

14

the results in favor of the Italian. Nevertheless we appreciated very much having Sawyer in the race."

Perhaps you are a bit puzzled about the references about the engine displacement. Obviously the reporter was saying in a polite way that Sawyer held a house cleaning with his 204 cu in. on the 172 cu in. Italian outfits . . . Lest you be a bit confused, let's remember that the BPM Racing Engine with that overhead set up is not a sewing machine. About the 158 Alfa Romeo that was mentioned . . . Paul says, "That is a real piece of racing machinery . . . it has a 'few' stages of supercharger and when they get that in a good hydroplane . . . just look out for some REAL speed."

We neglected to mention that in winning the Grand Prix at Milan, Paul broke all the records, turning a lap at 108.433 KPH against Achile Castoldi's existing record of 100.278 KPH. His new average for the race was 99.310 KPH against Castoldi's 96.021 KPH and Castoldi's records were set with the supercharged racing Alfa Romeo.

Paul and Erminie (Mrs. Sawyer) will treasure the prizes won on the continent, for these are not the enormous and gaudy monstrosities glittering with artificial gold plate, all too numerous in American Racing. The Sawyer's sweep of the International Circuit in Europe enriched their collection of over 200 cups with four beautiful sterling silver awards, dignified and a permanent remembrance of supremacy as the International Champion in the "Montonautico."

This yarn wouldn't be complete without the story of that beautiful gold chronometer that Paul is wearing (on dress occasions only, I think). Keeping a dinner engagement at Selva's apartment, the Sawyers were admiring their host's collection of boat racing trophies. In the center of the trophy case was the most beautiful gold wrist chronometer imaginable. Paul asked about the watch and was told that it was the first boat racing trophy Selva had won. Their host suggested that Paul take the watch out of the trophy case and examine it. After Paul and Erminie had admired the beautiful workmanship for several moments Selva suggested they turn it over and examine the back. Paul's own words best tell the rest of the story. "At first I was just conscious that there was engraving on the back . . . quite the usual thing on a trophy, of course. Then it occurred to me that the inscription would be in Italian. Suddenly two words leaped out of the inscription . . . those two words were "Paul Sawyer". Erminie says that I turned as white as a sheet and she thought I was going to keel over. She wasn't the only one that thought so . . . I did too. I glanced at Selva and his brother who were smilingly watching. It finally dawned on me that Selva was making me a present of his most prized trophy and that the engraving was an inscription to commemorate the gift. It was dated as of that particular day. I often wonder how Selva would have made the presentation if I hadn't asked to see the watch. This will always be one of my most prized posessions. I can't say enough about the wonderful treatment we received from every single person on the trip, including the contestants, officials, press, civil and military authorities and public."

I have neglected to mention just about a million things that the American boat fans always wants to know, such as prizes. In addition to the trophies, cash is paid on a standardized scale, but this scale is very different from our American system where all classes receive the same amount of money. Each class pays five places plus an added

The Sawyer racing team.

Clay Smith and Paul working on engine.

Paul's helpers, while trying for class X outboard record. L. to R., Forest "Bud" Lundy, Jack Mitchell and Sawyer.

Getting speeches the hard way. Interpreter whispering in Sawyer's ear.

amount to each of the other starters that **finish** the race, (not that **start** the race—as appearance money is often paid here.) Here is a run down of the classes, giving the first and fifth place prizes followed by the appearance money. Second to fourth place are the usual graduation from the highest to the lowest prize. Note: 100,000 lire is about $160.00.

					Appearance
Class X Outboard	70,000	down to	12,000		8,000
Freefor-All	100,000	down to	20,000		10,000
2800 cc Inboard	60,000		10,000	10,000	
Class cc Outboard	40,000		8,000	5,000	
Class A Outboard	25,000		6,000	3,000	

The comedy highlight of Paul's trip came when he arrived back in New York. After literally carrying the tow-ball for the trailer hitch in his hand thruout the tour, always looking but never finding a way to make use of it . . . he couldn't find it when they disembarked and had to go out and buy one in order to tow **Alter Ego** away from the steamship dock. The only racing Paul had done this season was his four victorious starts in Europe and he is now readying **Alter Ego** for the Salton Sea Regatta. Naturally, he would like to have the five mile 225 Class record* back (he lost it while abroad) and he isn't satisfied with the one mile mark.* It's a pretty good bet that Champion Paul Sawyer will be right out in front.

* Last month, Paul set a new mile record of 120.085 mph and a five mile record of 87.890 mph.—Ed.

Felix Del Porto (Lodi, California) "takes" another Olds (background) with winning time of 72.5 mph.

Kingdon Drags

San Jose Gearjammers' car clocked over 100 mph...Mrs. R. P. McKinney (Redwood City) expresses club's enthusiasm.

"A speed enthusiast's dream" . . . wrote Officer Ezra Ehrhardt of the California Highway Patrol in a letter to *Hop Up* magazine, describing the first Kingdon drag meet. The event (he went on to say) was held at Kingdon airstrip, located 9 miles north of Stockton and 4 miles west of Lodi, California.

The asphalt strip is 8/10th of a mile long and 150 feet wide, with an asphalt return strip, parking and pit area. There were 1196 paid admissions and a total of a 147 vehicles registered. Altogether 330 runs were made thru the electric-eye timer.

Sanctioned by the Valley Timing Association, timed by Al Clark, and promoted by Bill Hunefeld, this was one meet that was destined to be a perfect event . . . it was!

Cycles dig out at starter's signal.

18

Eldon Lange's "lightweight" took
its class trophy — 106 mph.

Oakland Clutch Busters promise to
return and avenge their rear-engined
conversion's defeat by Lange's car.

Before bright red paint job . . .

Norm Taylor (seated) and Jot Horn are the proud owners of this unusual roadster.

Airoadster

In the October *Hop Up* you read an article on the "Airoadster." The opening line asked, "Will it 'go' or 'blow'?" And now we're here to tell you . . . it goes!

Norm Taylor and Jot Horn, after many months of work, have at last got the roadster into running condition and are consistently turning in the high nineties (last week: 105.26!) at the ¼ mile Santa Ana drag strip.

"The engine," the October issue went on, "is a six cylinder 250 hp Ranger. The single overhead cam acts with roller rocker arms, on inclined valves. Rods are steel 'I' beam. Twin mags take care of the electrical system. "The dry sump oil system has a 17 qt. capacity and is cooled by an oil radiator. The engine is mounted *upside down* and *backwards!* A crank connector was made for the prop shaft and fitted to a Ford flywheel.

"The engine plate was made to fit a '49-'50 Ford bell-housing, and a '39 Ford transmission (Zephyr gears) was adapted to that. The rear end is '32 Ford with shortened drive shaft and radius rods, and Halibrand quick-change center section."

Norm and Jot built a five carburetor (Type 48 Stromberg) manifold; installed '32 Ford steering and '46 Ford hydraulics. The tachometer hands fell off the first time out, so they installed a Stewart Warner tach. The engine has "tached" 4000 rpm, but develops most of its power between 2000 and 3500. The bore is 4⅛ inches, with a 5½ stroke, for a total of 441 cubic inches . . . and a weight of 370 lbs.

A '27 T body on a '32 frame brings the entire roadster poundage to 1600. It has a dropped and filled front axle and split wishbones.

So now, after eight months' of work and approximately $800, Norm and Jot have one of the most outstanding and original roadsters in America. When asked if they had any "outside" help they would like to mention, they both replied almost in unison, "Yea, we'd like to thank our boss Roy Richter" (owner of Bell Auto Parts). And in conclusion, *Hop Up* would like to commend Norm and Jot not only for their ingenuity but also their trail-blazing in building a completely *different* roadster.

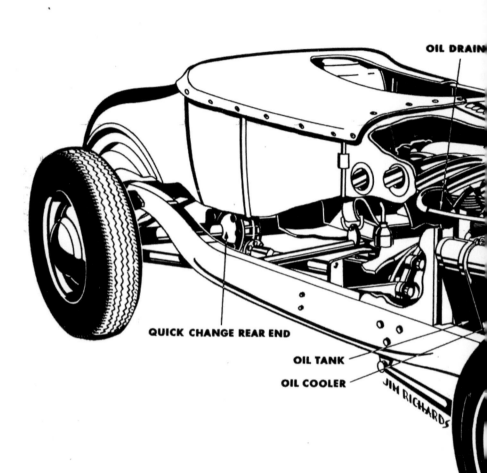

OIL DRAIN

QUICK CHANGE REAR END

OIL TANK

OIL COOLER

JIM RICHARDS

Roadster of the Month

GER AIRCRAFT ENGINE

FIVE CARBURETORS

Custom Ford

306

Harold Scott of Richmond, California, has spent his spare time for the last six months reworking his car—with this clean 1949 Ford as the result.

Harold, with the help of a friend, lowered the top 4 inches, installed a 1951 Pontiac grille, frenched the headlights and channeled the body 3 inches.

After that, Scott and his buddy molded the rear fenders into the body, nosed (see page 36) and decked it and followed that with paint—a "mad" pink!

Harold Scott has a lot of credit coming, not only for his originality, but because he did all the work at his own home—with a total expense of only $300.

Oh, yes! He installed a *bar* in the back seat!

Forrest Water Cooled Cycle

Article & Photos by Bagnall

Undoubtedly one of the most interesting and original two-wheeled vehicles in this country is the four cylinder (in-line) water-cooled, lightweight motorcycle designed and built by Howard Forrest of the Mustang Motorcycle Corporation in Glendale, California. (Forrest also has another two-wheeled masterpiece, an Ariel "Square Four" engine fitted into a Mustang frame: October *Hop Up*.)

Howard was first inspired to build this bike when he sold his midget race car in 1936. Being keenly interested in anything mechanical, he needed a project he could work on, since he no longer had the race engine to tinker with. This was the era when the motor scooter was first coming into popularity, so Forrest thought that a water-cooled "four" would be a nice power plant for a scooter. Consequently, the next two and a half years were spent in machining and constructing this engine. Practically everything within the engine was handmade. The crankshaft was machined from solid bar stock. Tubular connecting rods were

The "power house". Kickstarter is located at front of engine. Skill involved to produce this "jewel" is evident in this photo.

made and fitted. Steel dies were made to cast the aluminum alloy pistons. Incidentally, the engine is of single overhead camshaft design. The cam, however, was ground by Ed Winfield.

The distributor, intake and exhaust manifolds were also built by Forrest. A Henderson-Four generator and a Zenith carburetor from a Le Roi engine were about the only ready-made pieces fitted. As Howard progressed to the upper end of the block, he was confronted with the problem of finding spark plugs small enough to fit the combustion chambers. Packard solved this problem for him by coming out with 10 mm plugs on their '37 models.

When the engine was finally completed—after many a moon of burning the midnight oil—it was fitted into a Salsbury frame with

the power plant located underneath the seat. After a while, Forrest, still feeling the need for perfection, commenced construction of a complete bike for his "jewel" to be mounted in. Another year was spent in building the balance of this pint-sized motorcycle. The tanks were from a '29 Indian 101 Scout, the frame was all hand-made as were various other components.

A two-speed transmission was built by Forrest and fitted with 90 degree bevel gears in order to transmit the power from the engine to the sprockets.

The surrounding photos will show you that Howard Forrest's project was totally successful, and this little bike is a testimonial to the ingenuity and craftsmanship of its owner.

Some interesting specifications and data:

Clean lines of engine speak for themselves. Note exhaust manifolds, water return manifold and gauge on crashbar.

Engine
  4 cylinder, water-cooled, overhead cam
    (chain driven)
  1¾" bore and 2" stroke
  19.2 cubic inches
  12 hp at 5500 rpm
  Forced feed lubrication
  Battery ignition
  ⅞" valves
  3 main bearing crankshaft (all babbitt poured)
  Aluminum alloy pistons

28

Interesting gearbox design. Power is transmitted at right angle thru bevel gears.

Radiator capacity ½ gallon
  Thermo-syphon cooling system
Transmission
  2-speed, foot shift
  90 degree power change by bevel
    gears
Gauges
  Temperature (180 degrees running
    temp.)
  Oil pressure (45 lbs. running pressure)
Approximately top speed—65 mph.

HOP UP, February, 1952

Santa Ana Drags

With drag racing becoming more and more popular thruout the nation, *Hop Up* thought its readers would be interested in visiting one of the original drag strips.

C. J. Hart, Frank Stillwell and Creighton Hunter held their first meet July 1, 1950, and it was such a huge success that they have held a meet every Sunday since. The course (as in most cases) is an emergency landing strip for a nearby airport.

The meet gets underway at ten in the morning and ends as the sun goes down in the evening. One of the best features of a drag race is that anyone with any type vehicle can run. All you have to do is pay your dollar . . . get inspected for safety requirements . . . get in line . . . and run! There are free helmets provided and cars can run thru the traps as many times as time allows. Cars *must* have bodies!

A few of the record holders are: Paul Leon, who holds the modified roadster record of 132.00 mph; Mailliard and Cagle's full-

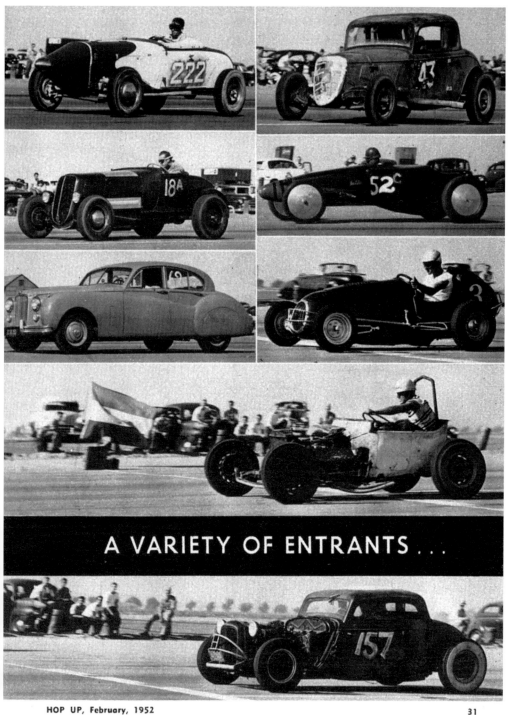

A VARIETY OF ENTRANTS . . .

313

Ready to roll.

Ken Droesbeke and Bob Funkhouser adjust carburetors in their coupe.

Sam Crooks, announcer

32

Ma, pa and Junior watch.

fendered coupe has that record with a 113.52 mph. Chet Herbert's cycle "The Beast" turned 135 mph to take the record. Harold Dawson in his full-fendered sedan holds *his* class with a 111.11 mph.

If you don't have a car or you're not interested in what your's will do, come on out to a drag race anyway. You'll find all types of hop ups running and with the commentators like Sam Crooks describing the cars and announcing their times . . . you'll have the afternoon of your life. One good example of the competitive spirit that prevails at all drag meets is when a Mr. Cagle of the "Dusters" club came up to me and asked if he could issue a challenge in *Hop Up*. I thought about it a second and said, "Sure, I guess so . . . what is it?"

"Well, the Dusters want to challenge *any* club in *any* association to a drag meet here at Santa Ana!"

So there's the challenge, what are *you* going to do about it?

Waiting their turn.

The Huth Muffler Company, altho new to mail order business, is one of the oldest muffler companies in California. Gerry Huth established his first small shop in Burbank in 1938 and after moving to better and larger locations 3 different times, he now owns and operates one of the most modern muffler shops in the country.

In addition to the Huth Custom Mufflers (which he manufactures in his Burbank plant), Huth also handles Belond Equa-flow headers, Mello-tone mufflers, Porter mufflers, Mallory ignitions, Stewart-Warner instruments, chrome accessories and Weiand speed equipment, plus a complete line of factory replacement stock mufflers and tailpipes.

Huth was a pioneer in the field of manufacturing custom mufflers of various tonal qualities . . . one of the first to supply his customers with any tone they desire on their cars: quiet, deep, mellow, rapper, etc.

"Your problem is our specialty." This is the slogan of the Huth Muffler Company.

Meet the Advertiser

Custom Hints

For the fourth in a series of articles on customizing your car, we have once again received full cooperation of the Valley Custom Shop (Burbank, Calif.). The subject this month: hoods.

One example shown here is a 1949 Merc which is relatively simple to fill. The holes are welded shut then filed down smooth. If a small area around the hole sinks while being welded, the sunken spot can either be filled with lead or hammered back out with a pick hammer before filing.

The '41 Ford hood presents a greater problem. The fill job has to run the length of the hood. The first step is to weld a few inches of the seam at the back of the hood and about 18 inches at the front. The two halves have been spot welded together at the factory but it is not sufficiently rigid to prevent flexing after the hood is filled.

Then, after the hood has been thoroly cleaned on each side of the seam, the metal is tinned and body lead applied. This is the spot where a lot of custom body men fall down on the job. *Cleaning* and *tinning* the surface properly so the lead will stick is of prime importance. Lead applied properly will last as long as the car but if it is applied improperly, you'll be lucky if it lasts two weeks.

The Valley Custom Shop uses very little lead. They prefer to weld joints or holes and after using hammer and dolly, file the surface smooth.

The exceptions: places where a dolly cannot be placed behind to hammer (such as windshield posts, when cutting a top; or Ford hoods, where the two halves are flange jointed instead of butt jointed).

36

HOP UP, February, 1952

What d'you Think?

The California Sports Car Club invited three roadsters from Southern California to compete with the sports cars in the road race at Del Mar, California . . . Russetta, S.C.T.A. and Bell Timing Associations, each entered a car.

How do you feel about the roadsters running with the sports cars?

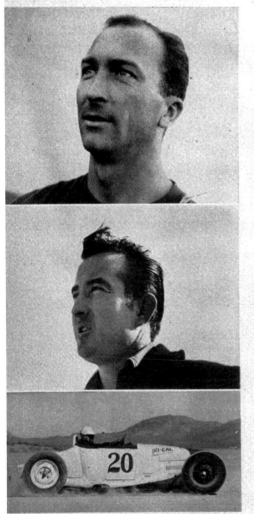

BILL LIKES

"I think it's a good idea, but, of course, there are complications . . . First of all, the roadsters are a highly specialized machine. For instance, the front end alignment is for straightaway running. The majority of us run with two-wheel brakes. The engines are tuned for hotter fuels than gas. Cooling is also designed for short runs . . . in other words, the lakes roadsters would require a lot of alterations to compete in that type of an event. If there had been more notice, the roadsters would have a better representation. How about an invitation to Pebble Beach?"

BILL DAILEY

"Great! It's a swell gesture on their part and I think it'll go far in improving the relationship between the roadsters and the sports cars. Of course, a roadster in reality is the American sports car and just because some people call them "hot rods" is no reason why they should be banned from competition. We may not do well this time, but with a little practice and time, we'll give 'em some stiff competition."

BILL BARKER

"I think it's great to run with the foreign cars. The roadsters won't handle as well in the turns, but I think they'll be faster on the straights. The only thing that will really hurt is the long distance of the race. Brakes not being as good and, of course, the cooling will be a problem. It'll be interesting tho and I sure hope we're invited to more races. I'd have got in this one, but I couldn't get running in time."

38

HOP UP, February, 1952

CORRESPONDENCE

SUSPENSION PROGRESS NEEDED

Barney Navarro's excellent article, "More Horses Thru Chemistry," was a concise and well-written criticism of an obvious and growing hazard and detriment to progress of the larger field of competition-car builders whose finances and "contacts" are limited. Furthermore, the special fuel path to higher output is contrary to the best benefits of design progress, as far as the public at large and transportation cars are concerned. For that matter, this single-minded concentration upon the straightway record type of car, frequently with no clutch, transmission, differential, front brakes or rear springs, is becoming farcial. Both car fanufacturer and hot rodders are losing sight of the greater need of progress in suspension and roadability brought about by faster autos, highways, and the increase of both.

Orinda, Calif.   M. H. Link

HUDSON TIPS

Being a Hudson enthusiast, I have collected some helpful tips for improving performance. Higher compression aluminum heads are available from Hudson factory, or use the 7.25:1 head which was optional on the 1941 model, series 10 Traveler Six, (3 x 4⅛), which must not be confused with the 3 x 5 Super Six.

Reground camshafts are available, and valve springs from a 1948 model Commodore Eight should definitely be installed. The breaker point gap should be set at .017 instead of the usual .020, and breaker spring tension increased. A richer mixture will increase top speed and aid spark advance. This can be accomplished thru the use of a richer metering rod.

An overdrive can always be installed, and if most of the driving is done in fairly level country, I would suggest a different rear axle ratio. The 1940 model 3 x 4⅛ size has a rear axle ratio of 4.55, which is more suitable for high speed driving in overdrive.

Alameda, Calif.   Paul E. Bricker

AUSTRALIAN PURSUIT RACE AGAIN

In reference to Mr. Willing's letter in your October issue, the term "Australian pursuit race" is an old bicycle racing expression. It refers to a race where two cyclists are matched on opposite sides of a track (one on the home stretch and one on the back stretch). The object of the race is to gain half a lap on your opponent—the first one to do so being declared winner—in races where the opponents are closely matched, a time limit may be set, the rider who has gained the most being the winner.

The term was introduced to this country around the turn of the century when Major Taylor (of Worcester, Mass.) who was world champion in 1901, 02, and 03, visited Australia and ran several of these races there. On its introduction in this country by Mr. Taylor, it got its name.

Ft. Devens, Mass.   Pvt. Thomas Epsstein

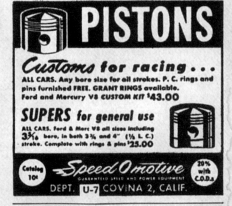

HOW DID THEY HOP UP THE MEXICAN ROAD RACE CARS? READ MARCH HOP UP

BOOK REVIEW

"HOW TO HOP UP FORD & MERCURY V-8 ENGINES"

By Roger Huntington   Pub. Floyd Clymer, $2.00

The latest publication of Floyd Clymer, who is well known in the field of automotive literature, is probably the best book to date on hopping up the Ford V-8 engine.

By referring only to the Ford products and not writing in generalities concerning all makes of cars, Author Roger Huntington has produced an excellent book for the Ford V-8 and Mercury owner who has not had much experience hopping up a car.

The book starts out with "What are we after and why," and runs the gamut thru performance fundamentals; planning the job, heads (both ohv and sidevalve), ignitions, induction systems (carb., injection and superchargers), porting, relieving, stroking, cams and (what is even more important to some), the cost involved for various stages of hopping up.

Taking everything into consideration, this book is excellent for the newcomer to the speed field and its reasonable price should make it a welcome addition to most automotive libraries.

CLASSIFIED

41

TECHNICAL TIPS

(Continued from page 2)

'49 MERC ENGINE IN '46 FORD?

Will a 1949 Mercury V-8 engine fit my 1946 Ford V-8? Will my Ford heads fit the Mercury engine? I want more power for hills but must still use my car for business.
Middlesboro, Ky.   R. E. Erwin

I do not advise using a '49 Mercury engine in your '46 Ford unless you can buy the complete engine. Reason: not many parts and accessories are interchangeable.

I suspect that the reason you want more power for hills is in the gear ratio. For some unknown reason the '46 Ford V-8 had a 3.54 axle ratio, the six had 3.78. Actually, this should have been the other way around, because the 6 has more torque or pulling power, and is supposed to be the economy model.

In view of this, I suggest you change to the 3.78 ratio which was standard on all V-8s and sixes built in 1947 and 1948.

If you still want more power, you can buy a new 1951 Mercury crankshaft and pistons for under $75. Even with a rebore and overhaul, I think you would come out cheaper than buying a complete new Mercury engine. These Mercury parts will fit your '46 engine with no problems involved and gives you a 4" stroke instead of 3¾".—Tech. Ed.

FORD 6 EXHAUST MANIFOLD

In the Oct. 1951 issue on page 42 you state there is nothing available for the Ford 6 to efficiently separate the front 3 cylinders from the rear 3 and still retain engine heat on the intake manifold.

This can be done by the simple method of splitting the exhaust manifold (using the stock manifold) and in this way heat can still be directed to the intake manifold in the stock manner. A very small hole is left to act as an equalizer between the front 3 and the back 3 as it has been found that it is impossible to muffle the noise enough to escape trouble with the law.
Marion, Ohio   Chas. A. Litell

This also requires a "Gotha" fitting welded on to the stock exhaust manifold.—Tech. Ed.

42   HOP UP, February, 1952

LATE NEWS

NEW RACING CLASS

Of particular interest is the new division recently announced by NASCAR: the Speedway Car Division, which is limited to passenger car engines (reworked within certain limitations) installed in one- and two-man Indianapolis-type bodies.

Debut of these cars will take place at Daytona, February 3 thru February 10, 1952. Ample prize money has been pledged for the season.

The official specifications allow unlimited bore (without sleeving); stock crankshaft and stroke, with any type camshaft. The engine must be American passenger car or approved truck type. Intake and exhaust manifolds may be any type. The limit on carburetors is two, of any type. You may raise the compression ratio, but the head must be stock and the ignition is limited only to battery-coil. Stock pistons are specified.

There are no limitations on spark plugs—any type may be used and the same is true of valve lifters. The water pump may be altered, and a stock generator must be run—or none at all. Any starter is permitted, whether attached to the car or not, but pushing and towing is outlawed. As long as the driver does not alter body shape, any type may be used. A de-clutching device of some type must be used and two forward and one reverse gear are mandatory. Special differentials are permissible (locked type, quick-change, etc.) but open drive-shafts are barred.

No stock frames will be run—only special racing types. Wheels must be racing type (Rudge, wire, magnesium, etc.) and the steering (if non-stock) must pass approval. Four-wheel brakes must be able to lock the wheels. Wheelbase: 96½ inches minimum; tread: 53 inches minimum; total dry weight: not less than 6½ lbs. per cubic inch of engine displacement.

Incidentally, NASCAR is staking a membership drive for all those who want to become Associate Members. You'll probably want to join to get the benefits of NASCAR's insurance and the NEWSLETTER containing all the inside dope on racing. The address to write is NASCAR, 42 South Penninsula Drive, Daytona Beach, Florida.

NEW PRODUCTS

HYDRAMATIC SELECTOR

Just what Hydramatic needs . . . . a manual selector! The Hydramatic Selector consists (as far as the driver can see) of a lever attached to the dash which locks the gearbox in 3rd gear, preventing the normal change to 4th.

Hydramatic Seleceter is a particularly useful device for ascent and descent of hills and trailer towing—where Hydramatics are notorious for their habit of bogging down in 4th, or worse, shifting back and forth between 3rd and 4th.

Further information from A. E. Nielson, 2139 N. Broadway, Dept. U-2, Los Angeles.

ROAD and TRACK
PHOTO QUIZ

1. The engine in this MG TC is a . . .

(a) MG

(b) Riley

(c) Offy

(d) Bugatti.

2. Lt. Col. A. T. Goldie-Gardner is flanked by his crew as he poses with his record-breaking streamlined car powered by a . . .

(a) Rolls-Royce

(b) Allison

(c) MG TD

(d) Ferrari.

3. This race car, of a type very popular in England, is powered by a . . .

(a) 250 cc Guzzi

(b) 500 cc J.A.P.

(c) 750 cc Crosley

(d) 1100 cc Fiat

ANSWERS: 1. (d) Type 40 Bugatti (Road and Track, Nov. '51). 2. (c) MG TD (Road and Track, Oct. '51). 3. (b) 500 cc J.A.P. motorcycle engine (Road and Track, Nov. '51). These and many other interesting articles are found in every issue of R & T Magazine.

SPEED POWER

● **IF YOUR CAR BURNS**
● **TOO MUCH OIL...**

HOLT'S **GET**

Piston Seal

AN ENGLISH IMPORT

Restore Engine Power ● Reduce Oil Consumption
Stop Piston Slap ● Restore Compression

Holt's Piston Seal is one of the finest discoveries to come from "Tommyland" in twenty years. Years of scientific research and experimentation have proven this product the best possible "first aid" treatment for old, worn out mills. By simply removing spark plugs and squeezing tube contents into plug hole, a self-expanding, pliable lubricating seal is formed around pistons. This restores compression and puts zip back in your engine. Will last 10,000 miles . . . more than a year of ordinary driving. Comes complete with rubber hose extension for application. Only $5.95 per tube.

SAVE GAS
with a
FUEL PRESSURE REGULATOR

END FOREVER:

● Carburetor Flooding ● Motor Stalling
● Fuel Waste ● Power Loss

DUE TO FUEL PUMP "PULSE"

For REAL gas economy try this amazing Regulator on your car. Many users claim up to 25% gas savings and that it pays for itself by eliminating carburetor tuning. It reduces gas waste caused by fuel pump pulsation and "surge," and the lost power and annoyance of "motor cut-cut" due to sudden pressure drop during acceleration or hard pulls. ONLY $5.95 postpaid (or send $1.00, balance C.O.D.)

BOOST MILEAGE WITH AN OCTA-GANE

When your engine starts to knock because of present lower octane gasoline, DO NOT set back the timing or retard the spark. Thousands of car owners are using the OCTA-GANE "50" water injection method for "top flight" performance. This all bronze, "fog type," exhaust pressure injector uses water, water & alcohol or Vitane as an "Anti-Knock," Anti-Detonant. Give car data. Send $2 deposit, balance C.O.D. $24.95 postpaid. Complete with 1½ gal. tank (Dual manifold installation kit $1.85 extra)

The "MOTOR MINDER" For Economy-Driving

New Stewart-Warner instrument tells at a glance how to save gasoline, how to drive efficiently, and how to locate and remedy engine troubles. Fits all cars and trucks. Includes complete kit for easy, quick installation. Special bracket mounts instrument above or below dash. A practical and beautiful accessory for any car.

Standard Model.................................$10.95
New Deluxe (Ebony Case)...................$13.95

Newhouse Stocks Complete Lines for All Makes of Cars

Thousands of items ready for "same day" shipment. Including all brands of Dual Manifolds, High Compression Heads, Ignitions, Valves, Cams, Crankshafts, Helmets, Pistons, Flywheels, Headers, Mufflers and Pipes and All Other Speed and Power Accessories. All equipment is fully guaranteed and prices are strictly competitive.

Newhouse
AUTOMOTIVE INDUSTRIES
Dealerships Available
WE SHIP ALL OVER THE WORLD

1952 SPEED EQUIPMENT CATALOG

Complete new catalog picturing and describing hundreds of speed equipment items for all makes of cars. 25c ppd. (Dealers please request wholesale catalog.)

DEALER INQUIRIES INVITED

Write today . . . become the exclusive Newhouse "Hop Up" Headquarters in your area.

Dept. HP-2, 5805 East Beverly Blvd., Los Angeles 22, California

World's Largest Firm Specializing In Hi-Performance and Hi-Mileage Equipment

MARCH 1952   15¢

HOP UP

Who's a Hot Rodder? . . . see page 20

Barris Kustom . . . . see page 18

TECHNICAL TIPS

BORING '49 FORD

What cylinder bore would you suggest for my 1949 Ford (for use in normal city traffic)?

Culver, Indiana   Bobby Claypool

The amount you can re-bore your engine depends on the amount of core shifting which occurred when your block was poured at the foundry. Usually, .125 oversize (3-5/16 actual bore) is safe on a late Ford V-8. Some can be bored to 3⅜, and occasionally 3-7/16 bore is possible. However, I know of a lot of engines bored 3⅜ in which the walls seemed OK, but soon gave trouble. Play safe and use 3-5/16! —Tech. Ed.

'36 BUICK TOP SPEED

I have a 1936 Buick Special (Series 40) four door sedan. I am told, when new, it developed 107 horsepower. What top speed, approximately, could this car have attained when new?

Chicago, Illinois   Robert Brockstra

The 1936 Buick 40 had a bore and stroke of 3-3/32 x 3-7/8, and the bhp was around 100. Beginning in 1937, the stroke of the "40" was increased to 4-1/8 and the bhp to 107.

85 mph under favorable conditions was possible. I drove one in 1936 that showed 92 mph but 83 to 85 is close to the actual speed of the Special, even today.

Incidentally, top speed of a car doesn't fall off much with age, because general looseness reduces friction, and even bad valves don't show much power loss at high rpm—this assumes that rings are still holding fair compression, and ignition and carburetion are in good shape. Another interesting "thing" about top speed is that speedometers tend to lose some of their optimism with age—Tech. Ed.

'35 CHEVY HOP UP

How can I improve the performance of a 1935 Chevrolet Standard? Would a 1941 (or later) Chevy engine "drop in" my '35 chassis.

Naval Base, So. Car.   H. A. Hughes

I would not recommend trying to hop-up any 6-cylinder Chevrolet built from 1934 to 1936. These had 3 main bearings, and 80 bhp, which was about all they could reliably stand.

The 1937 or later 4-main bearing engines can be installed in earlier chassis . . . altho not difficult, they don't just "drop in."

I once owned a '35 and I did mill the head .030. A free-flow muffler or a split exhaust would help and would not harm the engine in any way. However, 60 mph is just about as fast as this model could cruise, and still feel sure that the bearings would last.—Tech. Ed.

CUSTOM MERCURY

Would appreciate information on chrome molding as used on de Ville Mercury, October Hop Up, page 7 . . . A solid chrome strip above the grille just under the hood, running in an arc from parking light to parking light.

Clovis, New Mexico   C. L. Moody

The chrome piece on the Mercury in October Hop Up is actually part of the body.

If you will take a close look at the front of your Merc, you will notice a panel between the hood and grille adjoining the two headlights. This panel can be removed, chromed and then after replacing, it can be partially painted as Ellis has done his. Because of its size and proximity to the grille, the whole thing chromed adds too much bright work to the front of the car.—Dean Batchelor

If it's hopped up, it'll be in HOP UP

HOP UP

AHRC SEEKS UNIFIED RULES

A decade ago, a small group of individuals in Southern California banded together to run their hopped up jalopies on the dry lakes peculiar to this locale.

The Southern California Timing Association evolved from these outlaw deals, and because it was the only group of its kind in existence, they made their rules and regulations to fit their own needs with little regard to what other people thought, which was perfectly O.K.—then.

Since then, there have been numerous engine and body class changes and many *strict* safety rules set down. Also, many new timing associations and individually controlled drag strips have sprung up all over the nation.

The American Hot Rod Conference, which is composed of the seven leading timing associations in the California-Nevada area meet in Fresno on February 2. Most of the discussion will concern engine and body classifications, but car weight, distance for approach to timer, length of traps, and standing vs. running start drags will also be discussed.

The time is ripe to start standardizing rules among these groups and associations. It is imperative that action should be started immediately because this will be a large undertaking.

NEW PRICE . . . . . NEW POLICY

Due to a rise in costs, it has become necessary to increase the price of *Hop Up* to 20c, effective with the April issue. The one year subscription will be $2.

Concurrent with the announcement of *Speed and Spray*, a power-boat racing magazine edited by Kent Hitchcock and associated with the *Hop Up-Road and Track* groups, boats will no longer appear in *Hop Up*.

Unless there is an outstanding indication of interest in motorcycles by our readers, this subject will be dropped from *Hop Up*. How about it, shall motorcycles stay in *Hop Up* or not?

EDITORIAL STAFF

Editor ....Oliver Billingsley
Technical Editor................................John R. Bond
Associate Editors.................................Louis Kimzey
　　　　　　　Samuel Weill, Jr., Robert Dearborn
Staff Photographers............................Gene Trindl
　　　　　　　Ralph Poole, Jerry Chesebrough
Photographers............Bob Canaan, Joe Al Denker

PRODUCTION STAFF

Managing Editor....................W. H. Brehaut, Jr.
Production Director..........................Louis Kimzey
Art Director......................................Jack Caldwell

ADVERTISING

Advertising Manager.....................William Quinn
Southern California........................Dean Batchelor
Motorcycles...Bill Bagnall
United Kingdom.......................Kenneth Kirkman
　　　　　　　　　　　　2 Longcroft Avenue
　　　　　　　　　Banstead, Surrey, England
Italy ....Michele Vernola
　　　　　　　　　　　　　　　　C.P. 500
　　　　　　　　　　　　　　　Milano, Italy

CORRESPONDENTS

Italy ....Corrado Millanta

Vol. 1, No. 8　　　　　　　　　**March, 1952**

CONTENTS

HOP UP is published monthly by Enthusiasts' Publications, Inc., 540 W. Colorado Blvd., Glendale, California. Phone CHapman 5-2297. Entered as second class matter at the post office at Glendale, California, under the Act of March 3, 1879. Copyright 1951 by Enthusiasts' Publications, Inc. Reprinting in whole or in part forbidden except by permission of the publishers.

Subscription price $1.50 per year thruout the world. Single copy 15c.

Change of address—must show both old and new addresses.

331

HOW MANY 'POTS'?*

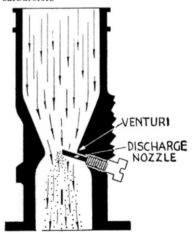

By Barney Navarro

If one more helps, a lot should do wonders. This is the line of reasoning that is often applied to carburetion. After installing a basket of carburetors, the budding mechanic expects his car to leap like a jackrabbit when he punches the throttle. However, such a procedure more often causes bitter disappointment rather than the fabulous performance that's expected. In fact, it is actually possible to add so much carburetion to an engine that the car will slow down if the throttle is floored under 35 mph in top gear.

There is much to be considered when selecting the proper carburetion for an engine. Of prime importance is the realization that your car was originally equipped for maximum performance within certain speed ranges. Any changes that you make will reduce throttle response in the low speed range. So, if you never intend driving your car faster than 15 mph in low gear or 40 in top gear, you will be more satisfied with the stock intake manifold and carburetor than with multiple carburetion.

The first thought that enters one's mind when thinking of adding more carburetors is that it's done to supply more gasoline. Indirectly this may be part of the reason, but more gas can be supplied in a much easier manner. If all that is desired is more gas, the installation of larger jets will suffice. We all know that gasoline is only one part of the combustible mixture, the other part is oxygen which is contained in the air breathed by the engine. Increasing the quantity of gas without increasing the amount of oxygen can be likened to the condition that arises when too much wood is placed on a fire. There will be too much fuel for the amount of oxygen, so part of it will not be burned. Consequently, this over-rich condition will lower power output instead of raising it. To effect an increase it will be necessary to supply more oxygen along with the gas. This is the eternal problem that is most difficult to solve.

*carburetors

VENTURI

DISCHARGE NOZZLE

Boiled down to simple terms, the number of carburetors is increased in order to increase the volume of oxygen that an engine breathes. Carburetor venturis cause a resistance to air flow. This resistance is reduced by increasing the area of the venturis by either enlarging them or adding to their number. Examination of the venturi diagram will illustrate why air flow is impeded.

In order to function, a carburetor venturi must offer resistance to air flow. Actually the resistance is a necessary evil, altho it has only an indirect use. It is caused by reducing the cross sectional area of the carburetor throat to produce the venturi. This reduction in size increases the velocity of air flow. At first glance it would appear that this would increase the pressure in the necked down portion, but it does just the contrary. The pressure drops below atmospheric and causes fuel to flow out of the discharge nozzle—the quantity being metered by a jet at the bottom of the nozzle. The greater the air flow thru the venturi the greater the pressure reduction and the larger the fuel flow. This function of a carburetor is more easily understood if it is looked upon as a means of metering the correct amount of fuel to go with the air that the engine breathes.

The carburetor isn't the only restriction in an induction system. It can readily be seen that the installation of a carburetor that has a much larger venturi than the size of the manifold passages will not be as great a source of resistance as the manifold. The same condition exists if two carburetors are fitted to a stock manifold originally designed for one carburetor. Multiple carburetion manifolds are designed to overcome this by using more direct flow paths, larger passages and lowered velocities. The key to the whole problem lies in the velocities encountered; for resistance increases with the square of the velocity. When the fuel mixture flow velocity is doubled the friction is not doubled but is quadrupled. Conversely, when the velocity is cut in half the resistance is quartered. This quartering is what takes place when dual carburetion is installed, but it must be remembered that this only takes place at the carburetor venturis.

Two or three straws will allow you to drink a bottle of soda pop faster by reducing flow resistance, but a mouth full of straws won't help matters any because you can't drink that fast. Your engine can suffer from the same condition by adding too much carburetion—if two will supply all that it demands, three will be of no greater help. An unported engine equipped with a stock cam will receive no added benefit from more than two carburetors. In order to use three or more carburetors, the engine must be "full race," and in the majority of cases must have the piston displacement increased.

The rpm range of operation must be given consideration when selecting a multiple carburetion system. The larger the total venturi area the faster the engine will have to operate to run smoothly. This is partially due to the fact that the air flow is slowed down too much at low speeds because of the large increase in cross sectional area. Instead of the air stream producing a fog, its flow will be so slow that droplets will dribble out of the discharge nozzle like they do from the nozzle of an atomizer or throat spray when the bulb is squeezed lightly. These droplets will be too heavy for the air stream to support, so they will strike the bends of the intake manifold and ports, collect to form puddles and then flow into the cylinders like a small stream. The cylinders that are fed by crooked passages will receive a different mixture than those connected to straight ones. Some cylinders will be rich and others will be lean, so the engine will naturally run roughly. This wetting of the holes will cause poor throttle response because the passages will have to dry out before the engine can pick up speed. Of course these conditions won't exist if you never allow your engine to idle to low rpm and never attempt to make it pull a load at low speed. Many race engines idle between 1000 and 2000 rpm and there are some that idle even faster. When operating on a race track they are never allowed to run slowly, so their performance is satisfactory within their operating range. When selecting a carburetion system it is best to realize that *some* of the principles embodied in a race engine can be applied to a passenger car engine, but you can't go "all out."

Crowd applause and checkered flag greet Ruttman, Smith as they finish 4th over-all at Juarez . . .

MERCURY

How did they Hop Up Ruttman's Mercury?

Some of the newspaper reports which came thru to the U. S. side of the border during and after the Mexican Road Race were misleading —to say the least. One press release, for example, stated that Troy Ruttman's Mercury was "2nd hand" and that he "bought it off a used car lot," which, of course, was probably true, but it was by no means the whole story. What the newspapers would have you believe is that Ruttman sauntered by a used car lot, bought a beat-up '48 Merc, climbed into it and walked away with the 4th place money in the 2100-mile race from the Guatemalian border to the United States.

All this made quite a hero of Ruttman in the eyes of the American public—which is as it should be. For nobody drove a greater race than the Southern California entrant. And he deserves all the credit he can get.

But calling the Merc a mere "used car" is insulting Ruttman's intelligence. Nobody with half a brain is going to enter a beat-up jalopy in a two-thousand mile race against $11,000 iron from Italy, nor against the best modified cars the North and South American mechanics can produce.

Furthermore, statements like those referred to above are even more slighting to the guy who modified Troy's Merc so that it not only ran fast but kept running thru the five grueling days, to place well up among the leaders. And the guy we are talking about is Clay Smith —one of the best engine wizards in the country.

HOP UP figured you would like to know the story behind Ruttman's car and behind Clay Smith's efforts. So we cornered the highstrung, nervous Smith and got the story from his own lips.

When Smith and Ruttman decided to enter the race, there wasn't any doubt as to the make of car they would drive. It would be a Mercury. They would have chosen a Ford because of its lighter weight, but the '48 Mercury had better weight distribution than the early Fords and firmer springing than the later Fords or Mercurys. And the car was sponsored by Ruppert Motors of Pomona. Remember, the car not only had to hold together at 100 mph averages over long stretches of flat, burning Mexican soil, but it had to handle well in the mountains. It had to accelerate fast out of corners and stop quick in emergencies.

There's quite a list of modifications that Clay made to the car in his shop in Long Beach. We'll take them in the order he told them to us.

To begin with, Smith tore the stock Merc down and, leaving the crank stock, bored the block $\frac{1}{8}$" over. The intake valves were enlarged from $1\frac{1}{2}$" to $1\frac{5}{8}$", while the exhaust were left at their stock size: $1\frac{1}{2}$". The flywheel was left alone too, but the engine was taken over to Electronic Balancing Company to be balanced. Belond Headers replaced the Merc set-up, and Smith used twin pipes which ran straight thru to the rear of the car (anything shorter would have endangered the driver and co-pilot with the chance of fumes getting up into the driver's compartment).

A Kong distributor (chosen because of its

Mexican Road Race

Ruttman snakes thru crowd after start at Mexico City, barely missing indifferent girl.

Shirt-tail flying as usual, Troy Ruttman steps from his Mercury at Parral finish line . . .

manual control) was fastened in place with Edelbrock heads of 8 to 1 compression ratio, and the manifold was a two-carburetor Evans. A dual was used instead of a triple because with a stock camshaft, three carburetors would have been too much. Clay kept the stock fuel pump on the Merc, but he also used an Auto Pulse for emergency. The fuel line was enlarged and surrounded by asbestos to prevent vapor locking.

The engine was, of course, ported and relieved and exhaust dividers were added. It might be worth while to note here that the car, during the race, got between 8 and 10 mpg—a very high average when you consider the speeds which were maintained. Mobiloil SAE 50 was used in the crankcase.

The only extra instruments were a tachometer and a vacuum gauge. Both of these were placed on the navigator's side of the car. And the navigator was Clay Smith himself. All during the race, Clay sat beside Troy and told him when to shift gears (among other things). The plan was to keep the engine between 2500 and 5000 rpm at all times, for best performance and durability. The only concession made to altitude (sometimes as high as 10,000 feet) was the manual spark control which Smith operated from his side of the car.

Air scoops were added to the stock Mercury brakes and a slight modification was made to the brake lines themselves. This took the form of a "safety lock" which was built in so that if the front lines went out, the rear brakes

8

HOP UP, March, 1952

would still be operative—and vice versa. The linings were heavy duty Johns-Manville, and they were riveted, not bonded, to the shoes. 6.50 x 16 Firestone racing tires were used on the coupe and, according to Smith, absolutely no trouble was experienced all the way. Steering was left as is.

For the front suspension, Clay substituted four Lincoln Houdaille shocks—50/50 action. Two Lincoln Houdaille 50/50s were used in the rear along with two tubular 30/70s.

The Mercury was not lightened in any way. Altho the rear seat was removed, the spare gas tank (demanded by regulations) was (when filled) enough to bring the overall weight of the car a good 100 pounds over stock weight.

One of the handy features Clay installed was the three-way fuel valve. At any time if the main tank ran out or got low, he could switch the reserve tank on. The switch also had a third position which cut both tanks off—in case of accident. And this switch was placed in the middle, between Troy Ruttman and Clay—so that either could reach it . . . if he had to. A small fire extinguisher was carried.

Notes and Comments

When asked which foreign driver impressed him the most, Clay immediately said "Ehlinger" (Mexico), and then added that "Troy Ruttman was the best American driver." Maybe you think he's prejudiced, but take it from us, Troy doesn't have to take a back seat for anybody. Clay also mentioned Faulkner and Sterling as outstanding in the way they handled their cars . . . however, he couldn't understand the Italian driving techniques. He said Ruttman almost ran over the Italians a couple of times. The Italian method of going into a corner was to drive up to the turning point full speed and then slam on the brakes, burning a lot of rubber needlessly. Then after the corner was rounded, they mashed on the throttle and burned more rubber getting away again. Ruttman invariably took these same corners without using brakes.

Smith felt that the cooperation of everybody in Mexico was great . . . he could hardly believe the amount of enthusiasm the crowd cooked up as the cars went thru the various towns. His only beef was the crowd control which he said was terrible. Huge mobs of people lined the road in each town and they only left a narrow lane for the drivers. It got so bad that Troy finally took to weaving down the road when approaching a town as if his car were out of control. That seemed to get the crowd back where they belonged.

We asked Smith if he would like to prepare a car for next year's race and the answer was an immediate affirmative. The only change he would like to see would be to have the cars either absolutely stock or with no limitations at all. One solution would be to have one class for absolutely stock cars and another for modifieds . . . all in the same race.

As far as the Merc was concerned, Clay Smith was more than satisfied with its performance. He felt that if a different rear end ratio had been available he could have managed three or four more mph top speed and consequently three or four mph cruising speed. Tho he doesn't think the higher gearing would have caught the Italian Ferrari, he does believe he and Ruttman could have beaten the rest of the Americans and made it a close contest with the Italians.

PACKARD

How did they Hop Up the Mexican Road Race Packards?

A prominent Mexican Packard dealer (Romuel O'Farrill) sent five Packard 160 engines to

Car 74, British-born Peruvian, Henry Bradley's Nash, awaits start of first leg . . . Tuxtla . . .

Ruttman's cornering technique saved tires.

Troy corners smoothly at Parral turnoff . . .

Howard Johansen to be modified for the long hard race from one end of Mexico to the other. Johansen's shop (Howard's Racing Cams) did the job and shipped the engines back to Mexico, where they were put into series "200" chassis. Of these five cars entered—only one finished. Doesn't sound like much does it? You'd think a good mechanic ought to be able to keep more than one out of five cars running, wouldn't you? That's what we thought too . . . . until we looked into the matter.

One of the five Johansen-prepared cars ran off the road and cracked up on the way to the starting line. You can hardly blame Johansen for this. Of the four which started, one more cracked up on the first leg of the race—driving too fast . . . . no fault of the engine. You might even say the engine was a little too good. That leaves three cars running from the second leg onward. Two of these went out, both with the same problem . . . . pistons. When the final flag fell, Trevoux in the remaining Packard crossed the finish line in fifth place—and the engine was in just as good condition as the rest of the finishers. They were all tired, with the possible excep-

tion of the $11,000 Italian Ferrari coupes, which were built to cruise at well over 110 mph . . . specialized road cars.

The first thing Johansen did when he received the five engines from Mexico was to put one of them on a dynamometer (to get an idea of the developed horsepower in these stock engines). It developed 138 hp. By the time Howard Automotive finished the modifications, one of the five engines turned up 192 hp on the dynamometer and the other four were not far behind.

The way this all was accomplished was to bore out the engines from the original 3½" to .100 oversize. The stroke was left stock and Pontiac 6 pistons were fitted. The blocks were ported and relieved and the stock ignition replaced by Scintilla magnetos. The heads were milled so that they averaged about 10 to 1 compression ratio, and Howard's Cams built log-type manifolds which equalized the pressure between all ports. The manifolds were designed to take four Stromberg Carburetors. Johansen's company also built the headers and the engines were balanced in his shops.

The stock hydraulic valve lifters were re-

Clay Smith fills auxiliary fuel tank.

Jean Trevoux of France crosses the finish line in 5th place.

placed by adjustable tappets, but the valves and springs were left stock. (There was no need for a different valve set-up because a stock cam was required in the race and this prevented the engines from winding high enough to need heavier valve gear.)

To augment the stock fuel pumps in case of emergency, hand pressure pumps were placed within reach of the navigators, and war surplus, aircraft oil radiators were attached to keep the oil temperature down. The stock Packard oil pumps put out fifty pounds pressure so Howard's modified them to develop 80 pounds per square inch pressure and the flywheel was lightened twenty pounds.

In the chassis department, Houdaille shocks were added to the rear suspension and Packard limousine brakes were used. As on many of the other cars, Firestone racing tires (8.00 x 15) worked out well thruout the grind.

Notes and Comments

Knowing how HOP UP readers are interested in modifying their stock cars, we asked Howard Johansen just how far a Packard owner could go in getting more horsepower from his engine —and still keep reliability. His answer was that the Packard engine's output could be increased 40 horsepower without losing its reliability. He feels that the Packard is an extremely rugged engine and very easy to work on. For the private owner to get this 40 extra hp, a cam is a must. And, of course, you recall from the Mexican Road Race rules that cams were barred.

About the race itself, Howard feels that it was run off in a very fair manner and he is completely satisfied with the press, the officials and the competitors. The Trevoux Packard (after winning the first leg) broke a front suspension A frame bolt (2nd leg). The driver and navigator tried to repair it but could only effect a temporary job. They lost 15 minutes beside the road and another 15 thru having to drive slowly for the remainder of the leg. And this 30 minutes may well have made thousands of dollars difference at the finish.

Next year, Johansen says he would like a chance to "go all out" on a car—with no limitations.

One of the largest groups of precision hop up equipment ever gathered together in one spot started from near the Guatemalian border and

Walt Faulkner's Lincoln gets bearings replaced after crossing starting line with pan removed.

Flores and Andrade's Packard steadily improved position until 5th leg . . . went out with engine trouble and did not finish . . .

raced the entire length of Mexico during this year's Carrera Panamericana Mexico (Mexican Pan-American Race).

The victory of the Italian Ferrari coupes (driven by aces Taruffi and Ascari) make it easy to overlook the spectacular performance of American cars and American drivers. Actually, the Italians were surprised. Chinetti (Ferrari team manager) approached three American drivers (Ruttman, Faulkner and Bettenhausen) after the race and opened discussions about the possibility of inviting these outstanding pilots to drive in next season's Grand Prix races. Contrary to previously published statements, no concrete invitation or agreement has been made, but the most likely choice of the Italians would be Ruttman, who pushed the Italians quite hard in the mountainous sections.

Ruttman's driving, plus Clay Smith's tuning and navigating, put the highly modified '48 Mercury in 1st place in part of the race and 4th overall at the finish . . . to be beaten only by the two Ferrari and Sterling's Chrysler. Sterling's car was an outstanding example of a car running in almost stock form—relying on the big 180 hp Chrysler engine to stay up in the top brackets. This school of thought—as opposed to the "all out" method of tuning the engine for highest possible performance—paid off. The final result: 3rd overall . . . right behind Ascari's $11,000 Ferrari.

The performance of the 5th place Packard, driven by the French ace Trevoux, must not be overlooked . . . Howard Johansen (Howard's Racing Cams) doing a remarkable tuning job in the limited time available. It is now understood that a Packard team will be invited to run at the 1952 Le Mans (France) 24-hour race—an event which has seen all too few American entrants in its long history of existence.

Among early retirements in the grueling Mexican run were three of the hot favorites: Her-

Modifications were allowed and most cars carried "extras" like this Chrysler's electric fuel pump, altitude adjustments on carburetors.

Bettenhausen finishes 1st on last leg (16th over-all) after burning up the road at 114 mph average.

shall McGriff, who was last year's winner; Bud Sennett, who placed 5th last year, and who this year was driving McGriff's Olds which scooped the field in 1950; and Jack McAfee, driving his Cadillac in which he placed 10th last year.

McGriff's Olds 88 caught fire this year and burned completely, tho the pilot and co-pilot slowed the flaming car and jumped clear with no injuries. It is difficult to understand an experienced pilot failing to carry a fire extinguisher. Bud Sennett went out with a broken fuel line. He was out long enough for repairs to prohibit his making the leg in the maximum elapsed time, and was accordingly disqualified.

McAfee ran into piston trouble and gear box failure. Tho he rebuilt his engine overnight, proper machining facilities were unavailable and before he had gone far, his pistons collapsed again, forcing his retirement.

Greatest trouble makers were tires. The famous Italian Pirelli tires fell down on the first leg of the race, forcing the Italians to run on Mexican Goodrich tires, which turned out surprisingly well. The **Road and Track** crew covering the race (**Road and Track**, January 1952) wore out 5 new tires in 3,000 miles of driving over the winding Mexican highways.

Bettenhausen, in the final stages of the race put on a spectacular display of driving, but was unable to overcome the time lost in early legs.

Notes and Comments

Piero Taruffi (1st place winner)

"The Americans are really good, considering their lack of experience on road courses. They are real gentlemen and a great credit to the U.S.A. Troy Ruttman demonstrated his sportsmanship by offering to help us get some badly needed tires after the 1st leg when we had 9 tire failures. We passed him at one time and he smiled and waved us on. In closing I want to say we invite Americans to compete in our European races and will try to show them the same courtesy and hospitality that we have received here."

Ruttman: (at Durango)

"I am having a wonderful time. The Mexicans are really treating us swell. But I wish they would keep off the road . . . it's really rough to drive 120 mph on a road lined solid with spectators. Without Clay Smith I wouldn't be up here (Troy was in 3rd place at this time). He's done a wonderful job. I would like to drive a Ferrari. They really go. Next year I'd like to see no restrictions on cam shafts."

When someone remarked that the Italians were using special fuel, Troy yelled, "I was right behind them at the pumps and they used Super Mexolina just like everyone else. A lot of the Americans are griping about the Ferrari. Hell, they're just doing what every American driver would do and that's to use the best equipment available in their country."

Greatest thrill for the **Hop Up** crew was finishing the final leg within the maximum time limit, for which we were presented an honorary plaque by the Mexican government.

The Hot Rod Shop's (Detroit) Cadillac rolled.

Victor Klette set a new 48 cu in. record . . . hitting 79 mph.

Rich Hallett

Salton Sea

The weather for the first three days was nearly perfect, tho occasionally the going was too choppy for record performances. The first day of competition was run under a heavy overcast and with a 30/50 barometer . . . literally perfect for records.

Speeds in new classes usually take substantial leaps in the first few years during the experimental and development stage. Then, gradually, the records "tighten up." As the contestants, engine experts and hull builders get near the point of nearly maximum power plant and hull efficiency the fight to raise a record is tough and the increases slight. Often a record set by an exceptionally good outfit under very favorable conditions will withstand assault for years.

Five of the records broken at Desert Beach were in the Utility Outboard Runabout classes. These classes are an exception to the rule in that with strictly stock engines plus certain hull limitations, development is limited to hull efficiency. Altho these classes are very new there have been literally hordes of them racing during the past year. The performance table shows that the average increase for the 5 records was only 1.4 mph, indicating that these stock utility classes reached the tightening up point in speed performance much faster than regular racing classes.

Three of the records were in the regular Outboard Racing classes and these were three of the toughest and oldest in the APBA record list . . . dating back from 1939 to 1946. Together they only produced an average increase of .66 mph. The inboard records, hydroplane and runabout alike were the very toughest in the books and, with the exception of the single Cracker Box mark, were in the largest registered classes in organized racing. Pete Pierce's 79 mph record in the 48's is actually only advance notice of what may be expected from this comparatively new class.

Paul Sawyer's terrific 120 mph 225 class record was the highlight of the year. Sawyer is making 120 mph with 260 cubin inches while the Unlimited world's record is only 160 mph made with 1710 cubic inches of supercharged Allison brute horsepower. Sawyer's performance won for him the Bobrick Trophy for the fastest mile set on Salton Sea, previously held by Guy Lombardo in his Allison-powered Gold Cupper **Tempo VI** with a speed of 118 mph. The going was so tough that a few of the boys who cracked the straightaway marks were able to win top honors in both heats of the competition . . . and so tough that only four of the 1950 winners of the Salton Sea perpetuals— Johnny Maddox, Doc Novotny, Rocky Stone and Ed Parsley—were able to defend their championships.

The three heat contest for the APBA Silver Unlimited Trophy didn't bring out any of the big thundering Gold Cuppers, but a fast field of 135's and 225's went out after the cup. Veteran Eddie Meyer in his **Avenger II** won the last heat.

Of the 79 official records that will appear in the 1952 APBA Year Book, 36 have been established by classes that have never been scheduled at Salton Sea, leaving a possible 43 records that could be held on that course. 27 out of that possible 43, leaves 16 scattered around the rest of the country. Yes . . . they do go fast down on the world famous Submarine Speedway, the fastest marine race course on earth.

48 cu in. Hydro......Louis Meyer Jr., Huntington Park, Cal.
135 cu in. Hydro.................Curtis Martens, Hampton, Va.
225 cu in. Div. II................Rich Hallett, Downey, Cal.
225 Class................Paul Sawyer Jr., Rochester, N.Y.
Cracker Box................Danforth Campbell, Long Beach, Cal.
B Rac. Inb. Run....................Jack Kelley, Oildale, Cal.
E Rac. Inb. Run.....Sherm Crichfield, St. Petersburg, Fla.
P.O.D.H................Doc Novotny, Los Angeles, Cal

Wee Willie holds both B Racing Runabout records.

Lou Meyer, Jr., holds the 48 cu in. competition record.

M	Out. Hydro	Dave Spies, Lido Isle, Cal.
A	Out. Hydro	Johnny Maddox, Imperial Beach, Cal.
B	Out. Hydro	Arnold Adams, Los Angeles, Cal.
C	Out. Hydro	Bud Wiget, Concord, Cal.
C	Ser. Out. Hydro	Bud Wiget, Concord, Cal.
F	Out. Hydro	George Peak, Los Angeles, Cal.
C	Rac. Out. Run	Rocky Stone, Willamina, Oregon
C	Ser. Out. Run	Manuel Carnakis, Bakersfield, Cal.
F	Rac. Out. Run	Ken Jolley, Burbank, Cal.
A	Utility Run	Buz Busley, Eugene, Oregon
B	Utility Run	Elgin Gates, Huntington Beach, Cal.
C	Utility Run	Cag Graham, Ventura, Cal.
D	Utility Run	Jack Loehead, Santa Ana, Cal.

Down in the California Desert on the Salton Sea lies the most famous boat racing course on earth. Here (Armistice Day week-end) twenty-one world records fell before the onslaught of racing's finest . . . from fourteen states and Western Canada.

World records don't ordinarily come in bunches like bananas . . . and now we have twenty-one broken records at one regatta. It is no wonder that the racing fraternity is a little ga-ga over the results.

Most boat racing courses are located where there is heavy water traffic and the buoys must be removed as soon as the race is over. The average regatta sponsor attempts to devise a course that will keep the racing right in front of the spectator but you can't set records on that kind of a course. Now let us look at Salton Sea. It has no permanent boat population; no traffic, and draws a very small crowd. This permits permanent courses engineered for speed. The competition courses are two in number, a 1 2/3rds miler for outboards and an overlapping 2½ miler for inboards—each with nine markers to the long sweeping turn to permit maximum speed.

Timing is done with the Crocker Photo-Electric Clock. This timing is exact. Weather is the biggest factor of all. Few racing boats can

get up to top speed in a "slick" (that condition when the water is like a mirror). Some classes can stand only a ripple and others will go like a bomb in a light chop. There are only two kinds of water on the Big Salton . . . either too rough or just right. One more very important factor is the humidity. At those times when a favorable barometer and perhaps a slight overcast occur, record conditions are perfect.

The Salton Sea has been aptly nicknamed "Submarine Speedway." . . . 250 feet below sea level. Salton's waters are high in salt content. With all other conditions equal an unsupercharged job will run faster at sea level than it will at 2000 feet of elevation, and so the slight minus altitude can be credited for a little help. Just how much more thrust a propeller could gain in water of a higher specific gravity is a point that still has to be proven scientifically. The final factor in record performance is the most important: the racing outfit.

Why is there only the one big regatta on Salton Sea each year?

First: weather. During winter and late fall there are violent wind storms and summer temperatures soar far above the hundred degree mark. This leaves only the early fall when the desert enjoys warm and sunny weather. Second: financial support. Most regattas are promoted by some civic or booster organization and many have the benefit of a large paid spectator attendance. Without the "gate" from a large spectator crowd and with no sponsor, this famous regatta is truly a "contestant's" event. Roy Hunter's miniature resort of Desert Beach furnishes and keeps in repair the course, pier and stand, the inboard launching harbor, and a crane. The racing men themselves, with a $5.00 entry fee per boat, pay the rest of the regatta costs and provide the trophies. This year the Southern California Speedboat Club took on the job of arranging the big event.

HOP UP, March, 1952

15

E Racing Runabouts

Paul Terheggen set a new mile record.

Doug Creech screaming along 55 mph.

Ed Olsen in Honey Bee Too.

Ed Brown sets new cracker box record.

ONE MILE RECORDS

Racing Class	Speed M.P.H.	Owner or Driver	Boat Make	Motor Make
48 cu. in. Hydro	73.589	Victor Klette, Norwalk, Cal.	Own	Crosley
	76.928	Lou Meyer, Jr., Inglewood, Cal.	Hallett	Crosley
	79.330	Pete Pierce, San Gabriel, Cal.	Hallett	Crosley
		(Owner: Kenny Harman)		
Old Record	72.727	Mulford Scull, Ventnor, N.J.	....	Crosley
135 cu. in. Hydro	97.494	Chuck Powell, Monterey Park, Cal.	Own	Ford
		(Owner: Jack Kirby)		
Old Record	97.351	Sid Street, Kansas City, Mo.	Hallett	Ford
225 Class Hydro	120.085	Paul Sawyer, Jr., Rochester, N.Y.	Hallett	Ford
Old Record	115.045	Paul Sawyer, Jr., Rochester, N.Y.	Hallett	Ford
225 Div. II	95.204	Art Maynard, Long Beach, Cal.	Wickens	Ford 6
	96.944	Rich Hallett, Downey, Cal.	Hallett	Ford
	98.901	Keith Black, Lynwood, Cal.	Hallett	Ford
		Black's engine was declared illegal and disqualified.		
Old Record	94.240	L. O. Turner, Provo, Utah	Hill	Ford
Cracker Box Run.	72.054	Ed Brown, Carmichael, Cal.	Wickens	Chevrolet
Old Record	68.562	Glen Miller, Long Beach, Cal.	Own	Ford
B Inb. Rac. Run.	62.803	Jack Kelley, Oildale, Cal.	Own	Ford
Old Record	60.430	Ed Parsley, Los Banos, Cal.	Speedliner	Ford
E Inb. Rac. Run.	74.572	Paul Terheggen, Lynwood, Cal.	Mandella	Ford
Old Record	72.828	Sam Griffith, Miami, Fla.	....	....
C Rac. Out. Hydro	64.888	Doug Creech, Charlotte, N. C.	Swift	Johnson
Old Record	63.549	Thom Cooper, Kansas City, Mo.	Fillinger	Johnson
A Utility Out.	42.881	Jack Corner, Los Angeles, Cal.	Own	Mercury
		(Owner: Bob Knapp, Pasadena)		
Old Record	41.277	Bob Batie, Seattle, Wash.	....	Mercury
C Utility Out.	40.113	Joe De Souza, San Diego, Cal.	Koehler	Elto
	40.684	Cag Graham,' Ventura, Cal.	De Silva	Elto
Old Record	39.154	Joe Michelini, Dallas, Tex.	Switzer	Johnson

FIVE MILE RECORDS

48 cu. in. Hydro	60.893	Victor Klette, Norwalk, Cal.	Own	Crosley
	61.771	Lou Meyer, Jr., Inglewood, Cal.	Hallett	Crosley
Old Record	58.121	Mulford Scull, Ventnor, N.J.	....	Crosley
135 cu. in. Hydro	75.598	Sid Street, Kansas City, Mo.	Hallett	Ford
	77.519	Morlan Visel, Los Angeles, Cal.	Visel-Moore	Ford
Old Record	75.157	Roy Skaggs, Long Beach, Cal.	Own	Ford
225 Class Hydro	87.890	Paul Sawyer, Jr., Rochester, N.Y.	Hallett	Ford
Old Record	83.488	Bob Rowland, Norfolk, Va.	Lauterback	Ford
225 Div. II	75.630	Art Maynard, Long Beach, Cal.	Wickens	Ford 6
	75.821	Rich Hallett, Downey, Cal.	Hallett	Ford
Old Record	75.188	Paul Sawyer, Jr., Rochester, N.Y.	Hallett	Ford 6
B Inb. Rac Run.	57.582	Jack Kelley, Oildale, Cal.	Own	Ford
Old Record	55.181	Pete Coffee, Los Banos, Cal.	Speedliner	Ford
E Inb. Rac. Run.	65.598	Ed Olsen, Long Beach, Cal.	Glazier	Ford
Old Record	63.875	Sherm Crichfield, St. Petersburg, Fla.	Glazier	Gray
C Rac. Out. Hydro	57.508	Bud Wiget, Concord, Cal.	Neal	Evinrude
Old Record	57.325	Vic Scott, New York, N.Y.	Jacoby	Johnson
F Rac. Out. Run.	53.160	Ken Jolley, Burbank, Cal.	Rockholt	Evinrude
Old Record	52.693	Ernie Millot, Stockton ,Cal.	Rockholt	Evinrude
A Utility Out.	35.827	J. Cunningham, Hawthorne, Cal.	Terrill	Mercury
	36.511	Buz Busley, Eugene, Oregon	Cates	Mercury
		(Owner: Elgin Gates)		
Old Record	35.267	Bob Knapp, Pasadena, Cal.	Own	Mercury
B Utility Out.	40.395	Thos Mitchell, Pasadena, Cal.	De Silva	Mercury
	40.577	J. Cunningham, Hawthorne, Cal.	Terrill	Mercury
	41.822	Elgin Gates, Huntington Beach, Cal.	Own	Mercury
Old Record	40.323	Jas. Coulbourn, Florida.		Mercury
C Utility Out.	37.460	Joe De Souza, La Mesa, Cal.	Koehler	Elto
	38.054	Cag Graham, Ventura, Cal.	De Silva	Elto
Old Record	35.985	Joe De Souza, La Mesa, Cal.	Koehler	Elto

Jerry's Purple Rage

Without a doubt this 1949 Mercury is about the lowest thing on wheels. The ground clearance is only two inches. But that is just the way Jerry Quesnel of Culver City wanted it. And that's the way we built it here at Barris Kustom Autos, Auto Carrozzeria of America . . . and in the following manner.

First, the springs were removed and inverted and lowering blocks positioned. Spring hangers (rear) were cut, heated and moved closer to the frame. An interesting attachment is the skids, placed under the rear end, since the car is so low it drags when entering driveways, service stations, etc.

Front (coil) springs were next cut and the A frames were sectioned. Spring sockets had to be moved to retain the car's original springing geometry. Frame and flooring were cut wherever the running gear had a tendency to rub or bump as the car moved along. This meant cutting into the body to allow room for the drive-shaft, front running-gear, rear-end housings, spare-tire well and so on . . . quite a lengthy job.

Once the full lowering was done, my brother Sam and I started restyling the car. The top, we chopped four inches in the front and 7 inches in the rear. Rear sections of the car were "stretched" and tapered by the insertion of special panels. The rear door posts and post sections were moved

forward four inches—and a swooping curve was added to the upper-rear door corners.

Headlights and parking lights were bolted into a one-piece unit, combining the bumper pan and grille assembly. Grille proper was then installed: and this consisted of one main bar (see photo) with full ball ends, and ½" x 3" chrome tips floating from the main bar. The complete grille assembly was mounted in heavy springs and rubber mounts—to take collision or shock action.

In the rear of the car, we molded the rear deck and tail lights and moved the fuel filler pipe inside the trunk compartment. The tail lights were installed in the bumper guards with molded, reflecting, plastic lenses.

All door corners were molded as were the pan creases. The doors and deck are opened by inside and outside electrical push-buttons. Paint consisted of 28 coats of lacquer; Ruby — Maroon — Purple metallic, with special toning colors.

When the outside of the car was finished, we got to work on the inside. The dash was done in chrome and two-tone purple metallic paint. Blue and grey mohair fabric was chosen for the upholstery. Jerry Quesnel mounted a special three-inch radio antenna on the rear bumper. Fully extended, the antenna is 10 inches long.

—GEORGE BARRIS
HOP UP, March, 1952

18

Flame throwers? The local Union published a small squib in which the following statement was made: "Hot rodders latest fad", and then goes on to explain in a mixed nomer how these "'flame throwers', 'jet jobs' emitted streams of flame from their exhaust pipes . . ." Same old deal—let any screwy "squirrel" start around town with such antics and he is immediately a "hot rodder". This attitude on the part of the newspapers and much of the public (due to their reading of such incidences as well as actual contact on the highways with these bums) is a tough nut *we* have to crack . . . (from the *San Diego Timing Association Bulletin*)

Hop Up agrees . . . It *is* a tough nut to crack but it's time that newspapers, magazines and newsreels wake up to the fact that there is a world of difference between the true motor enthusiast and the *silly jerks in junks* who *they* call "hot rodders".

Here is one roadster that vividly shows the difference between a fenderless junk and a clean, beautiful roadster.

This car belongs to Eddie Dye (owner of E.D.M. Lumber Co.) . . . body work by Gil's Custom Shop (Los Angeles). And the instructions were: Build a beautiful roadster . . . regardless of price.

Gil (Ayala) started with a '32 frame, on which he placed a '29 body: hammer welded the doors shut; molded a full belly-pan; and hand-formed the shell and grille.

The seating, instead of being in its usually high position, is down between the frame, "lower than the British Jaguar XK-120." Lights, nerfing bar are combined in one unit.

While all this was being done, Gil sent the engine over to Earl Evans (Evans Engineering) . . . for the works! After the engine and body were completed, the roadster was handed over to the Berry's Custom Upholstry who "did" the interior in beautiful white leatherette. Total cost of this beautiful roadster: (six months labor) $3400.

Who's a hot rodder?

349

Custom Roadster

JIM RICHARDS

Winner Jimmy Phillips in fast curve.

Del Mar Road Race

by Bill Bagnall

DEL MAR, CALIF., Dec. 9th. Fanned by a brisk Pacific wind, Jimmy Phillips today rode home winner of the 30-Mile Motorcycle Road Race event, held in this scenic Southern California resort.

A crowd of 6,000 enthusiastic fans braved the wintry winds to witness the California Sports Car Club program of sports car and motorcycle road racing.

At the drop of starter Ralph De Palma's flag, 24 motorcycles got underway to tackle the 2½ mile paved course. "Pappy" Ed Kretz jumped into the lead spot, followed by Jimmy Phillips and Bobby Turner—all three Triumph mounted. Turner was being chased by Kenny Brown and Wally Remmell, with the rest of the pack close behind. On the third lap, Phillips took over the first place position from Kretz, and on the fourth lap, Turner also got around Pappy. However, on the fifth tour of the circuit, veteran Kretz snatched the place position from Turner again, and Remmell had moved up to fourth with Don Hawley taking over fifth. At the halfway mark (6th lap), the leaders were: Phillips, Kretz, Turner, Remmell and Hawley. These positions remained unchanged until the tenth lap, when Hawley moved up to fourth and Marty Dickerson filled the fifth spot. On the eleventh lap, Kretz was forced out of the race . . . losing his oil tank plug and running out of oil. (His son was plagued with the loss of his carburetor bowl.) At the drop of the checkered flag, Jimmy Phillips raced under the wire at an average speed of 60 plus, to become the winner

24

of Del Mar's first motorcycle road race.

Results

1 Jimmy Phillips	40"	Triumph
2 Bobby Turner	40"	Triumph
3 Don Hawley	30½"	BSA G/S
4 Marty Dickerson	61"	Vincent
5 Joe Hostetter	40"	Triumph

Winner's Time: 29 min., 14.02 sec.

24 starters—9 finishers

Comments: Del Mar seems to be a lucky spot for Jimmy Phillips, as the last race held in this town (Crosby's Del Mar Race Track) in 1949, saw Jimmy (Triumph mounted) walk off with winning the Pacific Coast Championship. The sports car crowd (as well as almost everyone in attendance) was favorably impressed with the performance of the bikes, as well as the riders. This is rather remarkable due to the fact that the cycle riders have had very little experience on paved road racing circuits. (Let's hope this type of racing reaches even a fraction of the popularity that it holds in England and Europe.) Starter Ralph De Palma approached Ed Kretz, Sr., and asked him if his "father" was racing today. An interesting note concerns the fastest lap times of the motorcycles in comparison with the sports cars. Fastest bike was clocked at 2 min., 22 sec., and the fastest car was 2 min., 19 sec. for the 2½ mile course.

A day well spent . . . unenvied were the hearty riders who had to ride their bikes back to Los Angeles in the season's windiest, and one of the coldest, days of the year (very unusual weather).

For complete story of the sports car events, see *Road and Track*, February 1951.

HOP UP, March, 1952

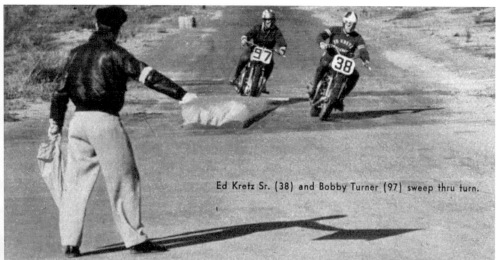

Ed Kretz Sr. (38) and Bobby Turner (97) sweep thru turn.

A little dirt track style slips in occasionally.

Kretz Sr. trailed by Jimmy Phillips.

Cutting corners in S bend.

Joe Reath in T-V8-60.

Roadster Rally

When anyone mentions the word roadster, the immediate impression you get is speed. However the Pasadena Roadster Club, along with the Pasadena Pacers have, for the last five years, sponsored an event which is not limited to hopped-up cars alone; but is the type of event which any club anywhere in the United States can organize and run off.

The fifth running of this event was carried out along the lines of former years' running —cars had to run over a pre-determined course, at a pre-determined speed . . . the course having checkers at secret checkpoints, to make sure every car followed the exact course.

The whole point of the run is not to determine whose car can go the fastest, but to find out which driver and navigator can come closest to an average speed—deter-mined by the club officials before the start of the run.

This explains the title above . . . calling the Pasadena event a *rally* instead of a *reliability* run. The term reliability run was started back around 1900 when any car while finished such an event was considered to be reliable. As the years went by and perfectly stock cars proved their ability to finish everything but a race against modified speedsters, the term *rally* came in world-wide use.

The "rally" under discussion, incidently, was won by Dave Cook—driving his father's Chevrolet. Dave carried as his navigator, Bruce Ivey . . . both seventeen years old. And credit—as always—must go to the Pasadena Roadster Club and the Pasadena Pacers for running off a meet *better* than clockwork!

Dave Mitchell's pickup

26

1st place (#13) and 2nd place, Mitchell's Oldsmobile Rocket-engined pickup . . .

Starting line-up at Rose Bowl.

Kenny Blake's clean channeled '32.

Scotty Murdock's 4-barrel. His
father acted as the navigator.

Gassing up in Palmdale.

'34 custom roadster.

Instead of designating a certain prize as first, another one as second, and so on down the list, as is usually done in contests, the complete prize list is posted at the finish line. The first place winner can choose any prize from the list, then it is crossed off, and the second place winner can have his choice of what's left. This seems like a fine idea for distributing the prizes in a fair manner. The prize the judges select for fifth place might be more valuable to the first place winner.

1/4 mile in 12.18 seconds!

Otto Ryssman's high speeds are due in part to the smooth starts without excessive fishtailing demonstrated by some contestants.

Pat Murphy's stripped lakester is already steaming as he gets under way, turned 17.06 elapsed time for the quarter mile. 82.56 top speed.

Jack Trousdale's modified T roadster did the standing quarter in 14.30 and hit 98.96 top.

The Doug Hartelt- Dawson Hadley modified coupe turned a top speed of 110.29.

Is Otto Ryssman's run a world record? It could very well be—except for the fact that there are no "world records" in the ¼ mile category. Minimum distances for International Records are, of course, a measured kilometer or a measured mile. In spite of that fact, it is quite possible that Ryssman's 12.18 seconds for the standing quarter have been bettered by no car to date.

The world kilometer (⅝ mile) record was set in 1937 by Bernd Rosemeyer—driving an Auto Union on the Reich autobahn in Germany. Rosemeyer's *elapsed* time for the distance was 19.08 seconds; his *average* speed (from a standing start): 117.3 mph—which is not only an International record, but a World record as well. The German driver also established the International and World records for the standing mile: 25.96 seconds, or an average of 138.7 mph.

When we speak of world records and in-ternational records, we differentiate between them by remembering that a *world* record has no specific limitations regarding class while an *international* record refers to a particular class. Rosemeyer was running in the International Class and because he beat all competitors in that class, he established an international record. Because he made the best time regardless of class: a world record.

For the kilometer, a short-chassis Grand Prix car was used—specially supercharged. The mile record was established with a normal chassis on which was mounted a streamlined body. The reason for using different cars was that a streamlined car is heavier and not quite as quick at the lower end of the acceleration range, but also known to be faster over the greater distance of a mile. The cross-over point of the acceleration curve on these two cars was approximately 1400 yards from the start. Since a mile is 1760 yards and a kilometer is 1100 yards,

K. Walker on A.J.S. 15.61 sec. standing quarter.

the streamlined cars could do. the mile quicker than the open car but the open car could do the kilometer quicker. Actually, two streamlined cars were used, a 5-litre and the normal 6-litre.

It is generally assumed by the layman that streamlining does little good until a car has reached high speeds. Actually, if a body can be streamlined without adding weight, acceleration can be improved from 0 mph right on up. If the streamlining does add weight (as in the case of the Auto Union) this would necessitate lightening the chassis. As a matter of fact, the two successful Auto Unions were not lightened for the record attempt.

Running a streamlined car, however, does present a serious stopping problem. There are few timing strips available in the world today which are long enough. A car of this type has comparatively little wind resistance . . . wind resistance which exerts such a tremendous slowing-up effect in a normal car's deceleration. In a streamlined car most of the stopping must be done by the brakes and engine compression—with no help from air resistance. This may be an entirely new concept to the average driver; but anyone who has driven both streamlined and unstreamlined cars will tell you

Ken Sunderland leaves start in cloud of smoke from burning rubber as officials give start signal.

32

During the day a 10 lap sports car road race was held on the airport circuit.

that there is a startling difference as soon as the throttle is backed off.

A word here about timing methods . . . *Hop Up* feels that the San Diego Timing Association's method so closely parallels that of the International system that other timing associations would do well to follow this lead.

The only way that a driver can compare his time with that of other drivers from other strips and other associations is by using the *elapsed time method*. This method times a car from the moment the car starts to move until it has crossed the finish line. Other methods lack uniformity (such as timing the cars during the last few feet of their run, etc.) and give no true indication of a car's ability to accelerate.

By making the elapsed time method universal, drivers from all clubs will have some way of comparing individual times. They will also be able to measure their acceleration runs against the international records.

In keeping with this whole discussion, it is believed that if Otto Ryssman were to streamline his Lakester, and if he had a 1 kilometer course to practice on, he would come close to challenging some of the International standing start records.

The San Diego Timing Association has had many large meets, but the December 2nd event (at which Otto set the new strip record of 12.18 seconds) was the largest yet and the most spectacular, as cars from all over the state met to vie for the $25.00 and $50.00 War Bonds . . . for best time of the day, and best elapsed time of the day . . . both of which were won by Otto Ryssman.

Ryssman's rocket was built strictly for accelerating and not for beauty.

Offices and factory.

Meet the Advertiser

In 1938 E. R. Lindberg started designing competition speed boats as a hobby, using information gleaned in the public library.

Thirty-eight months ago, Ed decided he would like to do something on this order for a living, but not knowing how much market there would be, a small $1.50 classified ad was placed in a popular West Coast magazine offering plans for a 135 hydroplane for $10.00. Lindberg sold one set of plans. This was then reinvested in more classified ads which brought in three sales. By this time, Lindberg knew he had the answer to what he had been looking for but it was just a matter of building the business up.

While acting as a West Coast Representative of Allis Chalmers Co., he continued operating the mail-order boat-plan business in the evenings at home.

For the last year, he has been devoting full time to designing racing boats and has a small staff to complete the plans and take care of the mail orders. The entire business

is based on competition racing hulls. Lindberg refuses to design commercial boats.

There are 64 powered racing boat classifications with 37 different type boats in these classes. Champion Boats sells plans for 18 of the most popular types. Plans have been sent to almost every major country except Russia.

Three months ago Champion Boats opened a small factory to start building boats in Southern California. Now a person can get anything from the plans on up to the finished boat, complete with engine, from one source.

By far the most popular class of racing and the one for which the most plans are sold is the Utility Class Runabout, and this would be comparable to a sports car in the automotive field because 2 or 3 people can ride in this type boat and yet it can be raced on Sunday in events with other boats and is very inexpensive to build and operate.

34

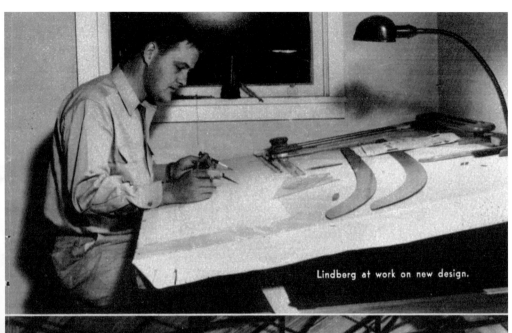

Lindberg at work on new design.

Utility hulls under construction.

Custom Grilles

Long ones, short ones, big ones, little ones, mostly they are horizontal, tho some are vertical.

One of the first things changed when customizing a car seems to be that part which is mainly used for letting air thru the front end to cool the radiator. Some favor replacing the old unit with a later (or earlier) stock or reworked model, while others prefer using their original grille—reworked.

36

365

What d' you think?

This month we have asked some of the leading custom shops for their opinion. "As far as styling is concerned, which of the 1951 automobiles did you like best and what changes would you like to see in the 1952 models."

Gil Ayala (Gil's Body Shop): "I like the Chevvy. With a little work, it could be made into a beautiful car. In '52 I'd like to see about 5 inches taken out of the sides of the body . . . lowered 2 inches . . . hood dropped 2 inches; larger windows and the seating position lower . . . possibly between the frame. I'd also like cut-away doors, up-sweep rear-fenders and a narrower body."

Neil Emory (Valley Custom): "Nicest '51 car (for the price) was the Ford Victoria. A good section job on one of those would really make it look great . . . say about 4 inches out of the side and, of course, lowered. I'd like to see larger windows, simpler grille, less chrome . . . and lower."

George Barris (Barris Kustom Shop): "The Chevvy and Mercury were the easiest to work on. The trend is toward higher front fenders, longer lines, dropped hood and deck . . . down between fenders. I like to see these changes and push-button didgets (doors, windows, seats, etc.) and the seating lower."

Sam Barris (Barris Kustom Shop): "I like the Chevvy and, of course, the Cad. The Chevvy was best to work on. Has good lines. I'd like to see it about 8 inches longer in back and 6 inches in front. Seating between frame, everything push-button, simple grille and less height between the ground and top of fender."

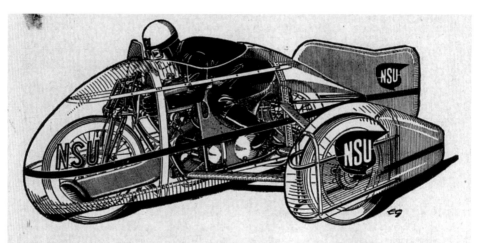

NSU BREAKS 22 RECORDS

Not content with capturing the absolute World Motorcycle Speed Record at 180.72 mph and 7 other records (see Hop Up, Sept. '51) . . . the German firm of NSU recently put a team of riders on an assortment of specially prepared motorcycles to take 22 more records.

The runs were made on the Munich-Ingolstadt Autobahn, which was also the scene of the previous record rides. And again Wilhelm Herz was riding . . . on non-streamlined supercharged 350 cc and 500 cc NSU solos. Herz set the following records:

Solo, Standing Start, 350 cc Class
1 Kilometer .... 90.5 mph
1 Mile ....102.0 mph

Solo, Standing Start, 500 cc Class
1 Kilometer ....102.0 mph
1 Mile ....113.5 mph

The 500 cc record was formerly held by Taruffi (Gilera), the 350 cc record by Sandri (Guzzi).

Hermann Boehm, NSU sidecar ace, was on hand to ride the streamlined 350 cc and 500 cc NSU sidecar outfits. The body shell closely resembled the record holding solo NSU . . . the wheel and fairing constituting the sidecar was attached to the motorcycle by three streamlined steel struts and carried 132 pounds of lead weights to fulfill the sidecar payload requirements. Records set by Boehm were:

Sidecar, Standing Start, 500 cc Class
1 Kilometer .... 84.5 mph
1 Mile ....97.5 mph

(These records broke the existing 750 cc and 1200 cc class records, thus accounting for four additional records)

Sidecar, Flying Start, 500 cc Class
1 Kilometer ....154 mph
1 Mile ....153 mph

(The 154 mph kilometer run established a new absolute speed record for sidecars. For both distances, Boehm not only broke his own 500 cc record of 125.4 mph, but also the 750 cc rec-ord of 129 mph (Ernest Henne, BMW), and the 1200 cc record of 137 mph (Eric Fernihough, 1000 cc Brough Superior). Thus, Boehm's ride set 6 new records).

Sidecar, Flying Start, 350 cc Class
1 Kilometer ....135 mph
1 Mile ....134 mph

Below, drive details of dual overhead cams on NSU 500 cc vertical twin 110 hp engine.

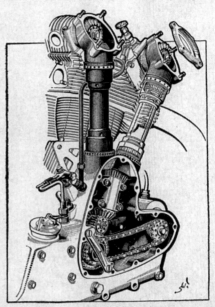

Below, Wilhelm Herz, world's fastest rider.

Wilhelm Herz, mounted on a 500 cc supercharged NSU, begins his record-breaking run.

Skillful streamlining on the 500 cc NSU helped Hermann Boehm smash the absolute World Speed Record for motorcycle with sidecar.

Compression Ratio

Would you like to know the actual compression ratio of your engine? Simply stated, **compression ratio is the volume of the cylinder, plus the total volume of the cylinder head combustion chamber, divided by the total volume of the cylinder head combustion chamber.** Compression ratio may be changed by milling the head, using thicker (or thinner) head gaskets, by "stroking" the crankshaft, or by boring the cylinders to a greater diameter. The new ratio may be found by the following procedure, in which a 1951 Ford V-8 engine is used as an example:

FIRST STEP . . . find the bore and stroke of your engine.

Example: bore, 3.1875 inches; stroke, 3.75 inches.

SECOND STEP . . . calculate the volume of a single cylinder (area of the bore times stroke).

1. To find area of the bore—square the radius and multiply by π (radius squared is ½ of bore times ½ of bore).
Example: ½ of 3.1875 = 1.5937″ (radius) 1.5937 times 1.5937 = 2.54″ (radius squared)
Then multiply the square by π (3.14), this gives you the area of the bore.
Example: 2.54 times 3.14 = 7.9756 sq in. (area)

2. Multiply the area of the bore by the stroke, this gives the volume of the cylinder.
Example: 7.9756 times 3.75 = 29.908 cu in. (volume)

3. Convert cubic inches to cubic centimeters to facilitate measurements (1 cu in. = 16.39 cc)
Example: 29.908 times 16.39 = 490.19 cc (volume)

THIRD STEP . . . measure the volume of the cylinder head combustion chamber.

1. Remove head from engine and thoroly clean the combustion chamber to be measured.

2. Insert sparkplug in chamber.

3. Place gasket (used) on head and seal, with light grease, to the chamber to be measured.

4. Be certain that head is absolutely level.

5. Using SAE-10 oil or hydraulic brake fluid, fill graduated beaker to 50 cc or other even mark. Pour into chamber until exactly level with top of gasket. Record total amount necessary to fill chamber*
Example: 85 cc

FOURTH STEP . . . add the volume of the cylinder to the volume of the cylinder head combustion chamber.

Example: 490.19 plus 85.0 = 575.19 cc (total volume)

FIFTH STEP . . . divide the total volume (as found by fourth step) by the volume of the cylinder head combustion chamber. The answer will be the compression ratio.

Example: 575.19 divided by 85.0 = 6.76
Therefore, the compression ratio of a 1951 Ford V-8 engine is 6.76 to 1.

*a. If piston does not go to top of cylinder at top dead center, fill space remaining and add amount to chamber volume.

b. If piston passes top of cylinder at t.d.c., measure amount of "pop-up," multiply by bore area, convert to cubic centimeters and subtract from the chamber volume.

c. If amount of piston "pop-up" is equal to head gasket thickness (and engine is ohv), just measure chamber volume without using gasket.

42

372

ROAD and TRACK
PHOTO QUIZ

1. This Ferrari coupe driven by Cornacchia in the Coppa della Toscana will go 130 mph with ease. What is the displacement of its engine?

☐ (a) 2325 cc   ☐ (c) 156 cu in.

☐ (b) 4100 cc   ☐ (d) 2 litres

2. Phil Payne's California-built Ford V-8 special was fastest sports car at speed trials held at:

☐ (a) Sydney, Australia

☐ (b) Gosport, England

☐ (c) Daytona, Florida

☐ (d) Yokohama, Japan

3. Max Hoffman's streamlined rear-engine Porsche made its debut at:

☐ (a) Watkins Glen, N. Y.

☐ (b) Elkhart Lake, Wisc.

☐ (c) Sao Paulo, Brazil

☐ (d) Palm Beach Shores, Florida

ANSWERS: 1. (c) 156 cu. in.—this is the Tipo 212 Export. 2. Phil Payne's Ford special was the fastest sports car at Gosport, England, Speed Trials, (b); see page 2, February Road and Track. 3. Hoffman's streamlined Porsche made its debut at Palm Beach Shores, Florida, Road Race (d) as reported in the February Road and Track, page 4.

HOW TO FIX
ANY PART OF ANY CAR

USED BY U.S. ARMED FORCES

QUICKLY-- EASILY-- RIGHT!

IGNITION · STEERING GEAR · BODY WORK · REAR END · OIL FILTER · GENERATOR · CARBURETOR · SHOCK ABSORBERS · DISTRIBUTOR · WHEEL ALIGNMENT · UNIVERSAL · AUTOMATIC TRANSMISSION · BRAKES · CLUTCH

NOW—Whether You're a Beginner or an Expert Mechanic —You Can "Breeze Through" ANY AUTO REPAIR JOB! MOTOR'S BIG BRAND-NEW AUTO REPAIR MANUAL Shows You HOW—With 2300 PICTURES AND SIMPLE STEP-BY-STEP INSTRUCTIONS.

Free 7-DAY TRIAL

Return and Pay Nothing if Not Satisfied!

COVERS EVERY JOB ON EVERY CAR BUILT FROM 1935 THRU 1951

YES, it's easy as A-B-C to do any "fix-it" job on any car whether it's a simple carburetor adjustment or a complete overhaul. Just look up the job in the index of MOTOR'S New AUTO REPAIR MANUAL. Turn to pages covering job. Follow the clear, illustrated step-by-step instructions. Presto —the job is done!

Over TWO THOUSAND Pictures! So Complete, So Simple, You CAN'T Go Wrong!

BIG NEW REVISED Edition covers everything you need to know to repair 800 car models. 771 giant pages, 2300 "This-Is-How" pictures. Over 200 "Quick-Check" charts — more than 38,000 essential repair specifications. Over 225,000 service and repair facts.

Even a green beginner mechanic can do a good job with this giant manual before him. And if you're a top-notch mechanic, you'll find short-cuts that will amaze you. No wonder this guide is used by the U. S. Army and Navy!

Meat of Over 150 Official Shop Manuals

Engineers from every automobile plant worked out these time-saving procedures for their own motor car line. Now the editors of MOTOR have gathered together this "Know-How" from over 150 Official Factory Shop Manuals, "boiled it down" into crystal-clear terms in one handy indexed book!

Try Book FREE 7 Days

SEND NO MONEY! Just mail coupon! When postman brings book, pay him nothing. Unless you agree this is the greatest time-saver and work-saver you've ever seen — return book in 7 days. Mail coupon today! *MOTOR Book Dept., Desk 53C, 250 West 55th St., New York 19, N. Y.*

Covers 800 Models—All These Makes

Buick	Henry J.	Nash Rambler
Cadillac	Hudson	Oldsmobile
Chevrolet	Kaiser	Packard
Chrysler	Lafayette	Plymouth
Crosley	La Salle	Pontiac
De Soto	Lincoln	Studebaker
Dodge	Mercury	Terraplane
Ford	Nash	Willys
Frazer		

Letters of Praise from Users "MOTOR'S Manual paid for itself on the first 2 jobs, and saved me valuable time by eliminating guesswork."
—W. SCHROP, Ohio.

Same FREE Offer on MOTOR'S New Truck and Tractor Manual

Covers EVERY job on EVERY popular make gasoline truck, tractor made from 1936 thru 1951. FREE 7-Day Trial. Check proper box in coupon.

HOP UP

APRIL, 1952 20 CENTS

PHOTO BY CHESEBROUGH

Custom Mercury *See Page 30*

TECHNICAL TIPS

FANLESS ROADSTER

In my 1934 Ford roadster chassis I have a 1941 Merc block, .040 bore, ¾ cam, ported and relieved, .050 milled heads, Lincoln valve springs, Mallory ignition, etc. My problem is how to eliminate the fan (because of excess noise) yet not overheat. Radiator and chassis are stock and I wish to keep them that way.

New York, New York   Fausto Guevaro

About 99% of the roadsters in the Southern California area run without fans and have very little cooling trouble (if engine and radiator are in good shape) unless the radiator is smaller than standard for that year car (such as channeled jobs and modified roadsters with race car type shells). The majority of drivers of these cars will avoid excessive traffic driving as much as possible, however. If you have to do much city driving, a fan is necessary—Dean B.

CANADIAN OLDS 6

I own a 1950 Canadian Oldsmobile 6-cylinder Hydramatic, 2-door sedan. The engine has the following specifications: bore 3-17/32″, stroke 4⅜″, displacement 257 cubic inches, 105 bhp @ 3400 rpm. Alloy pistons with two compression and two oil control rings.

Gas mileage seems poor to me, making 18 and 19 mpg on long country trips, 14 to 16 mpg in city and short trips.

I would like to have my engine modified to the extent that it would operate with the same ease at 70 and 75 mph speeds as it does now at 50 mph, and, if possible, at a gain in economy.

The car will remain strictly a family car to do a lot of slow city driving. What will be lost in modification?

Port Alberni, B. C., Canada   J. M. Pray

Your Oldsmobile specifications are identical to the last "6" built in this country. It's a good solid engine, with ample margin for modifications. Unfortunately, there is practically no speed equipment available for it.

I am a Rocket V-8 booster, and it would undoubtedly meet your requirements far better than a hopped-up 6. However, trading a late model car for a new one is a very expensive business. Objections to hopping-up are usually: (1) requires more frequent tune-ups, (2) very sensitive to fuel quality, (3) carbon removal required more often, (4) idle and low speed performance is sometimes rough, (5) engine is often more noisy, (6) economy drops if the added performance is used often.

Advantages are, of course, more performance, particularly at high speeds, higher maxima in the gears as well as in high, and usually better economy, if driven reasonably.

If you decide to modify the 6, here's an outline of what you can do, and still not be overly annoyed by the six objections listed.

1. Head—use an older model cylinder head to get higher compression. A 1939 Olds model 60 (217 cu in.) head with 6.2 compression ratio would give 7.15 to 1 on your 257 cu in. engine. Even the later 230 cu in. engine head will give a higher compression and it is better to mill a smaller amount off this one than to mill the '50 head. However, you can mill .050 to .060 from the '50 head if necessary.

2. Carburetion—leave it alone.

3. Exhaust—use one of the large Buick type straight-thru mufflers. Weld a divider in the exhaust manifold, then add a Gotha adapter to allow dual pipes and mufflers.

4. Cylinder block—should be relieved to eliminate obstruction to easy flow from the intake valve into the cylinders. This is particularly important with higher compression heads.

5. Camshaft—should not be more than a ¾ grind, nor have a timing overlap of more than 40°.

6. Fuel—if you don't go too high on compression, you can still use standard fuel by adding an Octagane or Vitameter injector unit.

7. Gear ratio—with Hydramatic transmission, you can use a faster gear with the modified engine. This will reduce low speed acceleration slightly, but the automatic transmission and engine modifications tend to cancel this out. A faster rear axle (lower numerical ratio) will also improve economy and increase the "quiet" cruising speed. Exact ratio will depend on availability of gears. Pontiac's 3.63 would be about right and will fit. I don't know exactly what Olds used in your '50 six, but 3.42 (as used in the 88) is rather "high" for a 257 cu in. engine. Your present mileage figures seem very good for such a heavy car.

8. Ignition—leave it stock.

—Tech. Ed.

HUDSON SUPER 6 HOP-UP

I have a 1949 super six Hudson. Does this engine have any basic commendable qualities as far as "hopping up"? Would I be better off starting with a Hornet engine instead? Will they interchange easily? I have no overdrive. What kind of performance can be expected from a Super or Hornet if a ¾ camshaft, 8:1 heads, ported and relieved, and dual carburetors?

Aurora, Nebraska   Robert Spencer

The Hudson is pretty much left out in the hop-up specialty business.

You can get good results by using the Pacemaker head on your larger engine. A dual intake manifold will be available from the factory soon and it undoubtedly will be well-engineered for good mixture distribution at all speeds and loads. I would wait for it.

I certainly think the 4-main bearing Hudson six engines are rugged and well-designed, tho they are somewhat heavy and unfortunately L-head design. Of course, the company president said some months ago that they had built experimental cars with 9.2 compression ratio and could go still higher with 100 octane fuel. I wonder . . . L-head engines develop combustion roughness at ratios of much over 8 to 1, and volumetric efficiency also falls off badly at high speeds.

If you can afford it, I would much prefer the 308-inch Hornet engine, even tho a change to the Hydramatic axle ratio is also advisable (since you do not have overdrive). As far as I can determine, the Hornet will use the same engine mounts as your present engine, even tho the cylinder block and heads are longer. I would advise a letter to the factory on this before you spend any money.

(Continued on page 43)

If it's hopped up, it'll be in HOP UP

H O P U P

INDIANAPOLIS

America's number one racing event, the Indianapolis 500 mile race, is held every year on Memorial Day, May 30. This year, as the date for the beginning of time trials draws near, feverish preparations are already under way for the battle for 33 starting starting positions on race day. Seasoned drivers and car owners foresee the hottest contest ever to gain the coveted starting positions. Added to last year's crop are many new cars. Shown this month (page 14) is the Cummins Diesel entry which, by special permission, is allowed a larger engine size than is permitted for spark-ignition engines.

Coming from Italy are two Ferrari-Grant Piston Ring specials, with possibly a third team member. Great things are expected of these 12-cylinder, 380 horsepower cars to be driven by Johnny Parsons, Alberto Ascari and another Italian

driver. Other new cars include one powered by a dohc Studebaker V-8, several others with Meyer-Drake 4-cylinder, 270 cubic inch engines which have proved so successful in past 500's.

Should a battle develop between the diesel-powered entry and any of the other cars, particularly the Italians, for the top position, there will probably be many protests against the 401 cubic inch supercharged diesel as the Indianapolis race this year counts toward the World Championship point standings. The victory at Indianapolis thereby is of paramount importance to anyone aiming at this objective. Since International regulations limit the size of blown engines to 91 cubic inches, the diesel may be claimed to be ineligible to claim points toward the World Championship, in which case perhaps the second place car would get the valuable points.

EDITORIAL STAFF

Editor ....Oliver Billingsley
Technical Editor................................John R. Bond
Associate Editors................................Louis Kimzey
Dean Batchelor, Robert Dearborn
Staff Photographers................................ Gene Trindl
Ralph Poole, Jerry Chesebrough
Photographers............Bob Canaan, Joe Al Denker

PRODUCTION STAFF

Managing Editor... ....W. H. Brehaut, Jr.
Production Director................................Louis Kimzey
Art Director................................Jack Caldwell
Art................................Gene Trindl

ADVERTISING

Promotional Director................................William Quinn
Advertising Manager................................Dean Batchelor
Eastern Advertising Manager......Robert L. Edgell
104 E. 40th Street, New York 16, N.Y.
United Kingdom................................Kenneth Kirkman
2 Longcroft Avenue, Banstead, Surrey, England
Italy.....Michele Vernola, C.P. 500, Milano, Italy

Vol. I, No. 9 **April, 1952**

CONTENTS

HOP UP is published monthly by Enthusiasts' Publications, Inc., 540 W. Colorado Blvd., Glendale, California. Phone CHapman 5-2297. Entered as second class matter at the post office at Glendale, California, under the Act of March 3, 1879. Copyright 1952 by Enthusiasts' Publications, Inc. Reprinting in whole or in part forbidden except by permission of the publishers.

Subscription price $2.00 per year thruout the world. Single copy 20c.

Change of address—must show both old and new addresses.

THE FLAME!

COMBUSTION CHAMBER DESIGN AND PROBLEMS

BY BARNEY NAVARRO

What happens in the combustion chamber? . . . Explosions, similar to dynamite blasts, causing fantastic pressures, are often pictured as being the power source of automobile engines . . . The only similarity between this concept and the truth lies in the fact that a form of combustion does the work, but violent reactions, such as we may imagine, would wreck any engine. Actually, the *burning* of the fuel is a slow process as compared to the exploding of a stick of dynamite, and pressures are only in the hundreds of pounds per square inch and not thousands as is popularly believed.

The loud report of the exhaust from an unmuffled engine may create the impression that explosions take place. Actually, the noise is produced by the sudden release of pressures when exhaust valves are opened . . . uncorking a champagne bottle produces the same effect. When the exhaust valve opens, all burning has ceased so it is impossible to hear any noise from the actual combustion of gases.

Fuel mixtures, instead of being ignited on the power stroke, are actually ignited on the compression stroke. Ignition takes place at varying distances before the end of this cycle. This distance is measured in degrees of crankshaft rotation and is referred to as spark advance or spark lead. Spark lead varies with combustion chamber design, engine load, engine speed and fuel. Early firing of the fuel charge is necessary because the burning takes a definite period of time. It must start before the beginning of the power stroke in order to have maximum pressures for this cycle. When the flame is started by the spark plug, it burns slowly at first and increases speed as the resultant pressure rises. Maximum pressure is produced a short time after the piston reaches top dead center. The maximum pressure at wide open throttle is rarely higher than 600 pounds per square inch in a passenger car engine. Race car engines and hot engines with high compression ratios may reach 900 or 1000 pounds, but these pressures only last for a very few degrees of crankshaft rotation. As soon as the piston moves a fraction of an inch the pressure begins to drop.

Spark lead is really a necessary evil because an engine could be made to produce more power if it were possible to commence the burning closer to top dead center. Due to the fact that an engine depends on heat to expand the gases which produce pressures, one can readily see that heat conducted to the coolant water thru the walls of the combustion chamber is lost heat that does no work. Heat loss is dependent on time . . . in other words, the longer the fire burns the more heat is carried to the water jacket. If the flame starts 45° before top dead center, a large amount of heat is conducted thru the walls of the combustion chamber to the water and is lost before the power stroke starts. Consequently, less pressure will be produced to push the piston down which will result in a power loss.

The burning rates of various fuels will have a very definite effect on spark lead because low octane gasoline burns faster than high octane. If an engine does not require high octane fuel, additional power cannot be obtained by using it. The use of high octane fuel in a low compression engine will *actually reduce* the power output. The spark will require more advancing to compensate for the slower burning and power will be lost. Quite often the improved throttle response received thru the use of aviation gasoline creates the impression that more power is available. This response at low speeds is only due to the fact that the fuel is more volatile (vaporizes more readily). High octane *does not* mean high power, it merely means high resistance to detonation (ping or spark knock).

Detonation is extremely rapid burning

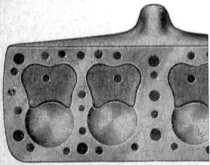

Flame starts at spark plug and radiates thru combustion chamber and quench area.

which produces a sudden shock similar to a dynamite cap. This shock is so rapid that it cannot be put to any use because it produces a hammer blow on the piston instead of a push. This condition takes place after the spark plug ignites the fuel but before the flame travels completely across the chamber. As the flame progresses, the pressure rises, causing the temperature of the unburned fuel to rise to a point where it is set off by the induced heat before the flame actually reaches it. When this happens, an entirely different type of combustion takes place with that part of the fuel. This sudden detonation produces a momentary temperature that is higher than the vapor point of molten iron. This high temperature cracks the lubricating oil at the top of the cylinder and produces a high hydrocarbon similar to some of the constituents of gasoline plus hard carbon deposits. The hydrocarbon burns and produces part of the smoke that is expelled from the exhaust when an engine pings. This burning actually increases oil consumption if allowed to continue and the drying of the cylinder walls increases wear.

Many methods are used to eliminate detonation, but the three principal ones are the use of high octane fuels, induced turbulance, and cooling of the unburned charge.

High octane fuels depend on certain types of chemical structure plus an additive (tetraethyl lead) to reduce detonation tendencies. The variation in structure and the quantity of ethyl fluid, produces the variations in octane ratings. Octane can be raised quite easily with the addition of ethyl fluid but there is a point beyond which very little effect is produced thru the addition of greater quantities. When this point is reached, more complicated refining processes are required to alter the chemical structure of the fuel. The processes, too expensive for automotive use, are presently limited to aviation fuel.

Turbulence reduces the tendency toward detonation by causing the fuel charge to circulate around the combustion chamber. In this manner, part of the fuel is brought to the flame instead of having to wait for the flame to travel across the chamber. Accelerated burning reduces the amount of spark advance required, so most of the burning takes place with the piston close to top dead center. In the L-head combustion chamber of the Ford V-8 engine, burning is so rapid that only 18° of spark lead is required at the rpm where maximum horsepower is produced. The combustion chambers of overhead valve engines do not provide as much turbulence, consequently they may require as much as 45° spark lead in extreme cases. Turbulence works hand in glove with the

quench area of the chamber (see illustration) because most of the burning is made to

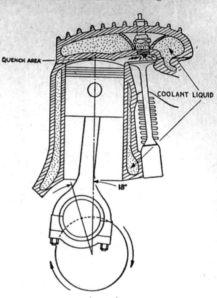

QUENCH AREA

COOLANT LIQUID

18°

Position of crankshaft and piston when fuel charge is ignited. Note how close the piston is to the head in region of "quench area".

take place during the portion of the cycle when the volume of this area is at a minimum. A small amount of fuel in this region is more easily kept cool by the water jacket than would be a large quantity . . . common practice is to keep the clearance between the piston and the head down to 1/16 of an inch at top dead center. This quench area keeps the fuel below the detonating temperature until the flame actually reaches it. The efficiency of this quench area is improved by using aluminum for the cylinder head and piston material because aluminum is a better conductor of heat. Higher compression ratios

(Continued on page 44)

CLEAN AND CHANNELED

by Bob Canaan

Here is a type that is fast disappearing from the streets and highways of California. With more and more roadsters being built especially for drag races, lakes or track use, a good, clean street job (like this beautiful example by Ray DeFillipi) is getting hard to find. There are all too few roadsters being used solely for transportation and the sheer joy of driving.

The overall appearance shows that Ray has spent a good many hours of thought and effort. All the details of the car have been given the attention they need so that everything is in good proportion and at the same time useful.

You'll notice that the radiator shell has been chopped to blend in well with the rest of the car which, of course, has been channeled. The "bubble" on the hood allows clearance for the dual carburetors.

Ray has used chrome extensively thruout the car, even to the extent of chroming the backing plates of the front wheel brakes. An interesting note is the windshield, which has been left stock as far as height is concerned. Altho a lower, "cut" windshield might give the car a better appearance in the eyes of some, Ray's idea proves itself when the top is up. The higher line gives ample headroom for driver and passenger.

The body has been channeled just enough to enhance the appearance and still retain a comfortable seating position, another point which brings out the unseen virtues of this roadster. Fire-Engine Red paint and white sidewall tires make an eye-catching combination.

Ray DeFillipi has handled the rear wheels in a manner which could be copied by more roadster builders. The rims have been removed from the wheels and reversed. When a roadster is channeled, as this one has been, the tops of the wheels ride up high and close into the body. Reversing the rims on the wheels gives ample clearance so that the tires do not rub on the body during sharp cornering maneuvers.

In the engine compartment you'll notice an Edelbrock dual manifold, twin Stromberg 97 carburetors, and Harrell heads. The cam is a Winfield, SU-I full-race grind and the ignition wires are carried in eight separate chrome tubes. Two Ford coils are used with a Kurten ignition, and the 4 inch stroke and $3\frac{3}{8}$ bore give all the power needed for street use. Fuel is supplied (from an aluminum tank in the turtle-deck) by a pressure pump.

One of the fine points of the car is the '40 Ford dash which maintains the clean body lines. Visibility over the hood is very good.

Ray says the roadster is not finished yet . . . for better handling he plans to install a longer pitman arm (faster steering) and a full belly-pan underneath.

6

The engine compartment of Ray De Fillipi's roadster is indicative of the care with which he handled all the details. Wiring, for example, is not scattered or haphazard, but is neatly arranged in groups, giving a neat appearance and making the engine more accessible for adjustments and repairs. The generous use of chrome also helps maintain overall neatness of the car and is an aid to keeping engine and all parts clean . . .

Altho this car was built specifically for the streets and was not intended for competition, roadsters with similar equipment often clock upwards of 125 mph in Southern California.

Right, low hood on Ray's roadster makes for excellent visibility as the driver looks over the 1940 Ford dash, steering column and wheel.

SUBSCRIBE TO HOP UP NOW!

8   **HOP UP, April, 1952**

Early Lakesters

The following is quoted from the *Southern California Timing Association Racing News and Program, August 24, 1941.*

"Albata-Bob Bebek, running an A V-8 roadster, took first in his class with a speed of 117.65 mph. Second was Vic Edelbrock of the Road Runners, who got 116.52 mph with his '32 V-8 roadster. Bill Burke of the Gear Grinders followed in third place at 115.24 mph in his '32 V-8 roadster with the engine that Vic ran last year. (These ran in Stock-Bodies class)

"Mel Ball in his D.O. McDowell, Willie West Karl Orr, Randy Shinn, Chauncey Crist in a in his A V-8, Sandy Belond, Tunney Shigekuni, rear-engine A V-8, Albert Rough, and many others have an equal chance at the five trophies and twelve point-winning places in the Roadster class.

"The Modified class boys were also very close together at the last races. Albata Jim White's Hudson 8, driven by Association treasurer Lowell Lewis, placed first with 124.14 mph. Danny Sakai's V-8 was second at 121.89 mph followed by Rod Pugh in the Pugh Bros. V-8, placing third at 121.20 mph. Babe Ouse squeezed 116.58 mph out of his Winfield flathead Modified and tied for sixth in his class.

"Ralph Schenck's Chevy 4, at 121.29 mph, was the only car in the Streamliner class to

Danny Sakai's V-8 Modified. Engine was built-up by Mal Ord, who made his own speed equipment—turned 125 mph in 1941. Radiator shell is from '39 La Salle.

Jack Lehmann's V-8 modified at Muroc in 1941. Drivers, on their way to the starting line would stop by this finish line stand to pick up their times.

Same car in 1946, then owned by Doug Caruthers. Photo was taken on a Road Runner Club cruise to the Jalopy Derby at San Bernardino. Mufflers, license plates, and lights were added for road use. Car now belongs to Harold Miller and holds the San Diego Drag Meet record at 120.80 mph.

qualify over 120 mph, which is the minimum speed for eligibility in that class. Ralph won twelve points, bringing the Albata total to 43.

"The Spalding Brothers, Bill and Tom . . . took the twelve (and only) points won in the Unlimited Class. Running a V-8 Modified with Riley Overheads and dual carburetors on a Roots-type blower, they set the day's fastest speed of 128.93 mph."

The speeds mentioned above may not seem very fast today . . . . but "way back then" the boys didn't have the speed equipment that is available now. Most of the "speed parts" were home-made—developed by the trial and error method.

Tony Capana in Marmon V-16 modified once the fastest car (145 mph) at the Dry Lakes.

#27—Karl Orr's Chevy modfied, #28—Ernie McAfee's Winfield flat-head 4-barrel streamliner. Men in photo are left (in white coveralls) Karl Orr, Wes Collins, Bob Rufi, Unidentified, Ernie McAfee. Ernie broke record first time out by turning 123 mph. Johnnie Junkin held previous record at 121.62. McAfee later turned 138 mph with same car.

This car once belonged to Fred and Bob Frame. Power plant was Ford V-8 with Dixon overhead valve . . . speed about 121 mph.

Spalding Bros. modified V-8 equipped with Riley ohv and a Roots type blower, clocked 132 mph. Car had a modified body but ran unlimited class because of the supercharger.

Karl Orr's modified V-8 carried #1 at El Mirage because of top position in point standings the last year of pre-war competition. Also held 133 mph modified record.

It was about this time (a little over ten years ago) that equipment manufacturers sprang into being and started the ball rolling. Edelbrock, Thickstun, Meyers, Ord, Weiand, Federal Mogul, Davies, Morrison, Betry, Spalding, Winfield, Bertrand, Porter, Smithy, Belond, and Huth—to name a few.

Custom body work was capably performed by Jimmy Summers, Roy Hagy, Linc Paola, and quite a few more.

When World War II interrupted lakes events, the roadster record was 123 mph and a streamliner had reached 140 mph. Now—in 1952—a roadster (even in the small displacement class) has to turn 120 mph or better to make points. Several *stock body* roadsters have passed the 150 mph mark and two bettered 160 . . . at Bonneville.

Three cars (two lakesters and one streamliner) have exceeded 180 mph at El Mirage; two cars (both streamliners) have topped the 200 mark at Bonneville. Marv Lee's "City of Pasadena" would undoubtedly be included in the over-200 class if it hadn't flipped at Bonneville.

Speeds and the quality of equipment are not the only things to undergo a radical change, however. Safety precautions and classes for bodies and engines are constantly being studied and improved—to make the running both safer and fairer to all. In fact—despite the bad publicity in the newspapers—the sport of amateur racing is actually one of the safest in the world . . . and there are figures available to prove it. Body and engine classes have been altered so often that it would be difficult to list them all. At the time most of the accompanying photos were taken, there were four main classes: roadster, modified, streamlined and unlimited.

12

Dick Ford's Chevy-bodied V-8 roadster ran as a modified because he narrowed body.

Members of the Bungholers Club helped Arnold Birner build up his 4-port Riley modified in about 2 weeks time. Top speed 126 mph. Engine was previously in a roadster.

Evolution of a car—the two views at right are Kenny Lindley's modified V-8 at El Mirage in 1946—Lower left, same car as owned by Dietrich and Thomas who added tail, putting car into streamliner class. Upper left, same car at Bonneville in 1949, entered by Walker and McAllister. New radiator shell added.

Freddie Agabashian tries seating position of the Cummins Diesel as owner Don Cummins (left) and designer Frank Kurtis (right) talk.

Cummins Diesel

BY BOB CANAAN

It is worthwhile reporting to you *Hop Up* readers that, as far as we know, the Cummins Diesel Company is the only American manufacturer of commercial engines which is currently using the annual 500 mile race on the Indianapolis track for experimentation and improvement of their product. A Cummins Diesel ran as early as 1931 and in 1935 a pair of Cummins placed.

Like the Cummins which ran in 1950 and 1951, chassis and body of this new car were built by Kurtis Kraft of Los Angeles. A glance at the chassis workmanship and the smooth body explains why Frank Kurtis builds more race cars than any one else in the world.

Specifications are probably more interesting than those of any car which has run at the famous "brickyard" for many years. With a 6 cylinder engine weighing 700 to 750 pounds (current Offenhausers weigh 535), the car is necessarily bigger, longer and heavier overall than its gasoline-powered competition.

To make for driver comfort and low seating position, the center of gravity is displaced eight inches to the left. The driveshaft passes to the left alongside the driver's seat and connects with the offset rear end —a design which is said to be favorable on tracks where the cars turn only to the left.

The tubular frame dips down alongside

the driver (who, this year at Indianapolis, will be Freddie Agabashian) so that the extreme right hand seating position will not cause the frame to interfere with his elbows.

The car is sprung by torsion bars front and rear—the front bars being attached to the upper A frame and the rear torsions connecting to the axle-housing in a fairly conventional manner. Two sets of shocks take care of the four corners of the car . . . one set: Houdaille, and the other: 50/50 Gabriel . . . the Houdailles are adjustable from the cockpit.

The open rear axle is a tube, as can be seen, which continues thru the rear axle bearing carrier and revolves with the wheels as an entire unit. The rear end is a Conze quick-change unit.

In wind tunnel tests at the University of Wichita, the car was found to be just about as streamlined as is possible without covering the wheels, and this led to problems in braking. A streamlined car requires more braking effort because the wind resistance does not help the car to stop. Then too, the turbo supercharger (driven by exhaust pressure) prevents the driver from using his engine as a brake. On the heavy Cummins, therefore, two sets of spot brakes are used —with separate lines and separate master cylinders. However, both sets are manipulated by the same pedal . . . the idea being not only increased braking power, but reliability—in case one of the brake systems

14

fails. Fading brakes have been a problem at Indy, also. Last year, drivers were seen to sail right on past their calculated stopping point during a quick pit stop . . . they had enough brakes to slow for the turns but not enough for severe braking. (Running past a pit stop draws a one lap penalty.)

At the present time, the four cycle 401 cu in. engine* is turning out 350 hp, but the aim of the Cummins people is 400 hp on regular Mobil commercial Diesel fuel—or 1 hp per cubic inch. Frank Kurtis has finished the body and chassis work and the car has been flown to the Eastern factory for further testing and engine tuning. After Agabashian has driven the car in the Memorial Day 500, it will be sent to Bonneville Flats (Utah) in an attempt to raise the World Record for diesel powered cars . . . which at present is held by the last year's Cummins.

*A "special" Indianapolis rule permits diesel displacements to 402 cu in. . . . limit for spark-ignition supercharged engines is 183 cu in. . . . for unsupercharged, 274.8 cu in.

Wheelbase	104"
Tread (front)	58"
Tread (rear)	56"
Weight (dry)	2150 pounds
Fuel capacity	50 gallons
Ground clearance	4"
Bore	4⅛"
Stroke	5"
Total capacity	401 cu in.

Above, transmission has two shift levers, one on the left for first and reverse and one on the top for second and third. Torsion bar is wrapped to avoid weakening surface nicks.

Below, quick-change rear end, open-tube axles, disc spot brakes make for lightness.

Above, large radiator is necessary for cooling big diesel. Air scoop feeds turbo-supercharger. Auxiliary fuel oil tank is located alongside dual master cylinders for brakes.

Below, lube oil tank is mounted over engine crankcase. Dual exhaust headers run directly into turbine chamber of turbo-supercharger.

Upper tube of right hand truss swoops to furnish elbow room for driver. Cross-tube behind seat jogs for rear end unit travel. Both tubular and vane-type shock absorbers are visible.

Below, with windshield and headrest removed, car can run upside-down on its own wheels.

Hop Up Test No. 1

BY DEAN BATCHELOR

Statistics		Owner—BILL FARIS
Chassis	1932 Ford V-8	
Wheelbase	108 inches	
Tread	57 inches	
Weight	2320 pounds	
Tires	5.50 x 16 front, 7.00 x 16 rear	
Rear end	3.27 to 1 '39 Ford with	
gears	Zephyr transmission gears	
	'40 Ford hydraulic brakes	
Body	1932 Ford Roadster	
Instrument	Reworked '32 Ford	
Panel	(by Danny D'Reagan)	
Engine	1940 Ford V-8 bored to Merc.	
Bore	3 3/16 inches	
Stroke	3 3/4 inches	
Displacem't	239 cubic inches	
Cam	Harmon & Collins Super M	
Manifold	Edelbrock Triplett with	
	Model 48 carbs	
Heads	Edelbrock 9.5 to 1	
Ignition	Spalding Zephyr type	
Flywheel	Chopped and balanced	

Valves   Stock size
    Intake 30°, Exhaust 45°
    Ported and relieved by Randy Shinn
    Exhaust dividers added to center ports
80 lb. oil pump
Clark Headers, Porter Mufflers

Upholstery by Roy Conyers
Paint by Ronnie Price
Bodywork by Valley Custom
Instruments—
    Fuel Pressure   Tach   2 engine temp.
    Oil Pressure
    Ammeter   Speedo Vacuum gauge
    Stock Ford fuel pump pumps air into tank
instead of pulling gas thru. Hand pressure
pump is on same line.
    Fuel selector valve in rear compartment
helps facilitate changing from gasoline to alcohol tank at Lakes.
    Car clocked 132.352 mph in July, 1951 at
SCTA Lakes Meet, fitted with cockpit tarp
and sans windshield, headlights, fenders and
mufflers.
    Straight methanol was used for fuel.

18

HOP UP, April, 1952

Owner Bill Faris (right) checking author out.

Interior of deck, showing selectors for fuel and air pressure lines—fuel line is 7/16".

Hop Up Magazine has had so many reader queries concerning the behavior and reliability of modified cars, that we decided to road test several . . . with various makes of equipment on them.

Because a hot roadster or coupe is an individually conceived machine, built to satisfy its owner's particular needs, it would be useless to use the same standard of measurement required in road testing a production vehicle.

In the first place, many things enter into the production car picture which wouldn't concern an owner of a hop up. The builder of a roadster (or coupe) is not generally concerned with such Detroit headaches as luggage space, gas consumption and depreciation.

Then too, the tester of a car such as we have in mind is bound to be confronted by a privately owned and well taken care of object of affection. So . . . he cannot subject it to the rigorous, sometimes backbreaking, tests of a factory-owned demonstrator. The roadster or coupe must be returned to its owner in the same condition in which he last saw it.

Anyone planning a special of this type has (or should have) a good idea of what performance he expects. He will know that a car built for acceleration will differ from a straightaway, high gear machine. And a car that is aimed at maximum speed will be different from one that is to achieve maximum economy. But the builder will also know that there are happy mediums that can be reached in most cases.

Engine compartment is not built for "show".

As Bill Faris of Burbank handed me the keys to his roadster he told me, "You probably won't like it. The gearing is too high and the steering is stiff . . . for town use. I'm going to change the rear-end gears as soon as I can . . . and have the front end re-aligned." I hadn't driven two blocks before I discovered what he meant. Those 3.27 gears were put in the rear end for straightaway runs at the dry lakes and are absolutely nowhere for town use—especially with 7.00 x 16 rear tires and Zephyr first and second gears in the transmission.

For a car that will be driven mostly in town, a 3.54 or 3.78 rear end, with smaller rear tires (6.50 x 16 or 7.00 x 15) would be more suitable, tho there is another alternative. If you're planning a car for street use, with an occasional cross-country trip, the 3.27 gearing and large tires can be combined with a stock transmission . . . which will provide good cruising and still give you better stop-sign to stop-sign performance in town than Bill's roadster does.

Aside from the gearing, the car is a pleasure to drive in traffic because of the seating position and placement of the steering wheel, foot pedals, and gear lever. Unlike many roadsters in my experience, the seats were not too heavily padded, but were upholstered to give the right amount of support.

Tho operating without the fan, the engine seldom ran over 170 F., even in traffic . . . probably due to the good condition of the engine and radiator. I liked the fire extinguisher which was firewall-mounted on the passenger side of the cockpit, directly in front of the instrument panel.

As I got out of city traffic and onto the open road, this little jewel really came into its own. The gearing that makes city driving a little less pleasant, makes highway travel just that much better. The legal speed limit of 55 mph is attained at 2000 rpm on the tachometer. At this engine speed, plenty of reserve power is there for passing or in case of emergency.

The excellent condition of Bill's car shows up when crossing railroad tracks or when on rough roads. The car is free of rattles and squeaks (bear in mind that this body is 20 years old). The carpeted floor mat reduces engine and road noise to a minimum.

After making monkeys out of some wise guys in a late model "mashed-potato-drive" Rocket (they seemed to think a roadster is a jalopy) I took to the hills. Bill Faris' roadster accelerates well and runs fast at the top end, but I wanted to see how it would

20

stick to the road on a turn . . . and I found out what Bill meant when he said the steering was stiff.

A car running at the lakes has the front aligned differently than a pleasure car. Lakes specials run 11 or 12 degrees castor as compared to the 4 or 5 degrees castor on a street roadster . . . and the toe-in on a car at the lakes is practically nil, whereas a car on the streets will ordinarily have a few degrees of toe-in. So, when I got into a corner with Faris' roadster, it took a lot of effort to wheel it around and when I got back in the straightaway the steering wheel wouldn't "return." This means that the car never steers itself—the driver has to do it all—which is alright in a quick steering car, but this roadster's steering was stock '32, which is just a little slow for fast cornering.

The car seemed to hold the road very well once you got the wheel pointed the way you wanted it, and the power available was more than sufficient to climb any hill encountered in normal driving. With the present gear set-up it was almost impossible to break the rear-end loose on a turn.

Night driving was helped by the sealed beam headlights—mounted high and fairly far apart. Many special-built roadsters, coupes and sports cars end up with the headlights mounted low and close together. Maybe they look good that way but they provide poor lighting at night . . . and even when the low beams are used, they blind oncoming drivers.

Notes and Comments

Taking everything into consideration, this roadster is a darn good machine. It has the power and speed to satisfy the sporting blood of most drivers and yet is conservative in appearance. Bill Faris will vouch for its reliability . . . three years since the engine was built, and the car has been thru two SCTA lakes seasons without a major overhaul. Bill finished number 39 in 1950 and number 55 in 1951—even tho he missed one meet altogether.

Sometimes I wonder whether it pays to have a good looking car anymore. I parked in front of a photographic shop to get film for the camera which would "shoot" the roadster. A woman, parked in the next space, threw open the door of her car. It soundly whacked the newly painted fender of the roadster.

"Oh, I'm sorry," she said as she stalked off down the street, "You've just had it painted, haven't you?"

And there *I* stood—with my #!$%*¼!! piccolo!   —DEAN BATCHELOR

Cornered well . . . .

Well arranged instrument panel.

396

What d' you think?

Roy Richter (Bell Auto Parts): "Of all the hundreds of special accessories that we have the opportunity to inspect, test and sell, there is one item that, in my opinion, stands above all others. This item is the new Stewart-Warner Deluxe Motor Minder. It has everything that is desirable to the customer and the dealer that sells it. It is practical, very attractive, of excellent design and construction, and popularly priced. Above all, the saving in gasoline will make this instrument pay for itself many times over, while giving a very personal insight into the condition and operation of your engine."

Alex Kraus (Eastern Auto): "In my opinion the best value in a custom accessory is one that: 1. adds a styling note to the car's appearance. 2. not over-priced. 3. easily installed. 4. does not require much body work or paint to effect its installation. If pinned down to a current popular item that meets these requirements. I'd pick the new 1951 Ford straight grille bar."

Milt Stanton (Auto Accessories): "I say the Select-O-Drive and the Select-O-Matic. They both give a person complete control of the car plus better mileage, braking ability, safety and versatility in the transmission. The Select-O-Drive is one of our most popular items and our new Select-O-Matic will be just as popular."

Ernest Newhouse (Newhouse Automotive Industries): "Well, I'd pick the Octa-Gane pressure injector. It not only keeps the engine free of carbon, but runs the cylinder heads cooler and eliminates pre-detonation that otherwise damages the engine. Plain water, fit to drink, works perfect, but if anyone wants "rubber-laying" performance, 100% methanol in the injector will satisfy even drag strip contestants. My second choice would be 'Liqui-Moly.'"

announcing

purchase of AUTOMOBILE TOPICS* by Floyd Clymer Publications

*America's Oldest Automotive Magazine . . . Established in 1900.

Published in Detroit . . . the *World's Motor Capital*

TO ALL CAR OWNERS and MOTOR ENTHUSIASTS !

AUTOMOBILE TOPICS, the oldest automotive magazine in America, having been established in 1900, is now a *Floyd Clymer Publication*.

You are invited to participate in our SPECIAL OFFER for new subscribers and old customers. Rates are $5 for one year and $8 for two years. With each new subscription, we offer AT NO EXTRA COST—any one of six $2 CLYMER MOTORBOOKS.

AUTOMOBILE TOPICS will come to you monthly with a new and enlarged format, full of news of interest to anyone connected with the automotive industry. Such features as complete car specifications, production figures, service helps, technical articles, news of the trade and factories, data on new products, all of which have been popular in the past, will be continued.

Clymer Motorbooks have become widely known throughout the world Now I PROMISE YOU A NEW AND DIFFERENT TYPE OF MONTHLY AUTOMOTIVE MAGAZINE, and offer you a SPECIAL DEAL for a limited time only. Those who know CLYMER MOTORBOOKS can visualize the type of magazine the NEW Automobile Topics will be, under Clymer management.

Please read details and MAIL YOUR ORDER NOW to secure a full year of interesting motoring information for ONLY 10 CENTS A WEEK . . . and a $2 CLYMER MOTORBOOK of your choice thrown in AT NO EXTRA COST!

Floyd Clymer

The New Automobile Topics will Feature:

THINGS TO LOOK FOR

398

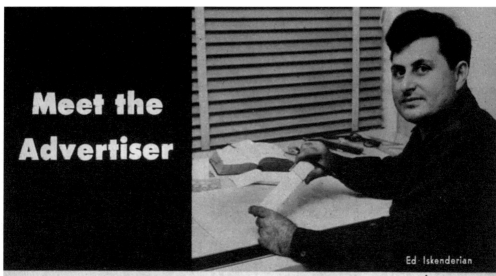

Meet the Advertiser

Ed· Iskenderian

From a humble beginning in a back corner of the Mercury Tool & Die Co. (owned and operated by a friend) former toolmaker Ed Iskenderian has built his cam grinding business into the respected position it holds today in the field of speed equipment.

Ed and his crew grind cams for nearly all cars and have on hand what is probably the largest stock of reground cams, for immediate shipment, of any shop in the United States.

Iskenderian gives credit for most of his success to the "track grind" cam and the "mushroom tappet" cam, both of which he introduced to the field. However, anyone who knows Ed will tell you that, in addition to designing good cams, he is also a guy who makes a practice of being honest in all of his business dealings — which has also contributed greatly to his success.

Ed is 30 years old, married and has two boys. He doesn't have any ambitions about expanding into other fields but would like to enlarge his present facilities for cam work. At present, altho his shop boasts the most modern precision equipment, Ed Iskendarian still keeps the old hand-operated grinder he started out with five years ago . . . just to remind himself of his humble beginnings.

Modern equipment . . .

26

Large shop

Grinder in action

401

Custom Hints

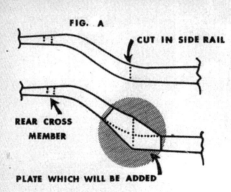

FIG. A

CUT IN SIDE RAIL

REAR CROSS
MEMBER

PLATE WHICH WILL BE ADDED

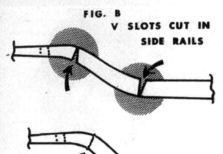

FIG. B

V SLOTS CUT IN
SIDE RAILS

WELD

by (Ghunga)—Dean Batchelor

There are two accepted methods of lowering Fords and Mercs prior to the 1949 models . . . and both systems are shown on these pages.

The first is commonly known as a "Z" frame—and "Z-ing" is accomplished in the manner shown in Fig. A and photos 1 and 2.

After the frame has been cut in this way, reinforcing should be added as was done on the frame of this 1934 Ford coupe.

The second method is the "Kick-Up" . . . as shown in Fig. B and photos 3 and 4. The width of the slot will depend on just how much you want to lower your car. For example: 1½ inch slot will result in a lowering of approximately five inches.

To avoid mistakes, a cardboard template can be made—to the size and shape of the side rails. Thus, experiments with various slot widths will determine exact results.

Kicking up the frame puts the rear cross member (spring hanger) several inches farther forward, so it will have to be re-positioned. The frame rails will be shorter in relation to the body . . . . they will have to be lengthened enough to support the gas tank and rear bumper.

Before performing any of these modifications, the rear deck floor will have to be cut out, whereupon the parts which need altering can be seen more readily. Lowering by either of these methods will decrease luggage space in the rear deck . . . . and the drive-shaft tunnel must be revamped —as far forward as the transmission.

Rear deck compartment of 41 Ford with floor cut away ready for next step of work.

Rear compartment of 41 Ford after job is complete showing addition on wheel well necessary when car is lowered this much.

28

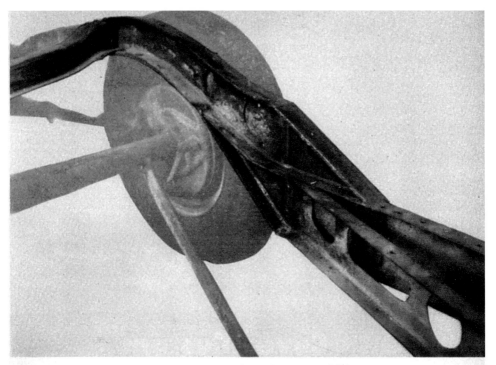

Inside of Z-frame with reinforcement added.

Outside of Z-frame with reinforcement added.

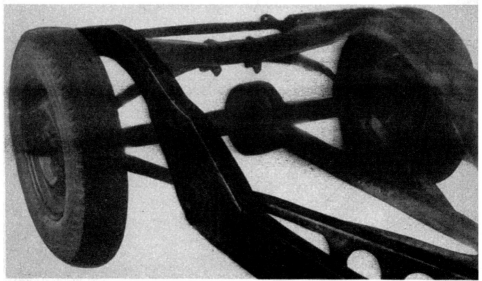

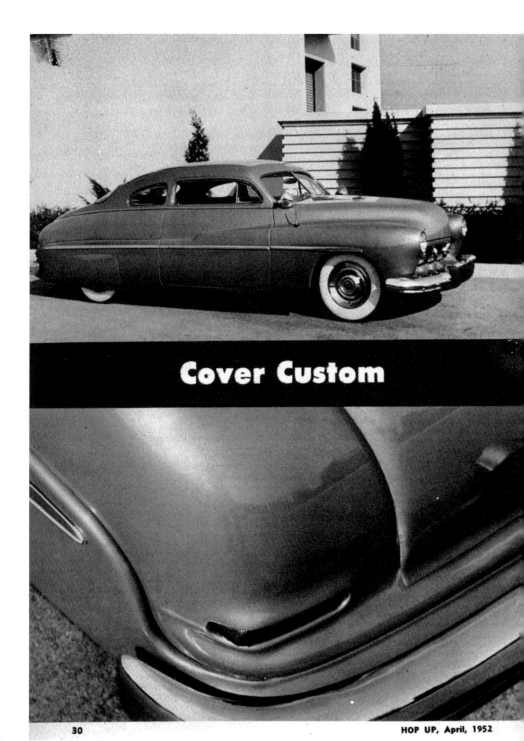

Cover Custom

In the rear of the Merc, the deck has been smoothed and the upper corners of the deck lid rounded . . . . in order to carry out the style of the hood and doors. The tail light case has been removed and the taillight lenses have been installed in the fenders.

The overall proportions of the Wally Welch custom present pleasing proportions and (in this writer's humble opinion) one of the big features of the car is that it does *not* drag its rear in the ground . . . . as do many customs which seem to have that "speed boat look."

And all this excellent body work was carried out by Gil Ayala of Gil's Auto Body Shop.

If it seems to you—from the appearance of recent custom photographs and articles— that the staff of *Hop Up* is a little "Merc-happy" . . . . you are right. But there's a good reason behind it.

As a matter of fact, next to the ever popular Ford, there are more Mercurys customized every month in America than any other car . . . and Wally Welch's Merc is one of the most outstanding examples to show up around these parts to date. By now you've seen the car in color on the cover, so you know what we mean in that department. Its really an eye-opener.

Let's start at the front of Wally's drive-in dream boat, and as we move toward the rear we'll check off what has been done to the car.

The headlights have been brought forward

three inches and the lower corners of the hood rounded off. The gravel shield has been molded into the body and fenders, the hood ornament removed, and a special grille formed and installed. *Hop Up* offers this hand-made grille as a good example of originality in design.

The top has been cut . . . . four inches in front and five in the rear, and the drip molding removed. You have probably noticed by now that the upper rear door corners have been rounded off. The doors, incidently, are electrically operated by push buttons.

Ordinarily, the push buttons on custom electric doors are mounted under the door, but Wally's are set in the chrome rub strip . . . . which results in a nice effect.

Chet Herbert (left) and Bill Walker.

GMC Dynaflow Ford

1932 Ford sedan chassis and body (channeled), 270 GMC engine burning butane with alcohol injection, 1950 Buick Super Dynaflow transmission, 1936 Ford rear end with 3.54 gears, 1940 Ford hydraulic brakes with 1950 Merc wheels and hub-caps and a Crosley steering wheel. Sounds like a wild conglomeration of parts but it was all very neatly assembled by Bill Walker (Walker's Garage, 12600 S. Main, Los Angeles, Calif.) for Chet Herbert.

Never one to be conventional, Chet wanted a car which would suit his whims, try out a few pet ideas, and still be usable as transportation. But it has taken Walker and Herbert two years to finish the job because Chet's friends continually talked him into running the engine at the lakes . . . with a great deal of success, I might add.

The GMC block is equipped with a Horning 12-port head of 12 to 1 compression ratio, Spalding dual ignition, Chet Herbert roller tappet cam, and at the lakes a Hilborn-Travers injection system is used with a hot fuel of Chet's own blend. The injector is replaced for town driving by two Century butane carburetors with a Cyclone heat exchanger common to butane rigs. There is also an alcohol injection system controlled by a switch on the instrument panel and fed from a one gallon tank also in the rear. An Autopulse fuel pump provides the "go juice."

To get back to the lakes, the engine has been timed at 154 mph in a Crosley sedan at Bonneville and 151 mph in a chopped "T" sedan at El Mirage during an SCTA

meet. It also holds the Russetta "B" coupe record at 138 mph in Ed Pink's '36 Ford coupe.

The starting system is 12-volt while the normal 6-volt unit operates the ignition and lights. Fuel is carried in a 50 gallon tank mounted where the seat usually is located. Fuel consumption is about 5 mpg.

Power is controlled by an Accellabrake unit hooked up to the Dynaflow shift lever. Pull the lever down into Drive to go, push up to apply brakes. Reverse is engaged by a hand lever on the floor. There are no foot controls, because Chet was left incapacitated by polio. Incidently, the installation of the Dynaflow was relatively simple. 1/4 inch was milled from the Dynaflow transmission adapter and the bolt holes were redrilled to match the GMC block. The only remaining step was to bore out the rear end of the GMC crankshaft to fit the end of the Dynaflow master shaft.

Red and white pleated leatherette upholstery and a Stewart-Warner instrument panel comprise the interior finish.

The front of the car is lowered by a dropped axle and race car type, split, adjustable radius rods are used. Shocks are tubular rear, Ford Houdaille front.

Engine Details

Bore	3 31/32 in.
Stroke	4 in.
Displacement	296 cu in.
Brake horsepower	
Fuel	275
Butane	198

34

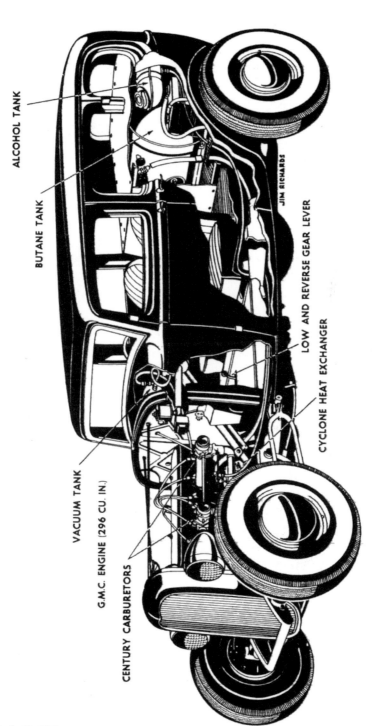

ALCOHOL TANK

BUTANE TANK

VACUUM TANK

G.M.C. ENGINE (296 CU. IN.)

CENTURY CARBURETORS

LOW AND REVERSE GEAR LEVER

CYCLONE HEAT EXCHANGER

JIM RICHARDS

Interior of rear, showing Butane tank, alcohol tank, battery.

Instrument panel — Vacuum tank is for Accelabrake unit.

410

Interior—tires are 7.60 x 15 rear, 6.70 x 15 front.

A group of Hot Dogs at Wilcap Automotive. Don Clark (left) and Clem Tebow (rear) holders of the Bonneville "C" Roadster record of 162 mph. Bill Walker, record holder at Bonneville in 1949. Bill Likes, holder of the "B" Roadster record at Bonneville. Tony Capana, who at one time had the fastest car at the lakes. "Red" Wilson, who helped pioneer track roadster racing in California and is active in boat racing activities. Chet Herbert in foreground.

Exhaust side, Spalding ignition visible just under headers.

Carburetion side of 296 cu in. engine.

Thunderbolt

The present crop of "Cars of the Future" fail to impress Ernest Newhouse (the fellow wearing the Xmas tie, above) of Newhouse Automotive Industries. Like Chrysler, General Motors, and Ford . . . Newhouse has a "Car of the Future." It's a 1941 Chrysler Thunderbolt, built in very limited production as a showroom teaser. The all-metal top automatically retracts into the rear deck. An air scoop under the bumper eliminates the conventional grille. The Thunderbolt beat Nash to fully-inclosed front wheels by eight years and the trap-door headlights appeared on the '42 De Soto. Seems, however, that the future has not yet entirely arrived.

413

Mail Box 110

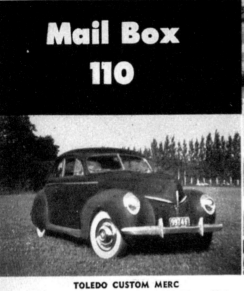

TOLEDO CUSTOM MERC

The hood and deck of my '30 Merc Club Coupe have been shaved, '51 Pontiac tail lights installed, and license plate dropped with a '49 Chevy bracket. Cadillac hub caps and teardrop skirts finish it off. It is in primer now but will be lacquered soon. The engine is a '48 Merc stocker.

Toledo, Ohio   Dick Imes

SHARP '39 FORD

For a car that is 12 years old, I think that the lines of a '39 Ford are really clean. Mine has a 3½" chopped Carson top, de-chromed, electric doors, running boards removed, '50 Mercury tail-lights, De Soto bumpers, spats, chrome dash and column, Zephyr gears, and a '48 Mercury engine.

Santa Barbara, Calif.   Pete Draper

TRACK ROADSTER

My track roadster has a 284 cu in. Mercury in it now but I am working on a Stude V-8 for this season. Will my 95 in. wheelbase pass California Roadster Association track car rules?

Osceola, Indiana   W. H. Sippel

CRA rules allow w.b. of 94" and up.—Ed.

IOWA '49 CHEVY

My '49 Chevrolet has shaved hood, decked rear lid, electric deck lid control. Three extra vertical bars have been added to the grille and the car has been lowered two inches. I plan to install an Edelbrock dual manifold. It already has a dual exhaust system.

McGregor, Iowa   Frank Davies

40

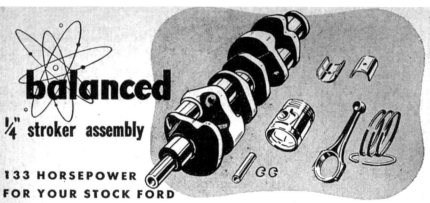

balanced ¼" stroker assembly

133 HORSEPOWER FOR YOUR STOCK FORD

WITH NO OTHER SPECIAL EQUIPMENT. This assembly comes either 3⅛" or 3⅜" bore giving your engine 275 or 286 cu. ins. respectively. Your stock Ford heads will then give you 7.8 to 1 compression and your engine will develop approximately 133 horsepower. This same engine will produce a smooth dependable 170 horsepower with addition of a ¼ cam, dual manifold and dual exhaust system.

Special PREPAID DELIVERY BY TRUCK FREIGHT TO ANY ADDRESS IN THE UNITED STATES

New Genuine 51-ICM Mercury Crank	40.98
New genuine Sterling 4 ring pistons, pins and pin locks (specify whether 3⅛ or 3⅜ bore)	48.00
New genuine Grant Rings	19.36
New genuine 29 A Ford Rods	26.48
New genuine Cadmium silver inserts	12.32
Complete assembly statically and Dynamically balanced	37.00

TOTAL PRICE $184.00

THE **404** CONSTANT ACCELERATION CAM . . . .

FOR FORD AND MERCURY V-8

Confidential experiments through long winter months of exhaustive tests in Florida and California have proven the **404 CONSTANT ACCELERATION** type camshaft to be the ultimate in design for full modified or sportsman competition, breaking all existing records in both track and drag strip racing. The **404** gives greater lugging power from 1,500 to 5,300 RPM. Ideally suited for short track competition.

Ask your dealer now for our special **404** data sheet and find out what this cam will do for you.

PRICE **$110** Plus Excise Tax, including 16 Special Radius Tappets.

AMERICAN HOT ROD CONFERENCE

On February 2, at Fresno, California, The American Hot Rod Conference passed another milestone—and an important one—on its path toward unification of rules for the West Coast associations.

The ranks of the Conference were swelled to eight member associations* as the Northern California Timing Association became a new member group.

Election results produced the following officers for the coming year: President, Felix Dal Porto (Valley Timing Association); Vice-Presidents, Dean Batchelor (SCTA) and Harold Bagdasarian (VTA); Secretary, Roy Rizki (Bell Timing Association); Treasurer, Lou Baney (Russetta Timing Association); Sergeant-at-Arms, Bill Likes (SCTA and RTA).

Thru the untiring efforts of California Highway Patrol's Chuck Pollard and Ezra Ehrhardt, cooperation between motor sports enthusiasts and state-wide law enforcement agencies is becoming better daily. The most recent step in that direction is a voluntary vehicle inspection system developed by Pollard and Ehrhardt. The plan, which has been approved by the highway commissioner, is now in the hands of the Attorney General. After approval by the latter, the plan will function as follows:

Members will go to an official light and brake station, have their lights and brakes inspected. They will then take the certificate of inspection to one of the Highway Patrolmen who has been authorized to inspect member's cars for further legal items. The inspecting officer will then issue a small windshield decal, which will be numbered and registered by the state.

At the February meeting a lengthy discussion was held concerning unification of competition rules of various member associations. Sergeant-at-Arms Likes read the newly proposed rules which were met with approval by the delegates. However, the rules are now subject to debate in individual association meetings.

ENGINE CLASSES

Class		
"O"	0"-91"	
"A"	91"-183"	
"B"	183"-260"	
"C"	260"-305"	
"D"	305" and above	

Dual overhead cams or a supercharger will advance the car into next higher class.

BODY CLASSES

Sedans and coupes will have the same regulations but will run in separate classes:

1. Stock body with fenders
2. Stock body without fenders
3. Modified body with fenders
4. Modified body without fenders
   Modified body can have no more than 2 of 3 possible modifications. Chopping, channeling or sectioning . . . no more than a total of six (6) inches.
5. Competition coupes: No restrictions other than no narrowing of body. Windshield must have 5" of vertical vision. No more than 1¼" of glass for each 1" of vertical vision. No fenders allowed, engine can be placed anywhere in frame.

Roadsters: Stock, Modified, Competition

Stock Roadsters . . .
Fenders optional, 1928 body or later on top of frame. Frame cannot be 'Z'd more than 6" in rear. Radiator may not be smaller than 1928 Ford. Must have conventional length drive line.

Modified Roadster . . .
Fenders optional, 1928 or later body, channeled or panned, any mixed body and frame. Conventional length drive line. Radiator must not be smaller than 1928 Ford.

Competition Roadster . . .
No fenders. 1927 or earlier body. No body modifications in back of cowl except rear wheel wells may be filled.

Lakester classes include belly tanks, fabricated body with open wheels. Body may not exceed 36" in width.

Streamliners with covered wheels.

Hop Up readers will remember that these rules are not final, not complete. When rulings have been decided and passed upon, Hop Up will publish them, along with complete safety rules.

Membership in the American Hot Rod Conference is open to everyone—$2.00 per year. For further information contact Lou Baney, 3346 W. Imperial Hiway, Inglewood, California.

*The other seven: Southern California, Russetta, Bell, and Valley Timing Associations, Cal-Neva Roadster Association, Oakland Schools Auto Clubs, and Fresno Rod Benders.

42

TECHNICAL TIPS . . .
(Continued from page 2)

U-TURN AT 60 MPH—PONTIAC CRUISING

What is the cruising speed of my '48 Pontiac "8" with Hydramatic, 3:63 rear end and 6.50 x 16 tires? Will my Pontiac Convertible go faster with the top up or down? Can any American stock car go down a four-lane highway at 70 mph and make a U-turn without rolling over?
Glendale, California   Wilford H. Day

Your engine turns 735 (7.10-15 tire does 735 revs per mile) x 3.63 (gear ratio or 2668 revs/mile. Therefore, 4000 rpm is equal to 90 mph and you can cruise at any speed up to the true top speed of approximately 88 mph. Most, if not all, convertibles will go the fastest when top is up and all windows closed.

I have seen movies of a '48 Stude going down the highway at high speed and the steering wheel spun. The car goes into a big wide slide that ends right side up and facing the opposite way. This was on pavement, of course. I think the stunt could be done with most any car, but it's dangerous because the sliding is what saves the car from turning over. If it happens to stick on a rough spot, you turn over!

'46 FORD ENGINE IN '40

Will a 1946 Ford V-8 engine fit a 1940 Ford?
Lacey Spring, Alabama   H. Edmonson, Jr.
Yes—Dean B.

HUDSON 8 HOP-UP

I would like to hop up a 1948 Hudson Commodore 8. What changes do you advise? With these changes would the economy be affected greatly when the car is driven at a steady 65? I would also like to know how fast a stock Hudson 8 will clock.
Valleyford, Wash.   Vernon Eden

Numerous tests and data that I have show that the Hudson 8 car will clock 91 to 92 mph. Because this engine has very light offset rods lubricated by splash, I wouldn't recommend doing anything to hop it up. You could use the optional head, but note that from the bhp/cu in., peaking speed, and valve timing, it's already hopped up to what might, in hot rod parlance, be termed a "semi-race" engine.

It takes just so much bhp to do 65 in any one car, so the fuel consumption should be the same either before or after hopping up. However, the modified engine usually gives more mpg because of higher compression ratio.
—Tech. Ed.

CUSTOM BUILT RACING BOATS
Finished or unfinished, inboards and outboards, hydroplanes and runabouts. Prices as low as $210. Let us build it or you build it yourself from our plans. Send 25c for our new, large, illustrated, catalog of plans.

CHAMPION BOATS
1524 W. 15th St., Dept. 46-C, Long Beach, Calif.

The Devil, You Say?

Yes, that little demon is out to get you. He has his hand in your pocket right now. He's stealing one dollar out of every six you are spending for gasoline. Who ever saw square turns on a race track? Yes, gas piles up on the turns, too. At high speeds it takes one horse out of every seven your engine develops to push the exhaust gas out. Yes, one gallon out of every seven that goes into your tank, just because your exhaust manifold is designed like a race track with square turns. Why continue to be fooled by false economy? Order those headers today while material is still available. Don't let that little demon put his hand in your pocket and stuff high prices down your throat either. Compare our prices with any. Yes, and our quality, too. If your high priced headers are even as good as ours, return them to us and we will refund your money.

THE FLAME . . .

(Continued from page 5)

are then possible before the detonating point is reached. Aluminum is used as the material for special heads because of this factor . . . not to make the engine run cooler.

The foregoing was not meant to imply that the overall efficiency of an L-head engine is always better than an overhead. Many other factors too numerous to mention also have a bearing on that subject.

Next month . . . "What Lights the Flame?"—Ignition fallacies explained.

NASCAR SPEED WEEK

The following are some of the speeds turned in by foreign and domestic cars during NASCAR's Speed Week time trials at Daytona Beach Florida. The famous Otto Crocker electronic timing system was used to accurately establish the true speed of cars running thru the hard-beach measured mile.

These times, recorded on the 5th and 6th of February, are not conclusive—the finals were run on the 7th. Readers will also bear in mind that sand is not always ideal for top speed running and that strong and gusty head and tail winds play an important part in various times.

Some of these cars (particularly in the South-bound only runs) were modified—official verification has not been received as to which of these cars was "strictly" stock.

RESULTS (Two Way Average)
AMERICAN CARS

Class 3, 201-240 cu. in.

M. Brown	'51 Stude. V-8	95.52 mph
C. Gilman	'51 Hud. Pcmkr.	88.96 mph

Class 5, Over 300 cu. in.

B. Shaw	'52 Chrysler	100.09 mph
B. France	'51 Packard	98.22 mph

FOREIGN CARS

T. McCahill	Mark II MG	79.49 mph
J. McMichael	MG TD	76.37 mph
G. Dodge	Sunbeam-Talbot	70.22 mph
J. Bird	Jaguar XK-120	119.83 mph
T. McCahill	Jaguar Mk. VII	100.94 mph

SOUTHBOUND ONLY (Fastest Way*)

P. Kirkwood	'52 Chrysler**	106.15 mph
J. Bird	Jaguar XK-120	121.79 mph
G. Kingshott	'52 Cadillac	104.56 mph
A. Thompson	'51 Oldsmobile	99.92 mph
B. Atchley	'52 Hud. Hornet	99.81 mph
M. Brown	'51 Studebaker	99.67 mph
R. Archer	'51 Nash	98.20 mph

*Note that the 2-way average speed of Bird's Jaguar XK is approximately 2 mph slower than the southbound one-way speed. This same difference, only to a greater degree (due to more frontal area), will apply to the American cars. So . . . subtract about 3 mph from the one-way speeds to get the approximate true speed.
**Modified

LAKES DATES FOR COMING SEASON			
SCTA			
Apr.	12-13	Aug.	25-31*
May	10-11	Sept.	27-28
June	14-15	Oct.	25-26
July	12-13	Nov.	8-9**
RUSSETTA			
Apr.	19-20	Aug.	16-17
May	17-18	Sept.	20-21
June	21-22	Oct.	18-19
July	19-20	Nov.	15-16**

*Bonneville
**Alternate meet (in case of rain)

TECHNICAL TIPS
HYDRAULIC BRAKES FOR '32 FORD

I have a 1932 Ford and would like to install hydraulic brakes. I was told I'd have to buy an $80 kit for doing this. Is there any other solution?

Detroit, Michigan   G. Impellizzeri

Suggest you try the junk yards in your area. There certainly should be enough wrecked '40 thru '48 Fords and Mercs to get a complete set. When buying brakes in this manner, they should be completely disassembled and inspected before using. They can be installed with a minimum of trouble.

As far as the price is concerned, I personally would value my neck at a bit more than 80 dollars, and safety items such as brakes, tires and lights should not be slighted on any car regardless of age. If a car is worth driving, it is worth spending money on for safety—Tech Ed.

'32 FORD BODY ON '41 OLDS ??

I wish to mount a 1932 Ford body on a 1941 Olds Hydramatic chassis. Can it be done?

Elwood, Indiana   Dick Hughes

I've heard that nothing is impossible so I have no doubt but what this can be done; however, the reason for this move is a little obscure. Why not put the Olds engine and transmission in the Ford?—Tech. Ed.

PAVED TIMING STRIP FOR MIDWEST

April 6 will be a milestone in the fast growing sport of speed in the Midwest . . . marking the opening of the first paved timing strip in that area. This strip, located at Half Day, Illinois (not far from Chicago), will give the motor-minded devotees a chance to settle their "hassles" in a legal and very exact manner.

Electronically operated timing equipment will give contestants accurate figures and each contestant will be given a certificate listing his speed. Safety regulations will be strictly enforced by a skilled technical committee in order to assure absolute safety for both participants and spectators. All types of vehicles will be allowed to participate including stock cars, racing cars, hop ups, motorcycles and miscellaneous cars of all sizes and types.

This paved timing strip at Half Day Speedway is 1⅛ miles long and 150 feet wide . . . it should prove to be a sure-fire magnet for those wishing to attempt new records thruout the summer season. Excellent sound equipment is also provided which will serve to keep both contestants and the public informed as to the times being turned in, and there are new facilities for serving refreshments.

ROAD and TRACK
PHOTO QUIZ

1. This sporty roadster was titled "A Gentleman's Speed Roadster" near the end of the last century. It was made by . . .

(a) Henry Ford   (c) Trindl-King

(b) Adams-Farwell   (d) Studebaker

2. No longer in production, the Auto-Union had a 16 cylinder engine that produced more than

(a) 250 hp   (c) 500 hp

(b) 380 hp   (d) 615 hp

3. This 2300 cc blown Alfa that is for sale is guaranteed to do at least . . .

(a) 90 mph   (c) 130 mph

(b) 110 mph   (d) 155 mph

Answers: (1) Built in 1898, the Adams-Farwell was a beauty for its day (2) This power-house put out more than 500 hp and still holds most acceleration records in the world. (3) With a 1937 chassis and engine and a body by Colli this Alfa will do an easy 110 mph. All these cars appeared in the March ROAD and TRACK. Subscribe now! $3.50 per year.

NOW! HERE'S MOTOR'S NEW, POCKET-SIZE "Trouble Shooter Guide"

Spot ANY Car Trouble *in a jiffy!*

MOTOR'S New Revised "TROUBLE SHOOTER" for AUTO MECHANICS

Yours ON APPROVAL For Only $1

Spiral Binding Opens Flat

Handy, Indexed Manual Helps You Find "What's Wrong" Quickly and Easily! Lists Over 2,000 Different Causes of Car Troubles

DON'T WASTE time and money trying to track down car and truck troubles. Let MOTOR'S Brand-New, Revised TROUBLE-SHOOTER find them for you — *easily* and *quickly*. This new handy guide — prepared by the Editors of the world-famous MOTOR'S Repair Manuals — lists over 2,000 specific causes of car and truck troubles! Includes valuable charts, crystal-clear cross-section PICTURES!

Saves You Time, Work, Money and Headaches!

MOTOR'S New, Revised TROUBLE - SHOOTER helps you track down noises, knocks, misses, and break-downs — *in a fraction of the usual time!* Suppose Fan Belt is noisy. Index leads you straight to the 7 things that could be making the noise. Suppose the engine won't start. Check index. Find *instantly* the most common causes of this annoying trouble. Save hours of *time* and *work* on these and hundreds of other jobs. And save money at the same time.

Only $1 — Money Back Guarantee

Tells Where to Locate Trouble in:

- Auto Engines of All Types
- Oiling System
- Brakes and Tires
- Ignition System
- Generator Circuit
- Clutch
- Cooling System
- Steering Gear
- Transmissions
- Overdrive
- Front Suspensions, Springs, Shock Absorbers, Rear Axle, etc.

Just A Few of the More Than 2000 Causes of Car Trouble Covered in this Work-Saving, Time-Saving Book

Tells how to spot 108 Automatic Transmission troubles. 7 causes of Fan Belt noise. Analyzes 12 conditions under which car won't start. 46 causes of Engine "Misses." 62 causes of Excessive Oil Consumption. 8 common causes of Engine Vibration, 11 causes of Slipping Clutch. 43 causes of Rear-Axle trouble. 29 common Brake Troubles . . . and where to look for cause. 58 checks for Faulty Springs and Shock Absorbers. 24 different causes of Wheel noises.

Also explains — with help of clear and simple cross-section diagrams and drawings — the inner workings of the Electrical System, Ignition System, Carburetor, Choke, Starter, Engine, Cooling System, Generator, Clutch, Transmission, Overdrive, Rear Axle, Automatic Transmissions . . . LOTS MORE.

Newest "Dope" On Automatic Transmissions— Worth More Than $1 Alone—Covers

HYDRA-MATIC
BUICK DYNAFLOW
CHEVROLET POWERGLIDE
FORD-O-MATIC
MERC-O-MATIC
PACKARD ULTRAMATIC
STUDEBAKER AUTOMATIC

SEND NO MONEY!

Just mail coupon. When postman makes delivery, pay only $1 for each copy of the book ordered, plus postage and C.O.D. charge. Then see what MOTOR'S TROUBLE-SHOOTER can do for you. If you are not convinced this handy pocket-sized guide can save you time and work—make locating car trouble a "breeze" for you — return book in 7 days for refund. Mail coupon today!

MOTOR Book Dept.,
Desk CK, 250 W. 55 St.,
New York 19, N. Y.

HOP UP

MAY, 1952   K   20 CENTS

PHOTO BY CHESEBROUGH

Custom Ford   *See Page 28*

TECHNICAL TIPS

OLDS 88 VALVES IN MERCURY

I want to put Olds 88 intake valves in a Mercury. I have taken out the valve seats. Do the Olds valves seat on the block or is there some insert to use? What is the valve spring to use and hook-up to get valve spring tension?

Light Street, Pa.   William Z. Utt

The best way to put Olds 88 intake valves in a Mercury block is to remove the intake seat insert completely. This permits only a narrow seat rather far out on the intake valve diameter. You can get by with this on intake valves but certainly not for exhausts. Either Ford or Lincoln Zephyr valve springs can be used without reworking. However, it is more convenient to use adjustable tappets. Actually, the Olds valves (¼" larger than Merc) are ⅛" too large because the intake passage restruction is the determining factor. Also, the resulting reduction in turbulence requires more spark lead. Olds valve stems must be cut to fit. Most speed shops carry special ⅛" larger valves for Mercury . . . a much better solution.—Tech. Ed.

DESTROKE V-8 FOR MORE BHP?

I am building a car (V-8 Ford) to run modified stock on ½ mile tracks. The fastest cars are stroked and bored to the limit and have special cams and distributors. However, the peak rpm is very little improved from stock.

If I bored to the limit and "de-stroked" (that is, shorten the stroke and decrease the piston speed), would I have a faster car?

Sidney, New York   H. N. Silvernail

Your question on destroking has been asked many times. In general, it doesn't work out too well. Experience with the Ford V-8 indicates that its bhp is limited by the intake valve size. With the same valve size, duration, and lift, you can bore, stroke, sleeve, or destroke and the maximum bhp doesn't change very much. The big strokers develop their power at a lower peaking speed, the small engines develop nearly the same power at much higher speed.

So, for your purpose (½ mile track), it all boils down to how to build up the engine at lowest cost, and how to build it to stay together. The different peaking speeds of various combinations are corrected by the gearing. For example, say all the engines gave 180 bhp, some peaking at 4000 rpm, some as high as 5000. So the 4000 engine "gears" to hit 4000 rpm at a certain point on the track, the 5000 engine "gears" to hit 5000 rpm at this same point. Both have substantially the same bhp all the way around. This is, of course, an over-simplification of the problem.

Ignoring piston speeds, the engine turning 4000 rpm is going to give less trouble than the one turning 5000 rpm. You can't ignore piston speeds entirely, so I'm suggesting you use the stock 3¾" stroke, and bore to 3⅜", if possible. This gives 268 cu in., or only 9.5% below the "Big Boys." So, if they use a 4.11 axle, you use 4.55, and you are right there—it says on paper!

If after all this you still want to try it, you can do it the cheapest by having the crankshaft metal-sprayed and de-stroked, use stock con rods, and de-stroker (longer) pistons.—Tech. Ed.

MORE GO FOR BUICK

I have a standard shift '49 Buick 56S Sedanette with 4.54:1 rear axle ratio (which I didn't like). Should I change to either the 4.1:1 ratio, which is optional, or use the 1951 ratio of 3.91:1 (if possible).

If I install the thin head gasket that is used on the Dynaflow models, the combustion chamber will be decreased .035, which should give 6.8:1 comp. ratio and about 5 more hp . . . according to table set up by Buick. Would you also recommended milling the head?

I intend using the '41 compound manifold, but instead of using Buick carbs, I would rather use Stromberg 97; but I am stumped on main jet size as I would like to keep gas consumption down.

I would like also to know what could be accomplished with a Gane water injection set-up.

Charles R. Koerniq   New York 21, N. Y.

The 4.10 axle is probably your best compromise, as a 56S is far too heavy to pull 3.9.

Try the thin head gasket without milling because you know how these Buicks can knock. Octa-Gane will make it possible to use regular gas where premium was required before. Then, if you want maximum performance, get everything working right, install the Octa-Gane, have the head milled when convenient, and use premium gasoline. If octane numbers go down more, you can go back to a thick head gasket. Stromberg 97's work fine on the '41 compound manifold. Start with regular Ford jets and check gasoline mileage, or have the car tested on an exhaust gas analyzer. This will indicate which way to go from there, but don't try to get 20 mpg from a 4000-pound car.—Tech. Ed.

LOWERING BLOCKS FOR '37 CHEVY

I want to use lowering blocks on my '37 Chevy. Would the lowering blocks be drawback in the roadability of the car? I am also thinking of putting a cutdown flywheel and ¾ camshaft in the engine. Would I have to change the valves because of the ¾ cam?

Hegganum, Conn.   F. H. Kozmon

Lowering blocks of about 1½ inches will improve roadability of nearly any American car. You can lighten the flywheel and install a ¾ cam with no change in valves.—Tech. Ed.

MALLORY AND VITAMETER ON '49 NASH

To pep up my '49 Nash Ambassador I intend installing Mallory distributor, Mallory coil and a Thompson Vitameter. Would there be any increase in mileage or performance?

Dayton 3, Ohio   Joe Moran

Adding a Mallory distributor and coil, and a Thompson Vitameter to your '49 Nash will make little, or no, change in performance because neither does anything to increase the horsepower. The only reason for better ignition is to improve the spark at high speed, and the only reason for a Thompson Vitameter is to permit using lower octane fuels with the same spark setting.—Tech. Ed.

2

426

If it's hopped up, it'll be in HOP UP

H O P U P

IRRESPONSIBLE PRESS

There will always be those who will do anything to make a fast buck. No matter who they hurt or who they defame—if it fattens their bankroll—they will anything, say anything, print anything.

A couple of years ago one of our "leading national magazines" decided to capitalize on the discovery that anyone who lambasted "teen-agers" and "hot-rodders" could get the nation up in arms.

A photographer was sent out on the story. He persuaded a bunch of innocent boys and girls to play a game immediately dubbed "chicken." He also talked them into climbing all over their cars as they drove along the public streets.

The magazine (which now piously editorializes about lack of fair-play in our government) recognized a sensational story and rushed the photos into an early issue, along with a story which claimed that stupid games were the chief activity of hot-rodders.

The staff of *Hop Up* has been connected with the sport of hopping up cars for many years, yet we have never known anyone who played these dangerous games with high speed automobiles. The average roadster or custom enthusiast thinks far too much of his car to jeopardize it with such nonsense.

However, the press . . . the *irresponsible* press . . . continues to publicize the shots printed by the "Great Magazine." And representatives of this magazine have frankly admitted that they thought the story was *good* because it was *sensational*. *Hop Up* is interested only in honest news and honest coverage of events.

So, for the best news in years, turn to page 48 and read the actual accident figures as taken from the files of the California Highway Patrol. The comparison between the driving record of teen-agers and the rest of the driving public is *very* interesting.

EDITORIAL STAFF

Editor ....Oliver Billingsley
Assistant Editor...............................Dean Batchelor
Technical Editor ....John R. Bond
Staff Photographers.................Jerry Chesebrough
Gene Trindl, Ralph Poole
Photographers............Bob Canaan, Joe Al Denker

PRODUCTION STAFF

Managing Editor ....W. H. Brehaut, Jr.
Production Director...........................Louis Kimzey
Art Director......................................Jack Caldwell
Art..Gene Trindl

ADVERTISING

Promotional Director......................William Quinn
Advertising Manager......................Dean Batchelor
Eastern Advertising Manager......Robert L. Edgell
104 E. 40th Street, New York 16, N.Y.
United Kingdom..........................Kenneth Kirkman
2 Longcroft Avenue, Banstead, Surrey, England
Italy......Michele Vernola, C.P. 500, Milano, Italy

Vol. 1, No. 10   MAY, 1952

CONTENTS

HOP UP is published monthly by Enthusiasts' Publications, Inc., 540 W. Colorado Blvd., Glendale, California. Phone CHapman 5-2297. Entered as second class matter at the post office at Glendale, California, under the Act of March 3, 1879. Copyright 1952 by Enthusiasts' Publications, Inc. Reprinting in whole or in part forbidden except by permission of the publishers.

Subscription price $2.00 per year thruout the world. Single copy 20c.

Change of address—must show both old and new addresses.

What Lights the Flame?

by Barney Navarro

Will a hot ignition make my stock 1952 family car accelerate faster? . . . An unconditional answer to this question is impossible. But—according to the reasoning behind this question in the majority of cases—the answer is *no*. If the stock ignition doesn't miss, and it delivers the spark at the right time, a hot ignition isn't going to make a perceptible increase in power output. The ignition merely "lights the flame"; it doesn't produce the pressure that determines horsepower output. It is like assuming that a firecracker will make a louder bang if it has a bigger fuse.

The expression "hot ignition" is very misleading because it satisfies a different condition than one is led to believe. Even the poorest ignitions of stock American production automobiles are capable of producing sparks that are hot enough to fire fuel charges at low rpm. Where they fail is in the high rpm range.

With a spark plug wire removed and the clip held ¾ of an inch from the terminal, you may observe that the voltage will be high enough at idling speed for the spark to jump the gap easily. Now wind the engine up to 5000 rpm and note how small the gap must be to get the spark to jump. Many stock ignitions will produce only an ⅛ inch spark or, even worse, none at all. This is the condition that we try to remedy with the so-called "hot ignition."

We say "so-called hot ignition" because some coil and distributor combinations don't produce a higher maximum voltage or hotter spark. They are only capable of supplying sufficient spark at high rpm. The dual coil systems fall into this category because they are—in effect—two separate units. And, on an eight cylinder engine, they function as if two 4-cylinder ignition systems were being employed. Each unit is only required to produce one-half the number of spark impulses in a given length of time. So, dual coil systems are better able to supply high voltage at increased engine speed.

Another, but less satisfactory, method of obtaining higher voltage at high rpm is to use a "hotter" coil. A hot coil will supply a higher maximum voltage. In other words, at low speed the spark will jump a larger gap. By the same token, there will be more voltage left after high rpm takes its toll. If you start with 30,000 volts and lose 15,000 as the engine "winds up," there will still be 15,000 volts available to jump the spark plug gaps. The stock coil may produce a maximum of 20,000 volts, so there will only be 5,000 volts left after the loss incurred thru increased rpm.

The voltage drop that takes place due to rpm is caused by the electrical characteristics of ignition coils. A definite period of time is necessary to energize or magnetize the iron core of the coil. As an engine increases speed, these periods of time become shorter and shorter. The number of "interruptions per minute" increase to a point where the points-closed intervals are too short to allow maximum charging. As these intervals shorten, the output voltage drops.

The fact should be inserted here that the spark plug "sparks" when the points are *opened*—not when they are closed as is sometimes believed. When the points open, battery current ceases to flow thru the primary winding of the coil, causing the magnetic charge of the coil core to break down. When this happens, the movement of the magnetic lines of force induces a high voltage in the secondary winding of the coil.

The high voltage thus produced is what makes the spark at the plug. The voltage induced is dependent on the strength of the magnetic field and the rapidity of its break down. This break down is further accelerated and intensified by the discharge of the condenser that is connected across the breaker points.

The problem can be more easily solved if we use an 8-cylinder, single-point distributor as an example. At 6000 rpm the points open and close 24,000 times per minute or 400 times per second. The mechanical action of the breaker points requires that they be open approximately two-thirds of the time. So, naturally, they are closed one-third of the time. One-third of 400 times per second results in the points being together for only 1/1200 of a second each time the coil is charged at 6000 rpm.

Dual breaker point, single coil ignitions improve this condition by using one point to make the circuit and another one to break it. In this manner, their mechanical action isn't changed but their contacting intervals are increased almost 1/3. This is accomplished by connecting both breaker arms in parallel (electrically) and staggering their positions in relation to the distributor cam lobes. The same number of cam lobes is used as when single points are employed, but the breaker arms are positioned so that they open and close at different times. Only one breaker point needs to be closed to make the circuit because both points are connected together. But both points must be open to break the circuit for the same reason. It is this mechanical overlapping that increases the dwell with this type of distributor. It is the same type that was used on Fords from 1932 thru 1948 and is now being employed in the dual point conversions for the 1949 thru 1952 models. This design eliminates quite a bit of the difficulty encountered with single breaker point ignitions but is still slightly lacking in the extreme rpm range. A well designed dual coil ignition is definitely superior but, of course, much more expensive.

Those people who demand the ultimate in performance, and are not frightened by high prices, usually prefer a magneto instead of the distributor and coil combination. Magnetos that are designed for high speed engines don't have much of the familiar tendency to drop voltage at high rpm. The reason for this lies in the fact that they are a combination generator, coil and distributor worked out in a very ingenious manner; for the primary coils also serve as field coils for its generating function. It is this arrangement that keeps the voltage from dropping when the charging intervals are reduced . . . because the faster the rotor turns, the higher the induced charge in the primary coils. This increase makes the magnetic charge greater, thereby offsetting the loss usually experienced from the shortened intervals of the coil and distributor ignition. At first glance, it may appear that there would be no limit to the speed at which a magneto would fire, but electrically and mechanically, it too is limited. There is a point beyond which the compensating effect will no longer effect a balance and the output will drop, but this will require an extreme high speed.

Mechanical limitations apply to both magnetos and distributor coil ignitions. The limiting factor is the speed at which the breaker arms begin to "float." When the breaker cam opens the points, the fiber rubbing block must follow the contour of the cam. If the speed becomes too great, the momentum of the breaker arm will become greater than the pressure produced by the return spring. When this happens, the rubbing block no longer follows the contour of the cam and the points will stay open too long. The charging interval is reduced, resulting in a weak spark. Cam contour, breaker design and weight, plus spring tension, all have a bearing on this condition and are interdependent. A simple solution is often attempted by installing double springs to increase the tension. Altho this procedure works with some ignitions, it is the wrong approach to the problem because it causes the fiber rubbing blocks to wear, the breaker arms to spring and, in some cases, the points to bounce.

The functions of ignition systems are not limited to merely supplying sufficient spark at proper intervals. They must incorporate some means of advancing and retarding the spark timing to conform to varying engine speed and load. When engine speed is increased, more spark advance is required and this is usually obtained thru the use of a flyweight governor. However, increased load requires less spark advance. To illustrate . . . assume your car is travelling at 60 mph on a level road, the spark may be advanced so that it fires 18° before top dead center. At a hill you depress the throttle to maintain the same speed. This supplies a heavier fuel charge to the cylinders. A heavier charge will burn faster, requiring less spark advance. So, most distributors are equipped with a mechanism for cancelling some of the advance (from 2° to 8°) to take care of this condition. This mechanism is controlled and operated by the intake manifold vacuum.

(Continued on page 43)

429

The scramble for lead on the first turn.

POMONA AAA STOCKER

By Sam Weill

Jim Rigsby, driving a '51 Oldsmobile, won his first big race when he took the checkered flag in the AAA 100-mile stock car race at the Pomona Fairground horse-race track. In second spot was Art Lamey, also driving a '51 Olds, while third place was taken by Louie Foy in a '51 Nash.

This race was of particular interest as it was the first West Coast stock car event in which 1952 models had competed.

Tony Bettenhausen's '51 Hudson Hornet, equipped with dual manifold, took first spot in the 17th lap and held it until the 109th, when he made his first of four trips to the pits to replace broken radiator hoses. After the fourth stop for the same reason, Tony had lost so many laps that he decided to call it quits. Allen Heath was see-sawing back and forth in first and second position

Jim Rigsby's winning '51 Olds which ran steadily and well thruout the entire race.

just before the axle on his '51 Studebaker V-8 broke, forcing him to retire on lap 115.

One three-way rhubarb occurred on the 90th lap when Ray Crawford, driving a '51 Mercury, slowed on the West turn (to avoid another car which had spun out) and was hit soundly in the rear deck by a Ford 6, driven by Jack McGrath. Bob Christie, driving the same '51 Nash that ran in the Mexico Road Race, was caught in the bumper-bending and retired with damage.

Over 17,000 fans turned out to see this race, which marked the AAA's resumption of a full calendar of events for the West Coast, and able J. C. "Aggie" Agajanian split a fat $10,374 purse among the drivers.

The official finishing positions (and the starting spots) were as follows:

1. Jim Rigsby (from 2nd), 1951 Olds; 2. Art Lamey (1st), 1951 Olds; 3. Louie Foy (20th), 1951 Nash; 4. Bob Scott (6th), 1951 Mercury; 5. Sam Hanks (23rd), 1952 Ford 6.

6. Troy Ruttman (14th), 1952 Plymouth; 7. Dick Zimmerman (9th), 1950 Ford; 8. Manuel Ayulo (15th), 1952 Mercury; 9. Roger Ward (3rd), 1951 Olds; 10. Dempsey Wilson (18th), 1951 Henry J.

11. Rosie Roussell (24th), 1951 Plymouth; 12. Joe James (12th), 1950 Ford; 13. Ralph Ruttman (22nd), 1950 Plymouth; 14. Norm Nelson (11th), 1952 Olds; 15. Jack McGrath (18th), 1951 Ford.

16. Walt Faulkner, 1952 Studebaker; 17. Andy Linden, 1951 Henry J; 18. Tony Bettenhausen, 1951 Hudson; 19. Gordon Reid, 1951 Henry J; 20. Johnny Parsons, 1951 Henry J; 21. Allen Heath, 1951 Studebaker; 22. Ray Crawford, 1950 Mercury; 23. Bob Christie, 1951 Nash; 24. Don Basile, 1951 Ford.

(Cars from 16th to 24th place did not finish race.)

Jack McGrath's '51 Ford suffering from the plague of the day . . a dirt-clogged radiator.

From L. to R.—J. C. Agajanian, winner Rigsby, Ralph DePalma, and Peter DePaolo.

Troy Ruttman, '52 Plymouth, being passed on the inside by Tony Bettenhausen, '51 Hudson.

PONTIAC CUSTOM

Don Roach (Reseda, California) has the distinction of owning one of the few customized Pontiacs seen in those parts.

Restyled by Al Ayala's Body Shop, this convertible has a Carson top which was installed after the windshield and windows had been cut three inches. Black and white leather upholstery is the only interior change, other than the hand controls for Don, who is a paraplegic.

The electric push button doors are identical with those discussed on pages 20 and 21, and are available in kit form. Olds 98 tail lights are set in the rear fenders above the exhaust tips which now extend thru the fender where the Pontiac tail lights once were mounted.

Headlights and grille have been frenched (*Hop Up*, December, 1951) and the gravel shields are chrome plated front and rear.

To lower the car, front coil springs have been cut and in the rear, the frame has been kicked up. This method of lowering puts the frame and body down together as a unit and does not alter the seating position as in a channeled job.

The only suggestion *Hop Up* would make is to raise the back of the car a little to make it ride level—doing away with the "speedboat effect."

This is a minor criticism and a matter of opinion, however.

Tommy Lee's 318 cu in. Offy with Cord body parts, clocked 123 mph with full fenders.

By DEAN BATCHELOR

They come and go at the lakes . . . clubs, club members and cars.

They appear . . . they run. Maybe they establish a record or two. Then they vanish from sight . . . as far as lakes activities are concerned. Of the original crowd of guys who first made the long dusty trip to Lake Muroc, few are left, around the lakes, that is. Most of the early small group of speed enthusiasts have gone their separate ways. Some of them to fame and fortune and some . . . well, nobody knows where they are.

Vic Edelbrock, Clay Smith, Eddie Meyer and others like them became nationally famous speed equipment manufacturers. Pete Clark, Rex Mays, Ed and Bud Winfield . . . the honor rolls of Indianapolis are full of the names of lakes "graduates."

Actual competition was different in those days, as different from the present as the personalities. For one thing, Muroc (which is now exclusively used by The United States Air Force) was a far superior surface to today's El Mirage . . . which has become practically unusuable. Harper Dry Lake, too,—before the late war—was smooth enough for top speed running.

In the early thirties, lakes events occurred whenever one or more speed fans got together and decided to run. That was all there was to it. There were no rules, no regulations, no judges, no officials, no committees, and (worst of all) no safety regulations. Cars of any type could run. Whether they were safe or unsafe made no difference. Many of the cars had fabric bodies, as do some of those seen on these pages.

It was a fabric belly pan, as a matter of fact, which caused the ruling about fire extinguishers.

Marvin Lee's beautiful Cragar roadster burned to the ground . . . tires and all . . . and just because of a canvas underpiece which burst into flame when fuel leaked down from the carburetors.

This and other similar events, caused many of the groups to band together to protect their equipment and in some cases their lives and limbs.

Just before 1937 it became obvious to the responsible element at the lakes that some type of organization was needed.

And it was in '37 that the first of these clubs was formed . . . some of which still exist and are among the foremost organizations at the lakes.

Followers of the sport are familiar with such names as Sidewinders, Road Runners, Albata, Gear Grinders, Gophers, Hornets, Stokers, and Lancers.

When you compare some of the clocked times of the middle thirties to those of the

Early Lakesters

Howard Markham's Cragar streamliner. At right, same car (then owned by Beck Bros.), but with a Winfield flathead engine.

past few seasons, you realize that the clubs and their members have made great strides.

In 1940, for example, Vic Edelbrock's roadster turned 119 mph and the Pugh Brothers modified roadster managed 127 mph. Clark and Tebow, Miller and Taylor, in the 1951 season at Bonneville had the speed up to 162 mph and turned 172 mph.

These increases are dramatic to be sure, and are only matched by the 1951 times of Earl Evans and Bill Kenz, respectively . . . 180 and 220 mph. Quite an advance in top speed running when you compare these figures to Rufi's and Seccomb's streamlined and unlimited entries of nearly 15 years ago, 140 and 125 mph.

In spite of these far superior records of today's speed experts, with what they had to use, the pre-war, 1930 to 1940 bunch deserve a lot of credit and praise.

Below—Stuart Hilborn's streamliner with '34 Ford V-8 engine was built from Bill Warth's Winfield flathead (see below).

Beck brothers acquired and rebuilt Bob Rufi's Chevy which had rolled at Rosamond in 1941.

Phil Remington's modified ... El Mirage 1946.

Above—Harold Kohler's modified four-barrel. Below—Ralph Schenk's Chevy 4 Streamliner.

Spalding brothers' streamliner, the "Carpet Sweeper," clocked (with V-8 engine) 129 mph.

Above—Ralph Schenk's Chevy 4 at Muroc.

Below—Fargo 4-port at Rosamond . . . 1946.

Hop Up Test No. 2

Chassis	1932 Ford V-8
Wheelbase	108 inches
Tread front	57 inches
Tread rear	58 inches
Weight as tested	2160 pounds
Tires front	5.50 x 16
Tires rear	7.60 x 16
Rear axle ratio	3.54 to 1
Transmission	Zephyr gears
Brakes	Ford hydraulic
Shocks	Gabriel tubular
Steering	'40 Ford (column shift)
Body	1929 Ford roadster
Paint	Ford Coronation Red
Instruments	
Tachometer	2 water temperature
Speedometer	Fuel level guage
Ammeter	Fuel-Oil pressure
Engine	'46 Merc 59-A block
Bore	.080 over Merc.
Stroke	3¾ inches
Displacement	251 cu in.
Cam	Potvin 282
Manifold	Evans dual
Heads	Evans
Pistons	Speed O motive
Ingition	Harmon & Collins mag.
Headers	Nates Muffler Shop

Ported and relieved, exhaust dividers added.

Fuel supplied by hand pressure pump.

Top speed: 121.46 mph . . . timed in 1950 by Bell Timing Assn. on straight methonol.

By DEAN BATCHELOR

To get a car for Hop Up Test No. 2, we called on our old friend Tom Glavis, who is also Secretary of The Bell Timing Association and member of the Dragons Club of Bell, California.

I 'phoned Tom we would like to take his pride and joy for a day . . . to do a little testing and to take a few photos.

"Sure! Anytime! When do you want it?"

"Right away, Tom. How about tomorrow? And remember, when I do the article, I'm going to tell what's wrong with your car as well as what's right."

At this point there was a significant pause on the other end of the line. I could feel the gears whirling as he thought this last one over. But he came thru like a trooper.

"Alright, I'm game as Tracy. But *you* remember . . . I built the roadster for myself, so there'll probably be a few things you won't like."

At Tom's house the next morning (with Chesebrough, The Intrepid Photographer) I couldn't see anything for him to be worried

12

about. This looked like one of cleanest A-V8's I'd seen in some time. Tom did all of the body and paint work. (He is a body-man at J. M. Taylor's Oldsmobile garage) . . . and a fine job he did too.

Workmanship thruout the car is tops and altho there were a few things I didn't go for, this roadster is pretty fine.

The first thing that bothered me was the lack of fenders.

"Tom, it isn't that I mind, but what about 'the law'?" (California has recently passed legislation which states: all vehicles over 1500 lbs must have adequate fenders.)

"I'm working on that situation now, but until I get the fenders finished, just drive sensibly. They won't bother you."

Windshield wiper works . . . horn works . . . emergency brake located in a place where you don't break your leg getting in and out of the car. There's a column shift which leaves a clear floor and plenty of leg room in an otherwise small interior. In fact,

on this roadster there seems to have been plenty of thought given to driver comfort.

Then I came to the one weak spot in the driver's compartment: the steering wheel was too low, making it hard for me to get my legs under it comfortably. And with the comparatively slow steering, it developed into work . . . turning sharp corners or driving on a winding road.

Those of you who read last month's test will remember how I complained of the super-high (for street use) gears in Bill Faris' roadster. Well, Tom gets a little closer to the ideal with 3.54-1 gears but he still has those big tires.

While I'm on the subject, the '48 Ford rear-end is wider than earlier models and therefore gives more clearance between the wheels and body. This is a good point to remember if you plan a channeled job.

Wending our way thru Los Angeles traffic, the roadster seemed right at ease and never overheated . . . in spite of the lack of a

14

fan. Driving a car of this type I am constantly worried that some careless joker would run into the back of us—and no bumper for protection: a common lack in many West Coast roadsters. But then maybe I worry too much.

I never will get over the lack of effort on the part of a good roadster to maintain cruising speed on the open road. Our path led Chesebrough and I over the Santa Ana Freeway, a big, new 6-lane Los Angeles highway. As we cruised along at an indicated 50 mph, we seemed to be passing cars quite easily (could have been a slow speedometer). (It occurs to me that the freeway system, when complete, would make a wonderful road race course someday!)

After making a qualifying lap thru Bob's Drive-In* (Burbank, California) and after a quick lunch, we headed for the spot that had been picked to shoot the photos of the roadster. On the way I noticed a minion of the law admiring our fine means of transportation. As we passed, he fired up his motorcycle and followed us along the street. My panic was overcome as I remembered Tom's words ("drive sensibly and they won't bother you"). I thought it was pretty nice of the officer to only give us "a warning ticket this time" with the admonition, "get those fenders on . . . pronto".

The photos having been taken, we started back to the town of Bell, via back roads and short cuts. We wanted to avoid the extra

*Watch for Dean's story about this spot. It's coming soon! "Bob's" is the place to be seen if you have a really sharp custom or roadster.

heavy traffic caused by dayshift defense workers on their daily road race home. It became apparent to me that this roadster, not only looked good but was *really put together right*. No rattles or squeaks . . . and those hydraulic brakes stop you on a dime with change to spare.

NOTES AND COMMENTS

On the whole, Tom's 29A V-8 is a good roadster. Sound construction, good bodywork, well maintained. But if it were mine, there are a few things I would change to suit my own whims. First would be the steering wheel and steering column. For a guy my height (6 ft.) to drive this car any length of time, would be very tiring because of the low position of the wheel. A small steering wheel would help some. For example, a '40 Ford wheel is 2 inches smaller in diameter than the Merc wheel that Tom is using. When a late steering system is mounted in a car of this type, the pitman arm is so low that ground clearance is inadequate to clear rocks and obstructions in the road. Next I'd change the fuel pressure gauge, which actually indicates air pressure in the fuel tank . . . the way it is now hooked up. Pressure readings on Tom's car mean nothing because there is a pressure drop between tank and carburetors that cannot be determined accurately. The fuel pressure guage should indicate actual fuel pressure at the carburetors and should be connected as near them as possible.

Third would be the addition of the legal fenders and some sort of bumpers—if I planned to use the car much in traffic.

When a Chevrolet owner from Ohio came to Barris Custom Autos of Los Angeles, and said, "I want something different" . . . he really got it.

Sam and George Barris got down to work. Weeks later, they came up with one of the nicest looking customs in the country. And here's how they did it.

After designs were sketched and drawings were made, the car was stripped down "to an empty shell"—and body production started.

The top was chopped in front 2½ inches. Windshield posts were slanted—2½ inches, and the rear of the top was lowered 6 inches, to give, as George puts it, "a tapering, swooping line. (And, incidently, George Barris has just returned from an extended tour of European custom shops. The eyes of custom fans all over the country will be on the Barris stables from now on . . . to see what ideas George accumulated over there.)

The windshield is from a 1951 Olds—and after this curved one-piece unit was aligned in the windshield frame assembly and installed, other windows were cut and fitted, as was the chrome stripping.

Rear fenders were lengthened 12 inches and raised 2 inches, while power-hammered panels were built around the spare tire mounting insertion. Bottom of the fender has been lowered 1½ inches and the skirts were sanded to give what George calls a "full round floating effect."

The spare tire swings outward on a pin to allow easy access to the rear deck . . . which has had its emblems removed, as has the hood. Tail lights are '50 Ford.

The grille, which is formed from that of a Canadian Ford "Meteor," is mounted in a

Fabulous Custom

441

special oval panel molded into the fender and pan assembly. What the Barris brothers have striven for is a "floating," or "free" look about the grille. And they seemed to have attained it.

Along with this grille treatment, the hood was lengthened and molded into one piece.

The headlights are removed and adjusted from the rear. "Half moon" shields have been placed over the lenses.

Chrome trim strips were taken from Chevrolet and Olds, door push-buttons are installed in body stripping. Rear springs were stripped and lowering blocks inserted. The body was channeled in the rear eight inches, so the flooring was cut and welded.

Front springs have been cut and shrunk and the shocks adjusted to a four inch drop.

Inside the car the Barrises have set off things with a special white and gray job by Glen and Bob Houser of Carson Top Shop.

That just about completes the description of the car—with the exception of mention of the exhaust pipes which protrude thru the bumpers; and the paint . . . which is two tone. The top is done in light metalic orchid and the body in blue, metalic, purple organic.

Custom Hints

After building up our courage to the required degree (and this took several months), we finally found ourselves prepared to delve into the mysteries of electric push-button doors . . . as installed by The Valley Custom Shop (Burbank, California).

We're glad to report that the job isn't nearly as difficult as we had first imagined.

One of the first things you'll need to know is that the solenoid (Delco Remy No. 1118019) must be mounted inside the door, and in a horizontal position . . . as close in line with the door latch mechanism as possible. In the case of most late model cars which have windwings, there is generally enough room to mount the solenoid with no strain. But in older cars with full roll-up windows, you may be forced to mount the solenoid low in the door and run the cable over pulleys or thru tubing as illustrated.

For all the mounts, it is best to use air-

Electric door latch button has been located in chrome stripping on Pontiac 4-door sedan.

craft control cable, obtainable from most surplus stores. If this 1/8 inch cable · is used, 1/4 inch or 5/16 inch tubing will be large enough to allow free movement and yet not so large as to allow sloppy play in the mechanism.

If a bend in the tube is necessary, use short radius bends. Contrary to what you might think, a long flowing curve in the tubing causes more friction between cable and tubing. About 2 inch radius is best.

When using pulleys, try to buy the type which are shielded so that the cable cannot jump off the wheel . . . or make a shield of your own design that will accomplish the same purpose.

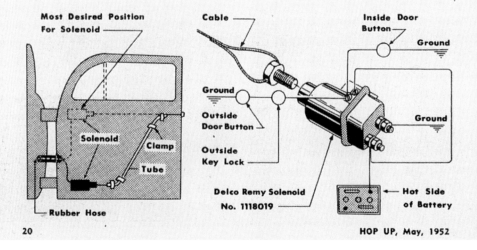

Most Desired Position For Solenoid

Cable

Inside Door Button

Ground

Solenoid

Clamp

Tube

Ground

Outside Door Button

Outside Key Lock

Ground

Rubber Hose

Delco Remy Solenoid No. 1118019

Hot Side of Battery

Typical inside mounting of door buttons. Middle button is for electric deck lid lock.

Where wiring. runs thru the door jam, a rubber hose is used to protect the wire. Drill a hole in the door jam the same size as the outside diameter of the hose . . . then clamp the hose on the back side of the door *post* to prevent slipping back and forth. Drill the hole in the door a little larger than the hose so it can slide thru the door as it opens and closes. The wire should be secured on both the door and the post (leaving slack to prevent binding) after it has been fed thru the hose. This is to prevent pulling it loose from the terminals.

For door locks, you may use any type of electrical locking which has two terminals in the rear, allowing key to be removed. Burglar alarm or ignition locks, which break the circuit when locked, may be purchased from most lock shops.

NOTE: Solenoid and tubing (if used) must be mounted securely if system is to work properly.

Outside door buttons and lock can be mounted in door, body, or out of sight underneath the running board, as desired. Installation at points other than in the door will require more wiring.

Wire from battery to solenoid and from solenoid to ground is No. 10. All of the other wiring is No. 14.

Solenoid in ideal position . . . 1941 Pontiac.

445

Drag'in Wagon

Engine: Mercury

bore	3⅜
stroke	4⅛
displacement	296 cu in.
cam	Potvin
ignition	Potvin
manifold	Cyclone 3 carb.
heads	Evans
flywheel	Potvin aluminum
clutch	Auburn
headers	Clark

Chassis:

1925 Chevy frame rails	
Ford rear end	4.11:1 gears
Ford front suspension	
four wheel hydraulic brakes	
transmission	Ford with Zephyr gears

Otto Ryssman has built this car (?) with one purpose in mind: to accelerate to top speed in the shortest possible distance. It would seem that his goal has been reached pretty well. This *gem* may not look like much . . . but it sure goes. To quote a few figures: elapsed time for a quarter mile at Paradise Mesa (near San Diego), 11.14 seconds from a standing start; elapsed time at

Cockpit was not built for comfort but driver does not spend a great deal of time in seat.

Superlight body by Ryssman is not beautiful but contributes much to the acceleration.

Santa Ana drags: 10:00 seconds flat with a rolling start) for a quarter mile; top speed at Santa Ana : 126:86 mph.

Having witnessed a few drag races ourselves, we are of the opinion that the smooth starts Otto gets contribute a great deal to his terrific speeds at the drags. Ryssman uses only second and high gear for the quarter mile for several reasons. The shift from low to second is harder than from second to high . . . and too low a gear will result in excessive wheelspin. Even when starting in second gear, full throttle is not applied until Ryssman is part way down the course.

At the present time, Otto is working on a new creation for the drags that will make this one look sick — both for beauty and speed. Most details of the car are a secret, but it will have a bellytank for a body and torsion bar rear suspension. All this is a far cry from 22-year-old Otto Ryssman's regular occupation as foreman of the curing room, at the Bridgeford Meat Packing Co. in Fullerton.

Neat (?) installation of battery and fuel tank is accomplished with aid of plumber's tape.

22

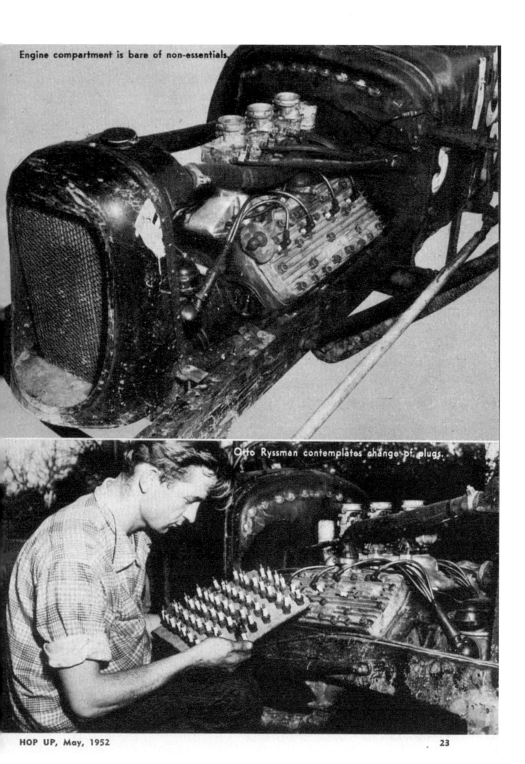

Engine compartment is bare of non-essentials.

Otto Ryssman contemplates change of plugs.

447

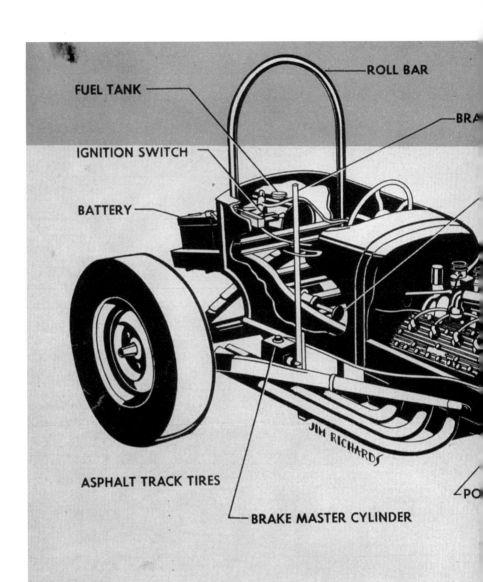

FUEL TANK

ROLL BAR

BRA

IGNITION SWITCH

BATTERY

JIM RICHARDS

ASPHALT TRACK TIRES

BRAKE MASTER CYLINDER

PO

Drag'in Wagon

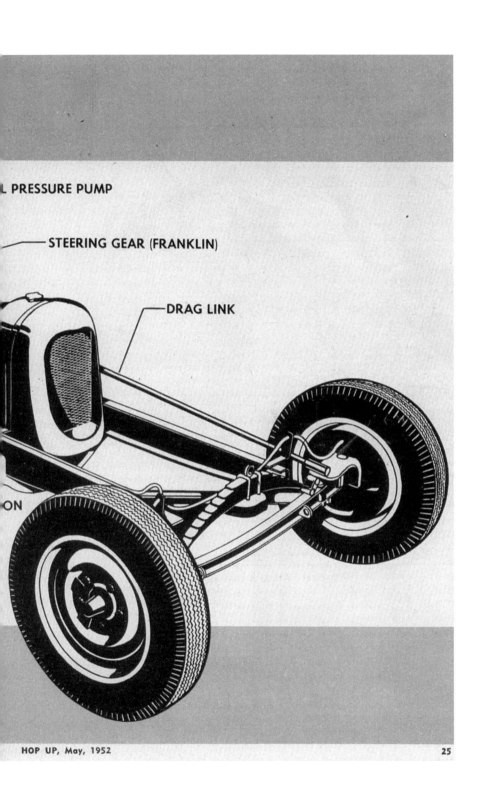

L PRESSURE PUMP

STEERING GEAR (FRANKLIN)

DRAG LINK

ON

449

Bob Lester perforates pattern for club jacket.

Bob Lester, after graduating from Whittier College in 1938, served as a high school athletic director until the late World War put him in uniform. Upon discharge from the service, he realized an ambition of long standing by starting Stylized Emblem Co.

This was five years ago and in the beginning most of Stylized's business was confined to lettering on sport jackets, shirts, etc.

In 1948 the firm turned its attention to racing emblems, decals, insignia, shirts and jackets until the majority of their business now centers in "the racing game" . . . catering to individuals and clubs alike.

Over half the starting drivers at Indianapolis in the last two years have worn emblems or jackets by Stylized. The largest selling single item (and the one that Lester attributes the success of his firm to) is the Lady Luck emblem which Les designed.

Silk screen process on the famous Lady Luck.

Meet the Advertiser

450

Above, club names and insignia on jackets are embroidered by hand operated machines. Right, checkered flags being silk screened.

Les (as he is called by his friends) does his own designing but quite often clubs or teams design their own decal or insignia and contact Stylized for manufacture. In either case Les is happy to cooperate.

Most of the production of emblems, decals, and T-shirts is done by the silk screen process. That, to the uninitiated, is a stencil made of silk instead of stencil paper and is much more accurate.

Special-order jackets and shirts are lettered in embroidery or chenille.

The firm is being enlarged constantly, not only in space occupied and equipment but in number of employees, in order to dispatch all orders quickly and efficiently. Bob has no intent, at the present time, of branching into other fields.

27

Mail Box 110

'51 FRAZER WITH OLDS 88 ENGINE

'51 Frazer convertible sedan. Blue calfskin and chrome interior, electric windows, Hydramatic, and Olds Rocket engine hopped up. 0-50 in 9 seconds. Blue nylon top (full automatic).
Bozeman, Montana   V. R. Hughes

ROCKETING ROCKET

My 1950 Olds has a dual exhaust system, Mallory high speed coil, special racing plugs, and a reworked high-speed Rochester carburetor. The rear end has been lowered 2" and the hood has been shaved completely. The finish is a bright, fire engine, red.

It has also taken numerous local drag races. There aren't too many Custom Olds "88"s around here and the guys sort of look up to mine, so its performance has, to be, more or less, "on the ball" all the time.
Cleveland, Ohio   Rufus "Spider" Weber

EASTERN HOP UP

I spent last winter building my "rod." The engine is built up to the limit. Have had lots of ignition trouble but solved that by building up my own distributor. The rear end is a Columbia two-speed.

We have just formed a club, (Eastern Custom Car and Hot Rod Association, Rhode Island).
Sharon, Mass.   Allen R. Littlefield

TEXAS CUSTOMIZED FORD

'50 Ford convertible coupe with stock engine, '50 Mercury grille, '51 Ford grille molding, a '51 hood, and '49 bumper guards. Deck lid has been smoothed.
Garland, Texas   John E. Range

(Continued on page 46)

Canvas tarp covers the rear seat when it is not in use and top is removed.

Cover Custom

Ray Vega of Burbank, California, can make his claim to fame as the owner of one of the latest fine customized jobs from Valley Custom Shop . . . also of Burbank.

The car gains in interest when readers recall that very few four-door convertible sedans serve as basis for "working over" (in comparison to other body styles), the reason

Lowness of car is emphasized by hood line which is only a few inches above front fenders.

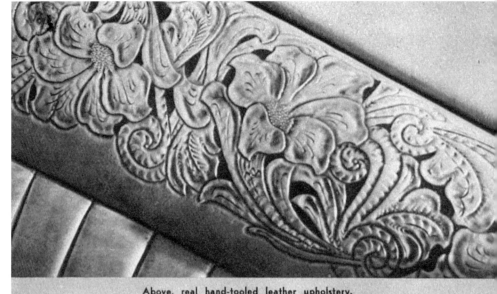

Above, real hand-tooled leather upholstery.
Below, '41 Studebaker tail lights and Chevrolet license bracket add to smooth contours.

With top removed, leather upholstery in natural brown stands out against maroon paint.

being that literally no four-door convertibles have been built since 1941—with the exception of Frazer.

Some of the details of Ray's 1938 Ford are: five inches of channelling, and a three inch cut out of the top. From a 1940 Ford, were taken the instrument panel, steering wheel, column shift, transmission, front fenders, grille, and hood. The latter was sectioned five inches and reshaped as shown in the accompanying photos.

All of the hardware was removed from the trunk lid and 1941 Studebaker Champion tail-lights replace the regular 1938-39 teardrop lights. Bumpers and guards are '47 Ford and are the normal distance from the ground, which places them 5 inches higher in relation to the body than they would normally be. At this point I would like to digress from the theme a moment to mention that a lot of custom builders, after lowering their cars, do not raise the bumpers back to normal position. Ground-skimming bumpers may look real racy but they give absolutely no protection to the car.

Upholstery, of genuine leather, was hand-tooled by Ray's mother and installed by the L & L Upholstery Shop of Glendale.

The engine compartment is fairly stock. Milled and filled heads, special ignition, and Huth headers and pipes being the only changes so far. But Ray says this won't always be the case.

The seats have been lowered 3 inches to take care of the difference in top height and to make for better visibility.

·A Carson padded top, chrome beading around the fenders, and rear fender skirts complete the exterior of this fine looking custom convertible.

Hopping Up the Chevrolet Engine

Almost every Chevrolet owner is interested in getting "just a little more" from his stock engine. But many have been confused by talk and diagrams of horsepower, torque, etc. There have been rumors that hopped up engines are not reliable and stories that the stock Chevrolet oiling system is not suitable for high-speed . . . . All of the foregoing are false and misleading.

First of all, it is a very good idea to start with a 1937, or later, Chevrolet block assembly. Earlier models had three main bearings instead of four, and were not too reliable when hopped up, due to extreme crankshaft flexing.

Chevrolet has made three basic blocks since 1937. The standard (3½" bore x 3¾"

stroke) 216 cu in. passenger car engine remains almost the same as it was in 1937 with only slight modifications. In 1941, a 235 cu in. "Hi-torque powerplant was offered to truck users. This engine had a 3 15/16" stroke and a 3 9/16" bore. In 1950, Power-Glide models were equipped with a new engine known as the "105". This engine was also used for most trucks built in 1950 (and later) and has the same dimensions as the Hi-torques built previously. The quickest way to spot the "235's" or 105 Hi-torques is to look at the side plate covering the

Properly modified Chevrolet engine provides hi power output needed for real performance.

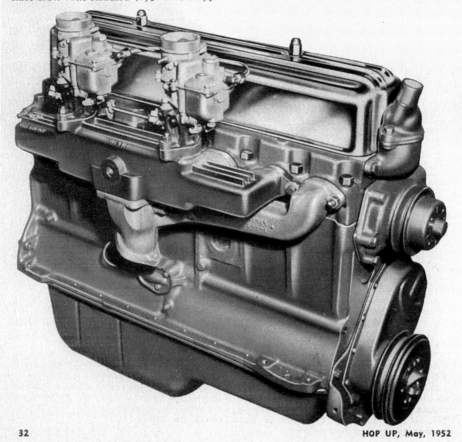

pushrods. Late Hi-torques have a short side plate which does not cover the spark plugs. Early Hi-torques and 216" standard engines have a pushrod cover which extends from the top of the head downward to cover the spark plugs and pushrods.

While the newest Hi-torques are considered best for hopping up (due to their newly designed head with large intake valves), any 1937 (or later) engine can be given a real shot in the arm quite successfully!

It's a good idea to mention here that the stock Chevrolet oiling system is much better than most hop up artists would have you believe. In effect, the Chevrolet engineers have combined the best advantages of splash oiling with pressure oiling. This gives Chevrolet the longest trouble-free bearing life of any car on the road. The crankcase is equipped with small spouts, which are adjusted with a "targeting tool" so that they will direct a stream of oil into the rod dips. As the engine is revved up, the pressure of the oil going into the dips on the rods is well over 75 lbs.

The only time that oiling or rod troubles occur on the Chevrolet engines that are hopped-up, is when the pan has not been properly targeted, the spouts are stopped up, or insufficient clearances are provided for the rods. Some oil additives also have bad effects on the Chevrolet rod bearings. We have had our best results using either plain oil (no additives) or the new Liqui-Moly oil.

By now most readers are wondering when we will get to the cam, carburetion, ignition, compression, and exhaust, a discussion that usually heads this type of article. Well, this oiling and lower-end discussion is important in order that Chevrolet owners will have no fear that their "bottom ends" will drop out when they really "turn it on".

The only thing that must be done with the rods is to increase the clearance from

Hartman dual manifold with Rochester carburetors provides fourteen more horsepower.

the stock .0015-.002" to at least .003-0035". Shims may be added to the stock rods to get this clearance, or you may get specially cut insert rods with bearings modified to give these clearances.

Because it is necessary to remove the crankcase to install camshaft or lightweight pistons, increasing these clearances imposes no extra work.

MANIFOLDS

A dual manifold is the quickest way to add more horsepower to your Chevrolet engine. By actual dynamometer tests, the addition of a dual intake manifold on an otherwise stock Chevrolet engine will add from 12 to 14 horsepower*. A triple manifold will add four horsepower more than a dual.

The installation of a dual intake manifold does not disturb gasoline mileage unless you are the type that has to "get on it" from every signal light. In fact, most owners report that dual carburetion has increased their hiway mileage by at least one or more miles per gallon.

Acceleration is improved measurably by the use of dual carbs . . . approximately 20% more from an otherwise stock Chevrolet.

COMPRESSION

The Chevrolet engine really rewards the owner who ups the compression ratio. There is ample bearing area to handle the increased "push" and the increase in mileage and performance obtained by raising compression are very worthwhile.

Perhaps the simplest method of boosting compression is to mill the head. A .125" cut on any 1941-51 Chevrolet head will

Mallory single coil dual point distributor for Chevrolet and GMC. Its use improves acceleration and top speed.

---

* Full details on tuning and installing dual carburetors are to be found in the latest edition of California Bill's Speed Manual.

raise the compression ratio to 7.25 on the 216" models and to 7.75 on the 235" models. Milling the 1937-40 heads is permissable only if the stock dome-type pistons are replaced with "flat tops". When making a cut of this magnitude, the intake valves must be "sunk" the same amount that has been milled from the head and ⅛" shims should be placed under each intake valve spring. No warping of the heads has been reported as a result of this treatment, and a lesser mill cut seems hardly worth the trouble as it would result in less than 7:1 compression.

On all models with the long side plate, it is necessary to slot the *lower* holes in the side plate and cut off the stiffening flange along the lower edge of the push rod cover. *Don't slot the upper holes!* This will misalign the spark plug holes and make spark plug removal difficult . . . or even impossible.

For further increases in compression, it is possible to obtain a head which has been milled and filled. This runs about $70 (with your old head in exchange). Milling and

8.25:1 high compression piston for use in '41 thru '52 Chevrolets. Can be used in 1937 and later models by changing over to a '41 or later head.

porting of your present head will usually cost in the neighborhood of $40.

If you have a Hi-torque engine already, the new hi-domed pistons can be easily installed. These are available in 3 9/16" and 3⅝" bore sizes and give 8.25:1 compression when installed with an unmilled head.

CAMSHAFT

Now that you have raised the compression ratio and installed two carburetors, the installation of a camshaft will *really* improve horsepower. By actual test on the dynamometer, an engine with 8.5:1 compression, two carburetors, and a ¾ grind camshaft gained 50 horsepower. The same should be true of any Chevrolet engine.

Semi-race cams are a lost cause, and few

34

Harmon & Collins "DIVCO" distributor is widely used on hopped up GMC and Chevrolet engines.

cam grinders still make them. At least a "Road" (¾ grind) should be installed—even if you still are using one carburetor. Investigate before buying and make sure that the cam you get will be quiet.

Most of the ¾ grinds now available are easy on the tappets, require little increase in valve spring pressure, and are as quiet as a "stocker". Many of them will idle just as smoothly as the stock cam. If you have a vacuum guage on your car, don't become alarmed when your vacuum drops off at idle with a reground camshaft. Due to the increased overlap, a reground cam will pump less vacuum at idle.

It is recommended that the installation of a reground cam be supplimented by a set of stock Chevrolet aluminum timing gears (getting a bit hard to obtain these days) and a set of tubular pushrods. The aluminum timing gears are much more dependable than the fiber gears, but do have a slight whine until they wear in. The tubular pushrods are almost 40% lighter than the stock pushrods and are 200% stronger.

Cyclone bell housing adapter permits use of Ford transmission on the Chevrolet engine.

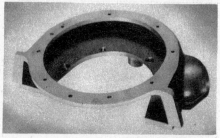

Stewart Warner instruments in '48 Chevy.

IGNITION

The stock Chevrolet coil and ignition work quite well when in good condition. Some improvement in high speed performance can be had by reducing the point gap from .018" to .012", however, this does tend to reduce point life. Many Chevrolet owners are now installing the two point conversion kits which have been on the market for the past couple of years. These give a hotter spark and longer point life by overlapping the points to give a longer period for the magnetic field to build up in the coil.

Cast aluminum side plate reduces noise.

EXHAUST

By actual test, the stock Chevrolet muffler will rob a slightly hopped up engine of 22 horsepower at 4000 rpm. Let's face it, those horses cost a lot to obtain, so why choke them to death in the stock muffler? You have several alternatives: (1) install two steel-packed mufflers with a split manifold; (2) install a single steel-pack muffler; (3) install a Buick straight-thru muffler; (4) install two stock mufflers. The latter is probably the best as it is quiet as well as efficient!

The use of exhaust headers is not recommended for the Chevrolet if it is to be used as a passenger car. Two reasons are involved here: (1) the isolation of the three front cylinders from the three rear gives a fantastically loud and sharp exhaust note which the law enforcement officers don't

seem to appreciate; (2) exhaust headers have no provision for heating the intake manifold, which gives rough operation and a slow warm up.

INTERCHANGEABILITY

All Chevrolet engines built in 1937 and later can be interchanged with only slight modifications*, such as exhaust pipe angle and flywheel mounting bolt holes.

POWER-GLIDE CHEVROLETS

A brief note about Power-Glides must be included! Dual carbs on a "P-G" greatly improve the ton mileage when properly installed. When a cam is installed, it is suggested that the hydraulic lifters be replaced with solid ones. The "P-G" Chevy reacts readily to hopping up, but we suggest that a ¾ race cam, dual carbs, exhaust system and more compression be the limit of modification because additional hop up work is only absorbed by the Power-Glide unit and is not transmitted to the rear wheels. Re-

* Details appear in California Bill's Chevrolet Manual

Edelbrock dual manifold for Chevy is popular.

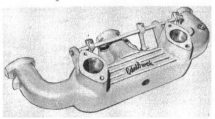

35

Marcad

Story and Photos by Norris Ewing

Whether you see it idling along Hiway 101 at an effortless sixty — threading Wilshire traffic like a low-rumbling ghost—or basking in the neons of a boulevard drive-in—Dick Songer's big, blue roadster rates your best double-take.

Your first glance tells you that here's a smooth hunk of metal. It's long, low and with an air of authority.

"Cadillac," you guess. "...Dropped a few inches. But...then...again..."

So, you take that second look. And, promptly, you find yourself in an analytical pickle! That upswept fenderdoo—that's Cad for sure. But the rear deck—not necessarily so. The hood packs extra length, somewhere. And the overall contour is un-Cadillac-ish somehow.

Nor does the name lend enlightenment. "Marcad," it reads, in neat metal letters along the front fender. "—Cad" gets you back to "Cadillac" — but wherefrom the "Mar—"?

Well, if you're at a drive-in, say, and if you speak politely to the young man behind the wheel, Dick Songer will raise the hood and your concusion will be "dispellusioned."

The "Mar—" comes from "Marmon," and appropriately, because that oversize engine room is jamful of a 1931 Marmon V-16 engine. It's the largest multi-cylinder engine ever put in an American stock car.

"Stock, it went 490.8 cu in., Songer will tell you. "With 3⅛ inch bore and 4 inch stroke. This one has been overbored .040 which produces about 502 cu in.

Talk to Songer and you find he masterminded his "Marcad" from drawing board to floormat in three years. And among other things, you learn that the engine was factory rated at 200 horsepower at 3400 rpm, but on Dick's version the heads have been milled .125 to raise compression from 6:1 to

has been replaced by a Songer-built, water-jacketed unit mounting four Ford "60" carbs; the stock flywheel has been traded for a Cadillac platter weighing exactly half as much; the heads have been ported; and the crank, rods, pistons, flywheel and clutch have been dynamically and statically balanced. So modified, the engine idles like a Swiss ticker but will show 4500 rpm in gears and will unstable about 275 lusty horses. Power is so great that the heavy Cad "75" clutch slips noticeably when everything is poured on at once.

This tidy package of torque is coupled thru a '41 Cad transmission, plus Chrysler New Yorker overdrive to the '41 Cad, 3:36 rear end. Result: six speeds forward, including a final ratio of 2.42 in high/overdrive. At 60 mph the tach shows 1650 rpm, and at 90 it shows a strainless 2400 rpm. Top speed has not been clocked, but Songer has seen 3600 rpm in high-overdrive, which figures 120-plus mph, including discount of a generous 10% for wheel slippage. Using optimum shift points, the "Marcad" can propel its 4500 pounds from 0-60 in 10½ seconds, and will skedaddle from 0-90 mph in 19 seconds. Songer thinks that he can "improve" these figures when he licks that

car gave 14½ mpg at substantial road speeds.

Songer is foreman of an electrical concern, so the Marcad rates special attention to things electric. Two Stewart-Warner fuel pumps are wired to operate individually or in parallel, depending upon the immediate thirst of those sixteen barrels. Two batteries and two generators are similarly selective, to insure juice for starting under all conditions. Dash-borne pilot lights indicate oil pressure, battery condition, fuel pump and generator selection and output rate of the cockpit-controlled, number two generator.

Visible and invisible parts from seven models of Cadillac put the "—cad" in Marcad. Songer started out with a '41 "62" coupe . . . the wheels, dash and front fenders (lengthened and deepened) are recognizeable holdovers. Also utilized were the '41 radiator, springs, axles and steering assembly (with modifications to steering post, tie rod and linkage). The grille is straight '46 Cad. Frame is from a '46 "62" sedan— but reinforced to support the mammoth Marmon engine.

Buick, Pontiac and Chevrolet parts also can be discovered in the car. In fact, parts from eleven different makes of car, plus

(Continued on page 46)

Muth Custom

It isn't easy to believe, is it? . . . Six months ago this car was a "total." And by *total*, we mean a total *wreck!*

By the time it had smacked into the rear end of a towering cement truck, careened crazily into an orange grove and rolled over several times there among the trees, not much was left but the running gear. The body resembled a sardine can opened by a starving man who had lost the key. It was a Ford—1950 Tudor—only you'd never know from the appearance.

You and I might look at a heap of junk like that and wonder who got out alive . . . but not Don Muth. He bought the car on the spot and proceeded to build a clean, practical custom, with the aid of Gardner-Muth Ford Agency, San Bernardino, Calif.

All totaled, Don sank $3,000 in his dream before it was a finished product. But is that a great outlay when you stop to consider

what you buy today in the way of a new car for the same amount?

Don planned to build of Ford parts exclusively, so he started with '49 club coupe and '50 convertible bodies, which he joined together. Then, he cut the windshield three inches in preparation for a Carson top. Parts of Fords as far back as 1936 are included, the most recent a '52 Ford steering wheel. The doors are '51 Ford Victoria, while the hood and fenders are vintage '51.

What makes the car unusual, of course, is the radiator inlet treatment: it's a combination of two 1951 Ford grilles. One American

and the other a Canadian Ford "Meteor."

Customizers will probably rush out now and start buying up Canadian grilles (if they can find them), particularly when they discover that the Canadian and American Ford installations are interchangeable.

The engine is pretty much stock. But don't let that fool you. Don Muth has fastened an Italmeccanica blower to that engine under the hood. So if you hear a snarling whine and a gorgeous custom flashes past, five'll get you eight that it's Don Muth—in what *Hop Up* thinks is one of the best looking customs to date.

What d' You Think?
How would you hop up an engine?
Girl spectators at the Saugus Drag Strip were asked . . .

Pat Titus: How would *I* hop up an engine? Let me see. First, I'd . . . let's see . . . I don't *know* what I'd do. I guess I'd get a book and find out. Oh, I don't know. I'd learn what I'm doing first. I don't like Edelbrock heads, but I *do* like Evans heads. Why? Well, because it sounds better. Oh . . . *I don't know!*

Nancy Zeier: You mean, what I'd put in it? Humm. Guess I'd start with a Winfield cam and a two carburetor (or I should say *dual?*) manifold. Then, let's see. I'd stroke it and . . . Oh, yes! All chromed heads— Edelbrock—because my boyfriend has them. I don't know what else. I'd put it in a '34 Ford, because my boyfriend has one.

Jann Perry: First, I'd get a '49 block, have it ported and relieved, bore it out an eighth over Merc. Then I'd stroke the crank an eighth . . . that makes it 1/8 x 1/8. Well . . . I'd get a set of Evans heads and an Evans three jug manifold, Harmon & Collins cam and mag and a set of headers. If it was just for me, I want a street and drag car because girls are not allowed to drive at the lakes, I would then drop it in a '40 Merc with Carson top.

Sue Rowland: Me? Humm . . . bore and stroke it. I'd use a cam (Weber). And an Evans manifold, Spalding ignition. Headers, I guess.
I couldn't put them together, but my brother has a lot of books at home. I guess that's where I've heard the names. I'd put it in a roadster. 27T maybe?

Pat Barbelen: Oh, fine! I haven't the slightest idea. I don't know. *Really!* I *don't* know! I guess I'd bore it out. I suppose I'd use Navarro heads and manifold, altho I have no particular reason to.

Kim: Hop up? My gosh, stupid! There's only one way to hop up on something and that's just to hop up . . . What's that you're saying? Oh, why didn't you say so? Well, son, I'd take it to one of the speed shops and have it done. Oh! How would *I* hop up an engine . . . man, who ever heard of a *cat* working on an engine?

40

464

HOPPING UP THE CHEVROLET ENGINE

(Continued from page 35)

moval of the hydraulic lifters will often raise the top speed, as these will "pump up" and hold the valves off the seats at speeds around 4000-4500 rpm.

MAGNETO IGNITION

The installation of a magneto on your Chevrolet is beneficial from the standpoint of added acceleration and top speed performance. Scintilla and certain other magnetos are now available with mountings specifically designed for the Chevrolet engine. Magnetos which fit a Chevrolet will also fit any GMC 228-270 engine.

GEAR RATIOS

More letters are sent in about gear ratios than any other modification. Almost everyone seems to be "high-speed gear" happy. Yet, few of the letters indicate the gears did any actual good at high speed.

The gear ratio which came stock in your Chevrolet was chosen by factory engineers for best all around performance. That means that top speed, mileage, and acceleration were all given consideration in choosing that particular ratio.

Chevrolets made in 1937-38 came with 4.22:1 or 4.11:1 in the Master models, while the Standard Models (being lighter) were equipped with 3.73:1 gear. Later models have nearly all been equipped with 4.11:1 gears, with the exception of the Power-Glides, which have 3.55:1 gears.

Gear-swapping on the Chevy is quite easy as the four available ratios interchange readily. A special, or re-machined, ring-gear carrier is necessary to install the Power-Glide gears in any other rear end.

Don't rush right out and buy a set of "P-G" gears and think that they will add speed to your "stove-bolt six"! That false idea has already gained too many followers.

Unless your engine is carrying a full load of speed equipment, the 3.73:1 gear ratio is probably the highest that you should install. If you are one of the boys who like to dig out from stop lights, then stick with the 4.11 ratio until you get enough equipment on the engine to handle a higher ratio easily.

So . . . . unless yours is a full-house Chevy or a good GMC engine, don't attempt to use the 3.55 ratio or you'll find yourself all bogged down in high gear at about 85 mph.

The world of speed has long looked down upon the trusty Chevrolet . . . practically called it a *dog*. But every dog has its day and it will be *real* fun to watch the amazement of owners of V-8s and suchlike as you go breezing past them in your hot Chevy.

What Lights The Flame? . . .
(Continued from page 5)

Maximum manifold vacuum is produced when your foot is off of the accelerator. The minimum, when the throttle is floored. This change is inversely proportional to the varying fuel charge that reaches the cylinders. The greater the vacuum, the less the charge. The smaller the vacuum, the heavier the charge. By using these changes to operate a diaphragm or piston, it is a simple mechanical problem to vary the spark advance accordingly.

One method of advancing the spark that causes considerable confusion is the system employed by the Ford Motor Company on the 1949 thru 1952 models. This series is equipped with distributors that use carburetor venturi vacuum to advance the spark. This vacuum differs from the manifold vacuum inasmuch as it is proby the air velocity thru the carburetor venturi. (See "How Many Pots" *Hop Up*, March, 1952). It is the same vacuum that causes fuel to flow from the carburetor jets.

It is not the same as the intake manifold vacuum!

The greater the air flow thru the carburetor, the greater the venturi vacuum and the more the spark advances. Load adjustment is obtained with this system by having a small bleed-back hole to the manifold side of the throttle body. When the vacuum in the manifold drops appreciably, the venturi vacuum can have less effect because the passages are connected with the same outlet to the distributor. When the venturi vacuum is low, the reverse takes place, for the manifold vacuum is then dominant.

When stock Ford, Mercury, and Lincoln distributors (or dual point conversions of these distributors) are employed, it is imperative that stock carburetors be used; or carburetors made for these models. *They cannot be operated by connecting a vacuum line to the manifold . . . or by drilling a*

(Continued on page 45)

YOU ASKED FOR IT!

Yes, you who have supported and enjoyed HOP UP Magazine have made it possible for us to make this wonderful offer. You can now add these beautiful 5x7 glossy prints to your collection by subscribing to HOP UP.

One foto with a year's subscription, two fotos with a two year subscription, or **all four** with a three year subscription. DON'T MISS THIS OFFER! Fill out subscription blank below and mail today to—

What Lights The Flame? . . .

(Continued from page 43)

hole in the venturi of a carburetor not designed for the purpose!

When dual carburetion is installed, a vacuum line to one carburetor is all that is necessary. Two venturi do not produce twice as much vacuum as one. Nor do they produce any more. So, an extra line is nothing but a waste of copper tubing. However, two carburetors divide the air flow between themselves so that the venturi vacuum is reduced considerably over the normal speed ranges. To obtain the proper amount of spark advance, it is necessary to have the distributor springs readjusted.

After studying the foregoing, one can easily see the implications and problems involved in answering the opening question of this article. There is no simple solution . . . the proper selection of an ignition requires more care and more thought than any other external part of an engine.

Next month . . . "WHY FORD'S THE FAVORITE." Barry Navarro explains why more Fords are hopped up than all other makes combined.

numerous handmade fittings, comprise the Marcad entire.

Songer gives large credit to metal craftsman O. W. Brue, of Meiner's Oaks, California, for guidance and assistance on the Marcad's bodywork. Several knowledgeable mechanics in Los Angeles, and in Songer's home town of Ventura (California), also contributed ideas which were put to good use.

—But it was young Dick Songer, a kid of nineteen, who tore down his plush "62" coupe to put running gear under a dream. It was Dick who spent all of his spare time, and most of his wages, over a three year stretch to shape that dream in metal. It was Dick who did the scheming, welding, wiring, fitting, worrying and cussing. And it was Dick—a few months ago—who sprayed the fourteenth, final coat of Corinth Blue lacquer and put his dream on the road.

MAIL BOX 110 . . .

(Continued from page 28)

UNPAINTED HORROR

Here are some snaps of my unpainted horror, a 1940 Willys coupe to start with.

I chopped the firewall 8", cut the hood to suit, then rolled the window sills over and welded them inside. Doors are welded and leaded shut. Lowered steering wheel into my

lap (sitting on the floor) and stuck an old DeSoto windshield up front.

The top may look ragged and torn, but that is just the way I got it for a buck at the junkie's. The whole arrangement was not meant to stand permanently—just to see how far to cut and all. The left side is primed, wait—it is the right side that is primed and the left side (drivers) is rusted. Grill is from a '46 Pontiac.

Boston, Mass.   Joseph E. Gibney

CUSTOM '40 PLYMOUTH

Enclosed three snapshots of my '40 Plymouth club coupe. The nose, deck and side panels have

been "shaved." Rear fender trailing edges extended 3", Pontiac tail lights installed.

The engine is a bored, stroked, and ported '46 Dodge with ¾ Iskenderian cam, chopped flywheel, dual carbs, and milled head. A 3:78 rear end is used.

The interior is in blue and white leather.

Oakland, California   Roland Davies

ILLINOIS CHEVY CUSTOM

Enclosed is a photo of my 1950 Chevrolet.

I added Cad fins, front & rear decks smoothed, other body chrome removed, grill

bars added, dual exhaust, defrosters on all windows, 2" blocks on rear, electric trunk latch.

Russel, Illinois   Jim Johnson

471

AMERICAN HOT ROD CONFERENCE

As announced in the last issue of *Hop Up*, the voluntary vehicle inspection program inaugurated by Officers Ezra Ehrhardt and Chuck Pollard of the California Highway Patrol, is about to become a reality. The plan, which had already been approved by Clifford Peterson, the Highway Patrol Commissioner, has now been given the green light by the Attorney General's Office. It remains only for the American Hot Rod Conference to issue decals (which are now being made — see design above right) to members whose cars can pass the inspection.

Because the California Highway Patrol is not actually authorized to test cars for safety, this campaign will be more of a safety pledge by AHRC members than a vehicle test. It is the first such plan on a large scale.

Pollard and Ehrhardt brought to the meeting a complete record of vehicle code violations in California from 1950 back to the time when auto traffic started in the state. It is of particular interest to hop up advocates everywhere, however, because California has the majority of America's hot-rodders (who are mostly in the younger age group).

| | TOTAL | | FATAL | |
Age Group	Number	%	Number	%
5-14	192	0.2	2	0.1
15-19	9,019	8.5	386	9.9
20-24	16,988	16.0	668	17.1
25-34	30,673	28.8	1078	27.6
35-44	20,680	19.5	750	19.3
45-54	13,341	12.5	434	11.1
55-64	7,544	7.1	294	7.6
65-	3,629	3.4	192	4.9

The above is an excerpt from:
State of California, Department of Highway Patrol, Annual Statistical Report, 1950 & prior.

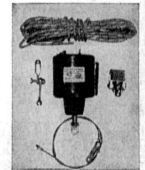

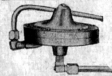

474

HOP UP

JUNE, 1952   20 CENTS

TECHNICAL TIPS

CORRESPONDENCE

Letters and answers in this column are those we believe to be of the most general interest.

Since its inception, *Hop Up* has been deluged with letters from the readers... gratifying, to say the least. But this mail has become too much for us to handle.

Hop Up checks over all reader inquiries carefully and tries to answer most of them, but naturally, there just isn't time enough to reply to all.

Hop Up enjoys hearing from you. So don't stop writing. But please don't do what one individual did. Don't get your car torn apart and then frantically write *Hop Up*, asking how to get it back together again. And don't be disappointed if you don't get an immediate answer from *Hop Up's* overworked staff.

Hop Up doesn't know all the answers, but it will do its best. Sometimes you will find that you can get a quicker answer by phoning or writing your local car dealer or parts supplier—not to mention *Hop Up* advertisers who are only too happy to answer your questions pertaining to their field.

HYDRAULIC BRAKES FOR '36 FORD

What Ford hydraulic brakes would fit a '36 Ford without too much alteration?

Austin, Texas   Joe Bob Simmons

Ford hydraulic brake systems are basically the same from '39 to '48; '39 Fords have the same wheel as your '36 so would present fewer problems.—Tech. Ed.

U-TURN AT 80 MPH

In referring to Wilford Day's letter asking about a U-turn at 60 mph (April 1952 Hop Up), I wish to state that in a 1951 De Soto station wagon (stock) I made such a turn in the middle of a pavement not at 60, but at 80 mph, besides being on only a two-lane highway. To back my statement are four other fellows who were riding with me. On an extra wide dirt road I accomplished an identical turn at almost the same speed.

So it appears to me that a U-turn at 60 should be possible, especially since I can whip a station wagon around at 80, and only being 16 years old.

Olney, Illinois   Donnie Fox

It's guys like you who stir up the wrath of the law and the public toward ALL teen-age drivers. Isn't life short enough without trying to kill yourself?—Tech. Ed.

(Continued on page 43)

If it's hopped up, it'll be in HOP UP

H O P   U P

With the big Memorial Day Speed Classic at Indianapolis descending upon us with lightning rapidity, the usual arguments among the bench racing fraternity are becoming more heated than ever before. Reason for all this difference of opinion is the entry of five Italian Ferrari . . . two entered by the factory and three owned and driven by Americans. Arguing for negative chances of the foreign entrys' winning are two schools of thought.

The first says: "A Ferrari is not built for this kind of racing, and—the Italian drivers are not accustomed to the track and will therefore be at a disadvantage too great to overcome."

The second maintains: "Those jobs are no good to begin with, and who do those guys think they are, bringing a car like that over to compete with our Meyer-Drake engined cars, which are superior."

The first of these two arguments has some merit but it will be partially offset by the three cars driven by Americans who are experienced on the track . . .

among them, Johnny Parsons and Johnny Mauro. The second is as ridiculous as it sounds and evidences a complete lack of knowledge as to what goes on beyond the Atlantic Ocean. The string of Ferrari successes are too numerous to mention here, but we on the staff of *Hop Up* believe the rail-birds at "Indy" are in for a bit of a surprise when the Ferrari cars hit the track this May.

We're as patriotic as the next guy and would like to see American men and machines invincible the World over. But it is the complacent and very unhealthy attitude of many Americans, coupled with the underestimating of the foe, that can eventually lead to our complete downfall . . . whether it be on the race track or battlefield.

So, if for no other reason than to shake up the short-sighted persons who would declare themselves "champions" without bothering to prove it, we would like the Ferrari team to come home one, two, three.

EDITORIAL STAFF

Editor ....Oliver Billingsley
Assistant Editor.........................Dean Batchelor
Technical Editor..........................John R. Bond
Staff Photographers.................Jerry Chesebrough
                          Gene Trindl, Ralph Poole
Photographers............Bob Canaan, Joe Al Denker

PRODUCTION STAFF

Managing Editor...................W. H. Brehaut, Jr.
Production Director.......................Louis Kimzey
Art Director.............................Jack Caldwell
Art..Gene Trindl

ADVERTISING

Promotional Director.....................William Quinn
Advertising Manager.................Dean Batchelor
Eastern Advertising Manager......Robert L. Edgell
          104 E. 40th Street, New York 16, N.Y.
United Kingdom....................Kenneth Kirkman
    2 Longcroft Avenue, Banstead, Surrey, England
Italy......Michele Vernola, C.P. 500, Milano, Italy

Vol. 1, No. 11   **June, 1952**

CONTENTS

WHY FORD'S THE FAVORITE

By

BARNEY NAVARRO

There are many reasons why the Ford engines are the all-time favorites among hop up fans. Ford has been the choice for many years. It is not a practice that started yesterday . . . but was inaugurated with the Model T's. Long before the current crop of enthusiasts was born, Model T's were being hopped up and in its day "Lizzie" was capable of being worked over into something that could show a clean pair of heels to the most expensive American-made car.

Two things are necessary before it is practical to hop up a car; there must be some romance connected with it and someone must make a profit.

Of the two, romance is the most important factor because it can produce the demand for speed equipment. One could say that it was this spirit that caused many sporty individuals during the twenties to want to hop up their T's. These functional cars had more ridicule heaped upon them than any car ever built. So it was only natural that people would get a bigger kick out of reworking them to a point where they could run away from the most expensive car in town. To be beaten by a T was the most crushing defeat possible!

The auto racing sport also contributed immeasurably to the popularity of Henry Ford's Great Innovaton: the Model T. In their day, the T's happened to fit the displacement limitations of the then current racing groups. They were simple inexpensive engines designed in such a way that they were very adaptable to modifications. The quality of material employed in their manufacture was superior to that used by the majority of manufacturers. Changes could be made that would cause other engines of

similar displacement to literally fall apart. Last, but not least, these engines were small in size which made them ideal for racing, from a weight standpoint.

Of course, a hopped up T was far from being a trouble-free mechanism. To obtain 140 horsepower from a T required that the safety factor be lowered considerably. In other words, the engine was originally designed to produce approximately 20 horsepower and was capable of withstanding the stresses imposed on it at this rating. A rating of 140 horsepower is 7 times the original 20 so the engine was much more apt to "come apart".

When one of these engines tossed a rod or broke a crankshaft, it wasn't too great a catastrophe. Everyone expected such things to happen and parts weren't expensive. So the romanticists of the era didn't let the disappointment of a "blown up engine" keep them from starting anew.

Some of the fabulous characters that operated Model T engines in track cars performed a very unique type of preventative maintenance to reduce this type of failure. After *every* race they replaced the crankshaft with a brand new one because a new one was less apt to break than one that had already suffered thru a race.

The Model A was the next Ford product to get the hop up treatment. The same characteristics appeared in this new Ford product, so the interest was kept alive. Passenger cars, race cars, and "hop ups" all received varying degrees of the same treatment. Model A's were designed to produce around 40 horsepower. So their safety factor didn't take as great a beating as the T's. This fact made the hopped up Model A a

4

bit more dependable . . . longer lasting.

At this point, it might be worthwhile to point out that stock Fords were considered to be quite snappy at accelerating. This was due to the fact that the engines were called upon to pull less weight than the majority of cars. Thus the performance obtained from Fords caused owners to be even more speed and performance conscious.

Of course, none of these cars would have been popular "hop ups" if it hadn't been for the fact that some engineers, mechanics, and business men visualized profitable returns from the production of speed equipment. There was very little interest in hopping up cars other than Fords so there was little point in producing parts for any others . . . . a business must show a profit or it soon goes out of existence. In spite of this, some equipment was made for others but there was very little demand for it. Equipment can be made for any car but a considerable amount of money must be invested in order to produce it. A manufacturer won't spend a few thousand dollars for patterns and machinery to produce speed equipment unless enough of it can be sold to repay the investment and then make a profit.

A large quantity of various types of speed equipment caused the Model A engines to remain popular for a long period of time. They were popular many years after the advent of the V-8's, and hot Model A's were capable of running away from stock V-8's.

During the first few years of production, the V-8's received nothing but criticism from the hop up enthusiasts. Even tho they were one of the snappiest performing stock cars, the majority felt that they would never attain the speeds that the "4-barrel" produced. At first there was very little speed equipment available for the V-8's so the 4-barrel owners still reigned supreme. A few observed that V-8's had many of the adaptable characteristics of the T's and A's. But the existence of these few visionaries wasn't enough to make it immediately possible to hop up a V-8. Instead, it was necessary to wait until some enterprising person felt that there was a market for the necessary parts. It wasn't until a number of manufacturers began to produce parts for the V-8s that they really came into their own. When sufficient parts were made available, Model A's became as obsolete as T's. Eventually, more equipment was produced for the V-8's than all other cars combined.

A large market for speed parts creates a high production rate which, in turn, lowers the cost of the finished products. The law of supply and demand snowballs and pro-

duction and demand get larger and larger. Of course, the production of speed parts has never been, and never will be, equivalent to that of standard or replacement parts manufactured in Detroit. This will naturally keep the price of speed parts much higher than regular automotive replacement parts. But, being that more speed equipment is produced for Fords, it is only logical that these parts will cost less than those for other cars.

The large demand for Ford speed equipment is not produced by hop up and race car enthusiasts. They only use a very small part of the total production. An overwhelming percentage is installed on late model passenger cars to improve their performance. It is this use that eventually determines popularity. If it wasn't for the fact that the major portion is used on family cars, it would be impossible to maintain the present popularity of hopped up Fords.

Some of the new rocker arm overhead valve V-8 engines may have greater potentialities for increasing horsepower, but it is very doubtful if they will ever be as popular as the Fords. Changes that can be made on a Ford for a reasonable sum cost a small fortune on these engines. The greatest deciding factor is the lack of hopping up interest by owners of passenger cars equipped with these engines. Of course, there are a few sports among these owners, but very few. Most of them are laboring under the delusion that they possess four-wheeled "rockets" that can't be improved upon—and most of them wouldn't care to re-work their engines if they could!

The new Chrysler V-8 strikes many as being an engine that will be very popular in hop up circles but the inescapable law of supply and demand reduces its potentialities considerably. The sale of speed equipment still determines the popularity of an engine. A dual manifold for the Chrysler V-8 costs $84.50 whereas dual manifolds for 1952 Fords and Mercuries range in price from $43.50 to $48.50. When you hop up a Chrysler, the manufacturer's own replacement parts prices strike an even harder blow. One measly carburetor 'costs $48.60 in Southern California; whereas, a brand new Ford pot costs a mere $12.60.

In some ways, overhead valve engines have less chance to become popular as hopped up jobs than L head (flat head) engines. Special heads will never be nearly as popular for the overhead engines. A good reason for this is that the limited production of speed equipment would necessitate charging approximately $500 per pair for

(Continued on page 47)

CUSTOM HINTS

by Dean Batchelor

Channeling is evidently becoming one of the favorite operations for customizing cars.

But before you get all steamed up about lowering your car by this method, let me explain a few things . . . .

You will lose seating and luggage space in direct proportion to the amount you channel the car.

Unless your car is such that you can move the seat rearward, and possibly down, you will have an uncomfortable driving position. In the case of a channeled roadster, you will be sticking out of the car from the waist up—unless you use a very thin seat, which is not too comfortable. You will be looking over the windshield instead of thru it.

You are not changing the appearance of the car in any way other than lowering it;

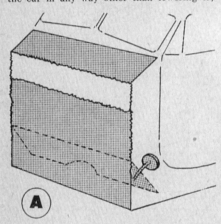

i.e., the contour and shape remain the same. When cutting top and/or sectioning body, overall contour is changed considerably.

First off, you may channel your car any reasonable amount . . . say, from one to six inches. Any more than six inches and you will probably need a glass dome in the top of your car to see where you're going.

Naturally, the seats, interior trim, bumpers (and anything else that could interfere with the operation) will have to be removed

before you start. If possible, the engine and fenders should be removed to make things easier to get to.

The metal floorboards are cut on the outer edges of the frame . . . so the body can be dropped. Next, the firewall is cut . . . the same amount as the car is to be channeled. Note: the cut across the firewall is made on the vertical section as shown in Figure A. The bottom of the firewall is usually a box section. Leave it in the stock position instead of dropping it with the body. Then it will help strengthen the body after all the hacking has been done. Also, the slanted part of the floorboards (under the foot pedals) should remain in the stock location.

The body-mounting brackets, which are usually riveted to the frame, will be cut loose and slid down with the body when it is lowered (Fig. B). When remounting these to the frame, be sure to use as many (or more) bolts as were formerly used. As a matter of fact, it is a good idea to weld the brackets onto the frame in addition to

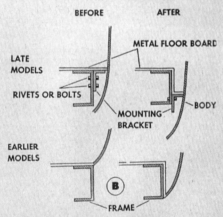

bolting. It might save the embarrassment of having the body come loose and be rattling around on the frame. Speaking of rattling, thin rubber pads or web belting between the frame and body will help prevent squeaks and rattles. These insulators can also be used to shim the body in spots

6

—if your channel job is not exactly perfect, and if the doors don't fit correctly.

After the body has been dropped and secured to the frame again, the floorboards can be welded back in. Because the floorboards are still on top of the frame and the body is a few inches lower than it was

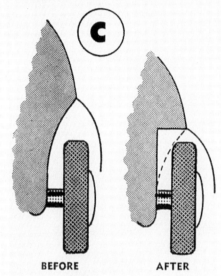

BEFORE   **AFTER**

previously, a slight addition will have to be made to bridge the gap. Don't weld the floor to the chassis. Weld it to the body . . . as it was originally (see drawings).

Channeled '39 Ford before floor is replaced.

There are three things you can do to the fenders after channeling your car. 1. Take them off (for roadsters and early model coupes only) and use cycle-type fenders. 2. Lower them with the body, in which case the front wheels will rub on the fenders when turning a corner, unless the cut-outs for the wheels are raised (Fig. D). 3. Raise the fenders on the body the same amount the body is channeled.

All three methods present problems, but No. 3 will be the most difficult to do. If the front fenders are raised in relation to the body, it means taking a section out of the hood—in the same amount the body was channeled. Because most hood sides slant

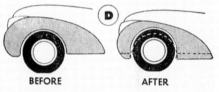

BEFORE   **AFTER**

inward, the sectioning of the hood will require a pretty good body man to make the job look like anything. In the rear it is not so bad, unless the car is a four-door sedan—in which case the rear door will have to be worked over to conform to the new location of the fender.

The steering column, unless lowered, will now protrude thru the instrument panel. On some cars the holes in the frame mount can be slotted and the column swung down enough to clear the panel. On others, a new bracket will have to be made. On cars

th column shift the rods from the column to the transmission will have to be reworked. What alterations they will need can readily be seen after the steering assembly has been relocated. Now, a new under-dash mount for the column can be installed. While the column is loose in the car, it is a good opportunity to position the wheel in the location that is the most comfortable to you.

The bumpers should still be mounted in the conventionel location to match the height of bumpers of other cars. To do this the body panel will have to be cut out directly above the bumper braces so the brace can still attach to the frame as it did originally.

When you decide to customize your car, consider carefully the final proportions. The owner of a custom job once told me he chopped the top 8 inches and channeled the body 6 inches. When I asked him why so much of a drop, he replied that he was afraid no one would know his car had been customized . . . . And I was under the impression car owners wanted custom work done to make the car look better! You should have seen this mess—it looked like a pill-box on the Siegfried Line. The only thing missing was the gun turret.

The information contained so far in this article will pertain more to the earlier model cars (with detachable fenders) than it will to the newer models.

Most of the newer cars are already, in effect, channeled. Too much of a drop, therefore, will cause the lower body panels to be very susceptible to damage if the car is driven over a high bump or on poor roads. And overhang on a channeled car must be watched when entering steep driveways.

As a last word of caution, if you have any doubt whatsoever about your ability to weld properly, or to estimate the strength required by certain structural members, do not try to do the job by yourself. Either take it to a reliable body shop or have someone help who knows the proper technique. •

Stock '39 Ford floor and seat before channel.

Channeled '38 Ford with floor mat extended down to cover the addition to floor boards.

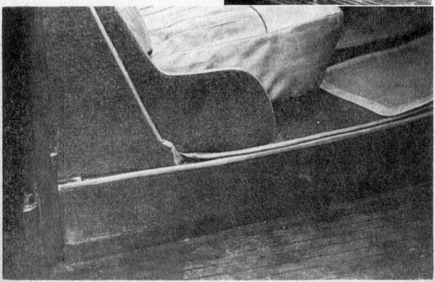

8

HOP UP, June, 1952

482

Hop Up Test No. 3

by Dean Batchelor

Realizing the tremendous amount of engine conversion that is going on, today, we are going to vary the road test this month . . . in order to give you some idea of the problems involved in "switching" engines. This article concerns the installation of a '52 Lincoln ohv engine in a '50 Merc station wagon. Naturally, the problems (of putting a different type engine in a chassis that was originally intended to carry something else) will vary with the make of car and the type of engine to be installed. But more of that in later issues.

Bob Stelling consumed approximately 120 hours in installing the Lincoln engine in his Merc. Weight of the station wagon, with the new engine installed, is 4180 pounds as compared to the former weight of just under 4000 pounds.

Looking back over the job, Bob decided that it would have been much easier to have used the Hydramatic transmission. He used the stock Merc transmission (with overdrive) with the idea of merchandising adapter kits for installing Lincoln engines in older model Ford products. Because of the

Air cleaner cut-out for generator and special headers required can be seen here. Note inaccessible spark plug location under headers.

difficulties encountered, the idea has been dropped indefinitely.

The late Merc bell housing adapter was utilized, but with considerable alteration. First, the adapter was rotated counter-clockwise so the starter mounting flange would line up with the cut-out on the Lincoln block (the starter on a Lincoln is located higher on the crankcase than on a Merc). Then it was found that the starter wouldn't mesh with the flywheel starter-ring gear because the Merc flywheel is smaller in diameter than the Lincoln. So . . . the block was ground out and the starter case was turned down in a lathe to allow it to move in closer to the flywheel.

This done, the holes in the transmission flange had to be re-drilled to put the transmission back on an even keel.

To mount the Merc flywheel on the Lincoln crankshaft, the four bolt holes in the flywheel had to be filled and new holes drilled. Lincoln flywheels have six bolts holding them onto the crank and the bolt circle is a different diameter than a Merc.

Those of you who are experienced in working on Ford products will remember the convenient location of the generator and fuel pump. On the older models they are right on top, in very accessible locations, but on the new Lincoln engine they are down low on the block. The fuel pump on the left, the generator on the right.

These were the next obstacles in the way of the new engine installation. Bob eliminated the fuel pump problem in a hurry by mounting an electric pump near the gas tank, eliminating the stock pump. The generator was not so simple a matter. One had to be used, so a new mount was made—on top of the engine and a little off-center to the left.

Everything seemed fine now, except for two things: The air cleaner wouldn't fit on the carburetor and the stock exhaust system

Under-hood view of stock Mercury engine....

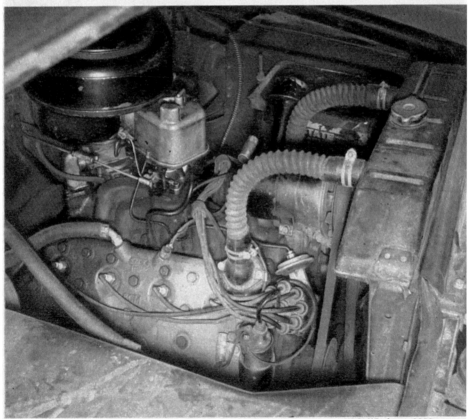

10

Same engine compartment with new Lincoln engine installed, new battery on right side.

wouldn't fit—both because the generator was in the way. The air cleaner situation was fixed by simply cutting a section out of the cleaner. As for the exhaust system, Bob wanted headers anyway, so this gave him a good excuse to make them.

The battery was next on the list of alterations. Mercs come standard with the square type battery. But the stock model wouldn't fit anymore. So a long battery was installed on the right side. The battery would have interfered with the exhaust pipe had headers not been built.

On the new Lincoln ohv engine the sump is located on the forward end of the pan. Unless the engine is moved to the rear when installed in the Merc (which is a little impractical) the sump would interfere with the crossmember. So Bob proceeded to turn the pan completely around,

putting the sump in the rear. This involved reworking not only the pan flange but the oil pump intake pipe. On the older Ford products the oil pump was inside the pan, but on the new Lincoln the pump is on the outside, much in the same manner as the in-line engines made by other manufacturers. When Bob turned the pan around, the hole for the intake line had to be filled in and the connection moved to the other side of the pan. Also, the pipe itself was shortened considerably. The dipstick now had to be changed, so an F-8 truck type has been utilized. These sticks are flexible and long enough to reach down thru the maze of "garbage" under the hood.

DRIVING IMPRESSIONS

As for the driving qualities of this station wagon, it seems to be even better than stock. On winding roads the tires howl quite a bit more than on a stock Merc but the front end goes where you point it regardless of the tire noise.

(Continued on page 46)

by George Essig

We're straying from the regular path this month (of having custom cars on the cover) by presenting Bud Crackbon's T pickup. The cover spot is well earned by Bud for he recently won the 8-Foot High Trophy at the Oakland Roadster Show. This trophy is billed as the largest in the world, and is presented to the car that the show judges think is America's most beautiful roadster.*

Bud is President of the Ramblers Club of San Francisco, which in turn is a member of the Cal-Neva Roadster Association and the American Hot Rod Conference.

The '25 T body and bed is mounted on a narrowed '32 Ford V-8 frame. Front end is '41 Ford with 50-50 Houdaille shocks and the rear end is '32 Ford with Gabriel tube

shocks. Transmission is stock '32 Ford. '39 Willys steering is used with a Crosley steering wheel (space in a T body is rather limited so a small diameter wheel helps the situation considerably). Tire sizes are 5.50 x 15 (front) and 7.00 x 15 (rear).

Metal work on the front-end was performed by Eddie Wendt, the two-tone paint job by Ross, and chrome plating by Standard Plating Co.—all of San Francisco.

In the engine department the '40 Merc block was bored .060 over, giving 248 total cubic inches, and was ported, polished, and

*This is assuming that the most beautiful roadsters in America are at this show every year. Bud's car qualifies as a roadster in this case because pickups run in the roadster classes at lakes events and drag races.

Cover Pick Up

487

Race car type front bumper adds to appearance as well as protecting front of pick up. Close attention has been paid all details.

Left, sturdy rear bumper does not distract.

Right, fan is driven by motor from car heater.

relieved. Inside the block is a Winfield full-race cam, Zephyr valve springs, Silvolite pistons, and a late model oil pump. The flywheel has been chopped and balanced by Al Blazic. Visible on the outside are Edelbrock 8.5:1 heads, Navarro dual manifold, and a La Mott dual coil ignition.

Chevy Custom

A few weeks ago *Hop Up* received a letter and a photo from a reader describing his Chevy custom job. Because the letter came from Link's Custom Body Shop, which is only a small stone's throw from *Hop Up's* offices, we beat feet up there to have a look for ourselves. The Chevy turned out even better than the small snapshot, so Ralph Poole, *Hop Up's* Staff Photographer, immediately proceeded to record it for posterity. The following is copied directly from Spencer Murray's letter to *Hop Up.*

"My car is a 1949 Chevrolet 2-door sedan. The top has been chopped three inches and the body channeled two inches. These modifications, with a lowering job on the suspension, makes the overall height of the car 4 feet 10 inches. The hood is filled, as is the deck lid. The door handles have been removed and the doors are electric push-button operated, while the deck lid is raised and lowered by an electric motor.

"The engine has been bored, ported, the head milled, and large valves with heavier valve springs installed.

"Quick steering was achieved by shorten-

16   **HOP UP, June, 1952**

Above, skirt and rear wheel can be removed even tho pipe is only one inch from fender. Below, bird's eye view of Murray's Chevy shows lines uncluttered by usual garbage.

18

ing the stroke of the tie-rod idler-arm—which is directly under the engine. This reduced the turning of the steering wheel from four and one-half turns to two and one-half turns, lock to lock.

"An original idea (I must confess) was the addition of outside tail pipes. Extending from the body at the rear of the rocker panel molding, they curve upward and to the rear—ending at a point directly over the rear bumper. The paint is enamel (most customs are lacquered) and the color is "Metallic Mustard."

"Altho I am employed at a body shop and the car was built at the same place, it is not a professional job. It was done by another fellow and myself . . . after hours and on Sundays. Neither of us is a body man by trade.

"The car is definitely *not* a copy of Cerney's car (*Hop Up*, January, 1952) which is quite similar. My Chevy was started in September of 1950; the top was the first thing to be done and nothing else was touched until that particular project was completed a month or so later."

Glendale, California   Spencer Murray
Link's Custom Shop

Palm Springs Road Race

Sunday, the 23rd of March, was a big day for the proponents of home-built sports cars, roadsters, or die-hards who just plain hate to see the flat-head engine disappear from the automotive scene.

Chuck Manning, driving his own home-built sports car with a Mercury engine, came home the winner in the fourth Semi-Annual Palm Springs Road Race. The good part is not so much the fact he won, but that he proved to the exponents of the expensive foreign sports car that a home-built car can get the job done . . . and with an L-head engine at that.

Quite a few people in the sports car clubs have been heard to remark at various times that . . . "a Ford V-8 engine wouldn't last a full race if it were hopped up enough to keep up with the best sport cars." I wonder

The Aston-Martin made a good impression on everyone, handled very well for a closed car.

what they think now. Luck? A few more races will tell.

It is quite possible that Mike Graham in the Cad-engined Allard or Don Parkinson in his modified Jaguar XK-120 could have beaten Manning. But they both spun out, losing valuable seconds regaining the course, when within striking distance of Manning's Merc. Both spin-outs were apparently caused by over-zealous driving while trying to catch the fleeing Manning who led from the sixth lap and was never headed.

There were three cars entered that could be considered as having come up from the hot rod ranks. Manning's, Seifried's, and the Cannon Special, all with Merc engines. Among the great number of foreign cars entered, there were many with American engines. Two Cad-Allards, one Merc-Allard, two V-8 60 engined MG's, and the Alfa Romeo chassis with a Merc engine entered by Keenan Wynn. Also present were the entirely American-built Edwards with a V-8 60 ohv, and the two Chrysler-engined Cunninghams.

For the first few laps of the main event it looked as tho the race could develop into an American free-for-all. Out of the first seven cars there was only Parkinson's Jag to represent the foreign contingent. Dick Siefried, Jr., driving his own car, took the lead right off the bat and was several hundred yards in front and going away, when a

20

Manning's Merc followed by Parkinson in a modified Jag and Graham in the Cad-Allard.

New owner, Robbins drove well first time out.

Graham in Cad-Allard follows Trousdale's V-8 60 MG and Parkinson's modified Jaguar.

broken fan belt forced him to retire. Phil Hill, driving one of the Cunninghams, lost a cardan shaft U-joint (DeDion rear end), after rounding the first turn of the first lap.

The race (101.2 miles) was 44 laps of the 2.3 mile circuit and Manning completed the tour in 1 hour, 45 minutes, followed closely by Don Parkinson and the Jag, Mike Graham (Cad-Allard), Jack McAfee (blown MG

TC), Irving Robbins (Cunningham), Howard Wheeler (Jaguar), Douglas Trotter (Aston-Martin).

By now the regular readers of *Hop Up* are probably wondering what's going on here . . . *What* is a magazine that is supposedly devoted to customs and roadsters doing reporting a *sports car* race? Well, now, podner I'm agonna tell ya. From the looks of the crowd at this race it is evident that the hop up and cycle lovers are becoming more and more interested in the grass on the other

Manning still being followed by those cars.

Coppel's MG (foreground) chases field down long straight to right angle turn at end.

22

Willet's MG, Barlow's Simca, and David's modified MG pass Hill's parked Cunningham.

side of the fence. So . . . without fear of sticking my neck out too far, I would say that within a very short time the sports car ranks will be swelled by new members . . . A lot of whom will be ex-hot rodders.

The most amazing thing to the hot rodders seemed to be the speeds attained by the small displacement cars. Especially John Edgar's blown MG (76 cu in.) driven by Jack McAfee, the Aston-Martin DB2 coupe (150 cu in.) Barlow's Simca (75 cu in.) and Bob Willet's MG (75 cu in.).

Performance of the remaining Cunningham was rather disappointing to the spectators; few knew that Robbins had owned the car for only six days and was just stroking around to get the feel of things. During practice, Phil Hill turned fastest lap in the Cameron Cunningham. This particular course is well suited to a small, light car, and the Cunninghams were at a disadvantage.

Pollack in the Siata leads McAfee in the blown MG coming out of right angle turn.

497

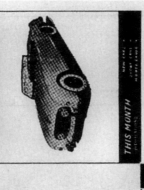

Automobile TOPICS

THIS MONTH

the Newest
yet......
The Oldest

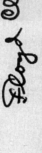

Meet the Advertisers

Phil Weiand is one of the oldest (from the standpoint of years in business) of all the speed equipment manufacturers. Starting originally in 1941, making a dual manifold for Ford V-8 and Mercurys, he continued until the war forced a stoppage of all such production. After hostilities ceased, Phil once more began to manufacture speed equipment but this time did not stop at just a dual for V-8s. He now makes dual, triple, and *quadruple* manifolds for Fords and Mercs, duals for Chevys, Studebaker Champs, and a new one coming up for the Stude V-8. The name Weiand (pronounced Why-and, *not* We-and) also appears on Ford, Merc, V-8 60, and Studebaker Champ heads.

Phil actually started his racing career in 1934 when the most popular engine for lakes use was the Model T Ford. In those days he made speed equipment for his own use and it was not until later that he put it on the market.

Weiand equipment is shipped all over world.

Zabel and Robinson at work on track roadster.

Many of you will probably remember the beautiful little bronze colored '27 T that Phil ran when the roadster boys first got started in track racing—immediately after the war. Weiand, who is 34 years old and married, has given up actual competition with his own cars. But Bruce Robinson, who works in the engine building department at Phil's company, carries on by running a '32 roadster at the lakes and a T on the track (*Hop Up*, January 1952). The '32, running in Class C, has turned 154 mph at Bonneville and 152 at El Mirage.

Above, castings are machined at Weiand's.

Below left, Weiand himself, closing big deal.

Below, last machine work before buffing heads.

A V-8 Coupe

by George Essig

There is a lot more to Ron Tehaney's clean little A coupe than meets the eye. It's like the old gag about a wolf in sheep's clothing. At first glance it appears to be merely a chopped A coupe with a V-8 engine. But let's go thru the list of alterations on this innocent looking car . . .

First, the chassis. The frame is '29 A . . . but with '32 V-8 crossmembers. Springs are '32 Ford in front and reworked Model T rear. The front axle has been dropped 2½ inches and the rear end assembly is Model A (3.27.1) but carrying a Halibrand quick-change center section. Transmission is from a '41 Ford with Zephyr gears installed and a '49 Ford column shift. Brakes are '41 Ford hydraulic.

The body is a '31 Model A five-window coupe that has been chopped 3 inches and has had a steel center section welded in—to take the place of the usual soft top on these models. Now . . . this is where the confusing part comes in (if you looked at the photos before reading the article):

A '32 V-8 gas tank and rear frame horn covers have been grafted onto the A body, making the rear view of the coupe look very much like a '32 instead of a Model A. Needless to say, the tail lights are '38-9 Ford teardrops and the bumper is '37 De Soto.

Doors are electric push-button—solenoid operated (May, 1952, *Hop Up*, "Custom Hints")—and the paint is *"Indian Pastel Brick Pink"* (so-help-me, that's what he said).

The engine is a '48 Merc 59A block, ported, polished and relieved. Valves are stock in diameter but have been ground thinner and polished. The guides have been tapered

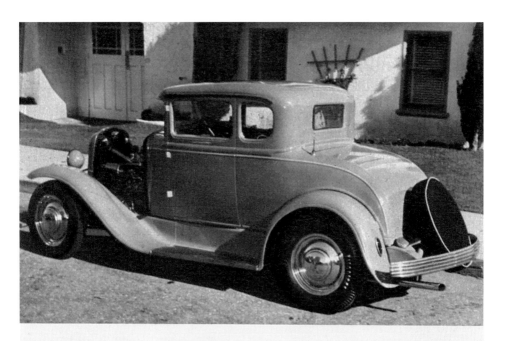

Above, chrome wheels, radio antenna mounted in rear deck are details that stand out. Excellent condition of body, fenders, running boards, etc. are shown in these photos.

503

Lavish use of chrome under hood includes chromed generator, water pumps, carburetors, voltage regulator, oil filter, dipstick, oil filler cap, headers, buffed heads, manifold, carburetor air stacks, and chrome-plated firewall.

on top to allow easier flow of the fuel and Zephyr springs are used. An Iskenderian 1015-B track grind cam works very well with the 3⅜ bore by 4⅛ stroke of the 296 cu in. engine. J. E. pistons with Grant rings complete the interior of the engine. Visible on the outside are Edelbrock 8.5:1 heads, a Weiand 4 carburetor manifold and a Harmon & Collins magneto. The entire engine assembly is electronically balanced and drives thru an 8 pound flywheel and a special reworked clutch.

Instrument panel is from a '34 Auburn. Fuel is supplied to the engine by a Stewart Warner electric pump from the '32 tank, and there is another tank in the rear compartment that works strictly by hand pressure pump.

30

Cad Pick Up

by Bill Bagnall

The old saying that "necessity is the mother of invention" certainly held true in the case of Jack Warner and Walt Ball, Portland Oregon motorcycle dealers. They were faced with the problem of finding a pickup truck . . . to carry their motorcycles to various race meets thruout the country. However, they weren't satisfied with the standard types available, as they were looking for the quality and heavy car riding characteristics found in the more expensive automobiles. This, plus the fact that they wanted something original, led them to

American

MOT

Jack Warne

5771 N.E. U

PORT

Spare tire location is both accessible and logical. Note well blended bed and rear fender treatment. Cab styling molds into contour.

building the Cadillac pickup truck which appears on these pages.

The project got under way with the purchase of a wrecked 1949 Cadillac 62 sedannette. After surplus bodywork was removed, the chassis and wheebase were lengthened one foot. Then the Cadillac front end was refitted and a GMC pickup cab installed. Two-and-a-half inches were chopped from the cab, and Oldsmobile doors fitter (requiring a 1½" cut in them). The pickup bed is standard GMC. This left a little "air" between the side of the bed and the Cad rear fenders, so a spare tire was neatly fitted

on each side.

In order that the rear tailgate might drop flush with the floor of the bed, it was necessary to make the rear bumper guards and license plate fold down. The under side of the guards also serve as a rest for the gate when it is folded down.

With the two motorcycles in place, it was found advisable to build up the rear springs, so two additional main leaves were added on each side. The car is equipped with a set of Smitty mufflers, and is finished with Olds Chariot Red lacquer.

More than eight months labor and an investment of $5000 . have gone into this "highway jewel." However, their efforts have been well rewarded as the car is a real "eye-popper" wherever it goes.

33

Hopping Up the Buick Engine

508

While there are still a few Buick owners who have not yet been "convinced" that Buick is *not* the fastest thing on the road, the majority are beginning to see the light! The Buick is basically a good engine, but it is handicapped by the heavy body and chassis it must lug around.

Certainly Buick acceleration is nothing to brag about . . . but it *can* be improved. Because acceleration is dependent on a little item known as *power-to-weight ratio*, we must raise the horsepower—or lower the weight—in order to better the acceleration. Gear ratio figures here to a certain extent, but we'll leave that factor alone.

Naturally, the average owner is not too interested in reducing weight by stripping the interior, substituting aircraft bucket seats, drilling holes in the frame, fabricating body panels of aluminum, and such-like. If you want a practical method of improving the "get-up-and-go" of the Buick, it will be necessary for you to turn to some means of improving the horsepower produced by the Buick engine.

LOWER END

Don't turn away aghast while exclaiming about the horrible things that are going to happen to the Buick poured rods! These will stand up adequately for mild road use. However, for really hot conversions, you can install the insert-type rods which came as a stock equipment on Buicks made in 1950 and later. These should definitely be used with Morraine bearings for best results. This is the factory bearing, available at your Buick parts counter.

Otherwise, the stock Buick lower-end, when well broken-in, is quite capable of standing up to continued high speed, high power output. From shop experience, it is recommended that you use "Liqui-Moly" in your regular oil. This is the *only* additive with which we have had any success.

If you are in the process of overhauling your Buick, the oil pump should be given a very careful going over to insure trouble-free operation. A new oil pick-up float should be installed as the old ones are invariably dirty and quite hard to get completely clean. The pump by-pass spring should also be replaced.

CARBURETION

The compound carburetor manifolds which came as stock equipment on 1941 Buicks can easily be adapted for dual carburetion on your 1936 to 1952 Buick. These are available for both the Specials and the larger models. There are *two* sizes, so get the right one!

In order to obtain the best performance from these manifolds, the stock carburetors should be removed and two Zenith No. 10167 1½" (SAE flange) carburetors installed with the following equipment:

	Small engines (to 263")	Large engines (to 340")
Main jets	#32	
Idle jets	#13	Same—only use
Power jets	#18	#33 main jets
Venturi	#30	

Because these carburetors use a two-bolt mounting flange, and the flanges on your compound manifold are of the three-bolt type, it will be necessary to use adapters to fit them properly. The adapters which are available were designed for fitting a V-8 three-bolt flange carb to a two-bolt flange, and thus the fit is slightly imperfect. It is usually necessary to slot the rear hole in the flange to get it to fit correctly and still get a nut on it.

Linkage should be of the ball-joint type. Adaption of the stock linkage to the dual set-up is easily accomplished. Naturally, the carburetors should function as a unit; that is, each should be fully opened or at idle at the same time. None of this stock baloney of one cutting in after the other if it's real performance that you are after.

As the stock set-up has the starter switch on the carburetor for most models, it will be necessary to install a two-wire type push-button switch on the dash panel to operate the starter. In our opinion, this is an improvement as it tends to eliminate much engine flooding.

Some readers will wonder why we don't recommend the old stand-by, the Ford 97

Concave turbulator pistons in later models will also raise compression in early Buicks.

carburetor, as these will fit the Buick manifold. The reason lies in the fact that the V-8 carbs do not have any provision for distributor advance vacuum, which is necessary for the best performance from any Buick.

A stock dual manifold, equipped as indicated above, will add approximately 20 horsepower to your Buick engine, even when no other speed equipment is installed. The mileage around town will remain about the same unless you become one of those stoplight clowns who has to "stand on it" coming away from every signal, trying to "shutoff" all comers! This type of driving not only knocks a hugh hole in your pocketbook from buying gas, but also attracts coupons from the local gendarmes.

COMPRESSION

"What do I want with more compression?" you may ask, recalling the spark knock that your Buick was giving as you drove home from work this evening. Well, the Buick really doesn't have enough compression for outstanding performance, and its tendency to spark knock can be lessened by installing an Octa-Gane Water Injector with a flange under each of your carburetors.

Early model Buicks (thru 1937) were equipped with flat-top pistons. Their compression ratio is 5.7:1. This ratio can be raised to 6.1:1 by merely installing the later model turbulator pistons. These pistons come in two types, one having a concave surface on the protruding dome—giving a lower ratio.

Concave turbulator pistons were used on all Buicks later than 1941. Earlier models back to 1938 used flat type turbulators which give slightly more compression when installed in the later Buicks.

By using 1938-1941 flat-type turbulator pistons in other models, compression is raised.

Early model Buicks (thru 1937) were equipped with flat-top pistons. Comp. ratio 5.7 to 1.

If you wish to raise the compression of your Buick to about 8:1, mill .080″ from the head of a Super model or .110″ from the head of a Roadmaster model. Always check to make sure that sufficient stock will be left on the head after milling. To compensate for the amount milled from the head, the rocker arm mounting brackets must be shimmed by *one-half* that amount, or . . . the same amount as milled must be removed from the valve stems. Be careful with 1941 models, as there were already milled to some extent (to give more compression) by the factory. Increasing the bore will automatically raise the compression ratio and, at the same time, will further improve horsepower and torque.

IGNITION

Ignition can be improved on Buicks by installing the dual-coil, dual-point set-up made by Spalding Ignitions. This is installed with two Bosch "Big Brute" coils for best results. If you can't quite stand the price of these units, then go for a Mallory single-coil, dual-point distributor. This overlapping of two points in conjunction with a single coil was described in Barney Navarro's article "Lighting the Flame" in the May issue of *Hop Up*. The Mallory distributor should be used in combination with the Mallory "Best" coil for best results. At least one step colder spark plug should be installed when the dual carbs and additional compression are added.

CAMSHAFT

By all means . . . if your Buick is now equipped with hydraulic tappets, throw them away—throw them away and get a set of stock Buick solid-type lifters, together with the proper pushrods for your engine. No other changes are necessary to use the solid

36

tappets in an engine originally equipped with hydraulic tappets. The solid type will permit rpm wind-up as far as your engine will go, whereas the hydraulic units pump up solid and hold the valves off their seats at about 4200 rpm (by actual test).

In choosing a cam, pick a type which will not excessively wear the tappets. A cam with a lot of duration, such as a full race or super grind, is not recommended for the average road car, because the more radical grinds need more than two carburetors for best results. The new ¾ and Super ¾ grinds, now being produced by many of the cam grinders, are really smooth and quiet, and perform quite nicely when used with two carburetors. If you plan to use only one carburetor, then order a road grind cam, which will have about the same duration as a mild ¾ grind.

EXHAUST

All Buicks can benefit by the installation of dual exhausts. Either two stock mufflers can be used or two steel-packs. The stock type will get you by in areas where the law frowns on excessive exhaust noise. Buick dual exhaust sets are not available in kit form. You'll have to build yours right onto the car. If you can't handle splitting the manifold, send it to one of the muffler companies which advertise in *Hop Up*. Nearly all of them are equipped to do the work .

If you have a 1947 or earlier Buick (back to 1936), you can use the 1941 style dual exhaust manifold and dual intake manifold without alterations. However, if yours is later than '47, the front motor mounts will obstruct the front manifold outlet. In order to use these manifolds on a 1947 model, it would be necessary to cut off the flange and weld it back on at an angle which would cause the pipe to clear the motor mount.

To use dual mufflers on a stock single-outlet manifold (by putting in a "Y") is a waste of time. However, you can adapt the stock single manifold successfully—by welding an additional flange onto the manifold and splitting into two units by tacking in a small piece of steel to give the dividing effect desired. One of the nicest sounding Buicks that we've heard had steel packs with a manifold division of 3/5 rather than 4/4.

CONCLUSION

Until you've ridden in a fully hopped-up Buick . . . one that has been given the complete treatment . . . you can't possibly imagine the fun that you've been missing. The Buick reacts readily to every item of speed equipment which is installed, and amply rewards the owner who lovingly bestows these items of equipment on it. You'll not go wrong hopping-up your Buick.*
*For further details consult California Bill's Chevy-Buick-GMC Speed Manual.—Ed.

California Bill

Mail Box 110

'33 PLYMOUTH—CALIFORNIA

My '33 Plymouth is painted metallic maroon and the interior is trimmed in dark red leather. Engine is stock except for dual pipes and 22 inch Porters. Car is lowered 3 inches by means of blocks, and Cadillac discs cover wooden spokes. '38 "tear drop" tail-lights and home-made direction lights.

Los Angeles, Calif.   Don Massie

DENVER—'36 FORD

My 1936 Ford has a '48 engine, Linc. trans. The body has '40 Chev headlights, boxed rear fenders, dual spotlights, has been dropped six inches, the rear spring torched, rear tire cover, dash and window frame are all chrome, blue and yellow leather custom upholstering, a white leather top—and dual Porter pipes. My car cost me $100 and up to date, I have $1600 in it— not including my wife (I just got married).

Denver, Colorado   Marvin L. Youngman

1947 BUICK—NEW JERSEY

. . . Custom '47 Buick Roadmaster owned by Nick DiTillio of Philadelphia and customized by Nick Mancini of Hilltop, New Jersey. Grille has: '49 Oldsmobile center bar, Buick frame, Hudson lower trim, and '52 Buick ornament. Headlights frenched, front fender tops built up for '49 Buick parking lights. Rear fenders faded into the body with tubular back-up lights. '49 Pontiac taillights faded into trunk lid, as is '37 Cadillac spare tire cover. Vacuum operated hood. Fuel tank fills from trunk compartment.

Two-toned, Cad ivory and Candiberry blue. Engine is hopped up and chromed. We hope to start a California Custom fad on the East Coast, and want to hear from Easterners who are interested.

Hilltop, New Jersey   Nick Mancini

'40 FORD—MINNESOTA

My convertible has been lowered (weighted down by cementing-in the trunk tool box), equipped with airplane shocks, completely de-chromed except for a spot light, all electric doors, trunk, and vacuum operated windows. Jungle Lime paint job of 5 coats. Engine is a '48 Merc stock with Edelbrock dual manifold and dual ignition. Interior is blue leather padded. '49 Ford accessories, chromed dash panel, radio panel, and clock panel. The dual ignition and manifold helps starting up here where it gets 30 below zero.

Fisher, Minnesota   Walt Lystrom

'50 NASH—TEXAS

James Samuels of New York is the proud owner of this '50 Nash. It was customized in El Paso, Texas, by myself and painted by fellow Californian. It features shaved hood and deck, taillights in fenders, frenched headlights, push-button doors, and a purple lacquer paint job.

Sunland, California   Milan Micka

'41 FORD—WASHINGTON

My car is a '41 Ford tudor with a '48 Pontiac grille and '50 Pontiac taillights. The chrome trim and bumpers are '48 Ford. It has padded leatherette upholstery and is running a stock '41 Ford engine.

Tacoma, Washington   Larry Rekdahl

38

1. **FORD, 1950** – Merc grille, bull nose, shaved deck, Pontiac tail lights, push-button doors, dual exhausts thru old tail-light openings. Owned by "Butch" Lockwood.

2. **CHEVROLET, 1949** – Custom grille, bull nose, shaved deck, Cad fenders, and stock engine. Bill Johnson, owner. Won first prize.

3. **FORD, 1935** – Chevrolet front and rear fenders, Chev. grille, chopped top, dual pipes, continental spare, custom interior, full house.

4. **MERCURY, 1939** – '50 Nash grille, chopped top, channeled body, continental spare, dual pipes thru fenders, '48 Chev taillights in bumper. Color bright rose. Bill Hill, owner.

5. **MERCURY, 1940** – Stock engine, dual pipes, recessed headlights, front air scoop, custom interior, padded dash, Jimmy Bishop, owner.

The cars above were displayed at the Custom Car Show held at the Cincinnati Race Bowl.

6. **FORD, 1951**—Bull nose, shaved deck, '51 Canadian Ford (Meteor) grille, dual pipes, full house, frenched headlights, and maroon paint.

7. **CHEVROLET, 1949**—Bull nose, continental type rear, Weber cam, Mallory ignition, dual Ford carbs, and 7.6:1 compression. Owned by Gene Young of Dayton, Ohio.

8. **CHRYSLER, 1949**—Dual pipes, fender skirts, oval port-hole in place of rear quarter window. Owned and styled by L. T. Patterson Co.

9. **BROWN'S ROADSTER**—Custom body and interior, '37 Cord hood and grille, Chev taillights, and '40 Ford instruments.

10. **FORD, 1949**—shaved deck, bull nose, custom grille and dual pipes. Owned by Schwartz Motor Co.

11. **CORD, 1937**—Supercharged—continental tire mount, custom finish and interior. Owned by Louis H. Philips.

The custom cars above were exhibited at the First Annual Custom Show, sponsored by the "Cam Lifters" of Cincinnati. Held at Downtown Mercury.

What d'you Think?

Men (and women), picked at random on the street, were asked . . .

In What Way Do You Think The New Cars Could Be Improved?

Walt Henry
Operates a hot dog stand. Drives a '40 Plymouth and would like a new Plymouth or De Soto.

Joe Van Shura
Service station owner. Drives a '48 Frazer but would like a new De Soto.

"Improve the comfort. Better riding qualities. The seats are too hard and don't fit the shape of your back. Brakes are not improving as fast as the rest of the car, in other words, the cars are too big and too fast for the brakes. Cars should be built stronger for the safety of the public and not any bigger than they already are."

"Most of the cars are too hard to service. Especially the lubrication and putting gas in. The filler spouts to the gas tanks have too many bends and the gas backs up and spills on the ground. The new Fords, Mercs and Willys have this licked now. The price is too high for what you're getting, too . . . this applies to all the cars."

Art Molen
Printer. Drives a '39 Plymouth and would like to have a new Ford or Chevy.

L. E. Donaldson
Printer. Drives a Dodge and would like a new car but is undecided as to what make.

"They should have sturdier construction and the body styling should be simpler. Ford went "gaga" on the new ones this year. I thought the '50 Ford was about the best looking one they made. Gas consumption is too high. The cars aren't economical any more."

"The automatic transmissions can be improved considerably. With an automatic transmission the mileage is bad. They creep at stop signs, cause cars to heat up in traffic and in the mountains, and the extra cost to have one in a car is too high. I still want a car with an automatic transmission myself but I think they can be improved a heck of a lot."

Jerry Stolp
Student at Glendale Junior College. Drives '48 Pontiac and would like to have an Olds 88.

Marillyn Webb
Receptionist. Drives a Ford. Would like a new Studebaker.

"Front tires seem to wear out too fast, even before the rear ones. They need better shock absorbers or something, maybe the suspension is wrong, I don't know. I think power steering is great. My car steers like a truck."

"I don't know what to say. I like them the way they are, but I do think that Studebaker has the most advanced styling of any new car. I would like to have a convertible if I could have two cars, othetwise a closed car would be better."

40

C. R. A. SPECIFICATIONS FOR THE TRACK ROADSTER

ENGINE LIMITATIONS—Cams in any position, 350 cu in. unblown 250 cu in. blown. American stock production auto or truck block.

CARBURETORS—No limitations.

EXHAUST PIPES — Extend past the driver's seat and safe distance from fuel system.

BODY—American standard size, stock, roadster body unaltered in contour.

FRAME—Tubular or Rail.

PICK-UPS—Pick-up must have a reinforced guard extending at least 6 inches below the bottom of the bed, or the bed must not be less than 17 inches or more than 26 inches from the ground at bottom.

BUMPERS—All cars must have rear bumpers to within 17 to 23 inches measured from the bottom of the bumper to the ground. All cars must have adequate bumpers to prevent underrunning. Stock bumpers will not be permitted. Only bumpers of steel or tubing to protect radiators and engines and arc welded or bolted to frame, which must not extend forward of the front wheels. Rear bumpers must not extend beyond the body more than 3 inches. **There shall** be no sharp corners.

PICK-UP BEDS—Pick-up beds must be a minimum of 3½ ft. in length and must extend not more than 20 inches past center of rear axle.

WEIGHT—Not less than 1200 lbs., not more than 2600 lbs. Car must have weight certificate.

WHEELBASE—Not less than 94 inches, maximum 115 inches.

TREAD—Minimum of 50 inches. Maximum of 60.

WHEELS—Maximum 20 inches. Minimum of 15.

STEERING WHEEL—All cars must be equipped with flexible steel spider type wheels placed so that driver has easy entrance and exit and can handle car without interference.

STEERING ASSEMBLY—Tie rods must be re- inforced or a truck tie-rod used. No welds will be allowed on pitman arms unless approved by Technical Committee. No brazing allowed on steering. Gearbox location optional.

FENDERS AND BRACES—All fenders and braces must be removed.

GLASS—No glass shall be allowed for wind- shields, only a soft pliable windbreak such as Pyrolyn or Plexiglas shall be used.

HEADLIGHTS & TAILLIGHTS — Headlights and taillights must be removed.

DOORS—Must be securely fastened or welded.

SAFETY BELTS—Each car entered must have regulation safety belt **bolted securely to frame.**

IGNITION SWITCH—Each car must have a cut-off switch within easy reach of driver.

FUEL LINE—Shut-off valve within easy reach of driver on all cars.

CLUTCH—All cars must be equipped with a positive neutral and pass the Technical Committee's approval.

BRAKES—All cars must be equipped with a suitable braking system and pass inspection.

LOCKED REAR ENDS—Optional.

TIRES—No factory built mudgrip or "knobbies" will be permitted.

FOUR WHEEL DRIVES—No four wheel drives shall be allowed.

SHOCKS—All cars must have double acting shocks on all four wheels.

FIREWALL—All cars must be equipped with fireproof firewall between driver and engine compartment.

HOOD—All cars must be equipped with full **hood** and radiator shells, securely fastened to body or frame.

ACCESSORIES—All exterior accessories must be removed from car.

CATCH TANK—All cars must have a catch tank on the radiator overflow of at least one (1) gallon capacity. Tank must be securely fastened to car.

IDENTIFICATION NUMBER—All cars must have identification number at least 12" block letters on both sides and back.

PAINT—All cars must appear at the track in a presentable condition. If all or partly painted with primer, may compete for one week only.

GAS TANKS AND BATTERIES—The location of gas tanks and batteries must be behind the driver. The gasoline tank must be behind the driver. Battery shall be a minimum of 12 inches from the gasoline tank.

SAFETY DISCS—A safety disc on the right rear wheel to prevent the wheel from being pulled thru the lugs.

REINFORCED BODY—All bodies must be re- inforced with tubing or steel rods, a minimum of one-half inch O.D. bolted to the frame.

NURFING BARS—All cars must be equipped with a suitable nurfing bar, extending forward of the rear wheels and bolted to the frame to prevent over-running or locking wheels.

CRASH HELMETS—All drivers must wear an approved crash helmet while on the race course. Driver must wear flexible shatter-proof goggles.

SAFETY HUBS—All cars must be equipped with safety hubs.

ROLL BARS—Every car must be equipped with a roll bar, to be of one (1) inch minimum chrome-molly or Shelby tubing. Bar must be braced to the frame either forward or to the rear, secured by bolts or welded directly to the frame and must be a minimum of 6 inches and a maximum of 12 inches above the body.   •

RIGHT-HAND MANIFOLD ON CHEVROLET

Regarding the Chevrolet engine pictured on page 32 of the May issue: I don't recall ever having seen a Chevrolet with the manifold on the right side of the engine.

Great Lakes, Ill.   J. R. Pasquale S. A.

It's not a 1953 Chevrolet, nor is it the Chinese version . . . the negative was reversed and the picture is printed backwards.—Tech. Ed.

COLUMBIA 2-SPEED REAR END

I have a 1947 Mercury Club Coupe with a Columbia rear end. When accelerating in first and second the engine sounds like it is racing.

Geneva, Ohio   Fred Inman

The regular installation of a Columbia rear axle uses an automatic down-shift mechanism which automatically places you in conventional every time you come to a stop. Therefore, your engine is racing in first and second somewhat, a condition aggravated by the fact that gear ratios of this model are rather on the low side. A simple correction for this is to install a three-pole two-position toggle switch in place of the spring-loaded switch used—Tech. Ed.

(Continued next page)

WHAT GEAR FOR BORED FORD?

I have a Ford standard coupe with a stock '40 engine and 4.33 gears in rear end (planning on a big engine later). Want pick up and good cruising speed for road and street use.

Would like to install a '41 Lincoln transmission and overdrive (have '40 Ford column shift).

Would it fit on a Ford bell housing? Should the same gears be kept in the rear end?

Canton, Ohio   F. Brookins

If it were mine, I would install 3.78 or 3.54 gears in the rear end and put the Lincoln gears in the Ford transmission.

This setup, coupled with a big engine (assuming you mean a bored and/or stroked V-8), will give you good all-round performance. —Tech. Ed.

NO FAN ON HOP UPS

In the pictures of these "hopped-up" engines I never can locate the fan. What happens to it, and what other provisions are made for cooling?

Helena, Montana   Bill Haselhorst

Some cars will cool adequately without a fan unless extremely heavy traffic is encountered. Some car owners just take the fan off during the winter months.—Tech. Ed.

HOW DOES HE OPEN THE DOORS?

In Hop Up (Feb. '52) on pages 24-25 is a '49 custom Ford by Harold Scott. I would like to know how he opens his doors! I don't see any door handles.

Seattle 3, Washington   I. N. Troyer, Jr.

Custom cars without door handles generally

44

have a concealed push button for an electric solenoid-operated latch mechanism. Some just leave the door unlocked and reach in thru the window to the handle. This is a bad practice, however, as it encourages car stealing and/or the looting of glove compartments.—Tech. Ed.

MERCURY ENGINE IN '32 FORD

I plan to put a new Mercury engine in a 1932 Ford. Will the engine mounts fit in the same spot? How about the old axle, will it be strong enough?

Detroit, Michigan   Walter Radecki

Your '32 engine mounts can be used on the Merc block in front, and the transmission will also fit, so the problems of installing a later model engine are minor. I assume you mean the front axle in asking if it will be strong enough. When Ford first brought out the V-8 in 1932 the engineers were evidently worried about the axle collapsing. They increased the size and strength of the front axle to make sure the extra weight of the V-8 engine (over the model A) would not cause failure in this very necessary part of the running gear. So the '32 Ford V-8 ended up with the strongest (and heaviest) axle ever put on a Ford passenger car to my knowledge. Starting with the '33 model the front axle was lightened to almost the same size as a model A. If you were referring to the rear axle, it too is plenty rugged providing the gears, bearings, key-ways, etc., are in good condition. In a car of this age it is a good idea (time, money, and facilities permitting) to replace vital parts of this nature to insure trouble-free motoring.—Tech. Ed.

COLUMN SHIFT FOR '39 FORD

Will a 1940 Ford steering column and transmission interchange with a 1939 Ford De Luxe?

Champaign, Illinois   Arthur Holt

Yes, and very easily.—Tech. Ed.

PHOTO CREDITS

Photo credits are given page by page, left to right and top to bottom.

6-11 .... Poole
12-15 .... Chesebrough - Essig
16-19 .... Poole
20-23 .... Chesebrough & Poole
26-27 .... Poole
28-30 .... Essig

Hills were overcome with the greatest of ease. Any normal grade that is presumed to be a high gear road was climbed in overdrive high without the slightest whimper from the engine. Steeper grades that would normally require second gear were pulled in conventional high. If the wagon was not overloaded with passengers or luggage, overdrive could still be used in most cases. The only sour point I could find in the driving qualities of this combination Lincoln-Mercury was a roughness of the engine at low rpm. Previously the car had a semi-race Merc engine in it and when Bob switched engines, he used the Merc's chopped flywheel. This light flywheel, coupled with the comparatively short stroke engine, could very well be the cause of the rough idling.

On the whole, this set-up makes a good combination but Stelling feels that it wasn't quite worth it. The end result is good but what it took to achieve this end hardly justified the effort. •

LATE NEWS
GOOD AND BAD

Bad news comes from Ed Almquist Eng. Co. of Milford, Pennsylvania to the tune of $6000 worth of stolen equipment. $1600 worth of it has been recovered, but it's still a pretty big blow to anyone who loses that much money. Most of the loot consisted of Almquist Cams, Hollywood Mufflers, Leonard No. 14E Spark Plugs, D & S Dual Manifolds, Sandee Dual Muffler Sets, Jahns Pistons and other miscellaneous items. A reward of $200 is being offered to anyone who can give clues leading to the arrest and conviction of the culprits.

Good news comes from the hill climb held last Sunday at Sandberg Ranch, by the Sports Car Club of America. First place was captured by Chuck Manning in his home built Merc Sports Car (see also page 20 this issue) with the time of 33.26 sec. Second was Carl Conway, Nash-Healey, 35.67 sec. Third, Ten Cannon in the Merc engined Cannon Spl. 35.88 sec. Total length of the climb is one-half mile. The results do not prove to us conclusively that American engines and/or cars are better than the foreign stuff but it does seem that we're not completely dead yet.

special overhead valve heads—this is a far cry from the $74.00 price for a pair of Ford flat heads. This high price may not scare off a race car owner but there are so few passenger car owners that would spend that much money that sales wouldn't even pay for a fraction of the tooling costs. The passenger car owners are still the backbone of the business so they are the ones that must be satisfied.

Head modifications for the rocker arm V-8's will of necessity be limited to reworking the stock ones. In some cases this will leave a lot to be desired; for there is a definite limit to what can be done to a stock head. It would take a lot more than imagination and ambition to transform a Cadillac head into a Chrysler hemispherical. Heads can be milled and the ports enlarged but basic design must remain the same. This is a limiting factor with all but the Chrysler heads. Their basic design does not require changing so they can be made to come closer to the ideal after reworking.

Quite often overlooked is the fact that engine size or cubic inch piston displacement is more important to performance and horsepower output than any other factor. Stock Ford engines don't excel in this department but greater displacement increases can be effected economically with these engines than any other produced in America. Bores and strokes can be increased more than those of any other car. Ford engines of 1946 vintage or later can be bored 1/8 to 3/16 oversize. Some are even being operated with cylinder bores that are 1/4 inch larger than stock. A handy Ford coincidence makes increasing strokes a very simple matter. Mercury cranks for the 1949 thru 1952 models have a 1/4 inch longer stroke than Ford cranks and are interchangeable. A very common practice is to grind the

Mercury pins 1/16 off center and to the diameter of early Ford bearings. So doing produces a crank with a stroke that is ⅜ of an inch longer than stock Ford and ⅛ longer than late Mercury.

Crankshaft juggling such as the foregoing is an impossibility with all but Ford and Mercury engines. A Mercury crankshaft only costs $45.00 and can be stroked ⅜ in. for $20.00. If a change of this nature is desired for any other engine, you can expect to spend at least $1,000 having a special crank made unless you will settle for a metal-sprayed job. This is perhaps the greatest example of Ford adaptability and low alteration costs.

If you still want to make a Hot Rod out of your 1940 La Salle . . . . if you want to bore and stroke it and make it compete with the hot Fords . . . . if you have a *big* fat bag of gold . . . . go right ahead!

CLASSIFIED

the *SLANT* that SAVES!

HORSEPOWER

ENGINE WEAR

OIL

The slanting vents in Grant Piston Rings are scientifically designed to allow only the excess oil to be thrown back through the ring passages. Patented collecting grooves constantly spray the preponderance of the oil on the cylinder walls, giving you "drag-free" lubrication for better compression, less maintenance and longer, more economical service.

Learn how these Piston Rings can put more power in your car by contacting your local Grant Distributor or by sending for Gerry Grant's free catalogue and literature on reringing and engine preservation.

Grant PISTON RINGS

GRANT & GRANT, 241 N. Westmoreland Ave., Los Angeles 4, Calif.

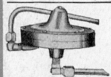

HOP UP

JULY, 1952   **20 CENTS**

PHOTO BY CHESEBROUGH

World's Most Beautiful 'Lakes' Roadster!
Install A GMC Engine in Your Chevrolet!

TECHNICAL TIPS

SPEED SHOP NEAR LOUISVILLE?

I am interested in having some work done on a 1950 Ford but I don't know where I can find a speed shop in or near Louisville, Ky. Can you give me any information?

Louisville, Ky.   Stanton Snodgrass

Sorry, we are unable to learn of a speed shop near Louisville. LOUISVILLE DEALERS NOTE: Seems like too many shop owners are missing a bet by not taking advantage of HOP UP's coverage.

REWORKED OIL PAN FOR LINCOLN

Would not friend Stelling's oil pan difficulties ('52 Lincoln ohv engine in '50 Merc—June HOP UP) been simplified by using oil pan and connections from the 279 ohv truck engine?

La Mesa, N. M.   Scott F. Yantis

It would have been easier to use a truck pan had they been available when Stelling made the change. The truck pan would require some alteration, however, because the sump would hit the cross member when installed in a Merc.

FORD FRONT END ALIGNMENT

I installed 1939 Ford hydraulic brakes on my '32 Ford. I used the '39 spindles on my '32 Ford axle. Should I align my front end like a '32 Ford or to 1939 specifications?

Oakland, Calif.   Arthur Griffin

Wheel alignment specifications for 1932 and 1939 Fords are practically identical but I would align it to '32 specifications.

SUPER CHARGERS ON CAD V16

Can I use two Graham superchargers on a Cadillac V12 or V16—1932 Model? Could I develop 300 hp?

Long Island, N. Y.   Benjamin Larke

You could use a set-up like this but the installation would be real work. Why not try a Roots-type blower? Either a SCOT or GMC blower could be adapted more easily and would come a lot closer to getting your engine up to the 300 hp mark. See ads in this issue—Bell Auto Parts and Ernie McAfee.

SOMETHING FOR NOTHING

I don't want a car for the track but would like to hop up my car some and still keep a certain amount of economy with it.

Petaluma, Calif.   Freddie Worthington

For the answer to this question, see Barney Navarro's article on Page 4—July HOP UP.

CHEVY GMC INSTALLATION

I am considering the installation of a 270 cu. in. GMC truck engine in my 1940 Chevrolet. I would like to know what alterations would be necessary to install this engine in my Chevy. Will my generator and starter fit on the GMC engine? If it would be impractical to install this large an engine, what is the largest engine that I could use without making larger alterations, and what changes would be involved?

Whittier, Calif.   James F. Ackley

See article by California Bill on Page 36.

REAR ENGINE BUICK

I have a 1939 Buick and would appreciate your advice on how to convert it to a rear engine job. It now has a '46 Buick engine and I would like to transfer it to the rear, or I would like to install a 65 hp airplane engine with an automatic transmission. I would start from scratch, strip the body off, do my rebuilding, and then make up my own body design. I am not so much interested in the speed as I am the style of a rear engine car, also the trouble-free driving and comfort.

Oneonta, N. Y.   Charles Tofinchio

In spite of the great success of Auto Union in the prewar Grand Prix Circuits of Europe,

(Continued on page 47)

If it's hopped up, it'll be in HOP UP

H O P U P

HOT ROD OR SPORTS CAR?

The old argument is back again: is a hot rod a sports car or not. We say yes, but with qualifications. Actually, what is the primary function of a hot rod but to engage in the sport of competition with other similar cars? The fact that the European type of sport is different from ours has no bearing on the subject. Across the ocean they build their sport cars to run in races on highways that are blocked off to public use for a day. Because this practice is against the law in most of the United States, the youth of America has built his sports car (roadster) for straightaway competition at the lakes or on the drag strips.

We can see no reason for either group to condemn the other as being wrong. If the many dry lakes in Southern California had been located in Italy or England, chances are they would have built cars for straightaway competion instead of (or in addition to) road racing. Conversely, if racing on the roads in this country were legal, we would be racing on them too.

Circumstances and environment play a large part in the development of automobiles or any other commodity. The two types of automobiles in question are tops at their particular type of sport but both are at a complete loss on the other's home grounds.

In this and the last issue we have covered the Palm Springs and Pebble Beach races in order to show our regular readers a little of what is happening on the other side of the fence. We do not intend to convert HOP UP into a sports car journal. We feel that an occasional article of this type is good for variety in the usual automotive diet. But the material presented in HOP UP is still dictated by you, the reader. If you like this type of article say so, if not, let us know and we won't repeat it again. The same goes for subjects we have not covered yet. If you have any ideas about what you would like to see in Hop Up, drop us a line.

STAFF

PUBLISHER	W. S. Quinn
EDITOR	Dean Batchelor
MANAGING EDITOR	Louis Kimzey
ART	E. C. Trindl
PHOTOGRAPHERS:	Bob Canaan
	Ralph Poole
	Gene Trindl
	Warren King
EAST	Robert L. Edgell
	104 East 40th Street
	New York 16, N. Y.
UNITED KINGDOM	Kenneth Kirkman
	2 Longcroft Ave.
	Banstead, Surrey, England
ITALY	Michele Vernola
	C. P. 500
	Milano, Italy

Vol 1, No. 12   July, 1952

CONTENTS

HOP UP is published monthly by Quinn Publications, 530 W. Colorado Blvd., Glendale, Califorina. Phone CHapman 5-4942. Entered as second class matter at the post office at Glendale, California, under the Act of March 3, 1897. Copyright 1952 by Quinn Publications. Reprinting in whole or in part forbidden except by permission of the publishers.

Subscription price $2.00 per year thruout the world. Single copy 20c.

Change of address—must show both old and new addresses.

Robbing Peter to Pay Paul..

Editor's Note: HOP UP feels that articles such as this by Barney Navarro show readers the real facts of modification, both good and bad. We'll try to give more of this particularly interesting reading.

By Barney Navarro

Performance has a price that must be paid—it can't be ignored. It's seldom possible to get something for nothing. In most cases to pay the price you must "rob Peter to pay Paul" because an improvement in one direction often means a sacrifice in another. The problem is to determine what you wish to sacrifice and to what degree. Going overboard in one direction is usually disastrous so most changes must be compromises.

Gear ratios required to accomplish different tasks will show quite graphically the procedure of taking from one to give to another. Low gears can be installed in your family car to improve acceleration. Instead of the 3.78 to 1 stock gears a ratio of 5.12 to 1 can be used as is done with some track cars. This will increase torque at the rear wheels so the car will accelerate much faster —if it can get sufficient traction. If you're not worried about the cost of this type of performance a set of gears may solve your problem. But, before you rush out and buy a set of gears, give some thought to the dis-

advantages. In this particular instance the disadvantages far outweigh the advantages. Top speed will be reduced considerably because the stock gearing was such that the engine produced maximum horsepower at top speed. Now the engine will be turning so fast that less horsepower will be available at high speed. Fuel consumption will be excessively high because of higher engine rpm. Oil consumption will be higher for the same reason. The engine will wear out much sooner because it will have to rotate many more times to cover the same distance.

Perhaps you want to swap your gears for some that will give a ratio of 3.27 to 1. This will have advantages too; the engine will rotate slower. Fuel and oil consumption will be reduced and the engine will last longer because less revolutions are required to cover a given distance. All this may be advantageous but the car will accelerate like a basket of snails. Top speed will again be reduced and second gear will be necessary for every little hill. Of course you will be able to pull these gears if you increase the torque of your engine—note—I said torque, not horsepower. *(Ed. Note: See Navarro's article in Feb. HOP UP, "No Miracles.")*

Horsepower can be increased, without increasing torque, by raising rpm. To pull high gears you *must* depend on greater torque.

Increases in compression ratio and piston displacement are the only things that will make an appreciable difference in torque for the purpose of pulling high gears. Of the two, displacement will make the biggest difference. As can be expected, there are still strings attached. Larger displacement means greater fuel consumption because it is only the increased quantity of fuel being burned that produces more power in this case. If all or part of the displacement increase was obtained from lengthening the stroke, greater wear can be expected. Higher compression too, has its price, for better gasoline must be used to eliminate ping.

Maximum power and maximum economy are never obtained at the same time nor are they obtainable from the same unit. Maximum power requires the proper burning of the most fuel in the least possible time. This ability is the most important factor in the design of a hot engine. You can work all you want to on an engine that is designed for maximum economy and your efforts may be quite noble but some wasteful fellow with a fuel guzzler will leave you in the dust.

Gas savers, regardless of claims, reduce horsepower if they increase gas mileage. Some of them improve mileage by introducing air in the induction system. This has the same effect as using smaller carburetor jets to lean down the mixture. Of course such a procedure will reduce power output and if carried to extremes, can burn valves. Another fraudulent method of obtaining better gas mileage is to insert a restriction, such as a screen, between the carburetor and manifold. A gadget of this type gives the same effect as placing a smaller carburetor on an engine. Obviously, maximum horsepower will again suffer.

The most misunderstood part of an engine is the camshaft. All sorts of magic and mystery surrounds this device. Reground cams are very often installed to accomplish a purpose for which they were never designed. Everyone expects something for nothing. The most common request when selecting a cam is to ask for one that gives maximum acceleration and maximum horsepower. These two conditions are as compatible as expecting an elephant to be as graceful as a deer. An improvement in one direction always means a sacrifice in another. If you want acceleration you can't have maximum horsepower. Conversely, if you want maximum horsepower you absolutely cannot have maximum acceleration.

Speed and economy are a pair that are as different as night and day. You may say that if I go fast I'll get there sooner, so even though the engine is burning fuel at a faster rate it won't take anymore to cover the distance. This logic would be fine if there weren't two factors called friction and wind resistance. These two power absorbers increase with the square of the speed. In other words, instead of becoming twice as great when speed is doubled, they become 4 times as great; double speed again, these resistances become 16 times as great. In reverse order, when speed is halved, they are quartered. It is for this very reason that an overdrive improves economy. Reducing engine rpm reduces friction so less power is wasted.

Wind resistance is a bit tougher to deal with; for we don't have the equivalent of an overdrive attachment to reduce this type of drag. Streamlining is of great assistance in reducing drag but it cannot eliminate it. Our modern automobiles are supposed to be streamlined but they fall short on this score. Of course the ideal streamlined shape would be impractical for a passenger car but there is considerable room for improvement in the average automobile. Many designs have reached a stage where they seem to change for the sake of change alone instead of improvement. With these designs one can expect to use from 60 to 80 percent of developed power to overcome wind resistance at top speed. Only 20 to 40 percent of the power is consumed in overcoming rolling friction. In considering these figures it is necessary to realize that rolling friction is the biggest factor at low speeds and that wind resistance overshadows it at high speed because it builds up on the square. It is this build up of resistance that quickly drains the gas tank.

Speed and performance are never obtained without some type of sacrifice. Your problem is to decide how much to rob from Peter to pay Paul.

This problem can be more easily understood if a thorough study is made of the technical articles in the last 7 issues of Hop Up Magazine.

Activity slows down at noon on the desert but
Ted Miller takes one more run before lunch.

SCTA MEET

Ak. Miller set C mod rdstr record at 160.14.

By George Hill

Southern California Timing Association officially opened the 1952 racing season here at El Mirage Dry Lake, May 3rd and 4th. Members were expecting a hard dry surface, due to reports that the lake bed had been flooded numerous times during our last winter's rainy season. Unfortunately, this was not the case, and many were disappointed at the rapid deterioration of the course on Saturday. In spite of this, many fast times were recorded, and Tom Beatty, of Glendale, Calif. led the parade by driving his supercharged Mercury powered wing tank through the course at 187 mph. This is the fastest time recorded at any dry lake meet to date, and was made possible, not only by the long run of 1.7 miles, but by the advanced design of Beatty's car.

By suspending the rear of the tank on swinging axles, and driving through a two speed transmission, Tom has solved the two problems facing most competitors running in the Lakester classes. Rapid acceleration and rear wheel traction are the two points most important in any fast run on a dry lake surface. (Hop Up Dec. 1951)

Ray Brown turned fastest time in "C" Lakester class at 180.36 mph, with Earl Evans a close second at 178.92 mph. With George Bentley at the wheel, Stanford Bros. class "B" Lakester hit an all time high for its class by going 162.16 mph. Mal Meredith, home on leave from the Army, teamed up with Doane Spencer, to take second place in this class at 158.17 mph.

In "B" Roadster class, top honors were taken by Don Clark and Clem Tebow, with the same car they ran at the 1951 Bonneville Nationals. The engine is equipped with

SCTA president Ray Brown at right, congratulates winner of drawing, held to raise funds.

over-head valves in a hemispherical combustion chamber, designed by Kenny Adams. Running with their home-built fuel injection system, they turned a time of 141.06 mph. Willingham and Franzman were second at 137.93 mph.

Running in the small engine classes, Barney Navarro drove his "A" Modified Roadster to a new one way record at 136.77 mph. Second place in this class was taken by K. Baldwin at 117.95 mph, and third by Butler Bros. entry at 113.92 mph.

During the winter months when cars are being altered or improved for the following season's competition, representatives of each club meet with the SCTA officials to discuss

Ray Calvi gets push from crew for 130 mph run. Later in the day, Ray flipped his car.

changes in the safety rules and the competition classes.

This year many demands were made to open classes that would allow the use of stock bodied coupes and sedans. Until now late model cars with hopped up engines have been unable to make use of Otto Crocker's efficient timing equipment.

With this in mind new classes were set up that would allow cars with unaltered steel tops to run without the addition of roll bars that are demanded in all open cars or cars with altered tops.

At this, the first meet of the season, a surprizing number of entries were present to record some fast times.

Sinclair & Beguette with a full fendered class "B" coupe went 109.48 while the team of Isom-Lapthorne & Evans received a time of 122.78 mph for their full fendered 1937 Ford sedan. The close competition in these classes should prove interesting as the season progresses.

SCTA has invited all sports car owners to bring their cars out to the dry lakes. If the cars pass the technical committee's thoro safety check, they will be allowed the use of the timing facilities. All open cars must be equipped with a roll bar along with the safety belt and fire-extinguisher required in all cars. Fastest sports car at this meet was a Nash Healey, at 102 mph.

Each day, more ways are being discovered to develop horsepower in the production engine. As horsepower increases, the damage to the lake surface becomes greater. With this, comes the possibility of greater speeds and more accidents.

Due to the loose course conditions on Sun-

Undaunted by rear end gear trouble, this crew proceeded to overhaul theirs in starting area.

day two cars were involved in accidents. Ray Calvi flipped his 29 "A" Roadster in the course, and altho the car was a total loss, the safety precautions built into the car for driver protection allowed Ray to walk away with a bruised elbow and skinned nose. George Bently went eight times end over end in Stanford Bros. Mercury powered wing tank, and walked away shaken, but unhurt.

The SCTA cannot be commended too highly for their strict safety rules and their close inspections.

532

Custom Merc

533

Custom Merc

This fine looking Merc convertible custom job was built for Ralph Testa of Hollywood, California, by George and Sam Barris, Barris Kustom Autos.

Ralph wanted his Merc low so work was started by lowering the front 5 inches and the back 7 inches. Front lowering was accomplished by cutting the coil springs and sectioning the spring cups. In the rear, lowering blocks were placed between the springs and axles, and the springs themselves were stretched. A "C" shaped section was then taken from the frame, directly over the rear axle, to give more clearance. To complete the low appearance of the Merc, 4" was cut out of the windshield. Side and quarter windows were also cut, but on a tapering line which started with the 4-inch cut at the windshield and ended with a 2-inch cut at the rear. A padded top was then put on.

The tapering peak of the hood extends down to the oval grille opening. Grille is the "floating bar" type, with built-in direction lights.

Headlight frames were frenched and extended forward 1½ inches with the sealed beam unit set back 1 inch into frame. Front fenders, gravel shield, and grille opening

Frenched-inset headlights & "floating" grille

Buick taillights and rectangular exhaust tips add to the rear view of Ralph Testa's Mercury.

were all welded together and molded.

A special key lock electric push button was inserted in the Buick chrome strip on the side of the body.

The tail light treatment shows imagination. It is different from the usual custom car tail lights in that '49 Buick lights were mounted horizontally instead of vertically as they were on the Buick.

Rear deck is filled, and all the body and pan creases are welded and molded solid. Another new touch is the exhaust pipes extending thru the bumper in the form of rectangles instead of the usual round tips.

After the body work had been completed a preparation of primer and sealer is put on and the surfaces made ready for the color.

The Coral Blue-Purple lacquer was put on over a metallic under base. Barris says there are 28 coats of lacquer on Ralph's Merc.

San Diego Drag Races

The swiftest all out drag session ever staged at the smooth Paradise Mesa air strip, just outside San Diego, saw twelve records fall on April 5th and 6th. This two day joint SCTA and SDTA invitational meet resulted when the first SCTA lakes meet, scheduled for the same week end was canceled. El Mirage Dry lake, of all things, was wet from recent rains.

Art Chrisman in the Miller Crank Special tries to regain record. Note roll bars on the cars.

Sports car owners also like to try their cars on the strip. Here a Nash-Healey starts down the smooth, wide course. Note the tire marks.

Regular meets on this strip, conducted by the San Diego Timing Association, are run under SCTA rules and classes. Consequently, co-operation between the two groups on this joint venture was evident from the start.

The entire meet ran smoothly and Otto Crocker's excellent timing apparatus performed in its usual perfect manner. Jarring feature, as far as Hop Up was concerned

12

Bud Fox makes adjustment on blown Merc

Fox & Cobb coupe sets record at 104 mph.

was the absence of an elapsed time set up used in conjunction with the top speed timer. * We still believe that the only true way to compare times with other strips is by the elapsed time method. (Elapsed timing starts the instant the car being timed begins to move and ends when the car crosses the finish line). Mr. Crocker agrees with us on this point. He said the only reason there were no elapsed times for this meet was the lack of trained personnel to man the necessary extra equipment.

* SDTA usually uses both systems

Ed "axle" Stewart in "A" class tank (V-8 60) has no transmission, so needs initial boost to get going. Reached 97 mph at end of quarter.

All runs at Paradise Mesa are made from a standing start, over a carefully measured quarter mile. The time traps are inside the measured quarter. When the contestant has crossed the finish line at the end of the quarter mile he has also passed the timing lights.

Fastest run for the meet, and a new record, was set by the Pederson brothers "C" lakester at 122.95 mph. In second and third place, also in this class was Art Chrisman, former "C" lakester record holder, at 121.95 mph, and Ralph Lynde at 121.68 mph. Ralph towed all the way down from Los Gatos, California, to run this meet, and was kept out of the final elimination by a severe case of water in the pan.

In the "C" modified roadster class an al-

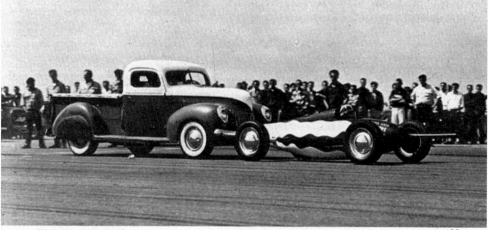

Tires smoke as Lynde's lakester gets going.   Power to weight ratio being a prime factor
Lynde has lightened by extreme methods.

Lynde carries enough water for one run only.

most unbelievable speed of 119.52 mph was turned in by the White brothers for a new record.

Easily the noisiest, and by no means the slowest car to run, was the "C" coupe of Bud Fox and Tom Cobbs. The engine is a 248 cu in Merc with a GMC roots type blower. Driven by Cobbs, this '40 coupe set a new record of 104 mph. If this doesn't sound fast, try a standing start quarter in your stock coupe sometime, and remember, this was clocked speed, not speedometer time.

Still amazing the assembled throngs are the little engines. Xydias & Baldwin with a V-8 60 engined 27T roadster set a new "A" class record at 96.97 mph for the standing quarter. Bob Willett in a super hot MG reached the terrific speed of 81.89 mph to easily outdistance the several MGs that also ran.

Present Records at Paradise Mesa

✿ "O" class—Bob Willett, MG	81.89 mph
✿ "A" class—Xydias & Baldwin, V8 60 roadster	96.97
✿ "B" Lakester—Arnett & Ortega, Ford V-8	98.56
✿ "B" Modified Roadster—Bert Reed, Ford V-8	108.50
"B" Roadster—Joe Barbara, Ford V-8	98.79
✿ "B" Modified Coupe—Sturdy & Miller, Ford V-8	99.22
✿ "B" Coupe—Lee Drake & Son, Ford V-8	96.00
✿ "C" Lakester—Howard & Pederson, Ford V-8	122.95
"C" Roadster—Don Little, Ford V-8	110.15
✿ "C" Modified Roadster—R. Brown & H. White, Ford V-8	119.52
✿ "C" Coupe—Fox & Cobbs, V-8 with blower	104.00
✿ "B" Street Coupe (gas class)—Roland Leischner, V-8	79.64
✿ "C" Coupe (gas class)—Jack Harper, Merc.	87.80
✿ "C" Stock Class—Louie Fleetwood, Packard 6	65.17

Motorcycles
✿ A class, Jack Ball, Harley..................104.52
✿ Indicates new record

Clyde Sturdy in "B" mod. coupe record holder.

Baldwin-Merc follows XK120 into home stretch.

Pebble Beach Road Race

To those who have never seen a road race we can only say, "You don't know what you're missing." And for those who have never seen a road race at Pebble Beach, undoubtedly one of the most scenic race courses in the world, here is a tip. Attend next year! You won't regret it! At this point we can almost hear the sneers of the big car fans, midget enthusiasts, and even the jalopy rooters, who are thinking: "Who the heck wants to watch a bunch of English kiddie cars (MG's to you) drive down a road?" Well, we have news for you. It's not as easy as it looks.

And no doubt you are asking, what the scenery has to do with a road race. It doesn't make the cars go any faster. Tracks don't rely on scenery to draw cars or spectators. Well . . . you're right, but there are lots of married men who could get to the races more often if their everlovin' wife had something to look at while the men are admiring the competition machinery. . . . And Pebble Beach has it.

Speaking of competition, sports cars aren't exactly toys as a lot of people seem to think. It takes a rugged, fast car and a good driver with plenty of guts to get the job done. True, there are some poorly tuned cars with drivers that are not too skilled, but they

Sterling Edwards' older car with ohv V-8 60 engine, Diedt aluminum body, special chassis.

16

Jim Seely coming out of hairpin turn in the Cannon-Merc. Note condition of road course.

soon drop by the wayside. In this respect, road racing is similar to any other type of competition.

These cars must handle well enough to negotiate all types of roads at maximum speed and there lies the difference between road racing and track racing. It's not just a matter of going around a track in one direction, lap after lap. There are left turns, right turns, uphill, downhill, fast curves, S-bends and straights.

The brakes and transmission take a terrible beating on every lap. Speeds change constantly, ranging from almost dead stops on some corners to 130 mph straightaways.

Escape roads are provided for cars that have brake failure or for the benefit of over zealous and under talented drivers. During a complete race, cars get more wear than most passenger cars would get in a year's driving. Not all cars are MG's, nor are they all stock. Almost all, regardless of make or model, are hopped up considerably and quite a few are specially built.

All cars entered, regardless of class, burn pump gas furnished to all competitors from the same truck. The tanks are then sealed to prevent other fuels from being used.

At most road courses all classes run simultaneously but are not actually competing

Hastings Harcourt in Baldwin-Merc special.

Special tube frame job has fiber glass body and Crosley engine with SCOT supercharger.

against each other. At Pebble Beach, however, there were three races. First was a short race for novice drivers, second was a 100 mile race for both stock and modified cars of under 91 cu in. displacement. And last was a 100 mile race for stock and modified cars over 91 cu in.

At Pebble Beach, just as last year, Bill Pollack in Tom Carsten's Cadillac engined Allard proved the unbeatable combination. This car is evidently very well prepared for

it has been entered in four races in the last two years and won all four. (Pebble Beach 1951-52, Reno 1951 all driven by Pollack; and the novice driver's race at Reno driven by Carsten himself.)

Pollack's driving was superb, but the large engines, running properly, seem to have things pretty much their own way. The Allard jumped into the lead at the start and led the full distance. Length of the race was 100 miles and Pollack covered it in 1 hr

Sterling Edwards' new job is built on a Henry J chassis and has a fiber glass body. The power plant is a Chrysler Firepower Vee-eight.

18

Reworked Crosley Hot Shot went very well.

and 34 min.

Chuck Manning, Palm Springs winner, went off the course and tried to climb a tree with his Merc special. No damage to himself but the car is a mess.

Most of the American built cars dropped by the wayside before the race was finished. Our honors, however, were upheld by Hastings Harcourt. Driving Willis Baldwin's Merc special in its first appearance since Palm Springs two years ago, he finished fourth.

This car seemed to have plenty of speed but lacked in handling qualities. Harcourt should be commended for his skill in bringing the car home so close to the front ranks.

The most impressive part of the Pebble Beach Race is the manner in which the Northern Region of the Sports Car Club of America conducted the meet. This is the first racing event we've seen where everything went like clockwork and where there was no delay between races.

Harcourt in the Baldwin-Mercury negotiating hairpin turn with the Ferrari in hot pursuit.

Cover Roadster

Without a doubt this black 27 T modified roadster is one of, if not the, sharpest looking and best constructed roadster in existence. A very strong statement, but the photos on these pages will back it up.

Body work, body structure supports, and the frame itself are the work of Jack Hagemann of Castro Valley, California. The frame is chrome moly, channel section .125" thick, with flanged edges. The front crossmember is made of the same material and constructed in the same manner as the side rails. The center member is a ⅜" thick steel plate which also acts as the rear engine mount. Chrome moly tubing makes the rear crossmember and spring mount. You will notice from the photos that this member is forward of the rear axle instead of the usual location behind the axle. This is to prevent the Halibrand quick change. center section from hitting the cross member when the wheels go over a bump. To accomplish this they put the right hand axle housing on the left side and left on the right, then rotated the housings 180°.

Radius rods and wishbones are thickwall chrome moly tubing connected to the frame by Ford truck tie rod ends. Front axle, rear axle housing, springs, radius rods, wishbones, and all steering apparatus is cadmium plated. Shock absorbers are .Houdaille 50-50 in front

and Gabriel 40-60 in the rear. Transmission is '32 Ford with Zephyr gears and the rear end center section is a Halibrand quick change. Second and high gears are used at the drags. Tires are 6.00 x 16 in front, 7.50 x 16 in the rear, and all are Firestone Indianapolis type. Brakes are hydraulic and on the rear wheels only.

As Al had originally intended the roadster for track use, safety hubs were put on the rear along with ¾ ton Chevy truck axles. Since the car was finished however, the sphere of activity has been limited to the dry lakes and drag races. At this point it might be added that it has been successful in both cases! 153 mph was clocked at the lakes and 118 mph in the quarter mile at Kingdom air strip near Lodi, California. The same engine in a super light draggin' chassis turned 125 at Kingdom. Ray Righetti is the regular driver but Al occasionally drives it himself. Al and Ray are members of the SCTA Sidewinders and the VTA Mid-Cal Stockers.

Steering is a converted Franklin which works a fore and aft drag link thru an L shaped idler arm to a transverse drag link. This drag link is connected to the right hand spindle arm as in a late Ford.

Instruments are set in an aluminum panel and consist of a Sun electric tach, oil

20

Portrait of a safe car. Fire extinguisher, roll bar, and safety belt securely mounted.

Neat dash, uncluttered cockpit aids driver.

Visible here are the fuel tank, quick change rear end, tube shocks and fine cotnstruction.

Panels fasten on by dzus fasteners on frame.

Clean lines of Al's roadster are apparent.

pressure guage, fuel pressure guage, and a water temperature guage.

The engine, built by John Errecalde of Stockton, has an Iskenderian 404 cam, Edelbrock heads, Weiand 4 carburetor manifold, Scintilla magneto and Speedomotive pistons. Bore is $3\frac{3}{8}''$, stroke $4\frac{1}{8}$, giving a total of 296 cu in.

Because the roadster is frequently run on drag strips, putting a terrific load on the clutch, John and Al are using a Ford truck clutch assembly. The larger diameter of the flywheel, clutch plate, and pressure plate on the truck assembly gives more surface to absorb the tremendous torque exerted on these fast starts.

Two problems occur when using an assembly of this type. Because of its larger diameter, the pressure plate cannot be installed while the pan is on the engine. Instead, the plate should be slid up from the bottom and the pan bolted on last. Second, the fingers on a truck pressure plate would hit the transmission housing unless the housing is reworked or moved back. By using a steel plate $\frac{3}{8}''$ thick for a center cross member and rear engine mount, they gained a space to move the transmission back the required distance. This important $\frac{3}{8}''$ keeps the pressure plate fingers from hitting the transmission housing.

There's a saying going around now to the effect that this or that car is "built for show and not for go." Here is an impressive exception. Al Dal Porto's roadster "goes" and it "shows". It's among the top cars for looks in spite of the lack of chrome "goodies".

Aluminum disc replaces front backing plate.

Cover Roadster

Owned by Al Dal Porto

24

JIM RICHARDS

25

549

Harry Weber being interviewed by the editor.

Probably the only woman cam grinder in U.S.

Meet the Advertiser

Weber racing equipment, while not as well known as some other brands, has a legion of followers who are almost fanatical in their loyalty to the product. Under the ownership and personal direction of Harry Weber, the Weber Tool Company lists many items not made by other manufacturers as well as the usual speed equipment.

Reground camshafts for any car, aluminum flywheels for Fords and Mercs, billet cams for Olds & Cad V-8s, special stroked crankshafts for Crosleys, special ½" stroked

Part of the office staff that handles orders.

26

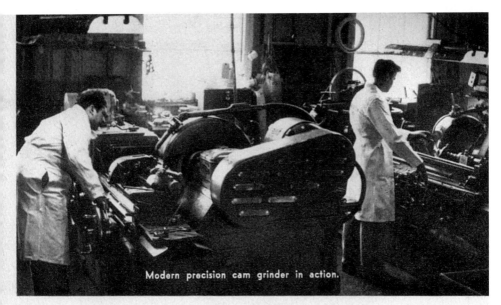

Modern precision cam grinder in action.

crankshafts for Fords & Mercs, and complete balanced crank-piston-rod assemblies. At the present time the company is also grinding cams for the Ford V-8 double overhead cam tank engine used by the U.S. Army.

In addition to his own equipment, Weber has now taken the distributorship for the English Lucas ignition for Fords and Mercs and liqui-moly.

Weber, who is a tool maker by trade, first started grinding cams in 1936. After a brief interruption in the speed business while he worked for Northrup Aircraft Co. and an automobile manufacturer in Detroit, he turned his shop into defense work during the war. Hostilities over, the Weber Tool Co. once again turned to manufacturing and distributing speed equipment.

A large office force helps to expedite correspondence and mail orders in the quickest possible manner. Present plans for the near future call for a building that will give more room for shipping, stock storage and production.

Starting machine work on aluminum flywheel.　　Complete balancing is done on this machine.

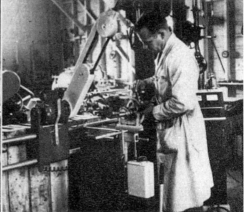

Hop Up Test No. 4

Hop Up's test roadster this month is the proud possession of Bob Longman, Bell, California. Because Bob is on active duty with the U.S. Navy at the present time, the test was arranged with the help of George Barris of the Barris Kustom Shop.

I've been looking forward to this test because it is the first we've done on a modified roadster. Where the others we've tested have been stock height roadsters, with the body on top of the frame in the original manner, this one is channeled.

The over-all appearance of Bob's roadster is very good. It sits low, and seems to have just the right amount of chrome which is emphasized by the purple paint job. You will notice from the photos that the stock '32 gas tank has been removed from the rear. The body was then paneled under to give a more rounded appearance to the rear of the car. In doing this the rear frame horns were cut off inside the body and new brackets made for the tubular nerfing bar type bumper.

The deck lid has been welded shut, and filled in, which greatly re-enforces the body but makes it necessary to take the seat out

to get into the back. The seat can be removed very quickly so it doesn't present much of a problem.

Metal work on the car, with the exception of the aluminum hoods, was done by John Manok who is now on the Barris staff. Hoods were built by Marvin Faw. To Bud Fine goes much of the credit for the mechanical work, according to Longman.

Very workmanlike is the complete bellypan which covers the underside of the car and adds considerably to the appearance of the roadster. The value disappears, however, when it only leaves three inches of ground clearance as it does on this car. A bellypan can add both speed and looks to a car, but one as close to the ground as this one adds little speed, if any, and is very impractical for everyday driving.

The battery is located under the floorboards on the passenger side of the car, and the horn is under the seat on the driver's side. These would ordinarily be visible from outside the car but are concealed by the bellypan on Bob's roadster.

Wishbones, tubular bumpers, headlight brackets and shock mounts were built by

28

Bob himself.

Bud Fine, right, helped Bob construct his car.

When channeling a car seating space is lost (see custom hints in June issue *Hop Up*), so the seat in Bob's roadster is merely

Functional rear bumper and license bracket.

Fine set of instruments compliment interior.

ROAD TEST STATISTICS

Chassis	1932 Ford V-8
Wheelbase	108 inches
Tread, front	57 inches
Tread, rear	58 inches
Tires, front	5.50 x 16
Tires, rear	7.00 x 16
Rear axle ratio	4.11 to 1
Transmission	'41 Ford (Zephyr gears)
Brakes	Ford Hydraulic
Shock absorbers	Tube
Steering	1932 Ford
Body	1932 Ford roadster
Paint	Deep Purple
Instruments	
Fuel pressure	Speedometer
Oil Pressure	Oil temp.
Water temp.	Ammeter
Tachometer	Fuel gauge
Engine	Mercury
Bore	.125 over Merc
Stroke	.125 over Merc
Displacement	268 cu in.
Cam	Spalding
Manifold	Evans triple
Heads	Edelbrock 9.5-1
Pistons	JE Edelbrock
Ignition	Spalding
Headers	Clark

Engine is ported and relieved, has a chopped flywheel and an Auburn clutch. Top Speed at the lakes: 120.68 and at the Santa Ana drags: 101.46.

30

a thin cushion. While not as comfortable as a regular seat it does well for short hops. A long trip in this car might become tiring.

In order to take photos while on the test run we squeezed Gene Trindl, *Hop Up* photographer, into the car with us. With the seat lowered and moved back as it is, space is no more cramped than in a stock body '32.

But my worst objection to Longman's roadster cropped up at this point. With the seat back as far as it is, and a Merc steering wheel used, the driver hasn't enough leg room. If the steering column was lengthened a few inches, and a little smaller diameter steering wheel used the situation would be relieved considerably. The gear shift is far away, too, and I found myself leaning forward to shift gears. The steering itself was one of the best I've seen; quick, positive, and turns with very little effort.

The rear end gear ratio is good for city driving. The 4.11 gears and 7.00 x 16 tires make a good combination, as long as Zephyr gears are used in the transmission. Acceleration away from stop signs was rapid and kept us ahead of traffic with no strain. If the stock ratio in the transmission had been used with the 4.11 rear end, the car would be geared entirely too low in 1st and 2nd gear. As it is city driving can be done without overworking the shift lever. This was my biggest complaint in the first two roadsters tested, as they were geared only for top speed running at the lakes.

Taking everything into consideration Bob's

HOP UP, July, 1952

Chrome "goodies" visible here are: drag link, pitman arm, spindle steering arm, wish bones, axle, tie rod, spring, shock absorber, spring perch, headlight bracket, and backing plate.

Engine has Edelbrock heads, Evans manifold, Spalding ignition and cam and Clark headers.

roadster handles well, looks good, and has more performance than anyone needs for normal driving. Altho it seemed to take quite a bit of pedal pressure, the hydraulic brakes work well and on a light car like this are more than adequate. An early pedal assembly was used and the arm that connects the brake pedal to the master cylinder may be too long for proper leverage.

A clean looking roadster certainly attracts attention. Everywhere we went we fell under the admiring glances of people driving stock cars. It's hard to tell whether they wish they could own a roadster, too, or are wondering how much money the owner has invested. It seems like the first thing people ask are "How fast does it go?" and "How much did it cost?". Invariably when the cost is told the person asking thoughtfully shakes his head and says "Boy, I would rather have a Cadillac." At this point all I can say is, "to each his own."

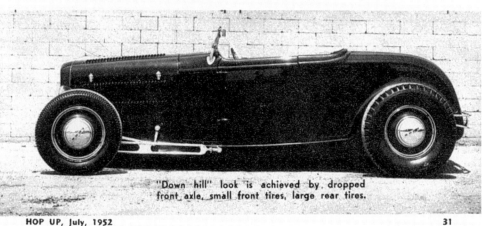

"Down hill" look is achieved by dropped front axle, small front tires, large rear tires.

Custom Hints

Powered deck lids are a custom feature not to be overlooked, and the choice of power and installation make it an interesting project. It is also a job that most of you can do at home.

There are many ways to install automatic lifts. They can be operated either by screw type electric motors, or hydraulic, or vacuum actuating cylinders. Most common installation has been by the removal of the regular spring and counter-balance lever on one side of the lid and connecting the power unit to these brackets. This method works reasonably well on deck lids that have a counterbalance spring on both sides. The remaining spring helps relieve some of the twisting strain on the lid when it is being lifted. If there is no spring on the opposite side to help with the lifting the lid will soon become sprung from the uneven force exerted on it. Two lift motors do not solve the problem because of the headaches in synchronizing.

The best installation seen so far is in Glad Ellis' Merc Coupe de Ville, featured in Oc-tober 1951 *Hop Up.* This car was originally a convertible. Because the convertible top is no longer used, Glad has utilized the hydraulic top lift motor for his deck lid. Instead of mounting the hydraulic unit on one side as is done in most cases, Ellis has mounted his in the center. As can be seen in the photos, a steel tube has been welded between the deck hinges, and a lever welded to this tube. An installation of this kind serves a dual purpose: 1st, it exerts the lifting force at the center of the lid, instead of at one side, eliminating strain; 2nd, it strengthens the hinges by fastening them together, preventing bending which occurs in some cars.

It would seem that in an installation of this kind, the lift unit takes up valuable luggage space. To a certain extent this is true, but on this particular car the unit is mounted in the space formerly occupied by the top when it was folded. On some models, especially coupes, the lift unit can probably be mounted high in the deck compartment and will be completely out of the way (Fig. A). A well braced mount is required for an installation of this type, as considerable force must be exerted to raise a heavy deck lid from this position.

To locate the position where the lower end of the unit will be mounted, raise the deck

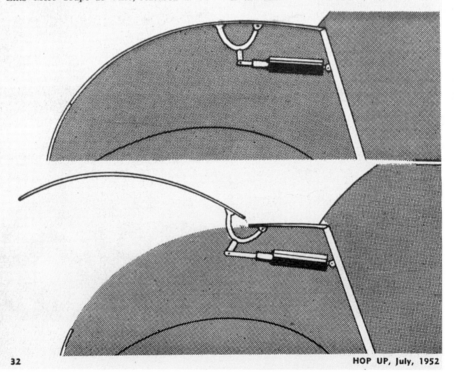

lid as far as it will go. Then, with the lift unit in its fully extended position, lower the deck lid about one-half inch and mount the unit. The deck lid is lowered slightly before mounting, to provide a safety factor when it is being actuated by the automatic unit. If the lid reaches its maximum opening before the lift motor reaches the end of its travel, damage may result.

More than likely the lift motor shaft will have more travel than is necessary to raise and lower the lid. A spacer will then have to be put on the shaft to prevent its pulling the lid too far shut (see photo). The length of this spacer can be determined by getting inside the deck and having someone close it, while you measure the amount of the shaft still sticking out. Too much closing pull can be as damaging to the lid as too much opening push. This applies to hydraulic and electric lifts more than to vacuum operated jobs.

A well planned and installed automatic deck lid lift can be a real custom feature. And worth all the time spent on it.

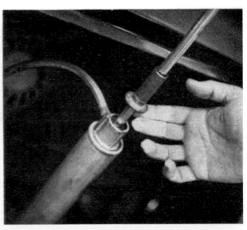

Spacer that prevents hydraulic arm from retracting too far when closing trunk lid.

Hydraulic unit as mounted in Ellis' Mercury.

Plymouth Custom

Common failing of many people who decide to customize their car is not knowing when to quit. If they had stopped somewhere along the line a much better looking car would have resulted.

Emory Bozzani of Burbank, California, whose Plymouth is shown on these pages certainly does not have that failing. His car is a good example of a conservative custom job. It is clean looking; an appealing car obtained without all the frills that could have been tacked on.

Bozzani wanted a good looking custom job but not one that was overdone. Simplicity was to be the keynote. Actually, the hood and deck lid are the only places where body work has been done.

The car has been lowered the same amount front and rear. This may not sound significant, but in the opinion of *Hop Up* it is important. We feel the "speedboat look" with the rear of the car dragging the ground should be reserved for the water where it has some function.

Many custom car owners are so wrapped up in what the outside of their car will look like that they ignore the interior completely. One of the best features, we feel, of

Beautiful upholstery sets off interior of car.

Removal of hood "garbage" helps appearance.

Bozzani's Plymouth is the custom upholstery done in black and white pleated leatherette. Naturally there are many different colors and combinations of upholstery that can be used, not all of them good. Emory's taste was a reliable guide. The car's interior goes well with the simple exterior. Altogether it makes an interesting car that receives lots of comment. The interior was designed and upholstered by the L & L shop in Glendale.

Shaved deck lid, Chevy license plate bracket.

Chevy-GMC Installation

Right side of GMC engine ready for installing.

Chevrolet owners no longer have an excuse when they are shut off by some big Merc, at top speed, or in a drag race. As is always the case, adding cubic inches is the cheapest way to obtain more horse power. In the GMC engine we find the answer to the frustrated Chevrolet owner's prayer for more cubic inches and, of course, more horse power. It also stands to reason that the added volumetric efficiency provided by overhead valves will pay off when competing against flathead engines.

Fortunately, the GMC truck engine is considered by many to be ideal for racing purposes. Why builders of high speed, reworked American engines have overlooked the "Jimmy" so long, is hard to understand.

Of currently available engines, the GMC is the easiest to adapt for producing high horse power output. At the same time it is one of the most suitable for high speed work, due to its extremely rugged lower end.

The stock GMC engine has all of the features that can be built into the Chevrolet engine, only with a lot of hard work. It is equipped with a heavy duty oil pump and a fine pressure oiling system. In addition, a large number of well engineered accessories are available.

The only engines with which we shall be concerned are the 228, 236, 248, 256 and 270.

The first three of these have a 3 13/16" stroke and the other two have a 4" stroke. Crankshafts are interchangeable between models and the rod and main bearings are the same size.

The 270 block seems best for racing or for a hot road job. This block can be identified by the first three digets of the serial number, as these will read "270." Most GMC engines carry a nameplate on the left rear side of the block near the oil pan flange. The 270 will be marked "4" stroke.

LH side of GMC engine. Equipment is Spalding ignition, Howard manifold, Clark headers and California Bill's special twelve port head.

3 25/32" bore." These engines are available through some war surplus agencies, or may be purchased thru a local GMC dealer. The problem is to persuade the dealer not to destroy one of the engines which has been turned in on exchange. If it were not for the "scorched earth" policy of General Motors, the GMC 270 engines would be quite easy to obtain. Anyone with a 270 truck who is planning to install another engine is a prospect. He can retain the block instead of turning it in. Exchange value of the old engine is only $10 to $15, and it will certainly be worth more than that in a Chevy. Now to get to the technical aspects of building this engine, let's start with the lower end.

The rod and main throws of the GMC

crankshaft are the same size as the Chevrolet. However, because the wrist pins are much larger, they give added stiffness to the piston. Most racing engineers feel that large diameter pins help keep pistons from breaking up in high speed engines.

The inserts used in the main bearings of a GMC are precision type and will not require align boring, providing the same main caps that were installed on the block in the factory are used. We recommend that the crankshaft be ground to a standard undersize if it is worn out-of-round. If the engine is to be used for a road job, standard clearances will be adequate. However, for the hottest racing engines, the crank should be

slowly thru the bushing when the rod is laid on its side, resting against the extended end of the wrist pin.

Whether the engine is to run as a road job or as a full race outfit, it is necessary to grind grooves in the crankshaft journals. Grooves should be about $\frac{1}{8}$" wide and about the same depth. These grooves should be placed so they coincide with the holes in the crankshaft. GMC engines, when properly set up, have terrific acceleration. The oil tends to pile up at the end of the pan, starving the oil pump, which drops the oil pressure below the danger point.

A horizontal baffle should be placed in the bottom of the pan, extending forward to the

This photo clearly indicates the rugged lower end of the GMC engine which is capable of withstanding outputs as high as 300 b.h.p.

ground one additional thousandth undersize, for clearance. This applies to both connecting rod and main bearing journals. Morraine Bearings are preferred over all others.

The stock GMC oil pump in good condition will pump about fifty pounds of pressure. If more presure is desired, the spring can be elongated by carefully twisting its coils over the pointed end of a chisel. This will evenly space out the coils in the spring. About $3\frac{1}{2}$" total length is usually adequate. The oil pump with a stationary oil screen should be used.

Connecting rods of the GMC will work as they are with no modification. The wrist pin bushings should be checked for fit. They should fit so that the wrist pin will travel

rear of the oil pump screen. This baffle should just clear the rods at the bottom of the stroke. A vertical baffle is then welded so that it meets the horizontal baffle. This should be installed carefully so that it will just clear the rear edge of the oil pump. A few $\frac{1}{4}$" holes should be drilled in each baffle. Do not put more than eight or ten holes in either the vertical or the horizontal part as doing so destroys the baffle effect.

A full flow oil filter should be installed to keep oil and bearings free of grit and dirt. The installation of this filter entails minor reworking of the block before the engine is assembled.

Much has been said about the advisability of using the 1950 model 270 GMC head, since it has a port area approximately 62% greater than that of the earlier models. For alcohol and all-out competition use, there can be no doubt that the use of this head

38

Rocker arm at left is the late model fabricated GMC rocker arm. On right is the early model and should not be used for competition.

is advisable. For road jobs the early head works out well, especially after it is equipped with large exhaust valves. The intake ports can be enlarged to take the late model intake valves. Big exhaust valves are a must for proper breathing. These can be installed quite easily by knocking out the hard seats and porting out the exhaust ports to the edge formerly occupied by the hard seat. Special oversized 1 11/16" exhaust valves are available for approximately $12.50 per set.

The GMC heads are seldom milled, as additional compression is obtainable thru the use of special pistons. Valve springs used on the GMC will depend solely on the camshaft which is chosen for the engine. However, it is a cheap form of insurance to install the special competition retainers which are available. Valve spring combination information is usually available from the companys who grind special cams. Valve springs should measure 1 27/32" from the base to the top after installation on the valve, with retainers in place.

The stamped type rocker arms are preferred for all-out engines, whereas road jobs can be successfully equipped with the early forged rocker arms. The cylinder head should be installed with a stock gasket, tightening the head bolts to approximately 90 ft. lbs. of torque.

PISTONS

Pistons for the 270's are available in 3 15/16", 3 31/32" and 4" bores. For best results the 3 15/16" pistons should be installed. This gives 292.5 cubic inches when used with the 4" crank. If the short 3 13/16" stroke crank is desired, it will be necessary to mill .093" from the top of the block. This combination gives 278.5 cubic inches. Solid skirt pistons work out quite well in a road job. Pistons are supplied for a specified bore size. Blocks may be bored for any of these sizes with assurance that pistons can be obtained quite easily. Some rebuilders feel that solid skirt pistons will not provide adequate oil control. If desired, the skirts of these pistons can be knurlized by any Perfect Circle dealer.

PUSHRODS AND TAPPETS

Tubular pushrods should be used in the GMC conversion, as they are lighter than the stock pushrods and, at the same time, much stronger. These pushrods sell for approximately $12.00 per set. For best results, used valve tappets or cam followers should be employed. These, of course, should be free from pits. Old tappets are preferred to new ones because they are glazed from use, and the pores of the metal contain grease and carbon. The face of an old tappet is much harder than a new one, and will last approximately three times as long.

Modified GMC pan for '49 Chassis.

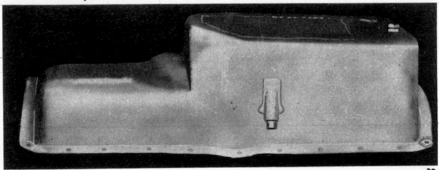

CARBURETION

There are many manifolds for GMC engines on the market today. Foremost of these are the manifolds produced by Nicson. They are available for two or three down draft model carburetors, and a three carburetor model is made for side draft type Zenith carburetors. This Zenith manifold, however, can only be used with a late head, whereas the other models are made for either type. The Howard 5 carburetor manifold has been tested and proved to be excellent for use with late heads, running in competition, using alcohol fuel.

IGNITION

For hot road jobs, the Mallory two-point conversion kit works out very well. For full race models the Spalding dual coil, dual point distributor is preferred.

CAMSHAFT AND TIMING GEARS

The GMC engine is rather touchy when it comes to camshaft timing. Strangely enough, these engines will idle quite well when even a lot of cam timing is used. Genuine GMC timing gears must be used, and under no circumstances should the Chevrolet crankshaft gear be retained, as this can not give proper camshaft timing.

292 cubic inch GMC installed in 1937 Lincoln Zephyr owned by Keith Wise, Ventura, Calif.

270 GMC installed in 1950 Chevrolet chassis with Mallory ignition and Nicson manifold.

INSTALLING THE G.M.C. MOTOR IN A CHEVROLET CHASSIS

If the Chevrolet is a 1937 thru 1948 model, little difficulty will be found in making this installation. However, if the car is a 1949 thru 1951 Chevrolet the oil pan will have to be carefully modified, so that it will clear the center pivot arm of the steering mechanism. To our knowledge, no 1952 Chevrolets have been equipped with GMC motors, due to the difficulty in motor mounts on these new models.

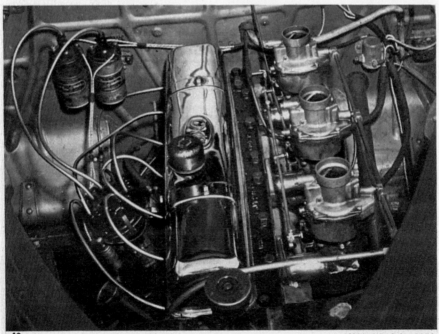

Regardless of the year, 1937 or later, the radiator must be moved forward about 1½″ in order to clear the fan. This is usually accomplished by moving the brackets on the side of the radiator, or by rehashing the radiator mount so that the radiator will clear these components.

Hooking up the accessories on a GMC installed in a Chevrolet might be termed a cinch—it's that easy! The starter and generator fit perfectly, however the starter should be in good working order to turn over this larger sized engine. The water pump should be a '37-'39 Chevrolet. The Chevrolet crankshaft pulley has a shank which is too long. ¼″ must be cut off the rear of this shank before the crank pulley will line up with the water pump and generator.

The Chevrolet distributor fits onto the GMC with no modification, however, a Mallory two point conversion kit should be installed for best results. For all out racing installations the Spalding dual coil distributor with Bosch coils is preferred.

The Chevrolet transmission mainshaft fits right into the GMC pilot bearing, or a new ball bearing pilot bearing, same as Chevrolet, may be installed. The crankshaft flange on the GMC is the same as that on 1937-39 Chevrolets. A 1938 Chevrolet truck flywheel, which has nine holes for mounting the pressure plate, should be used. The Chevy part No. is 838664. The flywheel should be chopped and balanced and then installed in conjunction with a 4038G Rockford clutch. These have been found to be the most satisfactory of all that have been tested thus far. The stock Chevy bell housing, 1937 and later, fits as is.

MOTOR MOUNTS

Engine mounts are easy to make. All that is needed are two pieces of ⅜″ steel about 2″ wide. Drill two holes in each. The holes should be 1 7/16″ apart. One hole should be 25/64″ and the other can be slightly larger to allow for any jockeying that is necessary to get the holes in place.

The rear motor mount plates should be drilled out to 25/64″ and heavy front motor pads used instead of the light rear ones which come as stock equipment.

EXHAUST SYSTEM

Exhausting through the stock Chevrolet muffler loses all that has been gained. Twin pipes with stock Chevy mufflers work very well, and give plenty of tone, when used in conjunction with a set of Clark headers or a split exhaust manifold. Steel-packs, used with these headers, are not for the city. We have tried this and it makes a jet plane sound like a toy by comparison.

CONCLUSION

If you now own a Chevy, at this point we can guess what is going through your mind. Here's some more "dreamin' stuff"!

Consider that the stock Chevy is capable of putting out only 55 hp at the rear wheels in its stock condition, and that a hopped up GMC, assuming three carbs, full race cam, and 292 cu in., will put out between 150-175 hp at the rear wheels. It is easy to see that your Chevy is going to be a real bomb once the GMC installation is complete. If your GMC turns out really hot, as so many of them do, it may be well to consider installing 3.73 or 3.55:1 gears in the rear end. The 4.11's usually are too low for all the horse power and you'll find that the rear end has a delightful tendency to "fish-tail" on you when full throttle is applied in low cog!! Have fun—we know that you will!

As this issue goes to press the Bonneville fever has struck in full force. Rumors creep in to the office from all sides about new streamliners, twin engined tanks, twin engined coupes, and just about any type of engine conversion you can think of. An "A" class streamliner with a supercharged cycle engine is being readied by two well known SCTA members. Anyone planning to go to the 4th annual Bonneville Speed Trials this year had better start making reservations, as it is sure to be a big meet.

LAKES DATES FOR COMING SEASON			
	SCTA		
June	14-15	Sept.	27-28
July	12-13	Nov.	8-9☆☆
Aug.	25-31☆		
	RUSSETTA		
May	17-18	Sept.	20-21
June	21-22	Oct.	18-19
July	19-20	Nov.	16-16☆☆
Aug.	16-17		

☆Bonneville
☆☆Alternate meet (in case of rain)

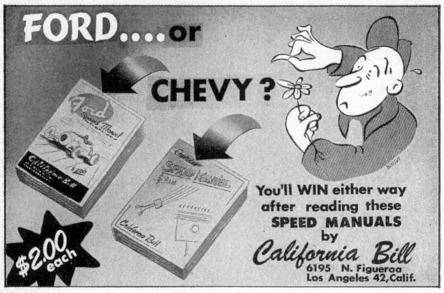

SPEEDY RAIL JOB HANGS UP NEW 128mph RECORD

Bakersfield, Calif.—The Pederson brothers of Los Angeles wound their Howard Cam Special up tight in the quarter-mile drag here May 4 and sent the Class K rail job scorching down the strip at 128.72 mph, posting a new record that gave them the fastest time of the day, a $25 savings bond and a trophy.

Lester Robertson, also of Los Angeles, came closest to the top mark by piloting his '25 T roadster, another Howard Cam Special named "Greased Banana," to 118.08 mph, in Class J. *From Motor Sports World, May 16, 1952.* **Both of these were V8's equipped with Howard M-14 cams. Cars with Howard Cams also hold drag records at San Diego, Pomona, Saugus and Santa Ana . . . Extra good cams for V-8 & GMC.**

SPECIAL CAMS FOR MODIFIED STOCK CIRCUIT . . . THESE CAMS ARE GUARANTEED TO BE BETTER THAN ANY OTHER.

HOWARD'S CAMS

10122-Q South Main St., Los Angeles

CORRESPONDENCE

Who is the "Chick" sitting on Tom Glavis' roadster (HOP UP Test #2, May) and Wally Welch's Merc (Ayala Custom) cover custom, April? Maybe some readers are curious about who rates such a position.

Morton, Pa. Ken Rummel, Jr.

With respect to the picture on page 32 (HOP UP, April '52) the undeniable beauty and comely lines of the Mercury cover custom are overshadowed by these same qualities in the blonde. Who is she, gentlemen? Being a true hot-rod-

der and also a normal male I feel, as must some of your other readers, that you have neglected us this once.

Providence, R. I. Kendrick Thayer

The reason for this letter is the girl on page 32 of the April issue and page 14 of the May issue. I have been trying to figure out if she is your wife or what (I noticed some rings on her left hand). At any rate I would like to have a picture of her that I could put next to the 8 x 10 photo of my '32 coupe in the barracks. Then I could look at them and tell these Yankees and Rebels "We haven't only sunshine but fine looking chicks and cars. Look at these pictures and tell me if you have anything to top that." P.S.: I'm from California.
Chanute Air Force Base, Ill.   A/2C Bill Trevino

The lovely young lady in the last three issues of HOP UP magazine is Miss Jeannie Chrisman of Sun Valley, California. She is 19 years old, graduated from Burbank (Calif.) high school last year and is a private secretary.

Jeannie is also a model in addition to her secretarial work. She has appeared in ads for Camel Cigarettes, Ivory Soap, Rose Marie Reid swim suits and will be on a forthcoming cover of Pageant magazine. Look for her also on the side of the Railway Express trucks in June.

Miss Chrisman is a natural blonde, stands 5 6", weighs 115 lbs. and measures 35" - 24" - 35" in the usual places. She likes to swim and ski and prefers the outdoor type of man.

PHOTO CREDITS
Photo credits are given page by page, left to right and top to bottom.

6 — 8	Art Dean
9 — 11	Gene Trindl
12 — 15	Art Dean
16 — 19	Bob Canaan
20 — 24	Jerry Chesebrough
25 — 37	Gene Trindl

TECHNICAL TIPS . . .
(Continued from page 2)

automobile engineers in general and racing car engineers in particular are still not convinced that rear engine cars are the answer.

Two of the greatest factors in road holding qualities, control and driving comfort of any car are weight distribution and driver placement. The weight distribution should be approximately 50-50 for maximum control of the car. The driver should be placed near the center or to the rear to get the proper "feel" of the car.

The light weight engines of the Porsche, Volkswagen, and Renault enable them to have the engine in the rear and still maintain the proper weight distribution. Also because of the small outside dimensions of these engines, the drivers seat can be properly placed in the car.

The use of a large engine such as you mention would seriously upset weight distribution, making the car tail heavy and the steering extra sensitive. Also, the absence of feel, to which we are accustomed, caused by moving the driver too far forward could be a serious disadvantage.

You state in your letter that you are interested in looks and comfort rather than speed. If you can hold yourself to this, you might be happy with the rear engine car you have outlined. But, if you are like most of us, a good stretch of road tempts us. At high speeds a car of this type would probably be about as dangerous a vehicle as you could get.

HOPPED UP '32 FORD

Can a '32 Ford V8 engine be hopped up with any degree of success? If not, what engine do you recommend? Would a '39 or '40 Chevy engine drop in a '32 without extensive work on the engine compartment?
Marwin, Missouri   Ronald Personett

A '32 Ford engine can be hopped up with some success but will not withstand the beating a later V8 engine will take. A recommend-
(Continued next page)

Our Newest Books

THE MODERN DIESEL

New, thoroughly revised edition describes and illustrates every Diesel engine currently built in England, U.S., and other countries. Text is clearly written in semi-technical manner for student or layman. All applications discussed—trucks, buses, railway service, marine, and aircraft, and industrial types. Such items as Diesel principles, fuel injection systems, lubricants are detailed. Some 200 interesting photos, charts, and drawings make this 280-page book handy for reference and well worth its price ....Postpaid $2.00 ☐

THE ABC's OF LUBRICATION

Most complete book dealing with every phase of lubrication, compiled by Chek-Chart Corp. engineers and authorities. Full information on different types of oils and greases, proper tools, best servicing transmission and differential service, body and accessories, special section on new automatic transmission care and lubrication. 89 charts, line drawings, 48 large 8½" x 11" pages. An aid to both service station operator and car owner-enthusiast ....Postpaid $2.00 ☐

HOW TO HOP UP CHEVROLET & GMC ENGINES

Complete manual on speed tuning these engines for high-performance. All latest equipment discussed, including Wayne and Nicson. Tells most economical means of getting more power and speed. 160 pages, 120 excellent illustrations ....Postpaid $2.00 ☐

HOW TO HOP UP FORD & MERCURY V-8 ENGINES

Outstanding handbook dealing specifically with "souping" these popular power plants. Compiled by Roger Huntington, noted authority. Over 120 authentic charts, photos, drawings, 160 informative pages.........Postpaid $2.00 ☐

SOUPING THE STOCK ENGINE

192 pages, over 150 illustrations. Covers everything from road to track units, how to get the most for your money. Postpaid ....$2.00 ☐

THE MODERN CHASSIS

Handy reference book gives details on suspension. shock absorbers, steering, weight dist., brakes. Over 160 illustrations. Postpaid ....$2.00 ☐

AUTOMOBILE TOPICS MAGAZINE

Established 1900—Oldest Automobile Magazine in America. Now owned and published by Floyd Clymer. More interesting than ever. Clymer's foreign car and Auto Show Survey of French, German, Swedish, Italian, English, and Russian cars (a report from behind the Iron Curtain). Feature articles, technical information, news direct from the World's Motor Capital—Detroit. Custom, racing, production news. Now revised for the automotive industry and car owners.

ONE-YEAR SUBSCRIPTION....................$5.00 ☐
TWO-YEAR SUBSCRIPTION....................$8.00 ☐
Sample Copy of Automobile Topics......Postpaid $ .50 ☐

FLOYD CLYMER MOTORBOOKS
1268 S. Alvarado, HU-1, Los Angeles 6, Calif.

All Books Postpaid
SEND FO RFREE MOTORBOOK CATALOG
FLOYD CLYMER MOTORBOOKS
1268 S. Alvarado, L.A. 6, Calif., Dept. HU-7
Please send books marked ☒ to:

NAME_____
ADDRESS_____
CITY & STATE_____

---

ed installation would be any V8 or Merc block from 1939 thru 1948. Because Ford parts are so interchangeable, about the only thing you would need to install a later engine, would be new water hoses. A Chevy engine could be installed without too much work but I believe the V8 engine would be more satisfactory and would certainly be less expensive to install.

AUTOMATIC vs MANUAL SHIFT

Which Ford transmission is faster—the automatic or the standard?

Los Angeles, Calif.   Lee M. Newton

Automatic transmissions are set to shift under normal driving conditions. Consequently, if maximum acceleration is desired they will shift too early to use the full power from the engine. Also it requires extra power from the engine to turn all the parts of an automatic transmission. All things considered, we believe the manual shift is better for both top speed and acceleration.

OVERHAUL YOUR MOTOR *in 10 minutes*

With a Motor "Renew" Kit
- Increase Compression
- Stop Piston Slap
- Stop Oil Burning
- Free Valves, Rings and Pistons

PREPARE NOW FOR SUMMER DRIVING!

"Renew" with "Compression Seal"

This proven motor treatment gives up to 15,000 miles of powerful, knock free performance to any car. Squeezed into cylinders, it forms a long wearing, lubricating seal by filling in worn places between cylinder walls and pistons. This increases engine compression, cuts oil and gas waste and eliminates the need of costly overhaul and ring jobs.

Cleanse with Motor "PURGE" Formula
Your engine will run smoother, cooler and more efficiently once flushed with Motor "Purge". It cleans, quiets and frees rings, valves and pistons from gums, carbon and varnish when poured into cylinders.

A Motor "Renew" Kit Treatment . . Revitalizes and Increases the Life of Any Engine!

FREE AUTO MANUAL WITH EACH ORDER! Manual tells how to save gas, oil, brakes and tires through economy secrets . . . introduces many new products.

Kit treats all 4, 6, 8, cylinder cars up to 1947. 8 cyl. cars from '48 to '52 require A DUAL KIT $11.90 ppd. FULL 10 DAY "MONEY BACK" GUARANTEE!

$6.95 Postpaid ($1 c.o.d. deposit)

Dealer Inquiries Invited!

Consolidated Engineering Dept. Huk-7
10407 W. WASHINGTON BLVD.,
CULVER CITY, CALIF.

48   HOP UP, July, 1952

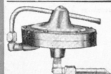

INDEX